MW00423742

JEWISH JUSTICES
OF THE SUPREME COURT

Brandeis Series in American Jewish History, Culture, and Life

JONATHAN D. SARNA, EDITOR

SYLVIA BARACK FISHMAN, ASSOCIATE EDITOR

For a complete list of books that are available in the series,
visit www.upne.com

DAVID G. DALIN

Jewish Justices

of the

SUPREME COURT

———

FROM BRANDEIS
TO KAGAN

Brandeis University Press
Waltham, Massachusetts

Brandeis University Press

An imprint of University Press of New England

www.upne.com

© 2017 Brandeis University

All rights reserved

Manufactured in the United States of America

Designed by Eric M. Brooks

Typeset in Bulmer by Passumpsic Publishing

Library of Congress Cataloging-in-Publication Data

NAMES: Dalin, David G., author.

TITLE: Jewish justices of the Supreme Court:

from Brandeis to Kagan / Dalin, David G.

DESCRIPTION: Waltham: Brandeis University Press, 2017. |

Series: Brandeis Series in American Jewish History, Culture, and Life |

Includes bibliographical references and index.

IDENTIFIERS: LCCN 2016049397 (print) | LCCN 2016049562 (ebook) |

ISBN 9781611682380 (cloth: alk. paper) |

ISBN 9781512600148 (epub, mobi & pdf)

SUBJECTS: LCSH: United States. Supreme Court—Biography. |

Jewish judges—United States—Biography.

CLASSIFICATION: LCC KF8744 .D35 2017 (print) | LCC KF8744 (ebook) |

DDC 347.73/26340923924—dc23

LC record available at https://lccn.loc.gov/2016049397

5 4 3 2 1

For my wonderful wife,

MIRIAM SANUA DALIN,

whose love and encouragement
I cherish more every day

CONTENTS

Illustrations follow page 114.

ACKNOWLEDGMENTS

The publication of this book affords me the welcome opportunity to acknowledge my thanks to several colleagues and friends who have spoken with me about material relating to the book. I would like to express my deep appreciation to each of the following individuals, whose sharing of their thoughts and general encouragement have helped make this a better book: Allan Arkush, Stephen F. Beiner, Judith Beiner, Gerard V. Bradley, Luis Fleischman, Robert P. George, Joseph R. Goldyne, Deborah Goldyne, Daniel Gordis, Michael A. Kahn, Carolyn Hessel, Yehudah Mirsky, David Novak, Michael Novak, Arnold Resnicoff, Daniel Rosenthal, Laura Rothstein, Edward S. Shapiro, Howard Shub, Kurt F. Stone, Daniel Terris, and Melvin I. Urofsky. I also wish to thank Andrew L. Kaufman, the Charles Stebbins Fairchild Professor at Harvard Law School, who served as Justice Felix Frankfurter's law clerk from 1955 to 1957 and who later wrote the acclaimed judicial biography *Cardozo*, for taking the time to meet and talk with me about Justices Benjamin Cardozo and Frankfurter.

For assisting me in my research, I am delighted to thank the staff of the Historical and Special Collections Division of the Harvard Law School Library and Linda Grant of the Harvard Law School Communications Office; the staff of the Manuscript Reading Room in the James Madison Building at the Library of Congress; the staff of the Lyndon B. Johnson Presidential Library in Austin, Texas; Clare Cushman, the director of publications at the Supreme Court Historical Society in Washington, D.C.; Charlotte Bonelli, director of the American Jewish Committee archives; and the staffs of the Jewish Theological Seminary Library in New York and the Florida Atlantic University Library in Boca Raton, Florida. Special thanks go to Kevin Proffitt and his archival staff at the Jacob Rader Marcus Center of the American Jewish Archives in Cincinnati for answering questions and sending me material relating to my research. Kevin and his staff also gave me permission to publish one of the photographs included in this book.

I would also like to acknowledge my special appreciation to Steve Petteway, the curator of the Photograph Collection at the Supreme Court of the

United States, and his staff for their gracious assistance in helping me locate and secure many of the photographs that I have included in this volume. I am likewise very grateful to Alan M. Dershowitz, the Felix Frankfurter Professor Emeritus at Harvard Law School, who served as a law clerk for Justice Arthur J. Goldberg, for giving me permission to publish a photo of him and Justice Goldberg, from his private collection, in this volume.

My son, Barry Dalin, helped locate digital copies of some photographs that have been included in this book. I shall always be grateful for Barry's wonderful research assistance and his continuing love and encouragement throughout the writing of this book. My daughter, Simona Dalin, who recently came to hear me speak about Justice Brandeis at her alma mater, Brandeis University, has also been a source of continuing love and encouragement throughout my researching and writing. Simona and Barry, who have enriched my life in so many ways, continue to be a source of support and inspiration in all that I do.

I was aided in travel and research related to this book by a generous grant from the Earhart Foundation.

I owe a special debt of gratitude to Phyllis Deutsch, my editor at the University Press of New England, for inviting me to write this book for Brandeis University Press. Her continuing faith in this book, and her many excellent suggestions for its improvement, have been invaluable throughout. Amanda Dupuis, the managing editor of the University Press of New England, showed unfailing patience in answering my many questions throughout the editing process. Jason Warshof did a superb and meticulous job of copyediting the final manuscript. I would also like to thank Gil Troy, who carefully read and gave numerous constructive and insightful comments on an early draft of the manuscript for Brandeis University Press. I am very grateful to Gil, a preeminent historian of the American presidency, who has a vast knowledge of American Jewish history, for taking the time from his busy schedule to critically review the early draft.

I owe a special debt of gratitude to my good friend Jonathan D. Sarna for graciously inviting me to include this book among the publications of the Brandeis University Press series on American Jewish History, Culture, and Life, of which he is the editor. Jonathan, who has read almost everything I have published over the past thirty-five years, carefully read and commented on every chapter of this book manuscript and made numerous suggestions for its improvement. His encyclopedic knowledge of American Jewish history, and his willingness to share his knowledge and insights with colleagues and friends, has been an inspiration to me in completing this book, as it has been in all my other published work in the field of American Jewish history. I remain ever grateful to Jonathan for his continuing advice, encouragement, and friendship.

I owe a special debt of thanks to John F. Rothmann, my cherished friend of fifty years, who also carefully read and commented on every chapter of this book manuscript. His invaluable suggestions and insights, deriving from his vast knowledge of American presidential and judicial history and biography, as well as American Jewish history, have helped make this a better book. I am additionally grateful to John for putting me in touch with San Francisco's Lowell High School Alumni Association, which graciously sent me Justice Stephen G. Breyer's high school yearbook graduation photo. The publication of this book gives me the welcome opportunity to express my enduring gratitude to John Rothmann for his continuing encouragement, wise counsel, and friendship.

My greatest debt of gratitude goes to my wonderful wife, Miriam Sanua Dalin, whose loving support throughout the process of my researching and writing this book has been a source of inspiration. Over numerous breakfasts, dinners, and evening walks, she has never tired of hearing and discussing my evolving ideas about the eight Jewish justices of the Supreme Court, their lives, and legacies. She has been forever patient during the long hours that I have been preoccupied with my work on the Jewish justices. A published historian and professor of American Jewish history, Miriam has read, commented on, critiqued, and helped me edit each chapter in this book. Her faith in me and in the importance of this book never faltered. I could not have written this book without her continuing support and encouragement. It is to her that this book is lovingly dedicated.

JEWISH JUSTICES
OF THE SUPREME COURT

1

BEFORE BRANDEIS

Presidents, Presidential Appointments, and
America's Jews, 1813–1912

FOR AT LEAST A CENTURY before President Woodrow Wilson appointed
Louis D. Brandeis as the first Jewish Supreme Court justice, other U.S. presidents had been laying the groundwork by naming Jews to other positions.
Indeed, the tradition of Jews receiving presidential appointments is almost as
old as the nation itself.

Most such appointments were to diplomatic posts. Presidents James Madison and James Monroe, for example, appointed Jews to several consular
posts, including in Scotland and St. Thomas.[1] The best known of Madison's
Jewish appointments was the political journalist and playwright Mordecai
Noah, who in 1813 was named U.S. consul to Tunis. Noah, who had lobbied
for the job, succeeded in part "because it was hoped that he might establish
beneficial ties with North Africa's powerful Jewish community."[2] The Muslim
rulers of Tunis, however, later protested his appointment because they did
not want to deal with a Jew. As a result, the State Department recalled Noah.
"At the time of your appointment as Consul at Tunis," then secretary of state
Monroe wrote Noah, "it was not known that the religion which you profess
would form any obstacle to the exercise of your Consular functions. Recent
information, however . . . proves that it would produce a very unfavorable effect."[3] Even though the administration had other compelling causes for recalling Noah, Madison explained his reason as being "the ascertained prejudice
of the Turks against his Religion, and it having become public that he was a
Jew."[4] Most Jews took Madison at his word, believing that anti-Jewish prejudice lay behind Noah's recall. To this day, Madison's recall of Noah remains
the only instance in American history in which antisemitism was a factor in
the rescinding or rejection of a Jewish presidential appointment.[5]

These appointments from the small, rather isolated Jewish community of the early eighteenth century were the exception, not the rule. The next major Jewish presidential appointment was made by Franklin Pierce, who named August Belmont, the influential Jewish financier and Democratic Party fundraiser, to be U.S. minister to The Hague. As the first Jew to hold this high of a diplomatic rank, Belmont served in the Netherlands from 1853 to 1857. Belmont would later raise more money for Democratic presidential candidates than any other nineteenth-century Jew. From 1860 to 1872, he would also be the first Jewish chairman of the Democratic National Committee.[6]

Between the end of the Civil War and the turn of the century, almost all Jewish presidential appointments were to diplomatic posts. Often their religion was important in the decision to appoint them. In 1870, President Ulysses S. Grant appointed Benjamin Franklin Peixotto, a San Francisco attorney and Jewish communal leader, as U.S. consul to Bucharest, Romania.[7] In sending Peixotto to Bucharest, then a hotbed of antisemitism, Grant endorsed the new consul's intention to use the American consulate to promote Jewish rights and political emancipation in Romania. The nineteenth-century Jewish lawyers Max Kohler and Simon Wolf cite a letter Peixotto carried with him from President Grant to Prince Charles of Romania: "The bearer of this letter, Mr. Benjamin Peixotto . . . has undertaken the duties of this present office more as a missionary work for the benefit of the people he represents who are laboring under severe oppression than for any benefits to accrue to himself. The United States, knowing no distinction of her own citizens on account of religion or nativity, naturally believes in a civilization the world over which will secure the same universal views."[8] Active in Republican presidential campaigns, Peixotto was later named U.S. consul to Lyon, France, where he served through the James A. Garfield and Chester A. Arthur administrations.

Peixotto was only one of several Jewish appointments made by President Grant, who named more Jews to public office, and to higher posts, than any previous president.[9] Grant appointed Simon Wolf, whose tireless campaigning during the 1868 race helped him carry the Jewish vote, to be Washington, D.C.'s recorder of deeds, a post Wolf would hold until 1877. Wolf, widely acknowledged as a national spokesman for American Jewry, advised Republican presidents from Abraham Lincoln up through William Howard Taft. He also served as Grant's main adviser on Jewish affairs, effectively making him the most important Jewish presidential adviser in U.S. history. Wolf not only represented the interests of American Jewry within the White House, he also frequently intervened with Grant on behalf of individual Jews seeking positions in his administration.[10] Among Grant's other notable Jewish appointments was Wolf's good friend Edward S. Salomon, who was appointed governor of the Washington territory in 1870 and thus became the first professing Jew to serve as governor of a U.S. state or territory.[11] Grant also reportedly offered the treasury secretary position to Joseph Seligman, a banker and longtime political supporter and friend. Had he accepted, Seligman would have become the first American Jewish cabinet member. But Seligman declined because, according to his son, "the bank needed him, and his brothers begged him to let politics and public office alone."[12]

On July 1, 1881, President Garfield appointed Wolf U.S. consul general in Egypt, rewarding him for his years of Republican Party service as a campaigner and an official. The appointment was, in a sense, timely. The next day, Garfield fell to an assassin's bullet.[13]

Oscar Straus Goes to Constantinople

In 1887, President Grover Cleveland appointed Oscar S. Straus U.S. minister to Turkey, the second Jew after August Belmont to hold this rank.[14] Born in Otterberg, Bavaria, on December 23, 1850, he immigrated to the United States with his parents and two older brothers a few years later. After graduating from Columbia University Law School, Straus practiced law before joining L. Straus and Sons, his family's china and glassware business. With financial help from his brothers, Isidor and Nathan—who later owned and developed R. H. Macy's into the world's largest department store—Straus was able to devote his life to public service. In 1882, he entered politics as the leader of a citizens' movement dedicated to municipal reform, which worked toward the reelection of New York City mayor William R. Grace. Straus also campaigned for Grover Cleveland when he first ran for president in 1884.[15]

When Straus's appointment to Turkey was announced in 1887, detractors pointed out that the U.S. minister in Constantinople was responsible for protecting Christian missionaries and colleges. Several Protestant clergy, however, supported Straus's appointment, including the enormously popular Brooklyn preacher Henry Ward Beecher, who wrote to Cleveland: "The bitter prejudice against Jews, which obtains in many parts of Europe, ought not to receive any countenance in America. It is because he is a Jew that I would urge his appointment as a fit recognition of this remarkable people who . . . deserve and should receive from our government such recognition."[16]

Straus was an immensely successful and popular minister to Turkey. His gift for diplomacy earned him the sultan's invitation to arbitrate a business dispute between the Turkish government and Baron Maurice de Hirsch, the Jewish financier and philanthropist who had built the first railroad connecting Constantinople and the cities of Europe.

In appointing Straus the first Jewish U.S. minister to Turkey, Cleveland established a precedent followed by Republican and Democratic presidents alike over the next thirty years, up through Woodrow Wilson.[17] The U.S. leaders recognized the symbolic importance of the Turkish embassy for American Jews, and especially for the growing number of Zionist voters, given that the Jewish homeland of Palestine, and holy Jerusalem, remained under direct Turkish control until midway through Wilson's tenure. Indeed, the Jewish diplomatic post in Constantinople can be said to have preceded the "Jewish seat" on the Supreme Court that began with Felix Frankfurter's appointment. Thus, when Oscar Straus resigned in 1890, President Benjamin Harrison invited Simon Wolf to the White House and expressed his desire "to appoint a representative American citizen of the Jewish faith to Turkey."[18] Upon Wolf's recommendation, Harrison appointed Solomon Hirsch, a Republican merchant and state legislator from Oregon, to succeed Straus. Hirsch held the position until 1892.[19]

Straus, meanwhile, remained close to Cleveland after his reelection defeat in 1888, thereafter advising him on his successful 1892 presidential campaign and serving in his Kitchen Cabinet. He and his brother Isidor, a major contributor to Cleveland's reelection campaign, were frequent White House guests, advising the president on monetary policy and Jewish-related immigration issues. Cleveland eventually offered Isidor Straus the postmaster general position, having considered naming him treasury secretary, but Isidor turned down the offer in order to run for Congress.[20] Cleveland strongly backed his campaign, and Isidor won and served a single term.[21] Owing to their views on monetary policy, and opposition to William Jennings Bryan's silver standard, the Straus brothers broke with the Democratic Party and campaigned for Republican William McKinley in 1896.[22] (In April 1912, Isidor Straus and his wife, Ida, would die on the ill-fated maiden voyage of the ocean liner *Titanic*.)

Under McKinley, Oscar Straus again served as a close presidential adviser on foreign affairs. And, in 1898, the president asked Straus to resume his post as U.S. minister to Turkey, an offer Straus accepted following initial resistance. The appointment was made during a tense period with the Turks, who had committed a massacre of Armenians in the mid-1890s that stunned the rest of the world. In particular, the sultan had refused American claims for property destroyed during the massacre, and American citizens in Turkey were calling for American warships to back up their claims. Straus enjoyed the sultan's respect, and McKinley flattered him by saying he was "the only man in the United States who could save the situation." In ultimately accepting the nomination, Straus concluded that "my destiny" was to return to Constantinople, and he wrote McKinley that "I deem it my patriotic duty to you and to the country to accept."[23] Straus remained in the position until December 1900. In 1906, President Theodore Roosevelt appointed Straus secretary of commerce and labor, the first Jew named to a president's cabinet. In 1909, President Taft prevailed upon a reluctant Straus to accept a third appointment as the U.S. diplomatic envoy to Constantinople, now with the rank of ambassador.

Shortly after entering the White House in 1913, Woodrow Wilson announced the appointment of Henry Morgenthau Sr. as ambassador to Constantinople.[24] Born in Mannheim, Germany, in 1856, Morgenthau knew not a word of English when he immigrated at age ten to New York with his parents and eleven siblings. In the United States, his father, Lazarus, who had made and lost a fortune in Germany, "tried a variety of wildly implausible business schemes, in the desperate hope of staging a spectacular comeback." None of his ventures proved successful, and Lazarus soon squandered the $30,000 in savings he had brought from Mannheim,[25] leaving his large family virtually impoverished. His brilliantly ambitious son Henry grew up shadowed by his father's failures, determined to redeem the family name and fortune. Following studies at New York's City College, and graduation from Columbia Law School, Morgenthau achieved major success as a real estate attorney and businessman, amassing a fortune that enabled him to retire before age fifty. By 1912, Morgenthau, who by his own account was "financially independent and rich in experience, and recently released from the toils of materialism," had decided to devote himself to public service. An early supporter of Wilson's presidential candidacy in 1912, when Wilson's nomination bid was still considered a long shot, Morgenthau contributed $5,000 a month for four months. By late spring 1912, before the Democratic National Convention in Baltimore, Morgenthau's friend Abram I. Elkus, along with William Gibbs McAdoo, Samuel Untermeyer, and a small group of Wilson stalwarts, was also contributing generously to Wilson's campaign.[26] Morgenthau was one of the single largest donors, giving more than $30,000.

After Wilson's nomination, Morgenthau chaired the Democrats' finance committee during Wilson's general election campaign. Hoping for the treasury secretary portfolio, Morgenthau was deeply disappointed by Wilson's offer of the Turkey ambassadorship. Twenty years later, his son Henry Morgenthau Jr.

would realize this dream, becoming America's first Jewish treasury secretary. Still, considerable evidence suggests, as the next chapter will detail, that Wilson wanted to make a Jewish appointment to his cabinet in 1913. But the eminent American Jew Wilson hoped to appoint was Louis D. Brandeis, not Henry Morgenthau.

Jews and the American Legal Profession

In modern times, disproportionate numbers of Jews, many of them the children or grandchildren of rabbis and interpreters of Jewish law, were attracted to the legal profession wherever they lived. As Ruth Bader Ginsburg, the first Jewish woman Supreme Court appointee, has so aptly put it:

> There is an age-old connection between Judaism and law. For centuries, Jewish rabbis and scholars have studied, restudied and ceaselessly interpreted the Talmud, the body of Jewish law and tradition developed from the scriptures. These studies have produced a vast corpus of Jewish judicial writing. . . . Jews prized the scholarship of judges and lawyers in their own tradition, and when anti-Semitic occupational restrictions were lifted, they were drawn to the learned professions of the countries in which they lived. Law figured prominently among those professions. Law became and remains an avenue of social mobility, a field in which intellectual achievement is rewarded. And, as it evolved in the United States, law also became a bulwark against the kind of oppression Jews had endured throughout history. So Jews in large numbers became lawyers in the United States, and some eventually became judges. Many of those lawyers and judges used the law not only for personal gain, but to pursue justice for others.[27]

In late nineteenth- and early twentieth-century America, however, while the law became an important avenue of social and economic mobility for immigrant Jews and their children, the oft-recounted Jewish ascent from "rags to robes" was not easily achieved. As Jerold S. Auerbach has noted, "The entry of Jews into the legal profession was prolonged and painful, strewn with obstacles of exclusion and discrimination set by law schools and law firms." During this era, Jewish attorneys faced deeply entrenched antisemitism in the profession.[28] Between 1874, when Louis Brandeis began his studies at Harvard Law School, and his appointment to the Supreme Court forty-two years later, a handful of Jews, including Brandeis, Frankfurter, Julian Mack, Marcus

C. Sloss, and Henry U. Brandenstein, were admitted to Harvard Law School and subsequently embarked on notable legal careers. During that same period, several German and Sephardic Jews, including Oscar Straus, Henry Morgenthau Sr., Louis Marshall, Samuel Untermeyer, Sol M. Stroock, Abram I. Elkus, Benjamin Cardozo, Irving Lehman, and Joseph Proskauer, attended Columbia Law School. Most of these lawyers, as well as Jewish law school graduates throughout the 1920s–1940s, found "the doors of most New York law offices were closed, with rare exceptions, to a young Jewish lawyer," as recalled by Joseph Proskauer, later a New York state appellate judge and Democrat Al Smith's campaign manager in the 1928 presidential election.[29] Upon graduation from Columbia Law School in 1899, Proskauer had unsuccessfully "made the rounds" of the top New York City law firms, eventually finding work in a small Jewish firm.[30] In 1902, he and his fellow graduate Abram Elkus, a future New York judge and U.S. ambassador to Turkey, formed the firm of Elkus, Gleason, and Proskauer, which soon became one of the city's two most influential Jewish law firms.

The experience of Proskauer and Elkus was far from unique. Moreover, prospective Jewish lawyers had "competed successfully with the Protestant elite in the national law schools," such as Harvard and Columbia, "only to discover that a law review editorship was insufficient for elite certification."[31] Upon graduation from Harvard Law School in 1906, even future Supreme Court justice Felix Frankfurter, a *Harvard Law Review* editor with glowing recommendations from Roscoe Pound, the law school's dean, was turned down by most elite New York firms. So spurned, many Jewish lawyers of this era created their own Jewish firms, some of which became nationally prominent. Even Julian Mack, one of the *Harvard Law Review*'s founders in 1887, began his legal career in a small Jewish firm in Chicago before embarking on a distinguished career as a law school professor and federal judge. At a Harvard Law School reunion, Roscoe Pound confided to Mack that he "was disturbed by the discrimination against Jewish graduates" by the elite New York firms, noting that even law review membership carried little weight.[32]

New York Jewish lawyers found other legal areas closed to them as well. When, in 1895, Louis Marshall moved from Syracuse to Manhattan to accept a partnership in Guggenheimer and Untermeyer, the city's first and most prestigious Jewish law firm, he was shocked to learn that few Jews had been admitted to the city's bar association and that "it was only in exceptional cases that men of my faith were appointed to committees of the organization."[33] Before Julian Mack's appointment to the U.S. Circuit Court of Appeals in

1910, and Louis Brandeis's appointment to the Supreme Court six years later, Jewish law school graduates, even with the most stellar credentials, could not expect to be chosen for the prestigious federal judicial clerkships, not to mention the even more coveted Supreme Court clerkships, which were important paths for legal advancement.

Judah P. Benjamin: The First Jewish Supreme Court Nominee

Along with being one of the nineteenth century's foremost attorneys and legal scholars, and the first professing Jew to serve in the U.S. Senate, Judah P. Benjamin was the first Jew to be offered a Supreme Court seat.

Benjamin is, of course, best known for his later political career. Yet during his nine Senate years, Benjamin was one of the Senate's most brilliant thinkers, and he eventually enjoyed a "towering" reputation as an orator.[34] Indeed, Benjamin has been ranked by some historians as one of the greatest orators in the Senate's history, on a par with Daniel Webster, Henry Clay, and John C. Calhoun. Joining his Southern Senate colleagues in seceding from the Union in 1861, Benjamin served in Jefferson Davis's cabinet as the Confederacy's attorney general, secretary of war, and secretary of state, gaining enduring fame —or infamy—as the "Brains of the Confederacy" and one of the foremost "Statesmen of the Lost Cause." At the war's end in April 1865, "in order to avoid capture and trial for treason, Benjamin disguised himself as a Frenchman and escaped to England."[35] Age fifty-four and penniless, he began life anew in Victorian London, where he stayed until his death in 1884. While establishing a lucrative practice as a barrister, Benjamin further enhanced his position as a legal thinker through his magisterial *Treatise on the Law of Sale of Personal Property, with Reference to the American Decisions, to the French Code and Civil Law*, better known as *Benjamin on Sales*, which "was immediately recognized as the leading authority on the subject" and "has maintained its reputation as a classic of English law." In his seminal study of the Jewish contribution to modern law, Arthur Lehman Goodhart, a U.S.-born professor of jurisprudence at Oxford University, has ranked Benjamin, together with Brandeis, Cardozo, and Frankfurter, as one of the most eminent "Jewish Lawyers of the Common Law."[36] Although Benjamin never served on the Supreme Court, he holds a distinction the other eight Jewish justices do not—he is pictured on the Confederate two-dollar bill, the only Jew to ever appear on U.S. currency.

It is, in some respects, unfortunate that Benjamin's association with the

Confederacy has clouded his remarkable legal achievements, both before his nomination to the Supreme Court, at age forty-two, and during his English exile. Born to a Sephardic family on the Caribbean island of St. Croix in 1811, Benjamin spent his childhood in Charleston, South Carolina, before entering Yale College at age fourteen, the first Jewish student to attend Yale in seventeen years.[37] Benjamin was ranked first in his Yale class, of which he was the youngest member, and received the prestigious Berkeleyan book prize, inscribed by Yale's president Jeremiah Day "for excellence in scholarship."[38] At the end of his second year in New Haven, Benjamin was abruptly and mysteriously expelled, with some historians suggesting antisemitism as a factor. Soon after his return to Charleston, Benjamin applied to Yale's president for reinstatement, but Day apparently did not respond, and Benjamin never resumed his studies there.

In 1828, Benjamin moved to New Orleans, where he worked odd jobs and studied law in his spare time. After passing the bar in 1832, Benjamin rose dizzyingly to prominence as an attorney, legal scholar, and politician in antebellum New Orleans, America's fourth largest city and "the greatest city in the South."[39] In 1834, when Benjamin was only twenty-three, he and his friend and law partner Thomas Slidell, a future chief justice of the Louisiana Supreme Court, published a major legal text, *Digest of the Reported Decisions of the Superior Court of the Late Territory of Orleans and of the Supreme Court of Louisiana*, which "immediately became a standard law book" for the state's lawyers and judges. Slidell's older brother John, a commercial and maritime lawyer who had become New Orleans's political boss, soon adopted Benjamin as his protégé. Within the next decade, with John Slidell as his political mentor, Benjamin became the city's leading commercial lawyer and entered politics as well. In 1842, he was elected as the Whig Party candidate to the Louisiana state legislature, and two years later was selected as the Whig delegate to the state's constitutional convention. Around the same time, Benjamin purchased a magnificent plantation called Bellechasse. Upon its completion, "it would house some 140 slaves and be one of the grandest, most architecturally significant mansions in the entire South."[40] The plantation would also symbolize Benjamin's acceptance into Louisiana's slave-owning aristocracy, thereby furthering his political career. In 1848, Benjamin was chosen as a presidential elector on the Whig Party ticket and "was a member of the delegation which accompanied Zachary Taylor on his triumphal trip to Washington to be inaugurated." President-elect Taylor was said to have been so impressed with Benjamin that he briefly considered appointing him to his cabinet.[41]

In 1852, Benjamin was elected to the Senate, along with John Slidell. Both would represent Louisiana until February 4, 1861, "when they would become the final members of the Southern delegation to resign their seats."[42] It was in the late winter of 1852–1853, before Benjamin began his Senate term, that outgoing president Millard Fillmore nominated him to replace the recently deceased John McKinley on the Supreme Court. As Benjamin's biographer Eli Evans has noted, the Supreme Court seat to which Benjamin was nominated "had been promised to a Southerner who could represent the Fifth Circuit (consisting of Alabama and Louisiana) held by the late Justice." Determined to reject the nominations of a lame-duck Whig president, the Democratic Senate had already turned down three of Fillmore's nominees, including the prominent New Orleans attorney Edward A. Bradford, soon to become one of Benjamin's law partners. In nominating Benjamin, Fillmore "was turning to the leading lawyer in the Senate in the probability that he would be confirmed, since the Senate could not reject one of its own members from the deep South, albeit newly elected."[43] To be sure, as Benjamin's biographers have suggested, he was likely to be confirmed, but he opted to remain in his active Senate role while reaping high remuneration from his private law practice, as compared to a Supreme Court justice's salary.[44] Yet if Benjamin *had* accepted Fillmore's appointment, antisemitism may well have played a part in the Senate confirmation process, as it would later in the confirmation battle over the appointment of Louis D. Brandeis. As a member of Louisiana's "slaveholding aristocracy" who eloquently defended the Southern position on slavery from the Senate floor, and "used every orator's tactic" to point out what he considered the inconsistencies in the abolitionist position, Benjamin drew antisemitic vitriol from Northern Senate colleagues such as the "leading abolitionists" William Seward of New York and Charles Sumner of Massachusetts.[45] Ohio's Senator Benjamin Wade famously vilified Benjamin as "an Israelite with Egyptian principles."[46]

On February 24, 1853, possibly on Benjamin's recommendation, President Fillmore nominated another of Benjamin's law partners, William C. Micou, to the still-vacant Supreme Court seat. But the Senate, awaiting Democratic president-elect Franklin Pierce's inauguration, was not eager to entertain a Whig nominee so late in the Senate session and did not confirm Micou.[47] Judah P. Benjamin is thus notable for being both the first Jewish Supreme Court nominee and a member of a law firm of which three partners had been offered Supreme Court appointments.

Louis Marshall and the Supreme Court:
The Appointment That Never Was

Although Louis Brandeis was the first Jew appointed to the Supreme Court, he was not the first Jew to actively seek a Supreme Court appointment. That distinction goes to Louis Marshall, one of the preeminent constitutional lawyers and Jewish communal leaders in early twentieth-century America.

Louis Marshall was born in Syracuse, New York, on December 14, 1856, one month after Brandeis. As Jonathan D. Sarna has put it, "The year 1856 was a vintage year for brilliant Jewish lawyers named Louis." Marshall's father, Jacob, a native of Baden, Germany, immigrated to the United States after experiencing antisemitism in central Europe. Both he and his wife were Orthodox Jews who observed the Sabbath and kept the Jewish dietary laws.[48]

Following Marshall's 1874 graduation from Syracuse High School, where he became fluent in four foreign languages — German, French, Latin, and Greek — he attended Columbia University Law School. Legends abound attesting to Marshall's brilliant law school career, which he completed in a single year rather than the allotted two, graduating before his twenty-first birthday. He "was long recalled as a prodigy who could rattle off cases, complete with precise citations and page numbers, when called upon in class." Returning home to Syracuse, Marshall joined the highly respected law firm headed by William Crawford Ruger, later chief judge of the New York Court of Appeals,[49] where he would remain a partner from 1878 to 1894. During those sixteen years, Marshall argued more than a hundred cases before the New York State Court of Appeals, reflecting his growing stature in the legal profession. At the same time, Marshall took a prominent role in the Syracuse Jewish community and by 1891 was important enough to be included in a national Jewish delegation to meet with President Benjamin Harrison. This delegation, which included Simon Wolf, Oscar Straus, Joseph Seligman, and the banker and philanthropist Jacob Schiff, sought to discuss with Harrison the state of czarist antisemitism and steps that the U.S. government might pursue to aid Russian Jews.[50] In 1894, Marshall's law school classmate and friend Samuel Untermeyer invited him to become a partner in his Manhattan law firm, Guggenheimer and Untermeyer,[51] with which Marshall remained associated to the end of his life.

Marshall, considered by many the preeminent Jewish communal leader of his time, served, at various times, as president of Manhattan's Temple Emanu

El, the most important Reform congregation in the United States, president of the American Jewish Relief Committee, and board chairman of the Jewish Theological Seminary of America, which he had helped reorganize in 1902. A cofounder of the American Jewish Committee, he served as its president between 1912 and 1929. Together with Jacob Schiff, Judge Mayer Sulzberger, Oscar Straus and other Jewish leaders, Marshall was central in the successful 1908–1912 campaign to abrogate the 1832 U.S. Commercial Treaty with Russia over the czarist government's refusal to recognize the passports of American Jews. In so doing, he helped ensure the religious liberty of American Jews seeking passports to travel freely in czarist Russia.[52]

Louis Marshall never really wavered in his support for the Republican Party.[53] During the presidential campaign of 1912, in which Taft, Theodore Roosevelt, and Woodrow Wilson, along with Eugene Debs, fought an epic battle, Marshall remained a vocal supporter of Taft's reelection, despite Taft's opposition to abrogating the Commercial Treaty with Russia. Oscar Straus bolted the Republican Party to support Roosevelt's third-party Bull Moose candidacy, while many other Jewish leaders left the Republicans to back the Democrat Wilson. Indeed, Wilson "became the first Democratic presidential candidate to crash the Republican hold over the Jews in half a century," enjoying the support of a majority of Jewish voters.[54] The *Boston Jewish Advocate* expressed the belief that Wilson deserved Jewish support because "he has made culture the shining purpose of his life," a sentiment shared by many American Jews.[55] The *American Israelite*, an early Taft supporter, "switched course during the campaign," attacking Taft's stand on the Russian Commercial Treaty issue and "finally praising the American people for their wisdom in electing President Wilson."[56] Much to Marshall's chagrin, Jacob Schiff, Henry Morgenthau Sr., his own law partner Samuel Untermeyer, and numerous other Jewish notables "climbed aboard the Wilson bandwagon."[57] Even Brandeis, himself a lifelong Republican who had avidly supported Taft in 1908, soon emerged as one of the Democratic candidate's most influential and trusted advisers. Among the few Republican stalwarts alongside Marshall were Judge Mayer Sulzberger and Julius Rosenwald, the Chicago Jewish merchant prince and philanthropist.

Marshall was especially distressed by his friend Schiff's nonsupport for the Republican Party and its presidential candidate. Concerned about the impact of Schiff's "startling action" in gentile Republican circles, he asked Schiff if he meant "to abandon the Republican Party entirely." Defending Taft's behavior on the Russian treaty issue, Marshall insisted that "the Republican Party in my judgment represents the principle of constitutional government as we have received it from the Fathers of the Republic" and, as such, still merited Jewish support. "It stands four square against socialism and radicalism," he reminded Schiff. "It is the protagonist of law. . . . It stands for representative government as contrasted with an unregulated democracy."[58] Taft, despite his faults, argued Marshall, would be better for the "protection of those principles which have made this country great than Wilson." Writing to Schiff on August 5, 1912, Marshall further cautioned him that leaving the Republican Party "when its political fortunes were at a low ebb" would be misinterpreted in Republican circles and could cause Jews to be branded as "unreliable and political opportunists," especially in view of the uniquely preeminent position Schiff occupied within American Jewry.[59] Ignoring Marshall's entreaties, Schiff continued backing Wilson and did so again in 1916.

Marshall's steadfast support for Taft in 1912 is especially noteworthy considering that, two years earlier, Taft had refused to consider appointing Marshall to the Supreme Court, despite a serious lobbying effort on behalf of Marshall's candidacy. The story of the campaign to promote Marshall to fill the 1910 court vacancy has never been fully explored by American Jewish historians or by students of the Supreme Court.[60] As Lloyd P. Gartner has noted, "Marshall's willingness to serve on the United States Supreme Court—and nowhere else —has been known," but, until recently, "not his active effort to get there."[61]

Louis Marshall was never interested in holding public office. The only governmental post to which he seriously aspired, and for which he considered himself eminently qualified, was that of Supreme Court justice. Marshall, age fifty-four in 1910, was one of the country's best-regarded constitutional and corporate lawyers. A long-standing member of the judiciary committee of the New York Bar Association, Marshall was elected or appointed a delegate to three New York state constitutional conventions, a record unequaled in New York judicial history. Marshall's advice was frequently sought concerning nominations to the New York state and the federal judiciary, advice he readily gave. His major role in revising New York state's corporation laws gave him "wide recognition" as an authority in the corporation-law field and as a skilled legal draftsman.[62] By 1910, when Marshall sought the Supreme Court appointment, his professional home—Guggenheimer, Untermeyer, and Marshall—had achieved renown as the nation's foremost Jewish law firm. Representing "a prospering clientele of German Jewish bankers, brokers and businessmen whose financial activities required legal intervention and protection, Marshall's inexhaustible energy, remarkable memory and verbal felicity quickly earned him an esteemed place at the pinnacle of the New York bar,"[63] as he developed a lucrative corporate law practice and litigated important cases before the U.S. Supreme Court.

Reflecting his expertise in constitutional law, Marshall argued many landmark cases affecting workers' compensation, immigration law, and church-state relations. His most famous legal victory was at the Supreme Court, which upheld his contention that a Ku Klux Klan–sponsored Oregon law denying Catholics the right to send their children to parochial schools was illegal. In this landmark case, *Pierce v. Society of the Sisters of the Holy Names of Jesus and Mary*, Marshall successfully challenged the constitutionality of the Oregon law, attacking as "an invasion of liberty" any attempt to make public schools "the only medium of education in this country."[64] He asked the court to affirm the basic right of parents to send their children to parochial schools and thus provide for their "religious instruction, the importance of which cannot be minimized." The Supreme Court overthrew the Oregon statute in what has been described as the Magna Carta for American parochial schools, establishing the right of nonpublic schools to do business and the right of parents to direct their children's upbringing and education.[65]

In 1910, Marshall's "towering reputation" in both constitutional and corporate law gave him reason to believe an appointment to the Supreme Court might be within reach.[66] Also buoying Marshall's hopes was his position as an influential Republican and staunch "Taft man," and a close associate of some of the highest-ranking New York Republican lawyers, such as Charles Evans Hughes and Elihu Root.[67]

Marshall's opportunity to realize his long-standing ambition came when Justice David Brewer died on March 28, 1910. In his single term as president, Taft appointed six justices to the Supreme Court—up to that time more than any other president since George Washington. Marshall's close friends within the Republican Party, such as Mayer Sulzberger and Jacob Schiff, were apparently well aware of his aspirations to sit on the Supreme Court. They acted immediately when Marshall asked them to speak to Taft on his behalf. Thus, on March 30, only two days after Justice Brewer's death, Schiff wrote to Sulzberger:

> Our mutual friend, Mr. Louis Marshall, has been to see me today, to discuss with me the propriety of taking up his aspirations for the United States Supreme Court, in connection with the vacancy which has just occurred through the death of Justice Brewer.

Mr. Marshall expressed the hope that you and I would go personally to see the President, in order to urge the nomination, and while between ourselves be it said, I do not think Mr. Marshall's chances to secure the nomination are very great, but if you are willing to do what Mr. Marshall hopes we will, I am ready to go with you to see the President. In such case, would you be willing to write the President, asking for an appointment, telling perhaps of the purpose of which we seek this?[68]

The published correspondence between Sulzberger and Taft, and between Sulzberger and Schiff, edited by the historian Lloyd P. Gartner, throws interesting new light on the effort to secure Marshall's appointment. Upon receiving Schiff's letter concerning Marshall, Sulzberger immediately wrote Taft:

> Would you be inclined to favor Mr. Schiff and myself to the extent of receiving us on Thursday, April 7th in order to give us an opportunity to advocate the appointment of Louis Marshall Esq. of New York as a Justice of the Supreme Court?
>
> When Justice [Rufus Wheeler] Peckham died, I wrote you in favor of Mr. Marshall's appointment and sent a full statement of his character, capacity and experience.[69]

Taft responded to Sulzberger in the affirmative on April 1.[70]

The result of the meeting, also attended by Colonel Isaac Ullman of New Haven, a leading Jewish Republican and close Taft supporter, was disappointing. Taft is reported to have said, "Schiff, if you were President, would you name Sam Untermeyer's partner to the Supreme Court?"[71] Taft's statement angered Schiff, while also making abundantly clear that Marshall had no chance. Marshall's partnership in the Untermeyer law firm was not likely the sole or primary cause of Taft's refusal to consider nominating him. But, to be sure, Untermeyer—an influential Democrat and civic reformer who urged regulation of public utilities and would later serve as counsel for the Pujo Committee, which enacted legislation establishing the Federal Trade Commission and other reform measures—was an ideological opponent of the president, who apparently detested Untermeyer personally as well as disagreeing with him politically—a view confirmed by Rabbi Stephen S. Wise, who visited Taft in the White House in 1911 to promote the candidacy of his friend Abram I. Elkus for appointment to the federal court.[72] While Marshall and Untermeyer do not seem to have shared legal cases, or to have agreed on politics, the American public "was not expected to realize this or accept as proper that Untermeyer, who was then receiving immense fees for arranging the widely detested trust combinations, could have his law partner on the nation's highest court."[73] Schiff's skepticism over Marshall's chances, conveyed in his letter to Sulzberger, probably came from knowledge of Taft's antagonism to Untermeyer.

Yet additional political considerations probably guided Taft's decision making. Indeed, Taft had apparently already promised Justice Brewer's seat to New York governor Charles Evans Hughes, who accepted the nomination later that month.

Taft had compelling political reasons to appoint Hughes over Marshall. Hughes was, in 1910, at forty-eight years old, "a bright new star in the Republican constellation" who already had his eye on the presidency. Taft had feared him as a potential rival in 1908; now he frankly regarded Hughes as "clear Presidential timber—stronger, indeed, than himself or Teddy Roosevelt."[74] When he learned, however, that Hughes "seemed prepared, indeed eager" to leave the political scene, Taft quickly wrote to him, offering him Brewer's seat.[75] Without question, Taft, mindful of his reelection prospects, felt that appointing Hughes offered greater benefits than appointing Marshall. Among his calculations was that the Jewish voters who had supported him overwhelmingly in 1908 would do so again in 1912. And even though he did lose significant Jewish support by his vacillation on the Russian passport issue, it is unlikely that he lost comparable Jewish electoral support by his decision not to appoint Marshall to the Supreme Court. It might also be argued that had Taft wanted to appoint a Jew to the Supreme Court to attract, or retain, Jewish support, he would have chosen Mayer Sulzberger rather than Marshall. A pillar of the Republican Party in Philadelphia, Sulzberger enjoyed the personal respect of Taft, who wrote that he was "proud to claim" Sulzberger as a friend.[76] More significant, perhaps, Sulzberger possessed an important qualification that Marshall lacked—prior judicial service. When Taft entered the White House in 1909, Sulzberger had served for fourteen years on the Court of Common Pleas, Philadelphia's principal judicial tribunal, the last seven of those years as president judge.[77] Such arguments notwithstanding, Taft seems unlikely to have considered Sulzberger for any of the six high court appointments he made during his tenure as president. According to Lloyd P. Gartner, the claim that Taft offered a Supreme Court seat to Sulzberger, "who politely declined on account of his age and desire to pursue Jewish scholarship," seems unfounded.[78]

Taft's decision was, of course, a personal disappointment to Marshall. It was, moreover, a disappointment for many within the Jewish community who would have been especially gratified by Marshall's historic nomination. Marshall's appointment would have, undoubtedly, invoked the same pride among American Jews as when Oscar Straus was named secretary of commerce and labor in 1906. Marshall, even more than Straus, held a rarefied position in American Jewish communal life. Thus, one Jewish paper could write that "the report that the name of Mr. Marshall has been presented to the President for appointment to the Supreme Court . . . has been received with great satisfaction by a majority of the Jews of America." It continued:

> It is no exaggeration to say that if Mr. Marshall should be appointed to this office, our Jewish population would view the appointment with more interest than any that has hitherto been made. We do not wish to say a single word against the Jews who have in the past been designated to high positions in this country, but we wish to say that none among them is as popular among all classes of Jews as Mr. Marshall, and that none of them stood as high as he stands in Jewish public opinion.
>
> Of all Jewish public men from "uptown," or among those who are referred to as German Jews, Mr. Marshall stands nearer to the East Side than any of them, and the virtue of Mr. Marshall in this regard is, that he has sought in all of his communal labors to pass beyond the boundaries of his class and to approach the Jewish Masses and to understand them. . . .
>
> The elevation of such a man to a high office would be the source of the greatest satisfaction to the Jews of this country.[79]

Taft's Choice: Julian Mack, the First Jewish Federal Judge

Along with Mayer Sulzberger, Taft might also have considered appointing Julian Mack—an eminent lawyer and jurist and family friend—had he wanted to appoint a Jewish Supreme Court justice. In 1910, Taft had already appointed Mack to the U.S. District Court of Appeals, making him the first Jewish appointee to a federal judgeship, a position he would maintain for more than thirty years.

Julian Mack was born in San Francisco in 1866, and three years later his parents moved to Cincinnati, where they joined Isaac Mayer Wise's synagogue, B'nai Jeshurun, and soon befriended the rabbi and his family. As Mack's biographer has noted, Wise became one of the young Mack's "greatest influences."[80]

President Taft himself had grown up in Cincinnati, where he established his close association with American Jewish life. Taft's father, and later Taft himself, was a friend of Wise's. The Taft family attended the First Unitarian Church, across the street from Wise's Plum Street temple. B'nai Jeshurun and the Unitarian Church, as Taft would later reminisce, occasionally "exchanged ministers,"[81] and the young Taft would sometimes accompany his father to listen to Wise's sermons.[82] Over the years, the Wise and Taft families dined at each other's homes.[83] It was through their shared friendship with Wise that the Mack and Taft families first became acquainted.[84] Other connections included Mack's father's cousin Henry Mack, a businessman and politician who "was elected State Senator and a director of the Cincinnati and Southern Railway, along with the father of William Howard Taft."[85]

In 1884, Mack began his legal studies at Harvard Law School, where he would become the protégé of James Barr Ames, one of the day's legal giants. A decade earlier, Ames had also mentored Louis Brandeis. In 1886, Mack and two of his classmates devised the idea of starting the *Harvard Law Review*, which published its first issue in April 1887. In the 1880s, as Melvin I. Urofsky has noted, "a number of law schools started legal journals, edited by students with the advice and oversight of faculty, to carry the latest in legal scholarship as well as reports of important cases."[86] At Professor Ames's suggestion, Mack and his classmates scheduled a meeting with Brandeis, by then a prominent Boston lawyer, "both for advice and the means to finance" the *Review*. This was how Mack first met the future justice, with whom he would later work closely as a leader of the American Zionist movement. Brandeis, who would become the *Review*'s treasurer, "gave a personal donation," connected Mack and his classmates with potentially helpful Law School alumni, "and raised the money to provide for the mailing of the *Review*."[87] Mack's friend Felix Frankfurter, a later *Harvard Law Review* editor, would write that Julian Mack was its "essential founder," its "moving spirit." When the *Review* published its first issue, Mack's name was listed twice on the masthead, as business manager and editorial board member. In 1919, thirty-two years after cofounding the *Review*, Mack would be elected to Harvard University's board of overseers, the first Jew to fill such a seat.[88]

When Mack received his law degree in June 1887, Harvard awarded him the prestigious Parker Fellowship for study at the Universities of Berlin and Leipzig following graduation. After returning in 1890 from his European studies, Mack moved to Chicago, where he practiced law for five years. In 1895, he became a law professor at Northwestern University and, in 1902, he accepted an offer to be an inaugural member of the University of Chicago law faculty, a position he retained, though usually in absentia, for nearly forty years.[89] Two years later, he won election as a Democrat to a judgeship on Illinois's Cook County Circuit Court. While serving in this position, Mack worked with Jane Addams to found Chicago's first juvenile court, located across the street from Addams's famous Hull House, and served as a part-time juvenile court judge, establishing a nationwide reputation as an authority on child welfare. In 1905, he was appointed to the Illinois State Court of Appeals, where he served until his 1910 appointment by President Taft to the U.S. Circuit Court of Appeals.

Mack's interest in the welfare of children led to his appointment, by President Theodore Roosevelt, as one of three cochairmen of the first White House Conference on Children in 1908. While in Washington for the conference, Mack renewed his acquaintance with fellow Cincinnatian William Howard Taft, then serving as secretary of war in Roosevelt's cabinet.

Back in Chicago, Mack had belonged to Rabbi Emil G. Hirsch's Sinai Congregation, the city's preeminent Reform temple. Together with the influential Hirsch and fellow congregant Julius Rosenwald, Mack helped found Chicago's Associated Jewish Charities, serving for years as director.[90] Through this leadership role, Mack first began to work closely with Rosenwald, the president of Sears, Roebuck & Co. and a leading Jewish philanthropist. Under Rosenwald's direction, Sears, Roebuck became the world's largest mail-order company and Rosenwald became one of Chicago's wealthiest citizens. A trailblazing philanthropist, he devoted as much energy to giving away his money as he had to acquiring it. Like the steel magnate Andrew Carnegie, Rosenwald saw himself as a public servant, the temporary steward of wealth entrusted to him for the purpose of bettering the world. To this end, Rosenwald gave tens of millions of dollars to the University of Chicago and the Chicago Museum of Science and Industry, as well as to Jewish groups such as the American Jewish Committee and the Joint Distribution Committee.

Mack and Rosenwald soon became close friends. Rosenwald came to trust Mack's judgment on philanthropic matters, and for many years Mack served as Rosenwald's closest adviser on philanthropies. In 1906, Mack and Rosenwald were among the founders of the American Jewish Committee.

A staunch Republican, Rosenwald contributed generously to the campaigns of every Republican presidential candidate of his era. Given that Rosenwald was Taft's friend and loyal supporter, rumors surfaced that, if reelected, Taft would appoint Rosenwald secretary of commerce.[91] In February 1912, following a dinner meeting with Taft, Rosenwald became the first American

Jew to be an overnight guest at the White House. Given his close ties to the president, Rosenwald could comfortably promote Mack's candidacy when a U.S. Circuit Court of Appeals seat became vacant in 1910. On October 11 of that year, the *Chicago Tribune* published a list of five "prominent prospects" for this vacancy[92] that included Kenesaw Mountain Landis, who would later achieve national fame as the iron-fisted first commissioner of Major League Baseball, and Mack, whose Jewishness presumably worked in his favor. This was because Taft needed to curry favor with Jewish voters after what was perceived as his unsatisfactory handling of the Commercial Treaty with Russia. Both Rosenwald and Rabbi Emil Hirsch, another Republican and the grandfather of future attorney general Edward Hirsch Levi (discussed later), made the case to Taft that Mack's appointment would please Jewish leaders.

Mack, who had several years of judicial experience, was respected by Republicans and Democrats alike. Indeed, as Mack's biographer has noted, his Democratic Party affiliation "worked in his favor" as "Taft pondered his choices cautiously."[93] For Taft, who had been a judge and a law professor before entering politics, Mack's judicial and academic credentials suited him well to the federal bench. The long-running friendship between the Taft and Mack families didn't hurt either. Mack's December 1910 nomination to the Seventh District Court of Appeals was confirmed by the Senate on January 31, 1911.

"Almost immediately upon ascending to the bench," as the political science professor William Lasser has noted, "Mack began a tradition of choosing his law clerks from among the top Harvard graduates, as recommended to him first by Roscoe Pound and then by Felix Frankfurter."[94] Mack and Frankfurter were especially committed to placing Jewish students who, because of the prevailing antisemitism in the legal profession, would otherwise have had few federal clerkship opportunities. Brandeis, after assuming his Supreme Court seat in 1916, continued Mack's system of having Frankfurter recommend his law clerks. Over the years, many of the Jewish clerks chosen for Mack would go on to become Supreme Court clerks for Brandeis. Frankfurter, during his Supreme Court tenure, continued Mack's tradition of appointing many Jewish Harvard Law graduates as his law clerks.

Despite the nineteenth-century appointments described in this chapter, American Jews still faced a glass ceiling that limited their participation in American government and public life. Although several prominent Jews served in ambassadorial positions, no nineteenth-century Jew attained cabinet rank or was appointed to a federal judgeship. Roosevelt's appointment of

Oscar Straus as secretary of commerce and labor and Taft's appointment of Mack to the federal bench thus broke important barriers in Jewish participation in American life.

Julian Mack would continue to serve on the U.S. Circuit Court of Appeals until his death in 1943. Mack, the first Jew appointed to a federal judgeship, would be the highest ranking Jew in the American judiciary until another, and seemingly more impenetrable, glass ceiling would be shattered with the Supreme Court appointment of Louis Brandeis in 1916.

2

LOUIS D. BRANDEIS

"People's Attorney," Presidential Adviser,
and Zionist

———————

ON AUGUST 28, 1912, Louis D. Brandeis, the nationally known Boston attorney and reformer, and Woodrow Wilson, the Democratic presidential nominee then serving as New Jersey governor, met secretly over lunch in Sea Girt, New Jersey, the coastal town where the governor summered. During their lunch, the two men forged a bond that would catapult Brandeis to great heights after Wilson's election as president.

Although they had never met before, Brandeis and Wilson had much in common. Born just six weeks apart in 1856, both were fifty-five at their Sea Girt meeting. Both were also Southern expatriates who had moved to the Northeast to pursue their education and stayed to further their careers.[1] For his part, Wilson had left his Augusta, Georgia, home in 1875 to attend Princeton University, to which he returned as a faculty member after earning his PhD from Johns Hopkins University and teaching for five years at Bryn Mawr College. Wilson was named Princeton's president in 1902 and elected New Jersey governor eight years later. Like Wilson, Brandeis, who was born in Louisville, Kentucky, moved north in 1875, to begin his Harvard Law School studies. Brandeis remained in Boston, where he established his legal career, until his appointment to the Supreme Court in 1916.

As the 1912 presidential campaign heated up, many Republican progressives had assumed Brandeis would support Teddy Roosevelt's Bull Moose Party.[2] Until then a lifelong Republican, Brandeis had backed Roosevelt in 1904, when he ran as a Republican, and William Howard Taft in 1908. Brandeis had also befriended and advised the insurgent Republican progressive leader Senator Robert La Follette of Wisconsin, many of whose supporters had now jumped on the Roosevelt bandwagon.[3] Yet to the disappointment of Bull Moose progressives, who had ardently courted Brandeis's support,

Brandeis was so impressed by Wilson that he endorsed the Democratic candidate, calling Wilson's July nomination "one of the most encouraging events in American history."[4] Brandeis first wrote to Wilson on August 1, praising his acceptance speech and his progressivism, noting especially "his discussion of economic problems"[5] and "his remarks about the tariff,"[6] which Brandeis lauded as "true statesmanship."[7] Wilson replied: "Your letter of August first has given me a great deal of pleasure. I have been very much cheered and reassured by the knowledge of your approval and support. I sincerely hope that the months to come will draw us together and give me the benefit of many conferences with you."[8]

Soon thereafter, Wilson sent word through a mutual friend, Charles R. Crane, a supporter of progressive causes and a major presidential campaign contributor, that he would like to meet with Brandeis, paving the way for the Sea Girt meeting.[9] On August 27, Brandeis took a night boat from Boston to New York, stopped for breakfast in Manhattan, and rode by train to Sea Girt, where he was welcomed by Governor Wilson at his summer cottage. Brandeis stayed for three hours, during which he persuaded Wilson to base his presidential campaign on the issue of monopolies and trusts, and helped formulate the basic tenets of Wilson's economic platform.[10] In so doing, Brandeis became the chief architect of Wilson's New Freedom program and Wilson's most important campaign adviser.[11] In some ways, Brandeis's involvement in presidential politics followed family tradition. Fifty-two years earlier, Brandeis's uncle Lewis Dembitz, a Louisville attorney, had been one of the delegates to the 1860 Republican National Convention, which nominated Abraham Lincoln for president.

The Brandeis Family of Louisville

Louis Brandeis was born in Louisville on November 13, 1856, the eldest of four children of well-educated German speakers who had emigrated from Prague following the antisemitic backlash to the failed 1848 central European revolutions. Not far from the Brandeises' Prague home had lived Sigmund Dembitz, a physician whose daughter Frederika would marry Adolph Brandeis in 1849, a few months after their arrival in America.

Before settling in Louisville in 1851, the Brandeis couple lived for two years in Madison, Indiana. The Dembitz family, for its part, had resided briefly in Cincinnati before joining the Brandeises in Louisville, where Lewis Dembitz began practicing law in 1853. Three years later, Adolph's brother Samuel and his family had moved to Louisville as well—and a decade thereafter they were joined by the attorney Otto Wehle, a younger cousin of Frederika's who arrived from Prague and later married Louis's sister Amy. In Louisville, Adolph Brandeis built a thriving grain and produce business, and the Brandeis children grew up in financial comfort. Propelled by the Union's demand for grain during the Civil War, Adolph's firm expanded rapidly, acquiring a tobacco factory, a flour mill, and a river freighter later named the *Fanny Brandeis*, after Louis's older sister. By the late 1860s, Adolph had become a leader of the city's Chamber of Commerce.[12]

Although Brandeis's grandfather and great-grandfather were leaders of Frankism, the cult movement adhering to the eighteenth-century false messiah Jacob Frank, and thus far outside the mainstream of normative rabbinic Judaism, Judaism played an insignificant role in the young Brandeis's upbringing.[13] And although his parents rejected Frankism and never denied their Jewishness, they did not belong to a synagogue or observe Jewish holidays. His mother especially "was averse to religious enthusiasm of any sort and raised her children to cherish the ethical teachings of all religions and the rituals of none."[14]

Yet before Brandeis emerged as a Zionist leader, some wondered whether he was Jewish at all. Such suspicions were fed because he tended not to live near or socialize with other Jews, did not belong to a synagogue, and contributed little to Jewish charities. In December 1900, Brandeis reassured his two young daughters, who were visiting relatives in New York, that "the Christmas tree and Santa Claus are very anxious to see you."[15] Even after Brandeis had become a leading Zionist, he did not follow Jewish dietary laws and was delighted to receive the hams his brother, Alfred, occasionally sent from Louisville. "There is great rejoicing over the ham—which has just arrived," he wrote.[16] Further, he seems not to have been troubled by the intermarriage by Alfred, one of his sisters, and one daughter.[17] Brandeis considered his son-in-law, Paul Rauschenbusch, the son of a famous Protestant leader, a "rare find" and a welcome addition to his family.[18]

Doubts about Brandeis's Jewishness were not entirely unfounded. His brother-in-law Felix Adler had earlier renounced Judaism to found the Ethical Culture movement. Throughout their lives, Adler continued to consider Brandeis, also an Ethical Culturist, a spiritual kinsman. Brandeis was far enough removed from Jewish life that when his name was proposed in 1906 for membership in the newly created American Jewish Committee, he was rejected because "he has not identified himself with Jewish affairs, and is rather inclined to side with the Ethical Culturists." Rumors suggested he and his wife had left Judaism for the Unitarian Church.[19]

Despite his parents' noninvolvement in Louisville's thriving Jewish community, the young Brandeis was very close to his favorite uncle, Lewis Dembitz, an Orthodox Jew said to have been the future jurist's greatest influence prior to Brandeis's departure from Louisville to study law at Harvard. Dembitz, a prodigy who read Greek and Latin and spoke several languages while still a teenager, studied law in Prague and, after moving to the United States, published highly regarded reference works about Kentucky law. He also combined law with public service, serving for a time as Louisville's assistant city attorney. A fervent abolitionist who had translated *Uncle Tom's Cabin* into German, Dembitz was a cofounder of Kentucky's Republican Party. He named one of his sons after Henry Clay and the other after Abraham Lincoln. Brandeis so admired his uncle, and his legal acumen, that he changed his middle name from David to Dembitz. It was also his great admiration for his uncle that led him to choose law as his career.[20]

For Dembitz, becoming "an ardent Orthodox Jew" happened suddenly at age thirteen, much to the chagrin of his freethinking sister Frederika.[21] A leader at Louisville's Orthodox synagogue, Dembitz offered a striking contrast to his assimilated relatives. Louis Brandeis had no experience of the Jewish Sabbath in his parents' home, but many years later he would vividly recall "the joy and awe with which my uncle welcomed the arrival of the [Sabbath] and the piety with which he observed it. I remember the extra delicacies, lighting of the candles, prayers over a cup of wine, quaint chants, and uncle Lewis poring over books most of the day. I remember more particularly an elusive something about him which was spoken of as the 'Sabbath peace.' . . . Uncle Lewis used to say that he was enjoying a foretaste of heaven."[22]

Dembitz also played a role in national Jewish communal life, helping establish New York's Jewish Theological Seminary and serving for years on its board of directors. A Jewish scholar of some note, Dembitz translated the books of Exodus and Leviticus for the Jewish Publication Society's Revised English Bible. He additionally wrote a detailed guide to Jewish prayer and worship, *Jewish Services in Synagogue and Home*, also published by the Jewish Publication Society, along with articles for the *Jewish Encyclopedia*.

However strong Dembitz's effect on his nephew, Brandeis never emulated his Jewish religious observance. Instead, the future justice was largely following the example set by his uncle's abolitionism, along with his backing of other liberal and humanitarian causes.[23] Brandeis would thus be inspired to be a Republican progressive reformer and Brahmin Boston's "people's attorney." Nonetheless, later on, the specifically Jewish example set by Dembitz would have a profound influence on Brandeis's Jewish legacy. Several years after his uncle's death, it was the comment by the journalist and Zionist leader Jacob de Haas that Dembitz had been "a noble Jew" and a Zionist "that piqued Louis Brandeis's interest, and started him down the road to Zionist leadership."[24]

Brandeis's path from Kentucky to Boston went through Germany, precipitated by the decline, and eventual closure, of his father's business in 1872, shortly before the economic crisis of 1873. Government contracts had dried up, and many Southern clients could no longer pay their bills. At Lewis Dembitz's suggestion, Adolph and Frederika planned an extended European tour to visit friends and relatives. Having allotted fifteen months, the family ended up remaining in Europe for three years, fulfilling the parents' desire to give their children a European education. During fall 1873, Louis, who already spoke German fluently, enrolled at the Annen-Realschule in Dresden, where he studied for three terms and graduated with honors. Before returning to Louisville in May 1875, the family visited friends in Brookline, Massachusetts. During this stay, Brandeis arranged to attend Harvard Law School that fall. Brandeis and his brother, Alfred, would exchange letters almost daily from the time Louis entered Harvard Law School in 1875 until Alfred's death in 1928.

Brandeis in New England

When Brandeis began his Harvard studies, he was just shy of his nineteenth birthday. He was then the only Jewish student at the law school, to be followed nine years later by Julian Mack. Graduating in 1877 with, as legend has it, the highest scholastic average in the law school's history, Brandeis was not yet twenty-one and thus needed a special action by the Harvard Corporation to get his degree. Brandeis remained in Cambridge in 1877–1878 for an additional year of study, and Harvard's new president, Charles William Eliot, named him a proctor at the college. The liberal Eliot would become a mentor and lifelong friend to Brandeis. In later years, Eliot, almost alone among Boston's Brahmin establishment, worked with Brandeis in support of progressive legislation to protect workingmen and consumers, and served with Brandeis as an officer of the National Civic Federation, "the most prestigious organization mediating between management and labor."[25]

One of Brandeis's faculty mentors, and his favorite instructor, was James

Barr Ames, who popularized the case study method of legal study and later was the law school dean from 1895 until his death in 1910.[26] Over the years, Brandeis, serving on the law school's committee of overseers and as *Harvard Law Review* treasurer and trustee, would work closely with Ames, who as a member of the Massachusetts Reform Club would share Brandeis's commitment to progressive reform. Brandeis would also work closely with Ames on behalf of the Harvard Law School Alumni Association, which Brandeis helped create in 1886.

One of Brandeis's close friends during his student days at Harvard was Frank W. Taussig, whose parents had run in the same Prague social circles as Brandeis's. His family, too, had immigrated in 1849, settling in St. Louis. An enrollee at Harvard College while Brandeis was at the law school, Taussig eventually became an internationally recognized professor of political economy at Harvard. He also became an advocate of the gold standard and free trade. In 1884, Louis's brother, Alfred, would marry Taussig's younger sister, Jennie. In later years, their close ties had important political and ideological ramifications, with Taussig helping shape Brandeis's evolving commitment to free trade and sound money.[27]

Brandeis also became close friends with his classmate Samuel Warren, who graduated second in their law school class, just behind Brandeis. Upon graduation, Warren, whose socially prominent New England family owned several paper mills, took a job in the Boston law firm Shattuck, Holmes, and Monroe, in which the legal scholar and future Supreme Court justice Oliver Wendell Holmes Jr. was a senior partner. A year later, Warren and Brandeis formed a law practice together.

Before he joined with Warren, however, Brandeis had to make a profoundly difficult decision—whether to settle in Boston or return to the Midwest, either to Louisville or St. Louis. During the summers of 1876 and 1877, Brandeis had gone back to Louisville. His family, especially his mother, had hoped he would return to Louisville and join his brother-in-law Otto Wehle in his growing law practice. His older sister, Fanny, his closest sibling, wanted him to come to St. Louis, where she had recently married Charles Nagel, one of the city's up-and-coming Republican attorneys and politicians. The Nagel and Brandeis families had known each other in Europe and had emigrated around the same time in the late 1840s. Settling first in Texas, Charles Nagel's father, a staunch abolitionist, had moved his family to St. Louis at the beginning of the Civil War. Charles had met Fanny through her brother Alfred, with whom he had attended Washington University in St. Louis. In September

1877, Fanny traveled to Cambridge and begged Louis to come to St. Louis, as she subsequently continued to do in letter after letter, along with suggestions that he join her husband Charles Nagel's law practice. There was much to recommend such a partnership. Nagel, already well established as an attorney in St. Louis, like Brandeis, "was uncommonly zealous in matters of the public interest, a strong fighter for good government and civic improvement."[28] As a further incentive, Nagel wrote to Brandeis that his parents "intended to build a spacious house . . . where he and Fanny would live and invited Louis to live there as well."[29] Above all else, Louis and Charles Nagel were brought together by their shared devotion to Fanny.[30] At least in the short term, Brandeis was swayed, and he moved to St. Louis.

But Brandeis wanted independence and turned down Nagel's offer to join his law firm. Nevertheless, Brandeis's first job was hardly free of attachments. Nagel helped him land a position with a prominent St. Louis attorney, James Taussig, the father of his Harvard friend Frank and of his brother Alfred's new wife, Jennie.

Brandeis's seven months in St. Louis were not happy ones. Having come to consider Boston the intellectual "hub of the universe," Brandeis saw that St. Louis didn't measure up.[31] After having spent several years in Europe and Boston, the home of Ralph Waldo Emerson, Henry James, and Henry Wadsworth Longfellow, Brandeis found Midwestern life provincial and unexciting. As he grew increasingly despondent, providence intervened through a letter from his law school classmate Sam Warren, urging Brandeis to return to Boston to open a law practice with him. Faced with this opportunity, Brandeis did worry about the financial insecurity of starting a new firm that would have to compete against Brahmin Boston's more established law firms. He also worried about his independence, not wishing to rely on Warren and his family's business connections. Fortuitously, Brandeis also received a part-time clerkship offer with Chief Justice Horace Gray of the Massachusetts Supreme Judicial Court, the state's highest tribunal, at a salary that would nicely supplement his small starting income with Warren. Brandeis thus enthusiastically accepted both offers.

Brandeis moved back to Boston in the summer of 1879, and he and Warren launched their firm in the fall. He also began his clerkship with Justice Gray, an arrangement that would last until Gray was appointed to a U.S. Supreme Court vacancy in January 1882.

For Brandeis, returning to Boston meant renewing old friendships and meeting luminaries such as Oliver Wendell Holmes Jr., Warren's former employer. On the July 1879 evening of Brandeis's admission to the Massachusetts Bar Association, Holmes celebrated with the two young lawyers at Warren's home. On this triumphant occasion, Brandeis wrote his brother, Alfred, Holmes toasted the new law partners with a "mixture of Champagne and Beer," one beverage to represent their dreams for the partnership and the other their reality. "Warren and Holmes talked, and I lay out on the ship's chair," wrote Brandeis of the evening.[32] During the early years of their law practice, Brandeis and Warren would occasionally dine with Holmes and his wife at their usual dinner spot, Boston's elegant Parker House, a popular meeting place for nineteenth-century Boston's politicians and literary elite, including Holmes's physician-poet father, Oliver Wendell Holmes Sr. Without his spouse, Holmes, before being appointed to the Massachusetts Supreme Judicial Court, would often meet Brandeis and Warren at the Parker House tavern for beer and conversation.[33] Thus was born Brandeis's fifty-year friendship with Holmes, who would later be Brandeis's closest Supreme Court colleague.

With their downtown offices on the third floor of 60 Devonshire Street, the new firm of Warren and Brandeis prospered in little time, thanks largely to the Warren family's network of business and finance connections. Their first client was Warren's father's paper-manufacturing concern, S. D. Warren and Company.

The Warren and Brandeis partnership continued for ten years, until 1889, when Warren left the firm to take over his family's paper-manufacturing business following his father's death the year before. Brandeis continued to prosper on his own, taking on other partners and associates, including George Nutter and William Dunbar, both of them Harvard Law graduates. After 1889, the expanding Brandeis law firm shared its offices, now located at 220 Devonshire Street, with S. D. Warren and Company. In 1897, Brandeis changed the firm's name to Brandeis, Dunbar, and Nutter. By 1904, the Brandeis law office comprised 3,500 square feet, seven lawyers, six other employees, and one telephone. One of the partners, Ezra Thayer, who had joined the firm in 1892, later became dean of Harvard Law School. The Brandeis firm moved again that year, taking over an entire story, with a library, conference room, and oak floors, in a fashionable new building on Devonshire Street.

In their expansion, Brandeis and his partners helped create a model for the modern twentieth-century corporate law firm, in which attorneys specialized in different areas of commercial and business law. Their firm also became Boston's first to make "it a rule that it would not hire anyone who had not graduated from law school," preferring graduates from Harvard.[34] In so doing, Brandeis and Warren set a precedent soon followed by other big city law firms nationwide. By the time of Brandeis's Supreme Court nomination in January 1916, "the firm's running log of cases had reached over 22,000," reflecting its tremendous growth over the years.[35] The day following Brandeis's Senate confirmation four months later, the firm was renamed Dunbar, Nutter, and McClennen. At Brandeis's retirement from the Supreme Court in 1939, the firm that he and Sam Warren had founded sixty years earlier remained one of Boston's top corporate law firms.

Throughout the 1880s and 1890s, Brandeis and Warren were active members of the Massachusetts Reform Club and the New England Free Trade League. After Warren's 1883 marriage to Mabel Bayard, the socialite daughter of three-term Democratic senator Thomas F. Bayard of Delaware and Grover Cleveland's future secretary of state, Brandeis and Warren both became Mugwump Republicans, supporting Democrat Grover Cleveland's presidential candidacy against Republican James G. Blaine in 1884. Brandeis's outspoken support for free trade was inextricably connected to the Warren family's paper-manufacturing interests, which Brandeis would represent for almost thirty years; in other words, the firm's interests and his philosophy dovetailed. In 1886, Brandeis staunchly fought to exempt raw materials imported for the Warrens' factories from certain tax duties. As late as 1908, while supporting Taft's presidential candidacy, Brandeis lobbied vigorously on behalf of the Warren family's manufacturing interests in Washington, D.C.[36]

Although Brandeis and Warren remained friends until Warren's death in 1910, their friendship cooled considerably after Warren's marriage to Mabel Bayard, who shared much of the social antisemitism endemic to upper-class young women in New England Brahmin society. For undoubtedly this reason, Brandeis was not among the hundred guests invited to the Warren-Bayard wedding, whose guest list was dictated by the bride, according to late nineteenth-century practice. Indeed, Mabel Bayard made her disapproval of her husband's friendship with Brandeis known by excluding him from future social events as well. Following Brandeis's 1891 marriage to Alice Goldmark, Mabel Warren did not invite the couple to a single one of the many elite social gatherings she hosted.[37]

Brandeis's marriage at age thirty-five was facilitated by a tragic event—his sister Fanny's death in March 1890. While attending the funeral in Louisville, Brandeis talked with Alice Goldmark, his second cousin on the Wehle side. Although Louis and Alice had met before at her New York home, they had never expressed much interest in each other.[38] After the Louisville encounter, however, a romance blossomed. Alice's father, Dr. Joseph Goldmark, a scientist at the University of Vienna, had participated in the Viennese revolution of 1848, and had briefly served as a deputy in the Austrian Reichstag, before immigrating to the United States in 1850. The two families had known each other in Europe, and although the Goldmarks had settled in New York, they remained in touch over the years, including through Brandeis family visits to New York and occasional shared vacations in the Adirondacks. Louis and Alice married on March 23, 1891, after a year's courtship. Alice's brother-in-law, Felix Adler, officiated at the civil ceremony.

Mabel Warren's blatant snubbing of her husband's Jewish friend and law partner was indicative of the prevalence of social antisemitism in late nineteenth- and early twentieth-century America. Reflecting such sentiments, Ralph Waldo Emerson, Henry James, Harvard president A. Lawrence Lowell, and other luminaries of the Boston intellectual elite sometimes expressed notably anti-semitic views. Emerson, perhaps Boston's most renowned nineteenth-century sage, and Brandeis's favorite Boston author, would compare Jewish law to "evil" and Judaism to a disease.[39] In 1916, Lowell would play a prominent role in the campaign opposing Brandeis's Supreme Court appointment, and would later famously impose a quota on Jewish admissions to Harvard. Brandeis was aware that as both a Southerner and a Jew he was still an outsider, and that there were limits to his acceptance into proper Boston society. The fact that Brandeis "had married a Jewish woman with a conspicuously Jewish name did not help him socially."[40]

To be sure, Brandeis was never completely ostracized. His continuing friendship with Sam Warren opened doors that otherwise would have been closed to him as a Jew. Sponsored for membership by Warren, Brandeis was admitted in 1887 to the socially prominent Dedham Polo Club, of which Warren was president, and, again following Warren, in 1900 purchased a country home in Dedham. All three of Brandeis's social club memberships in Boston, including to the prestigious Union Boat Club, were acquired as a result of Warren's sponsorship. When the 1891 volume of the *Boston Social Register* was published, with its listing of eight thousand "proper Bostonians," Louis Brandeis was the only Jew included.[41] Also, a few of the Boston elite social-ized with Brandeis, and welcomed him and Alice into their homes. Foremost among them was Oliver Wendell Holmes Jr., the most Brahmin of Bostonians. Shortly after beginning his law practice with Warren, Brandeis was invited to spend a weekend with Holmes and his wife at their summer home in

Mattapoisett. Brandeis was also a guest at their lavish second-floor apartment next to the Athenaeum on Boston's Beacon Hill.[42]

The influential Boston banker and philanthropist Henry Lee Higginson and his wife also briefly befriended Brandeis as the young lawyer's reputation grew during the 1880s and early 1890s. In fact, "when Brandeis married, Higginson's wife was the first person to call on the couple," and Brandeis was once invited to a Fourth of July celebration at the Higginsons' Lake Champlain summer home.[43] Brandeis's friendship with Higginson, however, did not survive Brandeis's eventual opposition to the interests of Boston's banking and legal establishment, which Higginson represented.

The irony, of course, was that Brandeis, the non-practicing Jew who celebrated Christmas, never joined a synagogue, and lived part of each year in the Yankee Protestant town of Dedham, was invariably viewed as an outsider, if not an intruder, by Mabel Warren and other such denizens of gentile society in old-line Boston. Brandeis and his wife were invariably excluded from the Brahmin social world of the Cabots, the Lodges, and the Lowells. Despite his Harvard law degree, his socially prominent law partner, and his increasing wealth, Brandeis was still denied membership in the most exclusive Boston social clubs, such as the Somerset, as was every other Boston Jew. "Anti-Semitism," he complained in a letter to his brother several years later, "seems to have reached its American pinnacle here."[44]

Undoubtedly, the most enduring legacy of the Brandeis-Warren friendship was their oft-quoted *Harvard Law Review* article "The Right to Privacy" (1890), which would profoundly influence Brandeis's jurisprudence during his Supreme Court tenure. The article reportedly came about because of Warren's anger at newspaper reporters and photographers who, disguised as waiters, sneaked into the lavish parties he and his wife hosted.[45] Warren was outraged that Boston's tabloid press was always ready to report, often incorrectly, on the couple's social life and their upper-class friends. Reports characterized "men and women who seemed to party constantly, had homes in the city and the country, rode to the hounds, sailed and had the money to support such a lifestyle."[46]

Like his uncle Lewis Dembitz, who helped found Kentucky's Republican Party and championed liberal causes, Brandeis was a steady progressive Republican in his early years, until the election of 1884. As a reform-minded Republican, Brandeis was deeply offended when the party nominated as its presidential candidate James G. Blaine, "the continental liar from the state of Maine," who as speaker of the House had been implicated in the Grant administration's bribery and corruption scandals. This made it easy for him to join the Mugwumps and support Grover Cleveland. Yet Brandeis's decision to leave worried his politically ambitious brother-in-law Charles Nagel, who, hoping for a career in Republican politics in St. Louis, wrote to Brandeis telling him of his decision to stick with the Republican ticket.[47] As a reward, Nagel would be appointed to the Republican National Committee in 1908 and, the following year, secretary of commerce and labor in the Taft administration.[48] Although Brandeis and Nagel would correspond less frequently after Brandeis's sister Fanny's death, their paths occasionally crossed in Washington during the Taft presidency and thereafter. Over the years, Brandeis would write to his brother, Alfred, of Washington gossip concerning the possibility of Nagel's appointment to the Supreme Court and to President Warren G. Harding's cabinet.[49]

Public Advocate

Shortly before marrying, Brandeis had told his fiancée that he hoped to earn enough from his law practice to eventually devote much of his time to public service. Such a reality played out, with the Warren and Brandeis firm prospering almost from the beginning and Brandeis continuing to do so after Sam Warren's departure. In 1890, when three-fourths of the country's attorneys earned less than $5,000 annually, Brandeis took in more than ten times that amount, which was well over $1 million in today's dollars (and with no income tax). By the late 1890s, he was one of the country's highest-paid attorneys. To ensure his financial independence, Brandeis lived frugally and invested conservatively. By 1907, he had made his first million dollars, and another million by his Supreme Court appointment a decade later.[50]

In his growing efforts as a reformer in the 1880s and 1890s, Brandeis led the opposition to the shady political aspects of the New England liquor industry, advocating and helping draft legislation for its reform. Over the next two decades, he became one of the leaders of the progressive reform movement, devoting himself to widely varying issues far removed from his corporate law practice, including antitrust law, railroad and public utilities regulation, labor relations, and civil liberties.

Throughout the first decade of the twentieth century, Brandeis increasingly spoke out for social justice, campaigning for a shorter workday and higher wages for women, trade unionism, women's suffrage, and liberal immigration policy.[51] In his emerging role as the "people's attorney," he also pioneered the idea of pro bono public interest work by attorneys, refusing to accept payment for any of the legal work he did on behalf of social and economic reform, and as an opponent of the corporate status quo.

In 1906, after leading an investigation of life insurance companies, Brandeis helped organize the Massachusetts Saving-Bank Insurance League and successfully campaigned for legislation to reform the life insurance industry. In so doing, Brandeis invented savings-bank life insurance in Massachusetts, which for the first time provided affordable coverage to the state's workers. Brandeis would always consider savings-bank life insurance his most successful reform effort.[52]

In 1907, Brandeis undertook one of his most famous public interest cases, the successful legal battle to prevent New England's largest railroad company, J. P. Morgan's New Haven Railroad, from gaining control of its chief competitor, the Boston and Maine Railroad. In attempting to take over the Boston and Maine, "the climax of J. P. Morgan's campaign to monopolize the transportation facilities of New England," the New York tycoon was supported by leading Boston bankers and business leaders, as well as Massachusetts's senior senator, Henry Cabot Lodge.[53] Alongside this fight, Brandeis began taking on some icons of the Boston banking and legal establishment as well, a few of whom were his former friends, including Henry Lee Higginson.[54] The son of a Cabot and a close friend of Senator Lodge, Higginson had opposed Brandeis on the savings-bank life insurance issue and now finally broke with him over their divergent views on the railroad merger.[55] The New Haven Railroad and its apologists, with considerable input from Higginson, "launched a personal campaign of defamation against Brandeis," much of it antisemitic in character, accusing Brandeis "of secretly acting for Jewish bankers in New York to 'wreck' the New Haven."[56]

The following year, 1908, while arguing the landmark case of *Muller v. Oregon*, Brandeis submitted to the Supreme Court a brief "that changed the course of American legal history."[57] Brandeis's sister-in-law, Josephine Goldmark, a social reformer who served with the National Consumers League, had asked Brandeis to defend an Oregon labor law establishing a ten-hour workday for women. In making this case to the Supreme Court, Brandeis developed what came to be called the "Brandeis Brief," which set out the sociological as well as legal aspects of an issue. In this effort, Goldmark and the National Consumers League had provided Brandeis with huge amounts of sociological data regarding the effects of long working hours upon women. While devoting only two pages of his brief to the legal precedents for regulating women's work hours, Brandeis spent a full 110 pages on social science data and analysis in support of his legal argument. The approach worked: the majority of the court, while hostile to labor legislation generally, upheld the Oregon law and specifically credited Brandeis and his sociological approach in rendering its decision.[58]

Brandeis's work on behalf of the Oregon law brought him into contact, for the first time, with Rabbi Stephen S. Wise, the Zionist leader and social reformer who had served a Portland congregation for seven years and who advised Brandeis based on his own experiences in helping get Oregon's ten-hour-day law enacted.[59] Brandeis and Wise would later work together closely when, beginning in 1914, Brandeis assumed the leadership of the American Zionist movement.

Brandeis's reputation as an attorney more concerned with people than corporations grew further in the years to come. Following the 1911 Triangle Shirtwaist Factory fire, Brandeis again worked with his sister-in-law, Josephine Goldmark, in defending New York's statute preventing women from being forced to work at night. By 1912, he had essentially given up his corporate law practice in favor of reform advocacy, although he still received an annual salary exceeding $100,000 for work he brought in to his Boston law firm. Long before his meeting with Woodrow Wilson at Sea Girt, then, Brandeis's readiness to fight big business and defend labor unions and social legislation, as well as his refusal to accept payment for his reform work, earned him the sobriquet "people's attorney" and enduring fame as a Progressive Era champion.

Advising Wilson

Prior to his meeting with Brandeis at Sea Girt, Wilson had never articulated a consistent policy toward big business. On some occasions, he had attacked the monopolies and trusts "as undermining democracy" while at others he had praised their contribution to America's wealth and well-being.[60] In formulating the details of the New Freedom, Brandeis provided Wilson with a campaign strategy to counter Teddy Roosevelt's New Nationalism—"instead of regulating the monopolies and trusts, Wilson and Brandeis proposed the regulation of competition to prevent the abuses by which the trusts and monopolies had come into being."[61] In creating this premise, Brandeis became Wilson's most important campaign adviser.

Their meeting at Sea Girt, Brandeis wrote to his brother the following day, left him "very favorably impressed with Wilson. He is strong, simple, serious, open minded, eager to learn and deliberate."[62] On his way back to Boston, Brandeis stopped at the Democratic National Committee headquarters in New York, where he "was very cordially received" by "a lot of fine fellows in charge there."[63] A couple of days later, Brandeis sent a contribution of $500 to the Wilson campaign, "a very sizable donation in those days (nearly $11,000 in current dollars)."[64]

During the following two months, Brandeis campaigned tirelessly for Wilson, writing articles endorsing the candidate's policies and traveling throughout the country speaking on his behalf. Between October 2 and October 25, Brandeis made twenty campaign speeches promoting Wilson's New Freedom in New England, New York City, Rochester, Buffalo, Cincinnati, Cleveland, Detroit, Chicago, Pittsburgh, St. Paul, and Omaha.[65]

Within days of Wilson's election, widespread speculation circulated that Brandeis would be offered a cabinet appointment, either as attorney general or secretary of commerce and labor. The very mention of Brandeis's name as a possible attorney general, where he would be in a position to shape antitrust policy, terrified and outraged business leaders, who orchestrated a campaign to prevent such an appointment. A decisive role in this effort was played by Brandeis's former friend Henry Lee Higginson, who mobilized opposition to Brandeis's nomination within the Boston legal and banking establishment.[66] Higginson now viewed Brandeis as "a most dangerous man" who lied and "is not to be trusted."[67] The month before Wilson's victory, Higginson had written a virulent letter to Wilson warning him against relying on Brandeis, for whom "no reputable lawyer here has a good word."[68]

After Wilson's election, Higginson personally contacted the president-elect's close friend, former Princeton classmate, and single largest campaign contributor, the industrialist and philanthropist Cleveland Dodge, asking him to use his influence to prevent Brandeis's cabinet appointment. Unfortunately for Brandeis, Higginson knew Dodge well, with their family connection going back to 1803, "when the first New York member of the Dodges became a partner in the firm of Higginson and Dodge, the largest dry-goods wholesaler in New York."[69] Dodge and Higginson now shared business interests, serving together as directors of the Old Dominion Copper Company, a mining firm headquartered in Boston.[70] Thus, Dodge personally intervened with Wilson and is credited with helping block a Brandeis cabinet appointment. Ironically, Dodge, one of America's wealthiest men, turned down Wilson's offer of the prestigious appointment as ambassador to the Court of St. James because to maintain his customarily lavish lifestyle in London would cost Dodge $100,000 a year.[71]

Also influential was the opposition of Wilson's close adviser Edward M. House, who recommended seven of the ten members to serve in Wilson's first cabinet.[72] A wealthy Texas businessman invariably referred to by the honorific "Colonel," House had enjoyed a reputation in Texas Democratic politics as "a kingmaker and power behind the throne" of several governors.[73] After retiring from his business career, House realized his ambition to play a similar role in national Democratic politics by becoming an early supporter of Wilson's long-shot candidacy. He further ingratiated himself with Wilson by supplying him with a bodyguard, a former Texas Ranger known to be a first-rate pistol shot.[74] In helping shape the president's cabinet, House met with Wilson ten times during the last several weeks before his March inauguration, often dining with the president and engaging him in long evenings of discussion.

Colonel House likely had an even stronger effect than Dodge in persuading Wilson against nominating Brandeis to his cabinet. Regarding the attorney general post, House contended that Brandeis "was more than a lawyer; he is a publicist,"[75] and warned that such a controversial lawyer "was not fit for [the attorney generalship]" or indeed for "anything of a legal nature."[76] House's opposition to naming Brandeis attorney general *or* secretary of commerce and labor was likely connected to Brandeis's Republican past and his support for Taft in 1908. Although House himself, according to his most recent biographer, was not antisemitic, he did note to Wilson in a postelection letter Brandeis's "curious Hebrew traits of mind" that "comes to the surface, now and then" and make one "hold something in reserve" in one's approval of him.[77] On the flipside, the opposition to Brandeis's appointment by several Jewish leaders, based on the notion that he was too radical on economic policy, may also have been a factor in House's opposition. One such opponent was the influential investment banker and philanthropist Jacob Schiff, a Republican who had switched parties to support Wilson's candidacy and who contributed large sums to the 1912 campaign. Schiff told House that he did not consider Brandeis a "representative Jew," perhaps helping sway Wilson and his adviser to remove Brandeis's name from consideration.

Whereas Brandeis derives much of his legacy from having been the first Jewish Supreme Court justice, along with one of the country's greatest justices, sometimes forgotten is his role as a pathbreaking early Jewish presidential adviser. Although denied a cabinet position, Brandeis remained one of Wilson's most trusted political confidants throughout the first three years of his presidency. While not attending Wilson's inauguration on March 4, 1913, Brandeis came to Washington a few days later to meet with Wilson. "Had a good private talk with the President this evening for an hour," Brandeis wrote to his brother.[78] A few weeks later, Wilson offered Brandeis the chairmanship of the Commission on Industrial Relations, recently established by Congress to study the causes of industrial unrest, an appointment Brandeis graciously declined. Separately, Wilson frequently sought ideas on economic policy from Brandeis, who was one of the people whose judgment on economic questions the president respected most.[79] In particular, Brandeis soon became Wilson's chief adviser on all antitrust and financial matters, including the regulation of monopolies and monetary policy, and Brandeis reliably helped draft and promote much of the landmark legislation and infrastructure of the New Freedom, including the Clayton Antitrust Act, the Federal Reserve Board, and the Federal Trade Commission, as well as other measures that helped transform Wilson's presidential campaign "antitrust rhetoric into reality."[80] As for the successful passage of the Clayton Antitrust Act, "after lobbying for it with the president, the attorney general and the Justice Department staff, Brandeis also defended the bill in hearings before the Senate Interstate Commerce Committee."[81]

Brandeis's influence was especially apparent in shaping legislation for the Federal Reserve System, and the Federal Reserve Board to supervise the system. A longtime critic of the "Money Trust," as the nation's biggest financial institutions were pejoratively known,[82] Brandeis strongly advised Wilson to support the more radical Federal Reserve proposal championed by Secretary of State William Jennings Bryan and by reform leaders such as Treasury Secretary William G. McAdoo and the New York attorney Samuel Untermyer, who had served as counsel to the Pujo Committee during its much-publicized investigation of the Money Trust. Wilson was convinced by Brandeis's arguments, and asked him to put them in writing for the following day. The Federal Reserve bill that Brandeis helped draft, which was passed by both houses of Congress and sent for Wilson's signature on December 23, 1913, is generally considered one of the Wilson's administration's most important pieces of legislation.

Although denied a cabinet post himself, Brandeis was given a major role in other cabinet appointments. It was on his strong recommendation, for example, that McAdoo, a Brandeis friend and political ally and later Wilson's son-in-law, was appointed treasury secretary. Attorney General Thomas W. Gregory also consulted Brandeis concerning Justice Department appointments.[83]

Throughout 1914 and 1915, Brandeis enjoyed a reputation as Wilson's indispensable adviser and problem solver.[84] Although still a private citizen, Brandeis "was widely viewed as an informal member of the Wilson administration."[85] For his part, Wilson did succeed in appointing other Jews to key positions, most notably Henry Morgenthau Sr. as ambassador to Turkey and Paul Warburg as a Federal Reserve Board member. By late fall 1915, however, Wilson was increasingly determined to appoint Brandeis to an important post in his administration. With the unexpected death on January 2, 1916, of Supreme Court justice Joseph Lamar, a new Supreme Court vacancy provided Wilson with just such an opportunity.[86]

Brandeis and Zionism

Although for the first half-century of his life Brandeis was a highly assimilated Jew who celebrated Christmas, did not practice Judaism, and had almost nothing to do with organized Jewish life, by 1910 he had begun to evince an interest in Zionism and by 1914 he had assumed the leadership of the American Zionist movement. His midlife "conversion" to Zionism, as it has often been known, and his meteoric emergence as America's preeminent Zionist leader, constitute an important chapter in Brandeis's life just prior to his Supreme Court appointment.

Brandeis's road to Zionism began in 1910 when, at the request of his client A. Lincoln Filene, the Boston Jewish department store owner, the future justice served as a mediator during the great New York garment workers' strike, which "had paralyzed the industry, thrown thousands of people out of work, and tied up millions of dollars of materials and partly finished goods."[87] Filene and other retailers feared their businesses would be severely harmed unless the predominantly Jewish garment workers and their employers could quickly reach an agreement. Brandeis, together with fellow mediator Louis Marshall, helped guide the parties toward the famous "Protocol of Peace," which brought stability to the garment workers' industry for the next several years. While mediating the strike, Brandeis first came into close contact with Jewish immigrants from Eastern Europe, an experience that affected him profoundly. He was deeply impressed with their democratic values and their passionate commitment to social justice. Brandeis came away from the strike realizing that he had more in common with many of these East European

Jewish immigrant workers than with the upper-class German Jews with whom he had long associated. He became fast friends with strike leaders such as Henry Moskowitz, a New York social worker with close ties to the labor unions. Moskowitz later became one of Brandeis's key supporters in his 1916 Senate confirmation battle, and subsequently advised New York governor Al Smith. Brandeis also became better acquainted with Rabbi Stephen Wise, who would become his close friend and ally in the leadership of the American Zionist movement, and in the campaign to confirm his appointment to the Supreme Court.

Shortly thereafter, in a December 1910 interview with a Jewish newspaper the *American Hebrew*, a reporter inquired: "Have you any interest, Mr. Brandeis, with those Jews who are working for the revival of a Jewish state in Palestine?" Brandeis responded: "I have a great deal of sympathy with the Zionists. The movement is an exceedingly deserving one. These so-called dreamers are entitled to the respect and appreciation of the entire Jewish people."[88]

As Brandeis related in a 1940 conversation with his authorized biographer, Alpheus Thomas Mason, the precise moment of his conversion to Zionism came two years later, when he met Jacob de Haas, a leading American Zionist who edited the *Boston Jewish Advocate*.[89] It was de Haas who fully awakened Brandeis's interest in Zionism, and who would play a crucial role in bringing Brandeis into movement's leadership.[90] When they met at Brandeis's Cape Cod summer home on August 13, 1912, to discuss Boston Jewish support for Wilson's presidential candidacy, de Haas remarked that Brandeis's uncle Lewis Dembitz, who had died in 1907, had been a "noble Jew." Asked to explain, de Haas discussed Dembitz's involvement with Zionism. Fascinated by what he said, Brandeis invited de Haas to stay for lunch, and for two hours de Haas recounted the history of the Zionist movement, and what de Haas termed the "epic story of Theodor Herzl," political Zionism's founder.[91] After this transformative encounter, de Haas and Brandeis began to correspond, and conversed more about Zionism the following summer. De Haas, who had once been Herzl's secretary, came to view Brandeis as a successor to Herzl in America. And Brandeis, in turn, would call de Haas his teacher, who had "kindled my interest in Zionism. He made me realize its importance, and to him, in large measure, I owe what understanding of it I have attained."[92]

That same year, a chance meeting with another important Zionist leader, the noted agronomist Aaron Aaronsohn, further helped inspire Brandeis to embrace the Zionist cause. Brandeis first met Aaronsohn, who was on a fundraising trip for his Jewish Agricultural Experiment Station in Haifa, after hearing him talk at a Washington dinner in his honor hosted by the Chicago philanthropist Julius Rosenwald, whom Aaronson had met through Judge Julian Mack during his first U.S. visit in 1909.[93] Riveted by Aaronsohn's stories of Palestine and its agricultural potential, Rosenwald had decided to finance his Agricultural Experiment Station, where experiments ultimately led to "a strain of wheat well suited to the arid soil of Palestine."[94] As Brandeis wrote his brother, Alfred, he was thrilled by Aaronsohn's talk and "the possibilities of scientific agriculture" it sparked.[95] He subsequently wrote his friend Norman Hapgood, the editor of *Harper's Weekly*, suggesting that Hapgood invite Aaronsohn to write an article about Zionism for the magazine.[96] Brandeis and Aaronsohn, whom Brandeis later described as "one of the most interesting, brilliant and remarkable men I have ever met,"[97] remained close friends until Aaronsohn's untimely death in a plane crash in 1919.

Brandeis was also influenced by the social philosopher Horace Kallen, who coined the term *cultural pluralism*. Kallen, who shared Brandeis's commitment to the liberal values and social idealism of the Progressive movement, had rejected the Orthodox Judaism of his youth in favor of what he termed Hebraism, which he understood as a Jewish approach to the modern world rooted in morality, democracy, and social justice.[98] Only in a sovereign state of their own, the Jewish homeland of Palestine, believed Kallen, could the Jewish people achieve their destined purpose of having Hebraism be a model for, and teacher of, democracy. In 1913, Kallen outlined his social philosophy this way in a letter to Brandeis: "In Palestine, we aim at a new state and a happier social order. But a state which from its very beginnings repeats the foreseeable and avoidable waste and misery throughout all the industrial forms and the injustice throughout human relations, is hardly worth aiming at."[99] Sharing Kallen's vision of a Jewish state in Palestine, Brandeis wrote to tell him so.[100]

Some scholars have alleged that Brandeis's conversion to Zionism resulted more from political ambition, and his hopes for a presidential appointment, than a sincere commitment to the Zionist cause. The Israeli political scientist Yonathan Shapiro, for example, has argued that Brandeis embraced Zionism only after he was passed over for an appointment in Wilson's cabinet.[101] According to this argument, Brandeis then shrewdly sought to become a "representative Jew," responding to the critique by Jacob Schiff, by embracing Zionism, and when he was later nominated for the Supreme Court, the overwhelming support of Schiff and other Jewish leaders led to his Senate confirmation. This argument, however, as we shall see in the next chapter, is deficient in that leaders such as Schiff played a relatively small role during the Senate confirmation battle, while some Jewish leaders such as Louis Marshall and Cyrus Adler remained silent, never publicly supporting Brandeis's nomination. Moreover, Henry Morgenthau Sr., among the closest Jewish leaders to Wilson and an active advocate for Brandeis during the Senate hearings, was a staunch anti-Zionist.

Brandeis's growing commitment to Zionism did not become publicly known until March 1913, when he introduced the European Zionist leader Nahum Sokolow, a member of the World Zionist Organization's executive committee, at a Boston rally. He was so moved by what he heard that, following Sokolow's talk, Brandeis said, "Thank you, Dr. Sokolow, you have brought me back to my people."[102] Impressed by Brandeis, Sokolow reported on their meeting at the World Zionist Congress in Vienna later that year.

Soon thereafter, Brandeis officially joined the Federation of American Zionists, which would later be renamed the Zionist Organization of America, and became a member of its associate executive committee. Now publicly recognized as a Zionist, Brandeis began to give speeches before Jewish and Zionist groups, and to spend more time and money in support of the Zionist cause. At the Federation of American Zionists' 1913 convention, Brandeis was elected as a delegate to the World Zionist Congress meeting to be held in Vienna that summer. Due to his political commitments advising Wilson in Washington, however, Brandeis could not attend.

By 1913, Brandeis came to view Zionism as having a basic affinity with the progressivism to which he was so deeply committed. In understanding Zionism as "the Jewish expression of democracy and social justice . . . he turned to Zionism as the Jewish expression of his progressive commitments."[103] The Zionist idea of Jews having their own homeland, a democratic state based on social justice and Jewish prophetic ideals, was one he could enthusiastically embrace.

Prior to Brandeis, the Zionist movement had confronted significant opposition from American Jews who claimed that Zionism was un-American. The key to Zionism's legitimacy for American Jews, as Brandeis understood it, was in its link to Americanism.[104] In speech after speech, in 1914 and 1915, Brandeis told Jewish audiences that his approach to Zionism came through Americanism and that the two shared common principles of democracy and social justice. Since embracing Zionism, Brandeis had been learning more about Judaism and proudly declared that "Jews were by reasons of their traditions and their character peculiarly fitted for the attainment of American ideals." This approach led Brandeis to make what would be his famous Zionist formulation, inextricably linking the movement with Americanism. "To be good Americans, we must be better Jews," Brandeis proclaimed to an audience at Boston's Symphony Hall in 1914, "and to be better Jews, we must become Zionists!" The historian Jonathan Sarna writes that by thus associating Zionism with Americanism, "Brandeis effectively pulled the rug out from under the movement's Jewish opponents and placed them on the defensive."[105]

Barnstorming the country to promote Zionism, raise money, and recruit new members, Brandeis became a prophet for the Zionist cause. Wherever he traveled, "his presence alone was usually enough to attract an audience."[106] There was a mystique about Brandeis connected to his charm and charisma, what some have even called a personality cult, that inspired Jews to join the Zionist movement. In his 1929 biography of Brandeis, Jacob de Haas captured this mystique in a description of the justice as "a Jew who is keen to feel and think with his people and who the world over, has come to be known as Israel's greatest spiritual guide and most practical adviser in this generation . . . whose private office in Washington is a temple to which men and women make pilgrimages from all the ends of the earth."[107]

On August 20, 1914, Brandeis assumed the top leadership position in the American Zionist movement, with his election to the chairmanship of the Provisional Executive Committee for General Zionist Affairs. Over the next few years, Sarna notes that Brandeis's leadership "helped to bring about an historic turning point in the movement's leadership."[108] Transforming Zionism into a major force in American Jewish public life, Brandeis brought much-needed order by reorganizing the movement's finances and greatly expanding its fundraising. He contributed immense funds from his own personal fortune: $171,538 between 1914 and 1921 and a lifetime contribution of more than $1.6 million.[109]

Brandeis's formal leadership of the American Zionist movement continued for seven years, from 1914 to 1921, a period that included ballooning memberships and fundraising, and the opening of new chapters throughout the United States. Brandeis strongly supported the work of Henrietta Szold, the founder of Hadassah (the American Women's Zionist Organization), and Hadassah's program of practical health care in Palestine.[110] Brandeis personally won for the Zionist movement the financial support of several wealthy American Jewish philanthropists who were his friends, such as the Filene's Department Store vice president Louis E. Kirstein, the financier and *Washington Post* owner Eugene Meyer, and Nathan Straus, the president of Macy's. Prominent non-Jews, such as the editor Norman Hapgood, became interested in Zionism because of their friendship with Brandeis, and for the first time the Zionist movement thus "gained access to major non-Jewish journals of opinion."[111]

Brandeis also personally recruited other prominent Jewish lawyers and jurists, including Felix Frankfurter, Julian Mack, New York state judge Benjamin Cardozo, and Benjamin V. Cohen, a former law clerk of Mack's who would help him lead the Zionist movement. So would Rabbi Stephen Wise, who would become one of Brandeis's closest Zionist lieutenants, with Mack close behind in importance. At Brandeis's behest, Mack would become cochair of the Provisional Executive Committee for General Zionist Affairs in 1915, and would succeed Brandeis as chairman after his Supreme Court appointment. Frankfurter, Brandeis's younger friend and political ally, who began his twenty-five-year teaching career at Harvard Law School in 1914, would likewise play a central role in the Zionist movement alongside Brandeis.

Beginning in 1917, Brandeis also played a crucial behind-the-scenes role in winning Wilson administration support for the Balfour Declaration, and helped author what became the official program of the American Zionist movement, the so-called Pittsburgh Program of 1918.[112] Brandeis became so devoted to the cause that, briefly in 1917, he seriously considered resigning from the Supreme Court to devote himself full time to work on behalf of Zionism. Even after stepping down from the leadership of the American Zionist movement in 1921, following a bitter dispute with the European Zionist leader Chaim Weizmann, Brandeis would continue to be discreetly involved in Zionist affairs throughout the 1920s and 1930s.

3

MR. JUSTICE BRANDEIS

The Court Years

_____

IN THE TWENTY-SIX DAYS following the January 2, 1916, death of Justice Joseph R. Lamar, Washington, D.C., buzzed with rumors as to whom President Wilson would appoint to succeed him.[1] Not since President Fillmore had offered a Supreme Court nomination to Judah Benjamin in 1853 had a Jew been singled out as a candidate. When Wilson announced Brandeis's nomination on January 28, he precipitated a four-month Senate confirmation battle, one of the most contentious in American history, unequaled until the 1987 battle over Robert Bork's nomination.

The Brandeis appointment came as a surprise to politicians and pundits alike. Very few people outside Wilson's small circle of trusted advisers would have anticipated that the president, facing what would be a tough reelection fight only eight months later, would make such a controversial appointment. At least one important member of Wilson's inner circle, Colonel Edward House, was apparently not consulted beforehand about the Brandeis nomination. When House later heard of it, he was reportedly "appalled."[2]

Brandeis had learned about the possible appointment a few days earlier but said nothing until the White House announcement was made. "I am not exactly sure," he wrote his brother, Alfred, in Louisville, "that I am to be congratulated, but I am glad the President wanted to make the appointment and I am convinced, all things considered, that I should accept."[3]

One of two Wilson cabinet members to initially push for the nomination was Secretary of Treasury William Gibbs McAdoo, a Brandeis friend and political ally as well as Wilson's son-in-law. McAdoo might have been seen to be returning the favor—it was Brandeis who had earlier urged Wilson to appoint him treasury secretary. Wilson's attorney general, Thomas W. Gregory, was the second enthusiastic backer, although Gregory, while praising Brandeis as "the greatest lawyer in the United States," warned Wilson that the nomination would result in a "tempest."[4]

Gregory's warning, if anything, underestimated the response, which included a storm of opposition. Brandeis would be serving until he died, or retired, according to the rules, and this meant a liberal president such as Wilson could impose his liberal judicial philosophy on his political adversaries well beyond his White House years. While this upset Wilson's conservative opponents, Brandeis's long record as a "people's attorney" committed to progressive reform upset them even more. Only fifty-nine when he was named, Brandeis, his critics feared—in the end, justly—might well enjoy a court tenure of more than twenty years.

Embodying the angry conservative response, the *New York Sun* denounced the appointment of a perceived radical to "the stronghold of sane conservatism, the safeguard of our institutions, the ultimate interpreter of our fundamental law."[5] Former president Taft, who had hoped Wilson would transcend partisan politics and appoint *him*, was livid when he heard the news. "It is," he wrote, "one of the deepest wounds that I have had as an American and as a lover of the Constitution and a believer in progressive conservatism, that such a man as Brandeis could be put on the Court, as I believe he is likely to be. He is a muckraker, an emotionalist for his own purposes, a socialist, prompted by jealously, a hypocrite . . . who is utterly unscrupulous . . . a man of infinite cunning . . . of great tenacity of purpose, and, in my judgment, of much power for evil."[6] Even the *New York Times* was unhappy with the appointment, lamenting that Brandeis "is essentially a contender, a striver after change and reforms. The Supreme Court by its very nature is the conservator of our institutions."[7]

On February 9, according to procedure, a five-member Senate Judiciary Committee subcommittee, chaired by Senator William Chilton of West Virginia, met to begin discussing Brandeis's nomination. Over the next four months, the subcommittee would hear testimony, discuss petitions and other correspondence, and evaluate criticism and support for the nomination before issuing a report to the full Judiciary Committee. The committee would then make a recommendation to the Senate, which the Constitution empowers to approve or reject candidates by a simple majority.

Day after day, the Senate chamber was standing room only, crowded with senators and witnesses, analysts and reporters, Brandeis's friends and opponents. Never present, however, was the nominee himself. Senate tradition dictated then—and would do so until Felix Frankfurter's nomination twenty-three years later—that Supreme Court nominees could not appear at their own confirmation hearings.[8] Thus, Brandeis could not speak in his own defense. In his absence, Edward McClennen, a junior partner in the Brandeis law firm, moved to Washington to lead the campaign for his colleague's confirmation.

While much opposition was directed at Brandeis's reputation as a social reformer and opponent of the Money Trust, some was doubtless antisemitic in origin, such as in the case of Harvard president A. Lawrence Lowell.[9] Immediately after the 1912 election, Lowell, an early supporter and national vice president of the Immigration Restriction League, had publicly opposed Brandeis's appointment to Wilson's cabinet, notifying the president that Brandeis did not "stand very high in the opinion of the best judges in Massachusetts."[10] When Brandeis's Supreme Court nomination was announced, Lowell wrote his good friend Massachusetts Republican senator Henry Cabot Lodge, "Are we to put on our Supreme Bench a man whose reputation for integrity is not unimpeachable? It is difficult—perhaps impossible—to get direct evidence of any act by Brandeis that is, strictly speaking, dishonest; and yet a man who is believed by all the better part of the bar to be unscrupulous ought not to be a member of the highest court of the nation. Is there anything that can be done to make his confirmation less probable?"[11] Lowell subsequently gathered a petition against Brandeis with fifty-five signatures, including most notably that of the Boston patrician lawyer Charles Francis Adams Jr., the descendant of two U.S. presidents, president of the Union Pacific Railroad, and treasurer of the Harvard Corporation. Besides Adams, the Lowell petition included the names of many of the most eminent leaders of Boston's business and legal establishment, such as Sargent, Gardner, Peabody, Shattuck, and Coolidge. Receiving the petition, Senator Lodge, on Lincoln's birthday, inserted a copy into the Congressional Record before presenting a copy to the Senate subcommittee's chairman, Senator Chilton.[12] The Lowell petition read:

We, the undersigned citizens of Massachusetts, are opposed to the appointment of Louis D. Brandeis to the vacancy in the Supreme Court of the United States. An appointment to this Court should only be conferred upon a member of the legal profession whose general reputation is as good as his legal attainments are great.

We do not believe that Mr. Brandeis has the judicial temperament and capacity which should be required in a judge of the Supreme Court.

His reputation as a lawyer is such that he has not the confidence of the people.

For these reasons we express the hope that the Senate will not confirm his appointment.[13]

Lowell, whose antisemitism was well known, later became notorious for trying to place a quota limiting Jewish admissions to Harvard. To Lowell's evident chagrin, the Harvard Law School faculty, with one exception, publicly endorsed Brandeis's nomination. Felix Frankfurter, appointed to the law school faculty the previous year, mobilized nine of his ten colleagues to support the Brandeis nomination. Throughout the confirmation battle, Frankfurter wrote a score of magazine editorials, letters, and articles in support of his friend. On February 5, the *New Republic* published an editorial, unsigned but written by Frankfurter, reviewing Brandeis's accomplishments, and praising him for his judicial qualities and for seeking "to make the great reconciliation between order and justice." At Frankfurter's suggestion, law school dean Roscoe Pound wrote to Senator Chilton praising the Brandeis appointment. So did Harvard University's former president Charles W. Eliot, who assured Chilton that "I have known Mr. Louis D. Brandeis for forty years and I believe that I understand his capacities and character." Recalling Brandeis as a "distinguished student" and referring to his "practical altruism and public spirit," Eliot concluded by saying "that the rejection by the Senate of his nomination to the Supreme Court would be a grave misfortune for the whole legal community, the Court, all American business and the country."[14] "Next to a letter from God," Brandeis's law partner Edward McClennen cheerfully declared of Eliot's letter, "we have got the best."[15]

Numerous other letters in support of Brandeis's candidacy were sent to the Senate subcommittee. Among those writing, or else testifying on Brandeis's behalf, were Cleveland's reform mayor Newton Baker, future secretary of labor Frances Perkins, recent ambassador to Turkey Henry Morgenthau Sr., *New Republic* editor Walter Lippmann, *Harper's Weekly* editor Norman Hapgood, and Rabbi Stephen Wise.

Liberals in both parties voiced support for Brandeis. Social reformers in the Democratic Party and progressive Republicans alike applauded Wilson's appointment, hailing its historic character. To gauge Republican backing for the nomination, Attorney General Gregory, at Wilson's instruction, had met with Wisconsin senator Robert La Follette, the only senator consulted about the nomination before the January 28 White House announcement. Gregory asked La Follette "whether Progressive Republicans in the Senate could be counted on to cross party lines and vote to confirm Brandeis. La Follette enthusiastically said yes."[16]

On the flipside, many Southern Democrats unsurprisingly opposed Brandeis's nomination. Edward McClennen "later placed anti-Semitism on the top of the list of the reasons for the opposition to Brandeis . . . among Southern Democrats."[17] Separately, Justice Lamar had hailed from Georgia, and the Senate's Southern Democrats had expected a Southern appointment to replace him. They were disappointed, and some angered, when Wilson did not fulfill this expectation. Also, as Colonel House reportedly told Henry Morgenthau Sr., some Southern senators feared that, if confirmed, Brandeis would try to undo the separate but equal doctrine.[18]

Throughout the confirmation battle, the anti-Brandeis campaign was largely organized and financed by Brandeis's former friend Henry Lee Higginson, who hoped to derail this appointment just as he had earlier helped derail his cabinet appointment. Alarmed by the Brandeis nomination, Higginson wrote his friend Senator Lodge, warning him that Brandeis "has not the judicial quality. It would be well to investigate sundry questions about him."[19]

At the same time, within days of Wilson's announcement, former president Taft and his onetime attorney general George W. Wickersham began mobilizing opposition to Brandeis among the American Bar Association's leadership. Taft and six other former Bar Association presidents, including former secretary of state Elihu Root, sent a scathing protest letter to the Senate Judiciary Committee stating that "the undersigned feel under the painful duty to say to you that in their opinion, taking into view the reputation, character and professional career of Mr. Louis D. Brandeis, he is not a fit person to be a member of the Supreme Court of the United States."

Taft, it should be remembered, did not share the antisemitic bigotry of A. Lawrence Lowell and other vocal opponents of the Brandeis nomination. Taft enjoyed close ties to the Jewish community of his native Cincinnati and was personally distressed by the anti-Jewish comments of George Wickersham directed at the *New Republic*'s "Hebrew uplifters," especially Walter Lippmann and Felix Frankfurter, campaigning in support of Brandeis.[20] And, while serving as Supreme Court chief justice from 1921 to 1930, Taft eventually developed a genuine affection for Brandeis, despite their longstanding differences on legal and political issues. Taft reportedly was "won over by the luminous mind and great learning of Justice Brandeis."[21]

Indeed, the strong opposition from Senator Lodge worried Brandeis backers more than that of Taft. In part, this concern derived from Wilson's breach of what was known as the rule of "senatorial courtesy," which dictates that a president, before announcing a Supreme Court nominee, should get approval from, or at the very least notify, the two senators from the nominee's state. In Brandeis's case, Wilson did neither. Lodge, a conservative Republican, had close ties to the Boston Brahmin establishment opposing Brandeis's nomination. As commentators then noted, Wilson was not so much defying Lodge as ignoring him. Lodge's position of influence as the senior senator from the nominee's state would probably have brought about Brandeis's defeat had Lodge invoked the rule of senatorial courtesy. But to the surprise of many of his Senate colleagues, despite his open disdain for both Brandeis and Wilson, Lodge did not do so.

Although Lodge did urge the American Bar Association leadership to oppose the Brandeis nomination, and shared Lowell's anti-Brandeis petition with his Senate colleagues, he did not vigorously mobilize political opposition against Brandeis, as many expected he would. Lodge may have feared the political repercussions in the upcoming Senate election of November 1916, when he would face Massachusetts voters for the first time since beginning his Senate career in 1892. This was because, with the 1913 ratification of the Seventeenth Amendment to the Constitution, strongly opposed by Lodge, he would no longer be chosen by the State Senate, which had selected him four times previously; now, he would have to campaign for the support of newly enfranchised voters, including many Catholics and Jews. He could not predict, so the speculation goes, the political impact of leading the anti-Brandeis fight on his reelection chances. Some of Lodge's friends and advisers appreciated this dilemma. Arthur D. Hill, a Boston lawyer who managed Lodge's personal legal affairs and investments, wrote the senator urging him not to publicly oppose the nomination and risk electoral defeat.[22]

Hill's advice was prescient: Lodge followed Hill's counsel and won a closely contested reelection bid the following November. His opponent, John "Honey Fitz" Fitzgerald, the flamboyant former Boston mayor, applauded Wilson's nomination of Brandeis, as did most of the city's Irish Democrats. Years later, Honey Fitz's grandson John Fitzgerald Kennedy would say the Supreme Court justice he most admired, and sought to emulate in his own court nominations, was Brandeis.

As for Jewish leaders such as Jacob Schiff, Wilson did not consult them before naming Brandeis to the court, as Theodore Roosevelt had done before appointing Oscar Straus to his cabinet. Nonetheless, Jewish leaders altogether, including former Brandeis critics, united to support his confirmation. Schiff praised the appointment both publicly and privately, predicting that Brandeis would become "an adornment" for the court and that his Senate confirmation would be "an honor to our people."[23] Henry Morgenthau Sr., who played an especially central role in orchestrating support for Brandeis, conferred in almost daily New York strategy sessions with Stephen Wise and Norman Hapgood and served as the Brandeis backers' liaison to Colonel House.[24] Oscar Straus's brother Nathan, a merchant and philanthropist, convinced the journalist Arthur Brisbane to write an editorial for the *New York Evening Journal* supporting Brandeis's nomination. Straus subsequently wrote Brandeis a personal note encouraging him to forbear the opposition's attacks, for "you will be most admired through the enemies you made."[25]

Some Jewish leaders, however, were less vocal in their support. For Louis Marshall, as Jonathan D. Sarna has suggested, Wilson's appointment of Brandeis was "particularly galling," given that Marshall had lobbied unsuccessfully for a Supreme Court nomination during the Taft administration. In a confidential handwritten note, Marshall's friend Cyrus Adler expressed views about the Brandeis nomination presumably shared by Marshall: "I do not view the nomination of Mr. Brandeis with complacency; he may have sufficient legal learning, but he seems to me to be a partisan and agitator and not the type of fair character and dispassionate type of mind which should be possessed by members of the most distinguished tribunal in the world."[26]

In public, however, Adler, like Marshall, remained silent. "I have kept silent for many months," Adler wrote Jacob Schiff, "because I did not want to be accused of endeavoring to injure [Brandeis's] confirmation. . . ."[27] It may well be, as Taft later claimed, that Jewish leaders like Marshall and Adler had "to praise the appointment and all hate[d] Wilson for making it."[28]

On April 1, the Senate subcommittee voted 3–2 in favor of Brandeis's confirmation. On May 24, after several weeks of further deliberation, during which Senate Republicans persisted unsuccessfully in trying to defeat the nomination, the full Senate Judiciary Committee recommended, by a strict party-line vote of 10–8, that Brandeis be confirmed. The full Senate followed its recommendation, and on June 1, Vice President Thomas Riley Marshall, in his role as Senate president, announced that Brandeis had been confirmed as an associate justice by a vote of 47–22. That afternoon, while the Senate was still in session, Brandeis had taken the train from his Boston office to his Dedham summer home. When he arrived, his wife, Alice, conveyed the news with the greeting "Good evening, Mr. Justice Brandeis." Among the flood of congratulatory telegrams received by Brandeis was one from his longtime friend and new colleague Justice Oliver Wendell Holmes Jr. It read simply "WELCOME."

Justice Brandeis Goes to Washington

At the suggestion of Attorney General Gregory, Chief Justice Edward White, and Justice Holmes, Brandeis traveled to Washington in early June so that he could be sworn in as a new justice on the last day of the court's spring term. In the late morning of June 5, he arrived in the Capitol courtroom where the Supreme Court held its sessions. The courtroom "was jammed with spectators and well-wishers," including Brandeis's wife, Alice, daughters, Susan and Elizabeth, and brother, Alfred, the last having traveled from Louisville to share in the historic occasion. A little before noon, Chief Justice White administered to oath of office to the court's newest member.[29]

Under typical circumstances, Brandeis would have been the most junior justice for at least a term or two. But only five days after Brandeis took the oath and the court recessed for summer, Charles Evans Hughes resigned his seat to campaign against Wilson for the presidency. Hughes, a 1910 appointee who would return to the Supreme Court as chief justice in 1930, was the only justice in American history to resign a court seat to seek the presidency. He vacated his seat on June 10, the same day he received the Republican nomination at the party's Chicago convention, having served six terms as a justice on the court.[30] During his relatively brief tenure, Hughes had written more court opinions, 151 in all, than any other contemporary justice. In doing so, moreover, "he almost invariably spoke for a unanimous bench."[31]

Justice Holmes, who had celebrated with Brandeis decades earlier after Brandeis's admission to the Massachusetts Bar, was especially delighted by his friend's Senate confirmation. Then age seventy-five, Holmes was a living legend, generally considered the greatest Supreme Court justice since John Marshall. A Civil War hero, seriously wounded three times in battle, Holmes had returned home to Boston to study and then teach at Harvard Law School for more than thirty years, and to simultaneously serve for two decades on Massachusetts's Supreme Judicial Court. The author of the magisterial work *The Common Law*, which helped modernize legal thinking in the United States, Holmes had been appointed to the Supreme Court by Theodore Roosevelt in 1902. By the time Brandeis joined him in 1916, Holmes "was at once the oldest man on the Court and its most vigorously youthful member."[32] Brandeis and Holmes lived a little more than a block from each other in Washington, D.C., and in good weather they would walk together to their Capitol offices.[33]

Worth noting here is that Brandeis did face antisemitism when he joined the court, especially from Justice McReynolds, who was part of the "Four Horsemen of the Apocalypse," as the conservatives who opposed the New Deal were sometimes known. (This antisemitism is covered further in the discussion of Cardozo.) In 1932, McReynolds, together with Justices Pierce Butler and Willis Van Devanter, urged Hoover not to "afflict the court with another Jew."

Brandeis and His Law Clerks

The hiring of Supreme Court law clerks began in 1882, when Horace Gray joined the court, having hired clerks, including Brandeis himself, when he served as chief judge of the Massachusetts Supreme Judicial Court. Gray and other Supreme Court justices "paid for [the clerks] out of their own pockets until 1922, when Congress allowed each justice to hire one clerk at an annual salary of $3,600."[34] In 1924, Congress made the Supreme Court law clerk positions permanent.

While on the Supreme Court, Gray relied on Harvard Law School faculty to select his clerks, as did Oliver Wendell Holmes Jr., who was appointed to fill Gray's seat upon the latter's death in 1902. After joining the Harvard Law faculty in 1915, Felix Frankfurter selected the clerks for Holmes, and Brandeis, following his own appointment in 1916, asked Frankfurter to do the same for him. The first law student Frankfurter chose for Brandeis, Calvert Magruder, clerked for one year. The next two, William A. Sutherland and Dean Acheson, stayed on for two years, and the rest of Brandeis's clerks served for a year each. It has long been assumed, correctly, that Brandeis, like Holmes, automatically took the clerks Frankfurter recommended. "As for choosing the man," Brandeis told Frankfurter, "I shall leave your discretion to act untrammeled."[35]

Brandeis encouraged his clerks to eventually go into law school teaching or government service. "Other things being equal," he wrote Frankfurter, "it [is] always preferable to take someone whom there is reason to believe will become a law teacher." Indeed, 52 percent of Brandeis's law clerks later obtained academic appointments.[36] Magruder, for instance, became a full Harvard Law professor at age thirty-one. He subsequently worked for several New Deal agencies before Franklin Roosevelt appointed him to a judgeship on the U.S. Court of Appeals. Another clerk, Paul Freund, who later taught at Harvard Law for more than forty years, was considered "the dominant figure of his time in the field of constitutional law."[37] Louis Jaffe, Brandeis's clerk during the 1934 court term, eventually taught at the University of Buffalo Law School, where he was named dean in 1948, before returning to Harvard, where he would teach until his retirement. Yet another, Nathaniel Nathanson, who had clerked for Julian Mack before clerking for Brandeis in 1934, taught law for decades at Northwestern University—the second Jew after Mack to serve on the school's law faculty. David Riesman, Brandeis's clerk during the 1935 term, began his academic career as a law professor at the University of Buffalo, where his scholarship focused on the interplay between law and society. With the publication of *The Lonely Crowd*, the best-selling 1950 book he published a year after joining the University of Chicago's social science faculty, and subsequent books, Riesman gained celebrity as one of the twentieth century's most influential sociologists. As for those clerks who entered government service, James Landis, on Brandeis's recommendation, served on the Federal Trade Commission and as chairman of FDR's Securities and Exchange Commission before teaching at Harvard Law, where he was dean from 1938 to 1946. Over the years, Brandeis would remain especially close with Dean Acheson, his law clerk from 1919 to 1921. Brandeis personally recommended Acheson to Roosevelt for appointment as solicitor general in 1933, and Acheson later served as assistant secretary in the Treasury and State Departments before being appointed secretary of state by President Harry Truman in 1948.

Especially for highly promising Jewish law school graduates from poor immigrant backgrounds, Supreme Court clerkships became coveted and prestigious attainments, and avenues of upward mobility, within the legal profession. Prior to Brandeis's appointment, no Jewish law school graduate had ever served as a Supreme Court clerk, and the new justice was well aware of the barriers to advancement in the legal profession posed by antisemitism. As the case of Nathaniel Nathanson attests, some of these clerks worked first for Julian Mack or other federal judges before accepting Brandeis's offer of a clerkship. Mack, as we saw earlier, pioneered the tradition of choosing clerks from Harvard Law, as recommended to him first by Roscoe Pound and then by Frankfurter. In addition to Nathanson, Freund, Jaffe, and Riesman, Brandeis hired three other Jewish law clerks, Harry Shulman, Henry J. Friendly, and Irving Goldsmith, during his tenure on the court.

The country's major law schools hired few if any Jews throughout the

1920s and 1930s, with Frankfurter serving as Harvard Law's sole Jewish faculty member during his twenty-five-year tenure. To remedy this situation, Brandeis, during his court years, "made a special project of finding law faculty positions for young Jewish lawyers whom he regarded as particularly talented."[38] Harvard's hiring of Paul Freund and Louis Jaffe within a few years of Frankfurter's appointment to the Supreme Court demonstrated the success of this effort, while also setting a precedent for the appointment of a growing number of Jewish Harvard Law faculty members during the 1950s and 1960s.

Also, before his appointment at Harvard, Jaffe would break a glass ceiling for Jews in the American legal profession by becoming the first Jewish dean of a law school, at the University of Buffalo, in 1948. Harry Shulman, who clerked for Brandeis in 1929, later broke another glass ceiling by becoming the first Jewish dean of Yale Law School in 1954. When Brandeis was encouraging Shulman to seek a teaching position, no Jews served on the faculties of the Yale, Columbia, Northwestern, or University of Pennsylvania Law Schools, with Frankfurter then the lone Jewish law professor at Harvard. In writing to Frankfurter regarding Shulman, Brandeis made his by now familiar case: "It seems to me that a great service could be done generally to American law and to the Jews by placing desirable ones in the law school faculties."[39] Brandeis further mentioned that a Yale faculty member had told him that "the right man there would find no opposition on the score of anti-Semitism."[40] Shulman, a Russian-born graduate of Brown University and a student of Frankfurter's at Harvard, thus joined the Yale Law School faculty in 1930, immediately following his clerkship. Although Shulman was considered for the dean position as early as 1939, when he was just thirty-six—and although the highly respected jurist Learned Hand contended, "My choice remains Harry Shulman," voicing a sentiment several other legal scholars and jurists shared—antisemitism blocked his appointment.[41] When, some fourteen years later, Shulman's name was again presented to the Yale Corporation to be the law school's dean, a new fight broke out "entirely because of the Jewish issue." An enthusiastic six-page letter of support sent by Dean Acheson to his fellow Yale Corporation trustees played a major role in securing Shulman's appointment.[42] Several Jewish Yale Law deans would follow in Shulman's footsteps.

Brandeis's law clerks served mainly as his research assistants, "checking points of law and earlier cases, but above all providing him with the massive amounts of factual material that he utilized in his opinions, especially his dissents."[43] Paul Freund would recall that after Freund had worked for weeks in researching and revising an opinion, Brandeis would often say: "Now I think the opinion is persuasive, but what can we do to make it more instructive?"[44] The clerks were central in what Brandeis viewed as his "educational strategy": although Brandeis would occasionally permit one to draft part of an opinion, the clerks' main role was "to provide him with the facts to educate bench or bar."[45] Dean Acheson would later recall that his research on a relatively minor prohibition case had resulted in fifteen pages of footnotes.[46] Brandeis presumably would have been appalled at the practice adopted by many later justices, including Frankfurter and Arthur Goldberg, of assigning clerks to draft decisions. All Brandeis's most famous court opinions, dissenting and otherwise, were written by him, and him alone.

Brandeis on Free Speech and the Right to Privacy

When Brandeis began his Supreme Court tenure, he joined Oliver Wendell Holmes Jr. as one of the court's two most liberal justices. They would often join together by attacking, in dissenting opinions, their more conservative colleagues' interference with the progressive social and economic reform legislation enacted by Congress. Brandeis passionately shared Holmes's belief that assessing and upholding the constitutionality of a law passed by Congress, especially one furthering progressive ideals, "is the gravest and most delicate duty that this court is called on to perform." Together, Brandeis and Holmes won the enduring gratitude of progressives for effectively letting reform-minded legislatures enact often-controversial measures. This was especially true after William Howard Taft was appointed chief justice in 1921, and the phrase *Holmes and Brandeis dissenting* became a well-known feature of the Taft court's decisions. The Holmes-Brandeis alliance led Taft to exclaim in frustration of the former, "I am very fond of the old gentleman, but he is so completely under the control of Brother Brandeis that it gives to Brandeis two votes instead of one."[47] Many of Brandeis's dissenting opinions, especially regarding the First Amendment right to free speech and the Fourth Amendment right to privacy, were destined in later years to become the law of the land.

When Brandeis came to the court, it had not yet developed a comprehensive jurisprudence in regard to the First Amendment. As late as 1907, Justice Holmes had written that the speech clause did little more than prevent government from imposing prior restraint on speech, and in 1915 he did not even question a state law punishing speech that tended to incite crime. When the first Supreme Court case testing the Wilson administration's wartime restrictions on free speech was decided in 1919, Holmes spoke for all his colleagues in upholding the restrictions. In his decision in the landmark case *Schenck v. United States*, Holmes, speaking for a unanimous court, famously wrote: "The character of every act depends upon the circumstances in which it is done. . . . The most stringent protection of free speech would not protect a man in falsely shouting fire in a theatre and causing a panic."[48] In his *Schenck* decision, Holmes, establishing the "clear and present danger" standard for determining constitutionally permitted restrictions on speech, attempted to cast a distinction regarding "whether the words used are used in such circumstances and are of such a nature as to create a clear and present danger that they will bring about the substantive evils that Congress has a right to prevent."[49]

Relatedly, civil liberties issues, including freedom of speech, had not been a major concern of the federal government or its courts since the Alien and Sedition Acts of the late 1790s. During World War I, however, Congress, responding to growing public anger about the antiwar movement, passed the Espionage Act in 1917. In *Schenck v. United States*, a trial court had used the Espionage Act to convict a Socialist Party official for sending draftees pamphlets encouraging them to oppose the draft. Writing for a unanimous court, Holmes had upheld the conviction, arguing that whether or not speech was permissible was "a question of proximity and degree. When a nation is at war, many things that might be said in time of peace are such a hindrance to its effort that their utterance will not be endured so long as men fight and that no Court could regard them as protected by any constitutional right."[50] While the leafleting might have been protected as free speech by the First Amendment during peacetime, the ruling held that no such right existed during wartime.

A few days after the clear and present danger standard was applied against Schenck, Holmes used it again against Socialist Party leader Eugene V. Debs, who, while speaking at a Canton, Ohio, antiwar gathering on June 16, 1918, had publicly questioned the legitimacy of America's war involvement in a way the government viewed as a treasonous effort to undermine the war effort. In *Debs v. U.S.* (1919), again writing for a unanimous court, Holmes upheld the Espionage Act conviction of Debs on the grounds that his Ohio speech's probable effect had been to prevent military recruiting.[51]

In their dissent in *Abrams v. the United States*, by comparison, another case resulting from the Espionage Act, Holmes and Brandeis transformed the clear and present danger standard from a doctrine restricting free speech to one defending it. In this dissent, against the court's 7–2 majority upholding the conviction of five men who had been accused of violating the Espionage

Act by distributing antiwar circulars, Holmes and Brandeis argued that an individual had the right criticize or verbally attack the American government. Congress, they maintained, can establish a limit on freedom of speech to counter an "immediate evil or an interest to bring it about" but not to counter some vague future possibility. Thereafter, Brandeis and Holmes wrote a series of dissents "outlining the right of the dissenter, the meaning of free speech and the promise of the Constitution."[52] Although Brandeis had concurred with Holmes in both the *Schenck* and *Debs* cases, he did not completely adhere to the clear and present danger standard Holmes had formulated. For Brandeis, the problem with this doctrine "was that it assumed that speech, while important, was not an absolute right and the government could, under appropriate conditions, restrict expression."[53]

In his 1920 dissent in *Schaefer v. United States*, which followed the Abrams case by four months, Brandeis described the clear and present danger standard as a "rule of reason" for which correct application requires the "exercise of good judgment." In this case, Peter Schaefer and his codefendants, who were officers in a Philadelphia German-language association, were convicted of publishing newspapers during the war that printed false reports and misleading articles. The articles, claimed the government, were openly contemptuous of the U.S. war effort, erroneously suggesting that President Wilson had illegally entered into the war, and thus violated the Espionage Act. Schaefer and his codefendants were also convicted of having obstructed military recruiting and having promoted the success of the enemy.[54] In his dissent, written on his and Holmes's behalf, Brandeis opposed the court's upholding of the defendants' conviction by arguing that the clear and present danger standard had not been met, and that the conviction should have been overturned. Brandeis contended further that judges should use a rule of reason to determine whether allegedly offensive or treasonous speech, said to violate the Espionage Act, should be restricted or defended. To exercise the good judgment necessary to apply the "rule of reason," Brandeis wrote, "calmness is, in times of deep feeling and on subjects which excite passion, as essential as fearlessness and honesty."[55] In Brandeis's view, the newspapers' publication did not present a clear and present danger to anything involving the American war effort and thus in no way violated the Espionage Act. No jury "acting in calmness," maintained Brandeis, could reasonably say the opposite. In the oft-quoted conclusion of his dissent, Brandeis cautioned the court that "the constitutional right of free speech has been declared to be the same in peace and in war. In peace, too, many men may differ widely as to what loyalty to our country demands; and an intolerant majority, swayed by passions or by fear, may be prone in the future, as it has often been in the past, to stamp as disloyal opinion with which it disagrees. Convictions such as these, besides abridging freedom of speech, threaten freedom of thought and of belief."[56]

A hallmark of Brandeis's dissenting opinions in the *Abrams* and *Schaefer* cases, and of his enduring contribution to First Amendment jurisprudence, was his contention that restricting speech during wartime only made it easier to suppress freedom of expression afterward.[57]

Also, when Brandeis joined the court, it had not developed even the beginnings of a jurisprudence regarding the right to privacy, a right Brandeis had first called attention to in his 1890 *Harvard Law Review* article on "The Right to Privacy," coauthored with Sam Warren. One of the most influential articles in American legal history, this study, according to Roscoe Pound, did "nothing less than add a chapter to our law."[58] In recent years, the idea of a constitutionally protected right to privacy, which has seen much public controversy and debate, played a key role in the defeat of Robert Bork's nomination to the Supreme Court in 1987.

While the Brandeis and Warren article contains a powerful indictment of press irresponsibility, it also pointed the way to a much more expansive understanding of what Justice Brandeis, in his dissenting opinion in the 1928 civil liberties case *Olmstead v. United States*, would later call "the most comprehensive of rights, and the right most valued by civilized man. In very early times, the common law gave a remedy only for physical interference with life and property. . . . Later, there came a recognition of man's spiritual nature, of his feelings and his intellect. Gradually, the scope of these legal rights broadened, and now the right to life has come to mean the right to enjoy life—the right to be left alone."[59] In what has been called one of their article's "most prescient parts," Brandeis and Warren warned that U.S. law must adapt to changing conditions given the threats posed by new technology to privacy. "Instantaneous photographs and newspaper enterprise," they argued, "have invaded the sacred precincts of private and domestic life; and numerous mechanical devices threaten to make good the prediction that 'what is whispered in the closet shall be proclaimed from the housetops.'"[60] While legal scholars and judges have often disagreed as to whether there is a constitutional right to privacy, Brandeis undoubtedly played a historic role in identifying and promoting the idea of such a right, both in this article and in his later rulings as a Supreme Court justice, especially in his famous dissent in *Olmstead v. United States*.

The Supreme Court had given little if any attention to this "right" to privacy until the 1920s, when government officials began using new technology to listen to telephone conversations. Brandeis hated the telephone in the first place and detested telephone wiretapping even more. In the *Olmstead* case, Brandeis sought to apply the principle of a constitutional right to privacy to changes in electronic technology, such as wiretapping. The *Olmstead* case grew out of the federal government's efforts to enforce Prohibition, which began in 1920. To serve their clients, bootleggers had availed themselves of the latest technology, including the telephone. For several months, federal agents in Seattle had tapped the home and office phones of several suspected bootleggers, including a policeman named Roy Olmstead, and had listened in on their conversations. Olmstead, who had sold $2 million worth of liquor smuggled from Canada, had set up an elaborate phone bank in an office building so that purchasers of his illegal liquor could call in their orders and then arrange for delivery. With hundreds of pages of incriminating evidence gathered from their wiretaps, the federal agents had arrested Olmstead and his colleagues, who were later convicted. Olmstead appealed the conviction, arguing that the wiretap evidence should have been inadmissible at his trial because it was acquired without a search warrant, thus violating his Fourth Amendment rights.

The court's 5–4 decision, written by Chief Justice Taft, upheld Olmstead's conviction, finding that the Fourth Amendment's prohibition against unlawful search and seizure did not extend to the wiretapping of telephone conversations. There had been no unconstitutional search of Olmstead's home and office, Taft ruled. No police official had actually entered the premises without a warrant, and no physical items had been seized. No one had forced Olmstead and the other defendants to talk on the telephone and thereby reveal information about the smuggled liquor. Therefore, Taft concluded, no unconstitutional search and seizure had occurred.

Brandeis, however, in his dissenting opinion, found the federal agents' wiretapping to be unconstitutional on grounds of being an invasion of privacy. "Whenever a telephone line is tapped," Brandeis wrote, "the privacy of the persons at both ends of the line is invaded, and all conversations between them upon any subject, and although proper, confidential and privileged, may be overheard. Moreover, the tapping of one man's telephone line involves the tapping of the telephone of every other person whom he may call, or who may call him."[61] Such wiretapping was unconstitutional, argued Brandeis, precisely because it violated the Fourth Amendment's search and seizure clause.

The writers of the amendment, Brandeis reminded Taft and his colleagues on the court who had upheld Olmstead's conviction, had not specifically mentioned wiretapping because neither the practice nor telephones had yet been invented.

In "The Right to Privacy," Brandeis and Warren had endeavored to protect the privacy of the well-off from unwarranted press intrusions. Now, in his *Olmstead* opinion, Brandeis sought to protect the privacy of the less well-off, accused of criminal activity, from unwarranted government intrusions. "The makers of our Constitution," Brandeis argued, "conferred, as against the Government, the right to be left alone—the most comprehensive of rights and the right most valued by civilized man. To protect that right, every unjustifiable intrusion of the Government upon the privacy of the individual, whatever the means employed, must be deemed a violation of the Fourth Amendment."[62]

These lines from Brandeis's dissent have been cited numerous times, by liberal and conservative judges alike, ensuring Brandeis's legacy as the father of the constitutionally protected right to privacy. Warren Burger, while still a member of the U.S. Court of Appeals, cited them in upholding the rights of patients to refuse medical treatment.[63] Justice William O. Douglas, who had first voted to uphold warrantless wiretaps, reversed himself in 1952, turning to Brandeis's "cause of privacy—the right to be left alone."[64] More recently, in 1990, three Supreme Court justices cited Brandeis on privacy in ruling on a right-to-die case.[65] Today, more than one hundred years after the publication of his famous law review article, Brandeis's historic role in promoting the idea of a constitutionally protected right to privacy can and should be considered one of the most enduring legacies of his distinguished Supreme Court career.

Holmes, like Brandeis, wrote a dissenting opinion in the *Olmstead* case, stating that wiretapping was illegal and that society must decide between arresting criminals and the government's own effective criminal activity through wiretapping in pursuit of alleged criminals. "We have to choose," said Holmes in one of the best-remembered sentences in all constitutional law,[66] "and for my part I think it is less evil that some criminals should escape than that the government should play an ignoble part."[67]

Chief Justice Taft was said to be angry about the Holmes dissent. "The truth is," Taft complained privately, "Holmes voted the other way till Brandeis got after him and induced him to change on the ground that a state law in Washington forbade wiretapping." Taft was correct in this claim. "I should not have printed what I wrote," Holmes confided to a friend, "however, if [Brandeis] had not asked me to."

Over his six hundred or so judicial opinions while on the Supreme Court, Brandeis's record on civil liberties, including the right to privacy, is considered stronger than his record on religious and racial rights. Both as a lawyer and a jurist, Brandeis never concerned himself specifically with the rights of blacks, Japanese, Catholics, or Jews as did Jewish jurists such as Louis Marshall and Julian Mack. Throughout his career, Brandeis focused primarily on the rights of the people at large, rather than those of racial minorities.[68] While growing up in Louisville, Brandeis, like most white Southerners, had little to do with the large African American population that supported much of the area's economy. Although Brandeis's parents had supported abolition, "civil rights did not play a major role in the family's thinking. While Louis left the city of Louisville as a boy of sixteen, it is improbable that he abandoned many of the racial attitudes that permeated it."[69] Later, as a progressive reformer, Brandeis never involved himself with civil rights groups such as the National Association for the Advancement of Colored People (NAACP), as did his friend Felix Frankfurter. During his Supreme Court tenure, Brandeis tended to vote with the conservative majority in cases involving race.[70] He was thus, as the legal scholar Robert Burt has noted, "within the Court consensus, but not ahead of it."[71] He signed majority opinions involving the religious liberty of Catholics and other religious minorities, such as the unanimous 1925 decision in *Pierce v. Society of the Sisters of the Holy Names of Jesus and Mary*, overturning as unconstitutional Oregon's Ku Klux Klan–sponsored anti-Catholic statute requiring parents to send their children to public schools.[72] But Brandeis did not write his own opinions in such religious liberty cases. Notably, never, during his twenty-three-year tenure on the Supreme Court, did he write an opinion that related specifically to the religious rights of America's Jews.

Bearing mention here is the 1935 case *Schechter Poultry Corp. v. United States*, in which the court unanimously upheld the right of Jews to produce and distribute kosher chickens—a ruling Brandeis strongly supported.[73] But the decision, which effectively backed the right of religious Jews to practice their faith, had another major implication: the rendering as unconstitutional of Franklin Roosevelt's National Recovery Act (NRA), a centerpiece of his New Deal program. The NRA, for its part, established production codes and wage controls for much of the nation's nonagricultural economy, including the poultry industry. As even Roosevelt's admirers have conceded, the NRA, created during the historic first hundred days of FDR's presidency, had established "thousands of intrusive price and production codes for industry."[74] One of these was known as the "Live Poultry Code," charged with regulating the city's kosher poultry industry.

Eating food certified by Jewish authorities as kosher is central to the observance of the Jewish dietary laws, and a religious obligation for observant Jews.[75] Joseph Schechter and his three brothers, whose father was a rabbi, had been born in Hungary and grown up in an Orthodox Brooklyn home. During the early 1930s, the Schechter brothers were kosher butchers who ran Brooklyn's two largest live poultry plants. In both, which adhered strictly to the Jewish dietary laws, they employed rabbis and Jewish ritual slaughterers, or *shochtim*, who attested that the Jewish dietary laws were being strictly observed.[76] The two slaughterhouses sold chickens to kosher markets and butcher shops throughout New York City.[77]

Beginning in June 1934, the Roosevelt administration expanded NRA inspections targeting both the poultry industry generally and New York's kosher poultry trade in particular. Commonly acknowledged was that "there were few industries, large or small, that warranted government regulation more than the kosher poultry trade," whose federal regulation came under the jurisdiction of the NRA.[78] Although the word *kosher* implied Jewish ritual purity and slaughtering under strict, rabbinical supervision, the kosher poultry industry, especially in New York, "was ridden with vile, contaminated facilities, wretched working conditions, and corruption."[79] Not infrequently, diseased chickens were sold at a discount to kosher butchers and retailers who reportedly watched the chickens "killed according to Jewish ritual (however loosely observed), before selling the tainted poultry to unknowing customers."[80]

In 1934, the Schechter brothers were arrested for allegedly peddling diseased poultry and trying to undersell their competitors, in violation of the NRA's New York Live Poultry Code. For the Schechters, the NRA allegation that they had sold sick poultry, which led to the case becoming known as the "sick chicken case," was especially offensive. To claim, as the poultry inspectors and government lawyers did, that the Schechter chickens were unfit was to suggest the Schechters "were not good Jews . . . that their kosher slaughterhouse was not really kosher, and so unworthy of customers."[81] The charge angered the Schechters and offended their dignity as religious Jews.[82] Thus, when the Schechter brothers were found guilty, fined $7,425, and sentenced to between one and three months in jail, they were determined to fight the NRA's verdict. The Schechters immediately appealed their conviction, and their appeal went all the way to the Supreme Court.

The Schechters' Brooklyn-based attorney, Joseph Heller, represented his clients well in what was his first Supreme Court appearance. The justices, we are told, "laughed heartily as Heller ridiculed the most byzantine provisions of the Live Poultry Code, his thick [Yiddish] accent enhancing his intended comic effect."[83] Brandeis and his colleagues listened attentively as Heller argued that the government's prosecution of the Schechter brothers was both excessive and unwarranted. The NRA bureaucrats, he suggested, had been persecuting as well as prosecuting his clients, on whose poultry business thousands of Orthodox Jews depended for kosher chickens. The Schechter brothers' fate, and that of the NRA itself, Heller intoned, was in the nine justices' hands.

By noon on May 27, 1935 — "Black Monday," as it came to be known by New Deal supporters — the Supreme Court room was filled to capacity, with an overflow crowd gathered in the hallway, as the Washington press corps, dozens of attorneys, and others awaited the decision in the *Schechter* case, and in two other cases challenging the NRA's constitutionality. In these two other cases, the court rendered unanimous rulings against the NRA. When Chief Justice Charles Evans Hughes began to read his *Schechter* opinion, a unanimous opinion signed by all nine justices, "there was a sharp, audible intake of breath by the crowd."[84] The NRA's Live Poultry Code, declared Hughes, was an unconstitutional expansion of federal authority. The conviction of the Schechter brothers had been overturned. Soon thereafter, the NRA lost hundreds of similar cases and, within a few months, had closed its doors. The NRA, a pillar of FDR's New Deal, was no more. To the surprise of many, Brandeis had joined the court in striking down a major piece of New Deal legislation, as did the court's other liberal Jewish justice, Benjamin Cardozo. The ruling shocked FDR, who on hearing the news asked his White House aides: "Well, where was Ben Cardozo? . . . And what about Old Isaiah [the nickname FDR used for Brandeis]?"[85]

Immediately after the *Schechter* decision was announced, Brandeis met secretly with Benjamin Cohen and Thomas Corcoran, students and protégés of Brandeis's longtime friend and top FDR adviser Felix Frankfurter and two major architects of the New Deal. "You have heard," the aging Brandeis reportedly told Cohen and Corcoran in the court anteroom, of "these three decisions," most notably *Schechter*. He warned that the rulings "change everything. The Court was unanimous." Then, in an act of questionable judicial propriety, Brandeis told them to ask Frankfurter to advise FDR that he would have to redesign much of his New Deal legislative program.[86] "The President," Brandeis said in what was possibly the day's most damning judgment, "has been living in a fool's paradise."[87]

Extrajudicial Activities and the New Deal

Brandeis's secret meeting with Ben Cohen and Tom Corcoran was not his only questionable act while serving as a justice on the court. Throughout his tenure, as even one of his greatest admirers has conceded, Brandeis would maintain "a level of extrajudicial activity that, by current standards of judicial ethics, would be either impermissible or at best questionable in judgment."[88]

But by engaging in such acts, Brandeis was continuing a Supreme Court tradition of justices engaging in extrajudicial political activity stretching back to the republic's beginnings. While the Founding Fathers may have sought to establish an independent judiciary, they did not prohibit judges from participating in extrajudicial political activities. Rather, as the judicial scholar Bruce Allen Murphy has documented, from the presidency of George Washington through much of the nineteenth century judges ran for political office, campaigned openly for other political candidates, and publicly advised presidents and cabinet members.[89] Between 1832 and 1860, John McLean was one of three Supreme Court justices to campaign for the presidency, while others publicly supported their favorite presidential candidates. In the post–Civil War era, Chief Justice Salmon P. Chase campaigned for the presidency in 1868 and 1872.[90] Three other justices, David Davis, Samuel Miller, and Stephen Field, each ran in two separate presidential elections, and Chief Justice Morrison Waite privately advised Rutherford B. Hayes in his 1876 presidential campaign.[91] The Chase court, in the late 1860s, also created a precedent permitting sitting justices to promote appointments for future Supreme Court colleagues, and for other federal-court judgeships as well. While by the 1880s sitting justices were no longer campaigning for the presidency or U.S. Senate, high court justices sought openly to influence judicial appointments, a practice that would be followed by Brandeis, Frankfurter, and later Supreme Court justices.

The public controversy over the disputed presidential election of 1876, in which the Republican candidate Hayes defeated the Democrat Tilden despite losing the popular vote, and the highly political role played by the Supreme Court in deciding the outcome of that election, resulted in restrictions being placed on the extrajudicial political activities of Supreme Court justices. Thereafter, court members would face "proscriptions against extensive informal political advising and open campaigning for office."[92] In the decades to come, only Justice William Moody, who had previously served as Theodore Roosevelt's secretary of the Navy, ignored the restrictions on extrajudicial political activity and continued after his court appointment to advise Roosevelt as part of his "Tennis Cabinet."[93]

Almost from the moment he took his seat on the Supreme Court, Brandeis tended to ignore or circumvent prevailing restrictions on extrajudicial political activity and, following Justice Moody's example, continued to advise Woodrow Wilson. As Wilson campaigned for reelection in 1916, he described Brandeis as "a tower of strength as an adviser and counselor,"[94] a role Brandeis continued playing throughout Wilson's second term, and for Wilson after he left the White House as well.

Along with Wilson, Brandeis often consulted the president's top adviser, Colonel House, and Wilson's cabinet members. After the United States entered World War I, Brandeis advised his old friend Newton Baker, who became secretary of war in 1917, on workers' conditions in the munitions industry. At Wilson's request, Brandeis "wrote a lengthy letter to Colonel House detailing the way the War Industries Board should be organized."[95] Generally speaking, members of Wilson's war government regularly sought Brandeis's advice "either for their own benefit or for transmission to the president."[96] In 1917, Wilson asked Brandeis to work with Colonel House to compile ideas for a postwar peace treaty, especially concerning the rights of minorities.[97] Despite two warnings from Chief Justice Edward White that "a member of the Supreme Court should confine his endeavors to the work of the Court,"[98] Brandeis continued working closely with Colonel House for the duration of the Wilson presidency.

In June 1921, shortly after his White House term ended, Wilson engaged Justice Brandeis "in a flagrantly political undertaking"—helping the former president draft a statement of progressive principles for the Democratic Party. This then-secret policy statement, which became known as The Document, was intended to define the partisan political platform on which Wilson hoped to campaign for a third presidential term in 1924.[99] However profound a conflict of interest, Brandeis apparently had no qualms that his judicial position should have precluded him from engaging in such blatantly partisan extrajudicial political activity.[100]

During much of his court tenure, Brandeis also secretly engaged in a wide variety of extrajudicial political activities through his now famous "political partnership" with Felix Frankfurter. The two had first met in May 1905 when

Frankfurter, then in law school, had attended a talk by Brandeis in Cambridge. They met again and became better acquainted in 1908, when Frankfurter was working as an assistant to Henry L. Stimson, then the U.S. attorney for the Southern District of New York. Brandeis, who would come to regard Frankfurter as his "half brother, half son," became one of Frankfurter's most important mentors, helping him secure his Harvard Law School professorship in 1914 and subsequently facilitating his appointment to the school's newly endowed chair in administrative law—a chair for which Brandeis had worked closely with Roscoe Pound to raise the endowment.[101] For the next two years, living as practically neighbors in Cambridge, their mutual admiration deepened.[102] In 1914, Brandeis personally encouraged Frankfurter's involvement in the American Zionist movement, with the younger lawyer serving as one of Brandeis's top lieutenants. At Brandeis's behest, Frankfurter attended the Versailles Peace Conference in 1919 as a legal adviser to the Zionist delegation, and as a liaison for Brandeis, who remained in Washington. By the early 1920s, Brandeis and Frankfurter's growing correspondence covered a variety of topics, including politics, law, and Zionism. And by 1928, Brandeis could say he believed Frankfurter to be the most talented, and, as we shall see, useful, lawyer in the United States.

The best known and most controversial part of the Brandeis-Frankfurter partnership involved finances. Brandeis, as we saw earlier, built a lucrative law practice, lived frugally, and was worth millions by the time of his Supreme Court appointment. His wealth had ultimately allowed him to forgo corporate clients in favor of pro bono work and advocacy for progressive causes. Frankfurter, too, had a passion for public service, demonstrated by his leaving a high-paying corporate law firm to work for Henry Stimson just ten months after graduating from law school. Prior to his 1939 Supreme Court appointment, Frankfurter "held a series of low-paying government jobs or taught at Harvard Law School at a time of notoriously low academic salaries."[103] While teaching full time at Harvard, and writing scholarly books for which he wasn't greatly reimbursed, Frankfurter worked without pay as counsel for the National Consumers League and other reform groups, and as the *New Republic*'s legal affairs correspondent. Aware of Frankfurter's financial constraints, Brandeis saw that he could underwrite much of Frankfurter's unpaid work as a progressive reformer and public servant.

Thus, in 1934, Brandeis confided to Julian Mack that he had "for years" been giving Frankfurter an annual allowance "for public purposes."[104] This allowance enabled Brandeis, while serving on the court, to continue exerting his influence in American politics, advising governors and presidents, drafting legislation, and generating public policy articles and editorials, often published under Frankfurter's name, for the *Harvard Law Review, New Republic*, and other publications. With Frankfurter thus on retainer as his "paid political lobbyist and lieutenant,"[105] Brandeis promoted his favored legislation, some pending in Congress, including laws to ban injunctions against unions and to apply workers' compensation acts to the railroads.

The entire arrangement began with a November 1916 letter by Brandeis to Frankfurter, with an enclosed check, stating: "You have had a considerable expense for travelling, telephoning and similar expenses in public matters undertaken at my request or following up my suggestions and will have more in the future no doubt. These expenses should, of course, be borne by me."[106] Frankfurter returned the check, but Brandeis sent it back with the following letter:

> Alice and I talked over the matter before I sent the check and considered it again carefully on receipt of your letter. We are clearly of the opinion that you ought to take the check.
>
> In essence this is nothing different than your taking traveling and incidental expenses from the Consumer League or the *New Republic*— which I trust you do. You are giving your very valuable time and that is quite enough. It can make no difference that the subject matter in connection with which expense is incurred is more definite in one case than in the other.
>
> I ought to feel free to make suggestions to you, although they involve some incidental expense. And you should feel free to incur expense in the public interest. So I am returning the check.[107]

Frankfurter then kept the returned check, and over the course of his career accepted a total of $52,250 from Brandeis, well over $1 million in today's value.[108] The arrangement was flexible, depending on Frankfurter's financial situation. In 1925, Frankfurter wrote to Brandeis about his "personal needs," and Brandeis wrote back, "I'll send the $1,500 now or in installments as you may prefer. Your public service must not be abridged."[109] When Frankfurter had to pay for medical treatment and psychoanalysis for his wife, Marion, who had suffered a nervous breakdown, Brandeis sent him money to defray the expenses.[110] The annual amounts "kept pace with inflation": Brandeis sent Frankfurter $2,000 in 1927 and $3,500 in 1934.[111] To facilitate this transfer of funds, Brandeis opened a special bank account for Frankfurter into which he made regular deposits.

The evolving Brandeis-Frankfurter partnership would first influence national politics in September 1917, when Frankfurter wrote Secretary of War Newton Baker suggesting that someone should chair the investigation of the causes of labor unrest. He recommended the labor leader Sidney Hillman, noting "the foregoing views have the support of Mr. Justice Brandeis."[112] Wilson accepted this recommendation and appointed Hillman to the post. The partnership had even farther-reaching effects, however, during the Franklin Roosevelt administration. Frankfurter had first met Roosevelt in 1906, and their personal ties deepened when FDR served as Wilson's assistant secretary of war and Frankfurter was in Washington advising the War Department. When Roosevelt served as New York's governor, beginning in 1929, Frankfurter was his political confidant. But it was during the gubernatorial campaign that Brandeis first used Frankfurter as a conduit to the future president. This channel would remain open during FDR's governorship and into his presidency, when the Brandeis-Frankfurter political connection would have its greatest influence.

When FDR entered the White House, Frankfurter remained a close political ally, adviser, and friend of the new president, enabling Brandeis to play a significant extrajudicial role in advising FDR on New Deal legislation and policy. In their first meeting, arranged by Frankfurter, on November 23, 1932, Brandeis offered him his help and "advised him to fund public works programs by taxing large estates."[113] Thereafter, FDR would refer to Brandeis affectionately as Isaiah, as would other New Deal officials in awe of his wisdom and demeanor.

Throughout the 1930s, FDR labor secretary Frances Perkins, interior secretary Harold Ickes, and other New Deal officials eagerly sought Brandeis's advice on issues of policy and government appointments. Brandeis was especially close to Perkins, an ally in several progressive causes whom he had enthusiastically recommended to FDR for the labor secretary post. According to his former law clerk Paul Freund, Brandeis "had devoted his entire meeting with President Roosevelt at the Mayflower Hotel in mid-January 1933 to arguing in behalf of Perkins's appointment to the position."[114] What became known as the "Brandeis-Frankfurter placement bureau" was especially successfully in filling positions in the Labor, Interior, and Agriculture Departments.[115] Upon Brandeis's recommendation, Ickes appointed Nathan

Margold, an NAACP lawyer and Frankfurter protégé from Harvard, as the Interior Department's solicitor. Margold, in turn, asked Brandeis and Frankfurter for advice on staffing his office.[116] With Brandeis's assistance, Abe Fortas, a brilliant, young Yale Law School graduate, was named director of the Interior Department's Division of Manpower and later the department's undersecretary. The many Jewish students of Frankfurter who, with Brandeis's help, were placed in important New Deal positions included Charles E. Wyzanski Jr., who was named the Labor Department's solicitor and became one of Justice Brandeis's key contacts in the Labor Department.[117] In the Justice Department, Paul Freund was appointed to a top post in the Solicitor General's Office. Another former Brandeis clerk, and Frankfurter student, Louis Jaffe, worked as an attorney with the New Deal's Agricultural Adjustment Administration and its National Labor Relations Board before beginning his academic career. Justice Brandeis convinced the Tennessee Valley Authority director to appoint another Jewish Harvard Law protégé of Frankfurter's, David Lilienthal, to the TVA board.[118] On Brandeis and Frankfurter's recommendation, Dean Acheson was named undersecretary of the treasury. An exception was the National Recovery Administration, with which Brandeis never successfully placed any political allies, perhaps spurring his anti-NRA stance in the 1935 Schechter decision.

Brandeis and Frankfurter were perhaps most notably successful in placing Ben Cohen and Tom Corcoran, acclaimed as the "greatest legislative drafting team in history,"[119] in positions of influence with New Deal government agencies. Corcoran, a student of Frankfurter's and a former law clerk to Justice Holmes, became general counsel of the Reconstruction Finance Corporation, whose chairman was Brandeis's old friend Eugene Meyer. Cohen, also a student of Frankfurter's and his deputy counsel to the Versailles Peace Conference's American Zionist delegation, became the Public Works Administration's general counsel. In regular consultation with Brandeis, Cohen, Corcoran, and Brandeis's former law clerk James Landis were instrumental in drafting major New Deal legislation, including the Securities Act of 1933, the Securities Exchange Act of 1934, the Public Utility Holding Company Act, the TVA Act, the Wagner Act, and the Social Security Act of 1935. All this legislation reflected, to some extent, Brandeis's proposals for economic recovery.

Speaking critically of how Brandeis influenced Roosevelt, Rexford Tugwell, a Roosevelt administration opponent of the justice who was well aware of his allies, wrote: "The first of these means was his disciples; the second was the threat of unconstitutionality. The first apostle in the Brandeis hierarchy was Frankfurter. . . . Through Frankfurter, mostly, the staffing of New Deal agencies was controlled and dissenters got rid of. And because Brandeis was, after Holmes's death, the most influential member of the court among intellectuals and liberals—and with Roosevelt—a word from him was nearly a command. . . . The blandishments of Frankfurter, the alternatives offered by Corcoran and Cohen, and the threat of judicial disapproval if they were not agreed to were sufficient . . . the results are plain enough."[120] In addition, with the help of Frankfurter, Cohen, and Corcoran, Brandeis secretly advised the Roosevelt administration on ways of securing Supreme Court approval of the New Deal legislation drafted by his surrogates. The "threat of unconstitutionality," noted by Tugwell, was most successfully used by Brandeis and his colleagues in the court's "Black Monday" 1935 rulings against the NRA.

Despite the undoubted influence Brandeis held over Roosevelt and his legislative agenda, critics such as Tugwell probably exaggerated this influence, and indeed FDR did not always follow Brandeis's counsel. The Hughes court, on which Brandeis was the most liberal member after Holmes's death, did not always uphold the constitutionality of FDR's legislative enactments. The conservative court's *Schechter* ruling was the first of many that would leave much of the New Deal agenda in ruins. Roosevelt was furious with Brandeis after the *Schechter* decision, and ever more determined to pack the Supreme Court in the hope of attaining the judicial rulings he desired. Thus, on February 5, 1937, FDR announced to Congress his highly controversial scheme to expand the court to fifteen justices and to pack the new seats with liberals who would rubber-stamp his New Deal agenda. Much to FDR's anger and chagrin, Old Isaiah did not support the president's court-packing plan. Brandeis immediately let Roosevelt know that "he was unalterably opposed to the President's action and that he [FDR] was making a great mistake."[121] Yet while Brandeis openly expressed his opposition to the plan, Frankfurter, ever loyal to FDR, actively promoted it.

That Brandeis should join his far more conservative colleagues such as Willis Van Devanter and George Sutherland in opposing FDR astounded some New Deal loyalists. By thus working with the court's more conservative members, however, Brandeis helped achieve greater civility and consensus on the court than would otherwise have existed. His success in doing so is part of his judicial legacy.

After Brandeis's open opposition to FDR's court-packing plan, which the White House considered an act of defiance, the Brandeis-Roosevelt friendship waned, as did Brandeis's extrajudicial role in shaping New Deal policy. Although he remained on cordial terms with the president, Brandeis never quite forgave him for what he considered the president's unconstitutional attempt to subvert the court's judicial integrity. Nor did he quickly forgive Frankfurter for supporting FDR's proposal. In the ever-ambitious Frankfurter's case, though, Brandeis likely acknowledged that his friend was protecting his own interests, remaining loyal to the president who would later appoint him to the Supreme Court. And after their brief rift, the annual payments from Brandeis to Frankfurter kept coming, as they had for the previous twenty-one years.[122]

Throughout the court-packing fight, speculation swirled that Brandeis might retire, thus giving Roosevelt an additional court appointment and effectively ending the court-packing battle. Roosevelt, one rumor held, wanted to appoint Frankfurter to Brandeis's seat. FDR loyalists such as Tom Corcoran and Harold Ickes, angered over Brandeis's opposition to the court-packing plan, expressed their view that Brandeis should resign so that Frankfurter could be named to his seat. Brandeis refused to step down, however, believing that "to resign in the midst of the struggle would harm the Court."[123]

Ultimately, it can be argued that FDR lost the court-packing battle but won the war to attain a liberal court majority to uphold the New Deal. With the retirement of Justice Van Devanter in June 1937 and George Sutherland in January 1938, Roosevelt's appointees to replace them, Hugo Black and Stanley Reed, ensured a clear majority in support of New Deal economic measures.[124] Five months later, Justice Benjamin Cardozo, who had been in declining health throughout his six-year court tenure, died. Since Cardozo's 1932 appointment by President Hoover, two Jewish justices had sat together on the court. Not until President Bill Clinton's nomination of Ruth Bader Ginsburg and Stephen Breyer in the 1990s would two Jewish justices serve together for as long a period. After several months of hesitation, FDR finally appointed Frankfurter to succeed Cardozo. And after Frankfurter's 1962 retirement, his seat would become known as the court's "Jewish seat."

Despite rumors since 1937 that Brandeis might retire, his announcement on February 13, 1939, somehow "was both sudden and dramatically unexpected."[125] Although eighty-three years old, he was in relatively good health. Friends suggested that he had wanted to retire before the court's term ended so that he could serve, however briefly, with Frankfurter. And their shared tenure was indeed brief, lasting just two weeks. FDR, for his part, replaced Brandeis with another liberal justice, William O. Douglas, a former Yale Law School professor then serving as chairman of the Securities and Exchange

Commission. Douglas and Frankfurter would be at times political allies, at times bitter rivals, during their many years together on the court.

Throughout the 1930s, Brandeis remained engaged and sometimes discreetly involved in Zionist affairs, speaking often to Julian Mack and Rabbi Stephen Wise about developments relating to Palestine and the Jews' increasingly dire situation in Europe. When after Hitler took power Wise proposed a boycott of German goods, Brandeis asked his clerk Paul Freund to research boycotts in colonial America "to show that it had an authentic American heritage."[126] After FDR appointed the newspaper baron Robert Bingham, who owned Louisville's *Courier-Journal* and was on old Brandeis family friend, ambassador to Great Britain, he asked Brandeis, a fellow Kentuckian, to administer the oath of office. After the ceremony, Brandeis talked to Bingham for close to an hour about the Zionist movement and Palestine, past and present, and about British obligations there.[127] "It was a moving discourse," Freund would later recall, including Brandeis's repeated refrain, "the age-old cry of the Jews, 'Next year in Zion.'"[128]

Following his retirement, Brandeis and Alice remained for much of the year in their Washington apartment, as during his time on the bench, while spending June through late September at their new summer home in Chatham on Cape Cod. After suffering a heart attack and lapsing into a coma for four days, Brandeis died on October 5, 1941. The following day, a private service was held at the Brandeis apartment in Washington, with the fifty or so attendees including former chief justice Hughes, Woodrow Wilson's widow, Edith, high court members and their spouses, American Zionist leaders, and former law clerks.

The eulogy was delivered not by a rabbi but by then assistant secretary of state Dean Acheson, the law clerk who over the years had remained closest to Brandeis. Felix Frankfurter also eulogized Brandeis, speaking briefly of how his friend "happily fused" Hebraism and Hellenism, quoting passages from the Greek historian Thucydides as well as from the Hebrew prophets Micah and Isaiah. Frankfurter also recited a passage from John Bunyan's *Pilgrim's Progress* on the death of Mr. Valiant-for-truth: "My sword I give to him that shall succeed me in my pilgrimage, and my courage and skill to him that can get it. My marks and scars I carry with me, to be a witness for me that I have fought his battles who now will be my rewarder."

Although born a Jew, "Isaiah" neither lived nor died as a religious Jew. No Jewish prayers or psalms were recited at the larger Brandeis funeral service, at which no rabbi officiated. Nor was the traditional Kaddish recited.

In its stead, a string quartet played Beethoven. Brandeis's parents, although never affiliated with a synagogue, had been buried in a Jewish cemetery in Louisville. Justice Brandeis's body, contrary to Jewish law, was cremated. On the anniversary of his death, his family placed the urn containing his ashes beneath the portico of the University of Louisville Law School.

Brandeis's Legacy

Louis D. Brandeis is widely acknowledged as one of the most influential justices ever to sit on the U.S. Supreme Court. The game of ranking high court justices has long been popular among legal scholars and historians, and they have consistently placed Brandeis's among the top three, often following John Marshall and Oliver Wendell Holmes Jr. During his twenty-three years on the court, Brandeis played a singular role in developing the modern jurisprudence of free speech and the doctrine of a constitutionally protected right to privacy. As Alan Dershowitz has noted, "The First Amendment's right of free expression, the Fourth Amendment's right to privacy and the due process clause's focus on personal liberty (rather than property) all owe their current vitality to the creative genius of Justice Brandeis, whose dissenting opinions have become the law of the land."[129] Also, if America's practicing lawyers were to be ranked in terms of "greatness," nearly every list would presumably include Brandeis, along with John Adams, Daniel Webster, Clarence Darrow, and Abraham Lincoln. Brandeis is thus the only name likely to land on both lists.[130]

As one of Woodrow Wilson's closest confidants and the architect of his New Freedom, as well as a shaper of some of FDR's most enduring New Deal programs, Brandeis also ranks among the top Jewish presidential advisers in American history. Relatedly, his political counsel was sought by a host of senators and cabinet members, including Robert La Follette, William G. McAdoo, and Frances Perkins. Before joining the court, Brandeis was known as one of America's preeminent social reformers, a leader of the Progressive movement who invented savings-bank life insurance, pioneered pro bono public interest work by attorneys, and demonstrated how the law could facilitate reform. The Brandeis Brief, the legal technique he developed when arguing *Muller v. Oregon* before the Supreme Court in 1908, was used by a generation of lawyers to support progressive legislation in the face of constitutional challenges and remains widely invoked today.

Appointees to the Supreme Court are nominated only sometimes for their judicial experience. Of course, some justices like Holmes and Cardozo were widely recognized as brilliant jurists before their appointment. Others, however, such as Brandeis, Frankfurter, Hugo Black, and Charles Evans Hughes, to name a handful, were appointed to reward their prior political service, either as presidential advisers or cabinet members, or as politicians who had held high elective office. Of the eight Jewish Supreme Court justices, Brandeis is one of only two—Frankfurter being the other—to have had no prior judicial experience or to have never served as an appointed official in a president's cabinet or subcabinet.

Especially in the 1930s and until his death, Brandeis was among the best known and respected Jews in the United States. Only Albert Einstein and the baseball superstar Hank Greenberg may have eclipsed Brandeis in celebrity. At his seventy-fifth birthday, his friend Louis Kirstein, a Boston philanthropist, publicly praised Brandeis as "a modern prophet," adding that "I am not the first, nor shall I be the last, to suggest that."[131] As noted earlier, FDR called Brandeis Isaiah, as did members of his White House staff. Some Christian admirers went so far as to praise him as "the Greatest Jew in the World since Jesus Christ."[132]

To this day, Brandeis remains the only American Jew after whom a great university has been named. When, in 1947, Middlesex University in Waltham, Massachusetts, was renamed in Brandeis's memory, its first president, Abram Sachar, explained that Brandeis "seemed to combine most felicitously the prophetic ideal of moral principle and the American tradition of political and economic liberalism." The Zionist leader Rabbi Israel Goldstein, who claimed credit for selecting the name, expressed the hope that Brandeis's "noble life might well serve as an inspiration to American youth."[133]

Brandeis's Jewish legacy is more complicated, given that he is considered the least Jewish of the eight Jewish high court justices. As the evidence shows, he was never observant. Of the first four Jewish justices, Brandeis's funeral was the only one at which the Kaddish was not recited. Yet notwithstanding his Christmas tree and the hams he enjoyed, he became intimately connected to the Jewish people through his Zionism. Indeed, he legitimized Zionism, making it fashionable among American Christians and Jews alike. Through his example, he persuaded American Jews, "who were generally unsympathetic to European Zionism, that one could be a patriotic American Jew while at the same time advocating a Jewish homeland for the oppressed Jews of Europe."[134] According to the historian Jonathan Sarna, Brandeis ranks with Theodor Herzl as "the most revered figure in the American—and for a time in the world—Zionist pantheon," probably doing more than any other American Zionist leader, with the possible exception of Stephen Wise, to help effect the establishment of a Jewish state.[135]

Furthermore, as the first Supreme Court justice to hire Jewish law clerks, Brandeis set a precedent that subsequent justices, Jewish and non-Jewish alike, would follow. In hiring Jewish clerks, and helping them find employment in academia and the federal government, Brandeis did much to promote Jews' advancement within the American legal profession. Moreover, through his leadership of the American Zionist movement from 1916 to 1921, and his continuing interest in Zionist affairs thereafter, Brandeis was and remains the only Jewish Supreme Court justice to have combined service on the court with a leadership role in American Jewish life. These achievements are a part of his Jewish legacy that should not be forgotten.

4

BENJAMIN N. CARDOZO

Redeeming the Family Name

ON MAY 1, 1872, Albert Cardozo resigned from the New York State Supreme Court, following a report a month earlier by the New York City Bar Association calling for his impeachment, along with that of his fellow judges George Barnard and John McCunn. The reason was their involvement in the corruption scandal led by William Marcy "Boss" Tweed. The report had followed weeks of public hearings. For their parts, Barnard and McCunn were summarily impeached and removed from office, and had Cardozo not resigned, he undoubtedly would have met the same fate.[1]

Albert Cardozo's resignation was a remarkable fall from grace for a lawyer and judge who was also a leader of New York City's Sephardic Jewish community—"an event of seismic significance in his life and that of his family, ending a brilliant public career and, according to some accounts, shaping the career of his son."[2] The resignation "dishonored the Cardozos and created in his son Benjamin a lifetime mission of restoring the family name."[3]

As a young lawyer during the 1850s, Albert Cardozo had become active in local politics, joining Tammany Hall, New York City's Democratic Party machine. In the next decade, when Mayor Fernando Wood fought Tweed for control of the city's Democratic Party, Cardozo "managed to keep a foot in each camp" and in 1863 was supported by both Wood and Tweed for a judgeship on the Court of Common Pleas, the city's highest court.[4] By the late 1860s, Tweed had emerged as the city's most influential Democrat, besting Wood. Through Tammany Hall, he also held sway in New York state politics, promoting "his allies and lieutenants to important political offices and forg[ing] what was known in the newspapers and caricatured by cartoonist Thomas Nast as The Tweed Ring."[5] Cardozo "did not put politics behind him when he went on the bench" and soon ingratiated himself with Tweed,

77

who subsequently supported Cardozo for nomination and election to the New York State Supreme Court, "professionally, a step up from the Court of Common Pleas."[6] The promotion was especially gratifying to the Cardozo family, given that his father, Michael Hart Cardozo, had been nominated for the same post but had died before the election.[7] Albert was the first Jew to serve on the court.

Between 1868 and 1872, at the height of his political influence as one of "Tweed's judges," Albert Cardozo lived with his family in baronial splendor at 12 West Forty-Seventh Street, kitty-corner from the even more palatial residence of Jay Gould, the Wall Street stock manipulator whose rise and fall would be inextricably linked with Cardozo and Boss Tweed.

During his reign as Tammany Hall's boss, Tweed, who began his political career as a New York volunteer fire company foreman, held a variety of posts, from state senator to deputy city street commissioner and commissioner of public works. By fall 1870, newspapers were vilifying the Tweed Ring as "the most licentious government ever known" and its boss as "the incarnation of all the vice in the City government."[8] Between 1866 and 1871, the Tweed Ring "plundered the City of New York with such precision that it has received the singular distinction of being labeled the model of civic corruption in American municipal history."[9] From Tammany Hall, Tweed and his cronies "systematically looted the city and state of New York of between 30 million and 200 million dollars."[10] Among Tweed's exploits was controlling the nomination and election of judges. In return for this support, Albert Cardozo readily did favors for Tweed, including employing his eldest son, twenty-two-year-old William Jr., as his paid assistant.[11] Tweed's political downfall began in summer 1871, when Nast, whose drawings appeared in *Harper's Weekly*, initiated a campaign against him and his henchmen. The subsequent investigation led by anti-Tammany reformers resulted in Tweed's indictment for perjury, grand larceny, and forgery and his eventual imprisonment.[12]

Amid the campaign against the Tweed Ring, even Cardozo's critics, and there were many, "conceded his impressive ability as a Supreme Court justice . . . whose sole defect—fatal, of course, in a judge—was a willingness to permit considerations of both personal gain and political loyalty to influence his rulings."[13] But after the newly formed Association for the Bar of the City of New York petitioned the New York State Assembly's Judiciary Committee, chaired by Samuel Tilden, to investigate "alleged abuses in the administration of justice"—and after the subsequent public hearings—the Bar Association called for Cardozo's impeachment.[14]

Some of the most serious charges leveled against Cardozo involved his appointment of receivers and referees to handle foreclosure sales and other real estate transactions. On this count, Cardozo indisputably used his appointive power "for political and personal patronage purposes."[15] Moreover, when it came to these appointments, Cardozo was oblivious to the fact that making one of his principal beneficiaries Gratz Nathan, his nephew on his wife's side, could expose him to nepotism charges. Of the 1,182 referee appointments Cardozo made between 1868 and 1871, 407 went to Nathan, who was also appointed by his uncle as a commissioner in municipal actions to open up new streets.[16] Nathan was often selected as counsel for other receivers appointed by Cardozo, who also "favored other family members and those closely associated with Tammany Hall."[17] Even though such blatant political favoritism was common practice in New York during the Gilded Age, it reinforced Cardozo's public image as one of Boss Tweed's unscrupulous partisan judges.

The bar association report also revealed Cardozo's involvement in the exploitation of the courts by the robber barons Jay Gould and James Fisk to further their illegal business schemes. In September 1869, Gould and Fisk, both railroad magnates and Tweed allies, were conspiring to drive up the price of gold and thereby substantially pad their fortunes. When this attempted cornering of the New York gold market collapsed on Black Friday, September 24, 1869, Gould and Fisk, to avoid financial disaster, "hatched a plot to prevent the clearance of transactions through the Gold Exchange Bank . . . to enjoin the Bank from acting as a clearinghouse for the Gold Exchange, and to place its assets in the hands of a receiver, on the pretense, known to be false, that the bank was insolvent."[18] Cardozo cooperated with their scheme, issuing an order giving them control of the Gold Exchange Bank, "which held millions of dollars of frozen transactions, and order[ing] the receiver to pay Gould's brokers and nobody else's."[19] Cardozo also issued several controversial injunctions favoring Gould and Fisk in their epic struggle for control of the Erie Railroad, on whose board they had placed Tweed, against Cornelius Vanderbilt. In his 1869 *North American Review* piece "A Chapter of Erie," Charles Francis Adams revealed the associated scandal, describing Cardozo as "inflexible . . . and unscrupulous . . . nominated as a partisan, a partisan Cardozo has always been, when the occasion demanded."[20] Many in the New York legal community shared Adams's sentiments about Cardozo's ethics.

Benjamin Cardozo was three weeks shy of his second birthday when his father resigned from the State Supreme Court. Following his resignation, Albert escaped disbarment through his Tammany Hall connections and continued practicing law until his death at age fifty-six in 1885. Seventeen years later, Benjamin would join this same law firm.[21] Separately, Albert's public disgrace "had an immediate impact on the family's comfortable style of living."[22] In 1873, the Cardozo family moved from its West Forty-Seventh Street brownstone to 62 East Fifty-Third Street and the next year to an even more modest residence at 212 West Forty-Fourth Street.[23] Nevertheless, over the next several years, Albert Cardozo's "friends at Tammany Hall did not forget him, and he was made a member of its General Committee and later he became one of its Sachems."[24] With these renewed political connections, Albert enjoyed a restoration of his fortunes: his law practice prospered again, and "in what appears to have marked something of a return to former comforts," the Cardozo family "moved in 1877 to a substantial home, still standing today, at 803 Madison Avenue," along with owning a summer home in the Jersey Shore resort town of Long Branch. [25]It was in this Madison Avenue home that Benjamin lived during his undergraduate studies at Columbia University, which he began at the precocious age of fifteen. As a rising New York attorney and judge, Benjamin would continue living in this home until his appointment to the U.S. Supreme Court in 1932.

A Proud Sephardic Heritage

The family of Benjamin Nathan Cardozo was part of New York's well-established Sephardic Jewish community, whose members were descended from Spanish and Portuguese Jews "who had fled from the Iberian Peninsula during the Inquisition and had come to America via the Netherlands and England."[26] According to Cardozo family tradition, "their ancestors were Portuguese Marranos—Jews who practiced their Judaism secretly after forced conversion to Christianity"—who settled first in Holland and then in London before immigrating to the New World. Both branches of the family, the Cardozos and the Nathans, had arrived in the colonies before the American Revolution and shared a "sense of superiority," considering themselves the elite of American Jewry.[27] Close ties amongst the Nathans and Cardozos, as well as the Seixas, Lazarus, Franks, and Solis families, were reinforced over generations by marriage within their close-knit Sephardic community. Benjamin Cardozo's grandparents themselves were first cousins, as were other partnerships within New York's Sephardic Jewish elite. The family's pride in being part of an American Jewish Sephardic aristocracy was not unfounded: the Nathans traced their ancestry back to Abraham de Lucena, one of the first

Jews to set foot on American soil, arriving in New Amsterdam from Holland in 1655.[28] Lucena, "who started out trading with the Indians for pelts, soon became one of New York's most important fur merchants." By the early 1700s, the Lucenas had become one of New York City's two most prominent Jewish families.[29]

Benjamin's great-grandfather Aaron on his father's side, the first Cardozo to settle in the American colonies, arrived in New York from London in 1752, and "his children scattered throughout the colonies."[30] Two of Aaron's six children, David and Isaac, who settled in Charleston, South Carolina, served in the Revolutionary War. Isaac Cardozo, who left Charleston after the Revolution, lived for a while in Philadelphia, where he married Sarah Hart, "also a Sephardic Jew, whose family was among the founders of Easton, Pennsylvania."[31] One of their children, Michael Hart Cardozo, and his wife, Ellen Hart, would welcome Albert Cardozo, their fourth child, in Philadelphia in 1828. Soon after Albert's birth, the family moved to New York.

After reading law with a prominent New York attorney, Albert Cardozo was admitted to the bar in 1849 at age twenty-one. On August 16, 1854, he married Rebecca Washington Nathan, whose grandfather Simon Nathan had moved to the American colonies from England "in time to fight on the American side of the Revolution, for which he also provided large sums of money."[32] Rebecca's father, Seixas Nathan, who hailed from another storied Sephardic family, served on the original board of the New York Stock Exchange in 1820 and as president of Congregation Shearith Israel (Remnant of Israel), known as the Spanish and Portuguese Synagogue and generally considered the country's oldest Jewish synagogue. Benjamin, the couple's youngest son, was born May 24, 1870.

Benjamin Cardozo was not religiously observant, but he remained a devoted, dues-paying member of Shearith Israel throughout his Supreme Court years, and he was proud of his family's Sephardic heritage. The Nathan-Seixas branch of his family had been intimately involved with the synagogue congregation almost from its founding in the seventeenth century. Cardozo's grandfather and uncles had served as synagogue presidents, and his father had been a vice president and trustee. His mother's oldest sister, Grace, was married to Jacques Judah Lyons, the synagogue's hazan (cantor) for thirty-eight years.[33] One of his most famous ancestors, his great-uncle on his mother's side, was Gershom Mendes Seixas, Shearith Israel's hazan throughout the American Revolution and for a generation thereafter. A standout clergyman and patriot, Seixas "led his New York congregation in special services to mark the adoption of the new federal Constitution."[34] Upon the recommendation of Alexander Hamilton, Seixas was appointed the first Jewish trustee of Columbia College, a position Seixas would hold for more than thirty years, until 1816. The first Jew to serve on the governing board of an American university, Seixas would also be the *last* Jewish Columbia trustee until Benjamin Cardozo's own appointment 112 years later, in 1928.

During Cardozo's lifetime, members of the city's Sephardic Jewish elite, many of them his relatives, were prominent in New York's economic, political, and cultural life. Cardozo's first cousins included Annie Nathan Meyer, the founder of Barnard College; the poet Emma Lazarus, famed for her lines welcoming immigrants — "Give me your tired, your poor, your huddled masses . . ." — engraved at the Statue of Liberty; State Justice Edgar J. Nathan Jr., who also served as Manhattan borough president during the mayoralty of Fiorello La Guardia; and the women's rights crusader Maud Nathan.

The Young Cardozo

The family instability into which Cardozo was born was not limited to his father's disgraceful resignation from the court. His mother, Rebecca, after many years of chronic illness, died in 1879, when Benjamin was only nine. Afterward, "and probably for several years before, a substantial amount of Ben's upbringing was left to his older sister Ellen, and perhaps to governesses as well."[35] Although Ellen, who went by Nell or Nellie, was eleven years older than Benjamin, "their relationship became so close that it occupied her whole life and a very substantial part of his."[36] Outside his busy law practice, and his subsequent judicial responsibilities, Benjamin gave much of himself to caring for Nellie, whose own health declined over the years. Indeed, for Cardozo, a lifelong bachelor, his devotion to his sister, with whom he shared a house until her death in 1929, was his single greatest priority outside the law. As one writer affirms, Ben and Nellie Cardozo "were one another's best friends."[37]

Cardozo was raised in the Orthodox Jewish milieu of Shearith Israel, a center of the extended family's social as well as religious life. Until shortly after his bar mitzvah, Ben followed Jewish Orthodoxy, neglecting "no detail of ancient ritualistic custom as to prayers, to food, and to special observances of religious holidays."[38] He began regularly attending Sabbath services with his father at age five, and like his Cardozo-Nathan cousins, he was "brought up to keep the Sabbath day holy, according to the literal rendering of the Commandments," walking to and from the synagogue rather than riding by horse or carriage.[39] Cardozo studied privately for his bar mitzvah with Shearith Israel's renowned rabbi Dr. H. Pereira Mendes, who led the congregation for more than forty years. Celebrating his bar mitzvah on June 2, 1883, Cardozo read his Torah portion from the Book of Numbers and chanted the prophetic reading, the haftarah, from Hosea.[40] His interest in the synagogue declined thereafter, even as he kept paying his dues and his seat for Sabbath and High Holy Day services, "albeit it was his relatives and not he who used it."[41] Also, through his Supreme Court years in Washington, he retained his hereditary voting status at the congregation.[42] He buried his siblings in the Cardozo family plot at the congregation's cemetery, where he would also be buried.[43] He also continued to follow some Jewish dietary laws, refusing to serve shellfish or pork in his home.[44]

Education and Law Practice

Shortly after his bar mitzvah, Cardozo was tutored by the rags-to-riches novelist Horatio Alger Jr., who was also a Unitarian minister, for his Columbia entrance examination.[45] A Phi Beta Kappa graduate of Harvard who knew Greek and Latin, Alger "had impeccable credentials as a tutor."[46] Albert Cardozo and his children had met Alger while vacationing at their summer home on New Jersey's North Shore. In enlisting him, the Cardozos joined Joseph Seligman, a wealthy Jewish banker and philanthropist who also summered in the fashionable beach town and whose five sons were all tutored by Alger.[47] Between 1869 and 1877, Alger lived in the Seligman brownstone on West Thirty-Fourth Street and occasionally visited the Long Branch summer home. For his part, Albert Cardozo "learned of [Alger's] effectiveness in preparing the Seligman boys for admission to college (four of whom attended Columbia)."[48] In fall 1883, following Albert's decision to hire him, Alger moved into the Cardozo home on Madison Avenue and tutored Benjamin full time over the next year. After completing his studies with Alger, Cardozo "took and passed the five-day entrance examinations and was admitted to Columbia."[49]

When the fifteen-year-old Cardozo began his Columbia undergraduate studies in fall 1885, he was his class's youngest member. A brilliant and diligent student, Cardozo in his first year received perfect scores in Greek, Latin, and German and a 99.6 percent in mathematics, and "in his junior and senior years, after Columbia changed to the letter-grade system, received an A in every class he took: physics, logic, literature, philosophy, ethics, political economy, psychology and history."[50] Of his professors, Cardozo was most influenced by the political economist Edwin R. A. Seligman, a son of Joseph Seligman, and the philosopher Nicholas Murray Butler. Nine years older than Cardozo, Seligman had graduated from Columbia in 1879 and, after earning both a law degree and a doctorate, taught economics at the school from 1886 until his retirement in 1931. The author of *The Economic Interpretation of History* and *Principles of Economics*, Seligman was one of his era's most influential academic economists, who wrote extensively on political economy and public finance and was a widely sought-after government adviser.[51] During his senior year at Columbia, Cardozo seriously considered pursuing graduate work in political economy with Seligman. As Seligman would later recall, Cardozo one day told Seligman of his decision to pursue a career in law. His father, while a pillar of his synagogue and a devoted family man, had been "a partisan judge motivated by political considerations who took money beneath the table," and in so doing brought disgrace upon his family and his tight-knit Sephardic community. As the young Benjamin contemplated his future, he felt that rehabilitating the Cardozo family name, still tarnished by scandal, required being a lawyer. In pursuing a legal career, Cardozo "set out upon a life plan designed to exonerate, or at least vindicate, his father, and bring back honor to the Cardozo family name."[52]

Nicholas Murray Butler, with whom Cardozo took classes on the "History of Philosophy" and "Ethics," would later serve as Columbia's president from 1902 to 1945. An influential figure in Republican Party politics, Butler would remain one of Cardozo's friends and, in 1932, would help mobilize political support for his Supreme Court appointment. Butler, not famous for mentoring or befriending Jewish students, was a passionate Anglophile who introduced the young Cardozo to the work of Matthew Arnold, about whom Cardozo would write a evocative senior paper. In 1916, Butler, known as "Czar Nicholas" during his lengthy Columbia tenure by his critics, would award Cardozo an honorary doctorate from Columbia, the first of several honorary degrees he would receive. Twelve years later, Butler would appoint his former student, by then chief judge of the New York Court of Appeals, to Columbia's board of trustees.

Cardozo graduated with the highest honors from Columbia in 1889, at age nineteen, and was elected vice president of his graduating class. Although his classmates did not elect him valedictorian, he was chosen to be a student speaker at Columbia's commencement exercises, where "his interest in government theory was displayed at this early date with an oration on 'The Altruist in Politics.'"[53] In this speech, Cardozo "attacked the unrealistic altruists who were advocating an absolute community and equality of wealth," arguing that "in almost every phase of life, this doctrine of political altruists is equally impracticable and pernicious."[54] While studying law at Columbia between 1889 and 1891, Cardozo simultaneously earned a master's degree in philosophy.[55]

Within days of being admitted at age twenty-one to the New York State Bar Association on June 26, 1891, Cardozo joined the Manhattan law firm founded by his father and Richard S. Newcombe, in which his older brother Albert Jr. had already become a partner. Newcombe died the next month, and thereafter the firm became known as Cardozo Brothers. In 1903, Cardozo and his brother Albert merged their growing practice with the small but successful firm of Simpson and Werner, which had a sizable real estate and business law clientele, forming the new firm of Simpson, Werner, and Cardozo. After his brother Albert's untimely death in 1909, Cardozo continued his increasingly lucrative private law practice until his election to the New York State Supreme Court in 1913.[56]

During his twenty-two years of law practice, Cardozo became one of New York City's top appellate litigators, a specialist in preparing elegant legal briefs for other lawyers and arguing their cases before the Court of Appeals, the state's highest court. Indeed, while still in his thirties, he argued cases before the New York Court of Appeals more frequently than most of the city's more experienced and better-known lawyers. When their clients were in trouble, "New York lawyers knew they could turn to Cardozo."[57] During his years of private practice, Cardozo was widely recognized, throughout the New York legal community, "for his wide learning, his analytical, logical mind, and his ability as an advocate."[58]

In his private-practice years, Cardozo participated in a few Jewish communal activities, including giving occasional lectures at Shearith Israel, despite attending Sabbath services very infrequently.[59] On June 5, 1895, he spoke persuasively at a special meeting of the congregation's hereditary electors, held at the new synagogue building on Central Park West. The occasion was a divisive public debate between traditionalists and reformers within the congregation. The issue of "modernizing" the traditional worship services was raised in the context of a controversial proposal by two of Cardozo's cousins, Gratz Nathan and Harmon Hendricks, and supported by his uncle Jonathan Nathan, a former synagogue president, to eliminate separate seating for men and women. Many congregants hoped, Gratz Nathan stated, "that in the new Synagogue the sexes shall sit together."[60] Those congregants supporting the proposal "wished to modify Orthodox practices, preferring a more Reform-like setting, which, they believed, would increase attendance at services."[61] After Rabbi H. Pereira Mendes and another congregant spoke out against the proposal, Cardozo offered a third speech in opposition, "impressive in its ability and eloquence," arguing that mixed seating would violate the congregation's constitution.[62] This document "forbade any boy from going into the women's gallery," and Cardozo argued that "the principle of separation of the sexes was embodied in the fundamental document of organization and that the electors could not violate the Constitution of Shearith Israel." Cardozo cautioned his fellow electors that "the law was on the side of the opponents of the motion and that if they were outvoted, there were laws outside to which the opponents could turn."[63] After Cardozo's address, the electors overwhelmingly defeated the proposal by a vote of 73–7. Separate seating was thus retained, and the Spanish and Portuguese Synagogue remained strictly Orthodox.[64]

As Cardozo's biographer Andrew L. Kaufman has suggested, it may have taken "some chutzpah" for the twenty-five-year-old lawyer, who "had long been absent from the synagogue," to take a leadership position on this issue.[65] But it also shows how Cardozo had not completely abandoned his Orthodox religious heritage, his Sephardic roots, or his family's synagogue. In helping resolve the dispute, he had "returned to his congregation in a moment of crisis, not to pray but to uphold a major feature of religious practice."[66] Although the question was never asked publicly of him, Cardozo may well have, if pressed, identified himself as a "non-observant Orthodox Jew."[67]

One of Cardozo's few close friends outside the legal community was Rabbi Stephen S. Wise. While much has been written about Wise's friendship with Louis Brandeis, and their shared leadership in the American Zionist movement, very little has been written about the much closer relationship between Wise and Cardozo, which began after Wise's marriage to Louise Waterman in 1899. Louise Waterman was one of Nellie Cardozo's closest friends, and one of her few intimate friends outside the immediate Cardozo-Nathan family. She and her husband were among the few people with whom Ben and Nellie Cardozo socialized. Stephen and Louise "would visit Nellie and Ben on the weekends, once or twice a month, and Louise visited Nellie regularly."[68] The Wises were also among the few friends with whom Benjamin Cardozo corresponded on a first-name basis.[69] Stephen Wise's unwavering friendship and political support would also help boost Cardozo's professional prospects.

Louis Marshall, another Jewish leader whom Cardozo first met in 1899, would serve as the future justice's mentor and help promote his professional advancement. Cardozo first became associated with Marshall, and his law firm Guggenheimer, Untermeyer, and Marshall, in a major case, *Mahoney v. Bernhard*, in which "Cardozo and Marshall each represented groups of stockholders of a failed bank seeking to avoid statutory liability for the debts of the bank."[70] Marshall's experience working with Cardozo in this case "and against him in another matter at the same time left him with a favorable impression," and he subsequently invited Cardozo to assist his law firm in litigation involving "a skirmish in a larger war between two giants in the American copper mining industry."[71] He later invited Cardozo to help his firm in other litigation, including cases before the New York State Court of Appeals, and referred clients to Cardozo's firm.

Marshall would assist the young Cardozo in another important way. In 1903, when Cardozo completed his first manuscript, *The Jurisdiction of the Court of Appeals of the State of New York*, he turned to Marshall, "who had widespread connections," for assistance in securing a publisher. After reading and praising the manuscript, Marshall wrote a letter of introduction for Cardozo to A. Bleecker Banks, an Albany legal publisher, urging its publication.[72] Upon Marshall's recommendation, "Banks undertook to publish the manuscript, and Marshall became negotiator and middleman between Cardozo and Banks. All matters, including suggestions for changes and even transmission of proofs, went through Marshall's hands."[73]

Redemption: The Second Judge Cardozo

By 1913, Cardozo had argued seventy-four cases before the New York State Court of Appeals and written a well-received book about the court's jurisdiction. He enjoyed a reputation as a "lawyer's lawyer," one of that "small group of lawyers to whom other lawyers regularly turn for help."[74] As one of New York City's most successful appellate litigators, his expertise was sought "by an ever-widening circle of lawyers, comprised largely of Jewish lawyers, who brought him their most difficult commercial work."[75] In addition to Louis Marshall, this influential circle included Irving Lehman, Abram Elkus, Samuel Untermeyer, Joseph Proskauer, Nathan Ottinger, Julius Goldman, Morris Hirsch, Morris Stroock, Sol Stroock, and Moses Esberg.[76] (Lehman and Elkus, who became Cardozo's close friends, would later serve with him on the New York State Court of Appeals.) As his reputation grew, legal work was also referred by some of the city's most eminent non-Jewish lawyers, some of whom Cardozo had appeared against in court, among them Alton Parker, the former chief judge of the New York State Court of Appeals and the Democratic Party's presidential candidate in 1904, and Harlan Fiske Stone, the future U.S. attorney general and later Cardozo's Supreme Court colleague. As Cardozo's biographer put it, "Cardozo was now litigating in the major leagues."[77]

Cardozo's prominence within the New York Bar, and especially among "the community of Jewish lawyers, was critical for his judicial career when in 1913 anti-Tammany Democratic reform leaders in New York City joined forces with the Republican Party to put together a fusion ticket to run against Tammany Hall."[78] Although Cardozo was a Democrat, "he was a conservative who had bolted his party in 1896 to support the Republican William McKinley over William Jennings Bryan . . . and an independent who had no ties to Tammany Hall. In 1913 these qualities translated into decided advantages when the newly formed, broadly based Fusion movement, sparked by revelations of corruption in Tammany-controlled City Hall, made a bid for control of municipal government."[79] Cardozo had another advantage—his Jewishness. The five-member subcommittee responsible for choosing judicial candidates for the fusion ticket decided that a Jewish lawyer was needed to balance the ticket religiously.[80] Upon the strong recommendation of Henry Moskowitz, the social reformer and labor leader who was mobilizing support for the ticket, Cardozo was selected for the Supreme Court candidacy. In recommending Cardozo, Moskowitz, a confidant of Stephen Wise, rejected the subcommittee's first choice, Julius J. Frank. "You haven't got the right kind of Jew," Moskowitz advised the subcommittee. "Frank is a Felix Adler Jew, a Modernist. The man you want to get is a *real* Jew. I'll tell you the man, Cardozo. He is [in] the Portuguese Synagogue."[81] Thus, ironically, Cardozo's future "turned on the Sephardic heritage whose religious tenets he had long since discarded."[82]

Another Jewish leader who aided in Cardozo's campaign for election to the New York State Supreme Court was Louis Marshall, the recently elected president of the American Jewish Committee (AJC). "Do not hesitate to call upon me for such assistance as it is within my power to render, to advance your candidacy," Marshall had written Cardozo immediately after his nomination.[83] At Henry Moskowitz's suggestion, Cardozo enlisted Marshall's help in seeking endorsements from various Jewish newspapers. Marshall also wrote lengthy letters on behalf of Cardozo's candidacy, which he published in the *Jewish Morning Journal*, *Jewish Daily News*, and the *Warheit*. Although Marshall deplored the concept of a Jewish vote and the assumption that Jewish candidates were automatically entitled to the support of Jewish voters, "he knew there were Jewish voters who might be instructed and advised on both candidates and issues, and he not infrequently sought to instruct and advise them."[84] This was his objective in vocally supporting Cardozo's candidacy. Writing of Cardozo's "extraordinary capacity," "preeminent ability," and "sterling character," Marshall urged a vote for Cardozo while eschewing the notion "that Jews should vote for a Jew on that basis alone." In this case, however, argued Marshall, "because of Cardozo's qualifications, if elected, he would shed luster upon the Jewish name."[85]

By this campaign, Cardozo had already successfully lifted much of the taint from the family name, as he had sought to do when he began his legal career. In 1913, "the name Cardozo at the bar was associated with the son and not the father."[86] On January 5, 1914, Cardozo took his seat as a justice of the New York State Supreme Court, the very court from which his father had resigned forty-two years earlier.[87] For the second Judge Cardozo, this was redemption.

After only five weeks on the State Supreme Court, Cardozo received an even more prestigious judicial appointment. New York governor Martin Glynn designated him to fill an interim vacancy on the New York State Court of Appeals, the state's highest court, to assist with the court's backlog of cases.[88] When Cardozo was appointed to this position on February 2, 1914, he became the first Jew ever to serve on the court. Upon his appointment, Cardozo received a "formal resolution of congratulation" from the trustees of Shearith Israel, who noted proudly that "the first Israelite" to be a member of the court had come from North America's earliest congregation and that he was "one whose ancestors had been faithful officers and members for two centuries and himself an Elector."[89]

In 1917, Cardozo was elected to a full fourteen-year term on the Court of Appeals "with the endorsement of both political parties," and in 1927 was elected its chief judge, "again with bipartisan support."[90] Throughout Cardozo's eighteen-year tenure, the New York Court of Appeals "was the nation's most distinguished common law tribunal," and Cardozo, "who from the outset was the court's brightest star,"[91] became widely recognized as the country's preeminent state court judge.

Cardozo's closest friend on the Court of Appeals was Irving Lehman, a member of the New York German-Jewish family that founded the Lehman Brothers investment banking firm. Cardozo and Lehman, both graduates of Columbia College and Law School, had been friends since their days as young attorneys in Manhattan, when they had often socialized and referred clients to each other. Over the years, their friendship expanded to include Irving's wife, Sissie—the daughter of Macy's co-owner Nathan Straus and a niece of Oscar Straus, Theodore Roosevelt's secretary of commerce and labor. Irving and Benjamin were each other's closest friends. Both in Manhattan and in Albany, Irving and Sissie would often join Cardozo for dinner and theater, and Cardozo was their guest for frequent weekend and summer vacations at their Port Chester estate in Westchester County. Like Cardozo, Irving Lehman had served on the New York State Supreme Court before being elected to the New York Court of Appeals. Their friendship continued after Cardozo's eventual U.S. Supreme Court appointment and move to Washington, D.C. As Lehman's nephew, the Oxford law professor Arthur Lehman Goodhart would later write, "The friendship that bound Benjamin Cardozo and Irving Lehman together was such an essential part of both their lives that it is difficult to remember the one without thinking of the other."[92] Moreover, through this relationship, Cardozo would also become a confidant of Irving's politically influential younger brother Herbert, who was elected New York's lieutenant governor as Franklin Roosevelt's running mate in 1928 and governor when FDR won the presidency in 1932, eventually serving four terms.

During his eighteen years on the Court of Appeals, Cardozo wrote 566 majority opinions and 16 dissents and, "unlike judges today, he did his own research and wrote his own opinions—and in longhand."[93] Cardozo remains famous not only for the substance of these opinions but also for his elegant literary style. "There are few judges on the bench today," noted one commentator on Cardozo's January 1927 election as chief judge, "who are capable of expounding the law with greater clarity. . . . When he renders an opinion or a decision, he tries to lay down a principle not merely for the present but one that may endure a hundred years from now. In consequence, he cultivated a style of expression . . . which for beauty and clarity of English, has seldom been surpassed in form and substance. In short, his opinions are masterpieces of literary style."[94] As a legal stylist, Cardozo is often compared to Oliver Wendell Holmes Jr., whose Supreme Court seat he would fill in 1932.

During his years on the Court of Appeals, Cardozo also achieved renown as a scholar who, as the author of *The Nature of the Judicial Process*, *The Growth of the Law*, *Law and Literature*, and *The Paradoxes of Legal Science*, made significant contributions to the study of jurisprudence. His most famous book, *The Nature of the Judicial Process* (1922), which became a classic of U.S. legal scholarship, "is the very first book ever by a judge who analyzed the process of judging,"[95] telling us "how he decides cases, how he made law, and, by implication, how others should do so."[96] Seeking to give a practical answer to the question "What is it that I do when I decide a case?" Cardozo developed "a model for judging that emphasized both its creative possibilities and its limits" which remains influential today, with most judges continuing to go about "the job of judging within the framework that Cardozo described."[97] Cardozo's *Nature of the Judicial Process*, which is often ranked with Holmes's *Common Law* as one of the top two works of legal scholarship by American judges, "helped make Cardozo well known to lawyers throughout the country and to generations of lawyers and scholars who have followed."[98] Between its publication in 1922 and the 1994 Supreme Court appointment of Stephen Breyer, who also wrote important law books while serving as a judge, Cardozo's *Nature of the Judicial Process* would sell 181,442 copies, making it the best-selling book ever written by a Jewish Supreme Court justice.[99]

In 1923, Cardozo was one of "five hundred legal luminaries—lawyers, judges, and law professors" who met in Washington, D.C., to found the American Law Institute.[100] The event marked, the *New York Times* announced, "probably the most distinguished gathering of the legal profession in the history of the country."[101] From the institute's inception until his high court appointment, Cardozo belonged to its governing council and executive committee, and was also elected its vice president.[102] Under the leadership of Cardozo and his colleagues, the institute undertook "the ambitious task of preparing restatements of the law—that is, of identifying the principles of the common law—in all major fields, such as torts, contracts, agency and property."[103]

Cardozo as Chief Judge

In running in November 1926 to succeed the chief judge of the New York State Court of Appeals, who had reached the mandatory retirement age of seventy, Cardozo competed with the Republican Cuthbert Pound, his colleague on the Court of Appeals.[104] The campaign had begun exactly a year earlier. In late 1925, Cardozo's friend Abram Elkus, who served as a New York Court of Appeals judge in 1919–1920, wrote letters to bar members throughout the state urging Cardozo's selection.[105] In making the same case to Governor Al Smith, Elkus assumed the Democratic governor, who enjoyed close ties to New York City's Jewish community, would support Cardozo's election. However, when he, along with Stephen Wise and other Cardozo supporters, "discovered that Smith had made some commitment to Pound, they mounted a strong campaign in the fall of 1926 to persuade Smith to change his mind and to obtain an agreement among leaders of both parties to name Cardozo for the chief judgeship, and a Republican as associate judge."[106] Wise, who would later take credit for Cardozo's election, later recounted: "I made fiery written protest to Smith; and then we had four hours together during which I hammered and hammered and hammered, inspired, if I may say so, but what I know was the rightness of my case, until Smith finally succumbed and named Cardozo."[107] While Wise thus "harangued the governor" on Cardozo's behalf, "Louis Marshall and others organized political support for Cardozo."[108] Even as compared to Wise's impassioned case, Marshall's campaign was likely more influential in Cardozo's election as chief judge. Marshall, although a Republican, was able to persuade Adolph Ochs, owner of the *New York Times*, to publish an editorial supporting Cardozo's nomination. The editorial declared that Governor Smith "could not excuse himself to his own conscience" if he failed to support Cardozo.[109] After Marshall and some New York Bar Association leaders also met with Smith, the governor finally announced his support for Cardozo, whom he praised as "an outstanding figure in the judicial history of the state."[110]

The fact that the Republican Marshall and the Democrat Wise, who shared little in common other than their friendship with Cardozo and who rarely worked together throughout their long careers in American Jewish public life, collaborated to promote Cardozo's election is a point of more than passing historical significance. Nicholas Murray Butler, like Marshall a Republican, also enthusiastically supported Cardozo's nomination, as he had when Cardozo first ran for a New York State Supreme Court seat in 1913. Cardozo's backers also believed that Al Smith's close adviser Joseph Proskauer, a fellow Columbia Law School alumnus who had referred clients to Cardozo when they were both in private practice, had effectively lobbied Smith on Cardozo's behalf. With Smith's crucial support, Cardozo was elected chief judge with the endorsement of both the Democratic and Republican Parties at the state's nominating convention in September 1926.[111] He took his seat on New Year's Day of 1927, becoming the first Jew to hold the state's highest judgeship.

Cardozo's Election to the Columbia University Board of Trustees

As chief judge of New York's highest court, and as one of the country's most influential legal thinkers, Cardozo was, "with the possible exception of [Columbia president Nicholas Murray] Butler, Columbia College's most distinguished living alumnus."[112] It was in this context that Murray, in 1928, began pushing for Cardozo's appointment to the college's board of trustees.

Much has been written about the history of antisemitism at Columbia during the 1870s and 1880s, the decades when Butler and Cardozo were students there.[113] This didn't mean Jews weren't represented: Butler's graduating class in 1882 "numbered fifty, of whom a half-dozen were Jewish."[114] Cardozo's graduating class in 1889 had an equal number. By the turn of the century, the Jewish student body had increased to 15 percent, with comparable proportions enrolled at Barnard and Columbia Law School. By the 1920s, however, "discriminatory admission practices were being rigorously enforced at both Columbia and Barnard, and even more so at the Columbia's medical school.[115] Moreover, in the post–World War I years, as in the preceding decade, there was a growing recognition of Columbia's seeming reluctance to welcome and properly acknowledge Jewish financial support, even from its wealthiest Jewish alumni. The school's board of trustees, meanwhile, had long been a virtual Protestant preserve. Some Jewish alumni alleged that Columbia and President Butler were antisemitic, a charge Butler hotly denied. Shortly before proposing Cardozo's name for the board, Butler had assured a newly elected trustee, Stephen G. Williams, whose law firm had once included among its partners Irving Lehman, that such a claim was baseless. "The statement that the University is anti-Semitic or that I myself am anti-Semitic," Butler wrote to Williams in November 1927, "was mischievously put in circulation downtown some fifteen or twenty years ago by two men of some importance on Wall Street, both of whom knew it was untrue and kept repeating it as if it were."[116] One of the men referred to by Butler "was almost certainly Jacob Schiff,"[117] the investment banker and philanthropist who had died in 1920.

For Butler, Cardozo's unanimous election to the board of trustees would publicly confirm that Columbia and its president were indeed not antisemitic. Butler passionately fought for the election of Cardozo, his top student, protégé, and now friend. The school's president likely invoked Cardozo's lofty qualifications, including his court position and his reputation as a legal scholar, as well as his often-expressed loyalty to Columbia, "to persuade the board chairman, William Barclay Parsons, despite his long-standing objections to the election of a Jew to the board, not to dissent from what the president had determined would be a unanimous vote in favor."[118]

Ironically, perhaps, Cardozo also recommended himself to some trustees based on a characteristic not shared by most earlier Jewish prospects: he was *not* wealthy.[119] Since the 1890s, at least another half-dozen Jews, "many of them alumni and all wealthier than Cardozo,"[120] including Irving Lehman, Oscar Straus, and the banker and philanthropist Otto Kahn, "had been mentioned as possible trustees—all to no effect." Some trustees viewed Cardozo's relatively modest financial status as a crucial factor in his favor, "not wanting to give the impression that they were on the lookout for Jewish money."[121] The trustee Stephen Williams had voiced this concern in 1926, when he suggested to Butler that the board should elect someone "not too obviously for his money, as election of Otto Kahn would be. I am opposed to the nomination of a very prominent and rich Jew."[122] On March 3, 1928, Cardozo was unanimously elected to a life term on the board, "thus ending a 114-year hiatus in Jewish membership."[123] The position more than a century earlier, of course, had been filled by Cardozo's ancestor Gershom Mendes Seixas.

Throughout the 1920s and early 1930s, Cardozo participated somewhat in Jewish communal affairs. Influenced by Brandeis and Julian Mack, and especially by his close friend Rabbi Wise, Cardozo joined the Zionist Organization of America, permitting the group to use his name in its Zionist publicity. Cardozo was also influenced to participate in Jewish affairs by his friend Irving Lehman, who was prominent in American Jewish communal life. In the 1920s and 1930s, Lehman served as president of the National Jewish Welfare Board and appointed Cardozo to serve with him on its executive committee. In 1929, Cardozo and Lehman were elected together to the executive committee of the AJC, and during the 1920s Cardozo served on the board of governors of the American Friends of The Hebrew University.[124] After his appointment to Columbia's board of trustees, he also served on the committee that met with the school's adviser to Jewish students.[125] "The requirements of his judgeship," however, limited his extrajudicial activity in these causes.[126]

Unlike Brandeis, Cardozo, both as a New York Court of Appeals judge and later while on the Supreme Court, was very concerned with the propriety of an active judge engaging in any extrajudicial activity, Jewish or political. Thus, when in summer 1927 President Calvin Coolidge offered to appoint him to a part-time position on the International Court of Arbitration at The Hague to succeed the recently deceased Oscar Straus, Cardozo declined. His main reason for doing so was that "acceptance might raise the question whether he was violating the provision in the New York state constitution that prohibited a state official from holding any other office or public trust."[127] As Andrew L. Kaufman has pointed out, "Cardozo's sensitivity may have reflected his memory of the disgrace that his father had brought on the New York judiciary and his desire to avoid controversy about an issue of propriety."[128] Likely because of his father's disgrace, Cardozo was always careful "to observe the proprieties regarding his judicial role."[129]

The Supreme Court Appointment

On February 15, 1932, President Herbert Hoover announced the nomination of Benjamin Cardozo to succeed the retiring Oliver Wendell Holmes Jr. as an associate justice of the U.S. Supreme Court. Since Holmes's retirement announcement a month earlier, a groundswell of support had emerged from legal scholars, fellow jurists, and politicians for appointing Cardozo, a man then widely considered "the preeminent judge in the country who was not sitting on the Supreme Court."[130]

Hoover's announcement generated initial controversy in seeming to "contradict most of the traditional 'rules of the game' that have come to be associated with the politics of judicial appointments."[131] Cardozo was a Democrat who had supported Al Smith for president in 1928 and who was by now regarded as a decidedly liberal jurist, while Hoover was a conservative Republican expected to replace Holmes with a conservative jurist. Geography constituted another factor, with Cardozo's appointment not furthering the "representation" of the court's membership. Quite the contrary: Cardozo would give the Northeast a majority of justices, not to mention being the third member from New York state, "a violation of the long standing tradition that membership on the Court represent as wide a geographical base as possible."[132] On first learning of Holmes's resignation, Hoover indeed appeared set to appoint a justice who would allow for greater geographical distribution. The West and the South had legitimate claims, considering that the court had just one Southern member and no one from the West Coast. Moreover, Hoover and his advisers recognized that the Republican Party could make gains, in the upcoming presidential election, "if he recognized the West or the South with a Supreme Court appointment."[133] Cardozo's religion was another factor. The idea that the court would include two Jews, with Brandeis having joined sixteen years earlier, was surprising to many — and quite distressing for some. While Hoover made several Jewish appointments during his presidency, and was apparently "devoid of any traces of anti-Semitism, he may have pondered the wisdom of having two Jews serving on the Court together just as he concerned himself with the problem of three New Yorkers on the bench at the same time."[134]

In the previous decade, Cardozo's name had been mentioned three times as a possible Supreme Court nominee, including in 1922, when Justice William Day retired and Pierce Butler was ultimately nominated to succeed him.[135] Columbia president Nicholas Murray Butler, who advised several presidents, had recommended Cardozo's appointment to President Warren Harding, describing his friend as an "independent Democrat whose record is, on the whole, the most distinguished of any man of his type in New York in this generation."[136] In a letter to Harding, Dean Thomas W. Swan of Yale Law School wrote "that there is no judge in the country of keener judicial intellect or of finer judicial temperament."[137] It was the unanimous opinion of his colleagues, Swan wrote, that "Cardozo had proven himself to be preeminently fitted for a place on the high bench."[138] Cardozo's colleague Frank Hiscock, who succeeded Cardozo as chief judge of the New York Court of Appeals—noting "rumors of the impending retirement of Justice Day and the possibility of the appointment of a Democrat"—also wrote urging Cardozo's nomination: "I simply content myself with saying, as a result of an intimate acquaintance and observation continued through nearly ten years, that he has such ability, learning and brilliance of mind as are possessed by few men. He would bring to the Court that degree and kind of progressiveness which I suppose should be lodged there—progressiveness which does not lead to radicalism or instability or undesirable experimentation with the fundamental principles of law."[139]

Cardozo's nomination, however, was unacceptable to Chief Justice William Howard Taft. In considering Cardozo and several other possible nominees, Taft consulted George Wickersham, his friend and former attorney general, who had earlier opposed Brandeis's appointment to the court. While concluding that Cardozo was "a man of sound learning," Wickersham had advised Taft that he did not think "it would do to have two Jews on the Supreme Court."[140] Taft fully agreed. In his letter to Harding strongly opposing Cardozo's nomination, Taft pointed out that Cardozo was "a Jew and a Democrat," and noted that while "I don't think that he would always side with Brandeis . . . he is what they call a progressive judge."[141] Determined to block the nomination of a progressive who might occasionally side with that "dangerous twosome," Holmes and Brandeis, Taft succeeded in helping defeat Cardozo's nomination.[142]

Cardozo's appointment was also suggested to President Coolidge on Justice Joseph McKenna's retirement in 1924. Once again, Nicholas Murray Butler recommended Cardozo's nomination. So did Coolidge's attorney general, the former Columbia Law School dean Harlan Fiske Stone, who was eventually named by Coolidge to the court to fill this very position.[143] Prior to appointing Cardozo in 1932, President Hoover had considered Cardozo for a Supreme Court vacancy in 1930 but had instead nominated Owen Roberts, who was Chief Justice Charles Evans Hughes's preferred candidate for the court.[144]

Almost immediately following the announcement of Justice Holmes's resignation on January 15, 1932, newspapers began speculating that the Hoover White House was seriously considering appointing Cardozo to fill the seat. The coverage was such that, by January 22, Mark Sullivan, a syndicated columnist with the *New York Herald Tribune*, wrote that the "universality of the applause for Judge Cardozo constitutes a unique condition, almost a phenomenon."[145]

Over the next several weeks, Cardozo's many friends and admirers, both within and outside the legal community, lobbied on his behalf, as they had done in support of his earlier court bids. For his part, Stephen Wise "used his many personal and political connections . . . and recruited other friends to promote Cardozo's candidacy."[146] One of Wise's successes on this front was winning over William E. Borah, the powerful Republican senator from Idaho, who would become Cardozo's strong advocate.[147] Four days after Holmes's resignation, Felix Frankfurter, who had worked as a top assistant for Henry Stimson, met with the former war secretary to promote his friend Cardozo's candidacy. At Frankfurter's behest, Stimson, now Hoover's secretary of state, conveyed his support for Cardozo as the nominee.[148]

In the month following Holmes's retirement, Cardozo's backers "flooded the White House with messages of support."[149] Samuel Seabury, Cardozo's friend and former colleague on the New York Court of Appeals, who had just been elected president of the New York State Bar Association, prepared a letter of support on behalf of the eight hundred bar association members urging Hoover to appoint "the most distinguished jurist of our age."[150] Another important letter to Hoover came from New Jersey congressman Franklin W. Fort, whose views as a member of the Republican Party "inner circle" were of special interest to the president.[151] In his letter, Fort noted that liberals viewed Cardozo "as their outstanding jurist since Justice Holmes retired," while conservatives saw him "as a Judge of the highest distinction and complete sanity."[152] Fort added another point: "The Jews seem to regard him almost as a saint."[153]

Members of the Senate, Democrats and Republicans alike, also wrote letters to the president conveying support for Cardozo. Because New York senator

Robert Wagner, a Democrat, was from Cardozo's home state, his backing was especially important to both the potential nominee and the president. Almost immediately, "on his own initiative," Wagner enthusiastically recommended the justice to Hoover.[154] Shortly after Wagner's "powerful statement" was reported in the *New York Times*, Jacob Billikopf, the executive director of New York's Federation of Jewish Charities, "approached Wagner and listed the names of people in the Jewish community who might be able to influence Hoover."[155] Wagner encouraged Billikopf in his efforts to make such contacts, adding that Billikopf could use the senator's name in mobilizing support.[156] Billikopf also wrote to top Jewish Republicans, hoping to enlist their support for the court candidacy of the Democrat Cardozo. One of Billikopf's letters went to former California Supreme Court justice Marcus Sloss, a scion of one of San Francisco's Jewish pioneer families and a Republican close to Hoover, asking Sloss to contact the president in support of Cardozo's candidacy.[157] The next day, Sloss telegrammed Hoover that a Cardozo appointment would please the "entire bench and bar of the nation."[158] Another letter went to the well-known Rabbi Abba Hillel Silver of Cleveland, who, although he would support FDR for president in the 1932 election, had close ties to Republican Party leaders in Ohio. In writing to Silver, Billikopf hoped the rabbi would persuade his close friend Morris Maschke, a high-ranking Ohio Republican official, to use his contacts in the Hoover administration to boost the Cardozo nomination.[159]

Cardozo's most influential supporter in the U.S. Senate was William E. Borah, who chaired the Senate Committee on Foreign Relations. Borah successfully urged Hoover to nominate Cardozo, even as many in their party were pressing for the appointment of a Republican. Thus, of the seven presidents to appoint a Jewish justice to the Supreme Court, only Hoover so transcended partisan considerations.

Meeting with Hoover the day before the president had indicated he would announce his nominee, Senator Borah reassured him that he should appoint Cardozo even though, as Hoover pointed out, "there is a great deal of anti-Semitism in the country and this appointment would mean two Jews on the Bench."[160] Borah reportedly continued: "Such an opportunity may never again come to you, Mr. President, to strike a blow at anti-Semitism."[161] In nominating Cardozo, Hoover ignored the tirades of high court justice James McReynolds, who had earlier opposed Brandeis's nomination and now urged Hoover not "to afflict the Court with another Jew."[162] With Borah's backing, Hoover did indeed "strike a blow at anti-Semitism" applauded by Jewish leaders from both parties. Borah also urged Hoover to ignore the overrepresentation of New York state judges on the court. When Hoover "expressed the feeling that three Justices from New York would be too many, Borah countered with the assertion that Cardozo's virtues transcended state boundaries."[163] Borah made his case thus: "Mr. President, the man you appoint to the Supreme Court represents every state, Idaho as well as New York. If you appoint Judge Cardozo, you will be winning the applause of the whole country and not merely one part."[164] In following Borah's advice, as the legal scholar Zechariah Chafee pithily wrote, President Hoover "ignored geography and made history."[165] Cardozo was universally recognized, in Felix Frankfurter's words, as the "rightful successor to Mr. Justice Holmes."[166] Judge Joseph Hutcheson, an appeals court judge who himself was often mentioned as a potential Supreme Court appointee, expressed the feelings of many in the legal profession in his note of congratulation to Hoover: "No one ever can, no one ever will take the place of Oliver Wendell Holmes; no one will ever try to. As a successor to him, however, there is no living man nearer qualified than the one you have chosen."[167]

The hearing on Benjamin Cardozo's appointment was brief, sailing through the Senate. The subcommittee and the full Judiciary Committee approved the nomination unanimously.[168] Unique among the eight Jewish appointees to the Supreme Court, Cardozo's nomination was confirmed by virtual acclamation, without even a Senate debate or roll-call vote, on February 24, 1932. Two weeks later, Rabbi Stephen and Louise Waterman Wise threw a surprise party for Cardozo, just after he had moved to Washington to begin his court tenure.[169] On March 15, Chief Justice Hughes administered the oath of office and Cardozo took his seat as the court's second Jewish justice. Senator Borah, along with Cardozo's relatives and friends including the Wises and Lehmans, attended the swearing-in ceremony.

When, on that March day in 1932, Cardozo took his seat on the high court, Hoover was widely praised. "Seldom, if ever, in the history of the Court," commented the *New York Times*, "has an appointment been so universally commended."[170] One Democratic senator called Hoover's appointment of Cardozo "the finest act of his career as president." History would concur that it was one of Hoover's most enduring presidential achievements.[171]

For his part, Stephen Wise "had perceived the personal meaning of the appointment" even before the Senate issued its confirmation: "The glory of it will be that [although his father] came under the malign influence of Tweed [and] made the name Cardozo synonymous with shame, [in] twenty years, Cardozo has effaced the memory of his father and his name can never more be used save in terms of reverence and honor. What an achievement for a man!"[172]

Mr. Justice Cardozo

When Cardozo took his Supreme Court seat, he joined Brandeis as one of the court's two most liberal justices. Cardozo had a liberal view of the state's power to regulate the economy, protect civil liberties, and ban racial discrimination. Issues concerning the last topic "began to appear on the Supreme Court's calendar more frequently during Cardozo's tenure, although they were still not a major focus of litigation. . . . However, [such cases] involved the efforts of the Democratic Party in the South to structure the election process to prevent African Americans from voting in the Democratic primaries that were effectively the final elections in many places."[173] In his first court term, Cardozo wrote one of his major opinions on voting discrimination against blacks by the Texas Democratic Party. This case, *Nixon v. Condon*, dealt with two Texas statutes "that explicitly made African Americans ineligible to vote in Democratic primaries."[174] Writing for the five-member majority, Cardozo struck down these statutes as violations of the equal protection clause of the Fourteenth Amendment. "Delegates of the State's power have discharged their official functions in such a way as to discriminate invidiously between white citizens and black," he wrote. "The Fourteenth Amendment, adapted as it was with special solicitude for the equal protection of members of the Negro race, lays a duty upon the court to level by its judgment these barriers of color."[175]

Franklin Roosevelt was president for most of Cardozo's court tenure, and the new justice's association with the administration began on FDR's first day. Hours after his inauguration, on March 4, 1933, when Roosevelt asked his ten cabinet members "to gather in the second-floor Oval Office for their swearing-in ceremony," he had "invited Associate Justice Benjamin Cardozo to do the honors."[176] Never before had a Supreme Court justice administered the oath of office to a new president's entire cabinet. Also for the first time in U.S. history, "the entire Cabinet was sworn in at the same time, in the same place, and by the same official."[177] Although he had not voted in the 1932 election, Cardozo, a lifelong Democrat, had considered it "very gracious" of Roosevelt to ask him to preside at the event.[178]

Cardozo's relationship with FDR dated to his service on the New York

Court of Appeals while Roosevelt was governor, with Herbert Lehman his lieutenant governor. During FDR's years as governor, he and Cardozo enjoyed a close working relationship.[179] Many of Cardozo's friends, including Wise, Frankfurter, and Lehman, had been among FDR's close advisers during Roosevelt's Albany tenure. Roosevelt had called Lehman "my good right arm" in running the state government.[180] Through these friends, Cardozo often had the governor's "ear" as well. Nonetheless, in July 1932, Cardozo remained undecided about Roosevelt's presidential aspirations, telling his friend Judge Learned Hand that "the nomination of FDR leaves me cold, though I like him personally."[181] Cardozo quickly "warm[ed] up" to FDR following his election, saying Roosevelt had "done magnificently" and that he was "increasingly impressed by both the man and his program."[182] During Cardozo's first three years on the court, however, most of the justices "held that the large part of New Deal legislation was unconstitutional," making these years among the most controversial in the court's history.[183] But Roosevelt's first two years in office provided no occasion for the Supreme Court to actually rule on the constitutionality of New Deal legislative measures. Cardozo, as one of the court's liberals, with "his affinity for the broad social objectives of the New Deal," was often "the most sympathetic to what Roosevelt was trying to accomplish."[184] More than once, he would join with Brandeis and Harlan Fiske Stone, another liberal, in voting to uphold the constitutionality of the New Deal's Social Security statute and other measures. In 1935 and 1936, though, when the court "finally ruled on the most fundamental aspects of the recovery program and frequently found them defective,"[185] Cardozo joined his colleagues in their unanimous 1935 *Schechter* ruling, which overturned the National Recovery Act, and in other notable decisions undoing important New Deal measures. So, too, in 1937 did Cardozo join his colleagues in opposing Roosevelt's court-packing plan, "viewing it as a personal insult and an affront to the independence of the judiciary."[186]

Despite the scale of his accomplishment, when Cardozo moved to Washington in 1932, he felt very much alone. His sister Nellie had suffered a stroke in February 1928 that greatly affected her speech and overall health. She died in the fall of 1929, leaving Benjamin "as the last of the children of Albert and Rebecca Cardozo."[187] Earlier that year, in June, Edgar Nathan, the justice's cousin and close friend, had also passed away. With Nellie's death, Cardozo "had lost his companion, confidante and mainstay" of more than forty years, whose emotional support, familial love, and companionship had given meaning and structure to his personal and professional life. Cardozo's remaining close friends in New York, especially Irving Lehman and his wife, Sissie, and Stephen and Louise Wise, "were constant in their attention, and after a while his spirits began to recover, although the memory of Nellie was never far away."[188] But alas, these intimates no longer lived nearby. Responding to a letter from Wise praising his judicial work, Cardozo replied, "Praise is precious even now—such is the vanity of human nature—though I ask myself in wonderment why I should value it, now that the one who would have shared it with me so fully has gone from me forever."[189]

As a lonely bachelor in Washington, Cardozo's Supreme Court years were not happy ones. In a letter to Louise Wise, he referred to himself as "the homesick exile" and to Washington as "my place of exile."[190] Even after leaving his three-room temporary residence at the Mayflower Hotel, and moving into his own apartment on Connecticut Avenue in fall 1932, "where he was joined by Kate Tracy, his housekeeper, and the maids who had worked for him in New York, he contrasted the dislocation he felt in Washington with his happiness in New York City."[191] Throughout his Washington years, he remained "wretchedly homesick" and despondent. "Washington is my legal domicile now, but not the domicile of my spirit."[192] At a dinner with Louis Marshall's son Robert, who was then working for the Bureau of Indian Affairs and one of the justice's favorite visitors, Cardozo confided: "I don't think there is much to live for when the people who have really mattered in one's life are all dead. I'm too old to make new friends who can replace those with whom I have lived for a lifetime."[193] The demands of his new job proved the best antidote to the justice's despondency.[194]

The loneliness in Washington affected him all the more "because the Supreme Court lacked the camaraderie he had enjoyed on the New York Court of Appeals."[195] By contrast with his earlier experience, "the Supreme Court was not a collegial body" and Cardozo "did not mingle much with his colleagues."[196] He never established the close personal relationships with his new judicial colleagues that had meant a great deal to him in Albany, where most of the judges "had resided in the same hotel, were constant companions, and trusted [and socialized with] one another."[197] He especially missed his long-cherished friendship with Irving and Sissie Lehman, and their evenings out and getaways in Port Chester. Cardozo did maintain friendships with Justices Stone, Roberts, and Brandeis but, surprisingly, "not to the point that he was ever on a first name basis even with them."[198] Of these relationships, the closest was with Stone, whom Cardozo had known in his capacity as Columbia Law School dean from 1910 to 1923, when Stone came "to see Cardozo almost weekly to talk about law school matters."[199] They had continued to correspond following Stone's appointment first as President Coolidge's attorney general and then as a high court justice. Although Cardozo "did not often go out socially" while on the court, "he traded dinners with the Stones several times a year, and they occasionally called on one another."[200]

Cardozo was also one of the "lonely bachelors" whom the Brandeises "regularly invited . . . to dinner and before Christmas," as well as for various teas.[201] The Brandeis-Cardozo friendship, however, never became especially close.[202] Memorably, Cardozo "did not like to go to the Brandeis apartment because he found it to be so overheated as to be uncomfortable."[203] The two justices disagreed on their approach to judging, "on just how certain a judge must be before deciding a case." Cardozo liked to be completely sure of his decision, and Brandeis once commented to one of Cardozo's law clerks, "The trouble with your Judge is that he thinks he has to be one hundred percent right."[204] Also, although Cardozo "respected and admired Brandeis," he realized that Brandeis's passionate attachment to extrajudicial causes, from social reform to Zionism, causes he did not as passionately embrace, "set them apart."[205] Some of Cardozo's New York friends, such as the Wises, were disappointed that the Brandeises did not reach out to Cardozo more regularly. On March 8, 1932, a few days before Cardozo had left for Washington, Louise Wise had written to Brandeis telling him that Cardozo was "the loneliest of men, having lost everyone in his family who was dear to him," and was now moving to "a strange environment, where there is no one who understands him or is interested in him as a human being, who I know hungers for sympathy and understanding, although he would be the last to admit it." We "so love Cardozo," she continued, and "would feel relieved to know you were to be his friend in a very real sense."[206] Brandeis, who was fourteen years older than Cardozo, "notably circumspect in his personal relationships,"[207] and estranged from the Jewish religious tradition that Cardozo still admired, did not befriend Cardozo in the way the Wises had expected. While the two justices "shared a religious heritage," they "differed too fundamentally in their Jewishness for it to unite them in the kind of friendship for which the rabbi's wife hoped."[208]

While his relationship with three of his conservative colleagues, Justices Willis Van Devanter, Pierce Butler, and George Sutherland, "remained cordial but distant," Cardozo's presence on the court was greeted with animosity by Justice James McReynolds, "a virulent anti-Semite and possibly the most unpleasant fellow ever to sit on the high court."[209] McReynolds had been a vicious opponent of Brandeis's court appointment, and had never accepted Brandeis as a judicial colleague. For McReynolds, the appointment of Cardozo, a second Jew on the court, was a further intolerable insult. McReynolds detested Brandeis and later Cardozo, "and there is no official portrait of the Court in 1924 because McReynolds would not sit next to Brandeis as protocol required."[210] On one occasion, McReynolds returned one of Oliver Wendell Holmes Jr.'s dissenting opinions "with the intimation that Brandeis had made him go wrong and then added a remark that the Lord had tried to make something out of the Hebrews for centuries, but finally gave up and turned them out to prey on mankind 'like fleas on the dog.'"[211] When Brandeis retired in 1939, McReynolds refused to sign the traditional letter of collegial farewell.

Both publicly and privately, McReynolds "treated Cardozo as discourteously as he had Brandeis."[212] When Cardozo was first nominated by President Hoover in 1932, McReynolds remarked at a public gathering that all one needed to become a justice was to be a Jew and the son of a crook, a "gratuitously nasty" comment understood to be directed at Cardozo.[213] At Cardozo's swearing-in ceremony, McReynolds "conspicuously buried himself in a newspaper."[214] During their few years as colleagues, McReynolds "emphasized his hostility" toward Cardozo by often holding "a brief or record in front of his face when Cardozo delivered an opinion from the bench."[215] Cardozo, a shy, retiring man accustomed to the civility of the New York courts, never got used to McReynolds's nastiness, which remained a source of discomfort throughout his Washington years. When Cardozo died in 1938, McReynolds did not attend any of the three memorial sessions at the Supreme Court honoring him.[216]

Cardozo's law clerks helped mitigate his loneliness, often accompanying him to dinner and the theater productions, especially those of Gilbert and Sullivan, that he loved. Cardozo "had his clerks to dinner once or twice a year, and they in turn usually invited him to dinner at their homes."[217] Like Brandeis and Holmes, Cardozo at first turned to Felix Frankfurter to recommend clerks from among his Harvard Law School students. Subsequently, to resolve the competing claims of friends on the Harvard, Columbia, and Yale law faculties, Cardozo "decided to select his clerks from among the three schools on a rotating basis."[218] Thus, the first clerk suggested by Frankfurter, Melvin Siegel, a recent Harvard graduate, clerked for Cardozo in 1932. Cardozo selected his 1933 clerk, Ambrose Doskow, from his alma mater, Columbia, and his 1934 clerk, Alan M. Stroock, from Yale.[219] Cardozo wrote all his judicial opinions by himself, however, and "made relatively little use . . . of his Supreme Court clerks."[220] Unlike Brandeis, he did not use his law clerks as his research assistants, or occasionally permit one to draft part of an opinion. While Cardozo would discuss cases with his clerk and "was receptive to the clerk's suggestions," he "delegated no opinion writing to the clerk and did most of his own research."[221]

Two of his four law clerks, Siegel and Stroock, were Jewish. Stroock, who served for two years and with whom he was especially close, was the son of Cardozo's longtime friend Sol Stroock, one of New York's most respected attorneys and Jewish communal leaders, who would later serve briefly as national president of the AJC. Although not Sephardic, Alan Stroock "came from the same social background in New York as Cardozo and had a long family connection with him," while "Stroock's wife, Katherine, was related to many members of the Nathan family," to whom of course Cardozo was also related.[222]

Cardozo's clerks generally venerated him, viewing him "not only [as] a great jurist" but as having "a saintly quality to him in that he didn't like to hurt people and was very gentle and very considerate."[223] Joseph L. Rauh Jr., Cardozo's last clerk, would later recall: "At that time I thought he was a saint, and came as close to being a saint as I would ever in my lifetime meet."[224] Alan Stroock would later remember his clerkship years as an "extraordinary experience" with a "brilliant, wise, cultured and gracious . . . human being. In both law and manners, he was the greatest teacher I have ever known."[225] His clerks were also impressed with Cardozo's knowledge of Judaism. Stroock, for example, would later recall that "once, when I told him that I was going to New York for our family Seder," Cardozo "recited to me without pause the entire *Mah Nishtanah* although I am sure that he had not spoken the words since he was a child."[226] During his six years on the Supreme Court, Cardozo "derived a great deal of pleasure from his daily contact with his law clerks," and although "it was not the same as the close life he had shared with his colleagues in Albany . . . it provided some warmth in the cold atmosphere of the Supreme Court."[227]

The *Bremen* Incident and Antisemitism

Although on appointment to the court Cardozo "resigned his connections with Jewish organizations," including his executive board memberships with the AJC and National Jewish Welfare Board, "both the times and specific incidents forced him to deal with anti-Semitism and his role as a Jewish judge."[228] In 1935, Jewish demonstrators boarded the German luxury liner *Bremen*, resting in New York Harbor, and tore down a Nazi flag, sparking a fight during which one demonstrator struck a policeman with brass knuckles. Ruling on this incident, Louis Brodsky, a New York Jewish magistrate, "created an international uproar when he dismissed the charge of unlawful assembly against five of the defendants . . . concluding that there had been no proof of unlawful assembly."[229] In this inflammatory judicial opinion, Brodsky "set forth what might have been in the minds of the defendants in seeking to tear down the Nazi flag." The Jewish defendants, argued Brodsky, "might have viewed the flag as emblematic of all the acts, which he listed, of the Nazi regime's destroying human freedom."[230] The Jewish lawbreakers were thus justified, Brodsky wrote, "because the flag provoked them, even though the U.S. government recognized Germany's National Socialist regime."[231]

Although outraged by increasing reports of Nazi antisemitism, Cardozo was personally distressed by Brodsky's judicial opinion, and by the favorable comments apparently made by two of his relatives, his niece Aline Goldstone and his cousin Maud Nathan, president of the National Consumers League, about Brodsky's ruling.[232] Writing to Aline Goldstone, Cardozo said: "I am disappointed that you and Maud . . . approve of Brodsky and his shameful utterance. What is the use of striving for standards of judicial propriety if you and she condone such lapses! It would have been bad enough if he had been a Gentile; but for a Jew it was unforgivable. Now our traducers will say — and with some right if such as you and Maud approve — that these are the standards of the race."[233]

Cardozo believed Brodsky "had failed to give the German ship the protection that it was owed under the law" and "viewed the matter all the more seriously because Brodsky was a Jew whose performance cast Jews, particularly Jewish judges, in a bad light."[234] Cardozo's jurisprudential point was "that Brodsky had no business letting his own personal views as a Jew affect his judicial judgment. . . . The law, in Cardozo's view, was clear, and the German ship-owners were entitled to its protection irrespective of the judge's personal reaction to Nazism."[235]

Cardozo expressed his own unequivocal antagonism to Nazism in a letter to Felix Frankfurter shortly after the Brodsky incident: "There are few, even among the intellectuals, that are burning with indignation about [Hitler's] treatment of the Jews," he wrote. "They deprecate such narrowness; they would put an end to the persecution if they could do so with a word; but they do not lie awake at night about it. I found a man the other day who said it made him sleepless. But there are not many of his type. We need another Garrison who will cry out unceasingly until all the world shall hear."[236]

In 1930, when the AJC was discussing ways to combat antisemitic hiring practices, Cardozo, then a board member, "expressed the view that while little can be done with private businesses, it may be possible, by suitable legislation, to curb the practice of discrimination in the matter of employment on the part of public service and utility corporations."[237] In a 1935 letter to his cousin Annie Nathan Meyer, Cardozo "expressed undisguised contempt for [the lawyer] Madison Grant, an implacable nativist, and his 'notorious' attitude toward Jews."[238]

Although Cardozo's "notions of judicial propriety or perhaps his own lack of a crusading spirit kept him from public action in attacking Adolf Hitler's policies," he did join several other Jewish judges in 1933 in urging President Roosevelt to change U.S. government policy so that Jewish refugees from Nazi Germany "could more easily be admitted to the United States."[239]

Even as Cardozo rarely spoke out publicly against the Nazis' antisemitism, he took a stand when antisemitism struck closer to home. When his law clerk Alan Stroock signed an agreement to purchase a home in the Spring Valley section of Washington, D.C., a real estate agent told Stroock "that the agreement violated a restrictive covenant against Jews."[240] On learning that Stroock was ready to cancel the agreement, Cardozo was incensed. Such a covenant in the nation's capital touched a nerve for Cardozo both as a Jew and a Jewish justice on the high court, eliciting an uncharacteristically impassioned response. When Cardozo asked whether the real estate agent "knew that Stroock was his law clerk," and "Stroock replied affirmatively, Cardozo became even more angry, taking the incident as a personal attack."[241] He encouraged Stroock to bring a lawsuit, "saying that he would issue a public statement of support." Stroock, however, did not bring the lawsuit.[242]

Palko v. Connecticut

Although Cardozo's Supreme Court tenure was brief, he authored more than a hundred opinions, some of them landmarks in U.S. constitutional history. In 1937, for example, he spoke for a unanimous court in upholding several key provisions of the Social Security Act of 1935. Later that year, Cardozo wrote the celebrated majority decision in the case of *Palko v. Connecticut*, which constitutional law scholars have called "the most significant basic decision ever pronounced by the Court on behalf of the application of the federal Bill of Rights to the several states."[243] *Palko v. Connecticut*, read from the bench on December 6, would also be Cardozo's last judicial opinion, as well as possibly his most important.

Palko v. Connecticut involved a man, Frank Palko, convicted by a Connecticut court of second-degree murder. The defendant had initially been charged with first-degree murder for killing two policeman who had tried to question him about a robbery. The trial judge, however, "excluded a confession and other important evidence offered by the prosecution, and the jury convicted Palko of only murder in the second degree."[244] The state of Connecticut, alleging errors by the trial judge, proceeded to try Palko again, "this time obtaining a verdict of first-degree murder, punishable by death."[245] When this conviction was affirmed by the Connecticut Supreme Court, Palko's attorneys appealed to the U.S. Supreme Court, contending that the statute permitting a retrial after the state's appeal violated the double-jeopardy clause of the Fifth Amendment to the Constitution, which applied to individual states, such as Connecticut, via the due process provisions of the Fourteenth Amendment.[246]

In 1833, Chief Justice John Marshall had written a historic opinion for a unanimous Supreme Court that the Bill of Rights was binding only on the federal government, not the individual states. Attorneys for the defendant in *Palko v. Connecticut*, however, argued that "whatever would be a violation of the Bill of Rights if done by the federal government, is equally unlawful if done by a state, by force of the Fourteenth Amendment guarantee that no person shall be deprived, by any act of the state, of his life, liberty or property without due process of law."[247] Cardozo, in upholding Justice Marshall's ruling, disagreed, concluding, "There is no such general rule."[248]

In rejecting Palko's contention, Cardozo held that "the double jeopardy provisions of the Fifth Amendment were not binding on the states in toto, if at all, and that, therefore, Connecticut could constitutionally give to the state . . . a right of appeal on a question of law in a criminal case."[249] Cardozo followed legal precedents in concluding that the only Bill of Rights provisions applicable to the states were those "of the very essence of a scheme of ordered liberty."[250] The Bill of Rights protections *not* applicable to the states, argued Cardozo, were those that "might be lost, and justice still be done."[251] Jury trials, the right to an indictment, and the privilege against self-incrimination had all been justly held as inapplicable to the states, argued Cardozo.[252]

As Judge Richard Posner has suggested, Cardozo's landmark opinion in *Palko v. Connecticut*, arguing that the "ordered liberty" concept should dictate which Bill of Rights protections apply to the states through the due process clause, although rejected by some subsequent Supreme Court decisions, remains "of enduring interest."[253] For decades thereafter, the *Palko v. Connecticut* opinion would loom large in the debate over how judges should decide which Bill of Rights protections were binding on the states.[254]

On December 10, 1937, just four days after delivering his *Palko* opinion, Cardozo suffered a serious heart attack, the first of two in less than two weeks.[255] Indeed, Cardozo had been in physical decline since beginning his court tenure, experiencing his first heart problems in June 1930, shortly after his sister Nellie's death, while still serving on the New York Court of Appeals. Although the 1930 event was considered a "mild attack of angina,"[256] Cardozo's heart "had sufficiently weakened that . . . one of the specialists who examined him the following year later said that Cardozo had lived longer than was reasonably to have been expected at the time."[257] He suffered a severe recurrence in summer 1935, "and his physician then warned him to retire from the Supreme Court because failure to do so would shorten his life expectancy by two-thirds."[258] He "ignored this advice," and continued to follow an exhausting schedule until his attacks in late 1937.[259] Thereafter, he contracted severe influenza and was, at the same time, stricken with an excruciating case of shingles. On January 7, 1938, he had yet another heart attack and the following day suffered a stroke that resulted in the partial paralysis of his left arm and left leg. Over the next few months, even as his health outlook appeared increasingly dire, he did not mention the possibility of retirement.[260]

In May 1938, Sissie Lehman "suggested that Cardozo be brought to the Lehman home in Port Chester," hoping "that living in the country would help his recovery."[261] Cardozo was thus taken from his Washington apartment to the Lehman estate, where Irving and Sissie cared for him "and helped him immeasurably during his final illness."[262] It was appropriate that he should spend his last two months with the Lehmans, whom he had missed so desperately while in the nation's capital.[263] On Saturday July 9, Cardozo died of a massive coronary thrombosis at age sixty-eight.

Two days later, a funeral service was held at the Lehman estate, where a rabbi from Cardozo's Shearith Israel congregation officiated. The Orthodox service, which lasted only ten minutes and was conducted entirely in Hebrew, consisted of the Twenty-Third Psalm and Hebrew readings from the Book of Proverbs.[264] Cardozo had asked "that there be no eulogy, and there was none."[265] After the service, the funeral procession "made its way down the Hutchinson River Parkway, detoured to Manhattan," and stopped before Shearith Israel, "which opened its doors and gates wide in respect, and then continued on to the Shearith Israel cemetery in Long Island," where the mourners recited the traditional Kaddish.[266] Cardozo's coffin was then "lowered to his final resting place, near the gravesites of his mother, father, his brother and all his sisters excepting Emily, his twin, who had married a Christian and who, according to Orthodox Jewish law, could not be buried in holy ground."[267] More than two hundred family members, friends, and associates, including three of Cardozo's Supreme Court colleagues, attended the service. Whereas Cardozo's friend Stephen Wise, at the time perhaps America's preeminent reform rabbi, attended, the Lehmans and some of Cardozo's other friends were disappointed that Wise "had not officiated or been assigned any role," as it was believed "Cardozo had wanted."[268] Nevertheless, at a service of the venerable Orthodox Spanish and Portuguese Synagogue, a reform rabbi, no matter how distinguished, would not be invited to participate.

Among his bequests, Cardozo left money for the perpetual care of his and his family members' graves, $25,000 to the Federation for the Support of Jewish Philanthropic Societies, "the umbrella Jewish organization in New York City," $7,500 to Mt. Sinai Hospital, and generous gifts to several friends, his chauffeur, his cook, and his sister Nellie's nurses. To Irving Lehman, he left his library, one of the foremost private law libraries in the United States. To Sissie Lehman, he left the loving cup presented to him by the New York Court of Appeals, one of his most treasured possessions. He left the remainder of his estate, approximately $188,000, to Columbia University for "the foundation or maintenance of a chair of jurisprudence in the Law School of the University, to be associated with my name, and to perpetuate the scientific study of a subject which has been one of my chief interests in life."[269] Columbia honored this wish, and the Cardozo Professorship of Jurisprudence still signals his enormous contribution to the legal field.

Cardozo's Legacy

As a result of his illness, Benjamin Cardozo's time on the bench was even shorter than the six years history records.[270] Of the eight Jewish high court justices, only Arthur Goldberg and Abe Fortas had briefer tenures.

Cardozo's appointment as Oliver Wendell Holmes Jr.'s "anointed successor" was especially noteworthy in marking "one of the few times in our history that the most qualified candidate to fill a vacancy on the Supreme Court was the one actually picked. . . ."[271] Cardozo, then serving as chief judge of the New York State Court of Appeals, was also the only Jewish high court justice to be appointed by a Republican president—not to mention a president whose candidacy Cardozo had not supported. Cardozo's ties to the Democratic leadership through his support for Al Smith in the 1928 campaign, as well as his kindred friendship with Irving Lehman, the brother of New York's Democratic governor, made Hoover's appointment even more remarkable.

Through his service on the New York Court of Appeals, Cardozo would join the top echelon of American jurists, as assessed by legal scholars, a list that included Marshall, Holmes, and Brandeis, along with Learned Hand, the only one of the group to never reach the high court.[272] But it was during Cardozo's eighteen years on the appeals court, the "most highly regarded state court in the United States, [that he] became the most famous and most esteemed state court judge in the country."[273] His greatness, thus, predated his Supreme Court service.

Yet when Cardozo died in 1938, many court analysts predicted that, due to his short tenure, his legacy might be unremarkable. A consensus, however, has emerged among judicial scholars over the past several decades that Cardozo should be ranked among the "greatest" justices to sit on the Supreme Court. "Although fate allowed him little more than six years on the high bench," noted the Supreme Court scholar Henry J. Abraham in 1999, "he is eminently deserving of the recognition of greatness bestowed on him. Those six years were among the most emotion-charged and contentious in the Court's history, and Cardozo demonstrably did his part in recording the history of that period with his more than 100 opinions for the Court, written with the pen of legal scholar and philosopher as well as of poet and teacher."[274] Most recent judicial scholars would likely agree with Abraham, who has concluded that "no justice in the annals of constitutional law and history ever rendered a more enduring contribution in so brief a span of years."[275] It was Cardozo, for example, who "lucidly and carefully spoke for the Court in 1937 in upholding the key provisions of the landmark Social Security Act of 1935."[276] Of these rulings, "one sustain[ed] the unemployment insurance provisions of the act, and the other, the old age pension."[277] It was also Cardozo who, as we saw, authored the landmark 1937 Supreme Court opinion on *Palko v. Connecticut*, one of the century's most frequently cited court rulings.

For his part, Judge Richard Posner has suggested that Cardozo's judicial legacy might have been greater had he, during his final six years, continued serving as chief judge of the New York Court of Appeals rather than on the Supreme Court. Although his high court appointment "may have conferred a slight halo effect," notes Posner, "six more years on the New York Court of Appeals might have raised Cardozo's reputation to an even higher level than it has attained—and as with Learned Hand and Henry Friendly, people would be saying what a shame it was that Cardozo was never appointed to the Supreme Court and what a super job he would have done if he had been. He did well on the Court, but his performance was an anticlimax."[278]

Notwithstanding such gentle critiques, in 1939, in an "unprecedented" tribute, the Columbia, Harvard, and Yale law reviews published a joint issue devoted to examining Cardozo's work. And in 1941, the New York City Bar Association endowed an Annual Benjamin N. Cardozo Lecture Series in his memory. In the decades since, his major judicial opinions, theoretical writings, and approach to judging have remained a subject for study by legal scholars and Supreme Court observers alike.[279] Moreover, Cardozo's opinions have consistently been among the most frequently cited of twentieth-century jurists. In his 1990 book, *Cardozo: A Study in Reputation*, Posner provided a detailed quantitative analysis of law review citations of Cardozo's judicial opinions during the 1980s that powerfully confirmed his continuing importance.[280]

As for Cardozo's particular ranking as a Supreme Court justice, it has generally been bolstered in the decades after his death. In 1970, for example, sixty-five law school deans and professors of law, history, and political science, who were asked "to evaluate the performance of the 96 justices . . . on the Supreme Court from 1789 until 1967," rated Cardozo as the sixth greatest, behind Marshall, Joseph Story, Roger Taney, Brandeis, and Stone.[281] An article in the April 1983 *American Bar Association Journal*, which distilled "everyone's choice for the greatest justices of the United States Supreme Court," produced "a new roster of the all-time, all-star era Supreme Court nine," which ranked Cardozo fifth, after only Marshall, Story, Holmes, and Brandeis. Subsequent rankings by "various groups of experts and lay observers of the Court" have been "remarkably similar in their judgments," consistently rating Cardozo among the top ten.[282]

Cardozo also continues to be regarded as one of the foremost legal scholars to serve on the high court. Harvard Law School dean Roscoe Pound considered Cardozo one of the top legal minds in American history.[283] Only Storey, Holmes, and Frankfurter made enduring contributions to legal scholarship and jurisprudence comparable to or exceeding that of Cardozo. Moreover, Cardozo's *The Nature of the Judicial Process* remains today, almost a hundred years after its initial publication, the most influential work by a judge on the art and process of judging. A text that "established him as one of the leading jurists of our time," *The Nature of the Judicial Process* "has become a classic of legal education, and is continually recommended to aspiring law students on the . . . ground that it still possesses the same validity and vitality . . . as it did when published."[284]

Cardozo's Jewish legacy is also significant. He was, for example, alone among the eight Jewish Supreme Court justices to follow the religion's dietary laws in his home. His observance of kashrut separates him clearly from his predecessor, Brandeis, who enjoyed hams, whose funeral did not even incorporate the Kaddish, and who was cremated, in opposition to Jewish law. While two of the other Jewish justices, Frankfurter and Fortas, were raised in Orthodox homes, only Cardozo maintained a lifelong affiliation with an Orthodox synagogue, despite his drift from overall observance.

Reflecting his devotion to Orthodox Sephardic tradition, as well as his acute legal thinking, Cardozo offered his judgment against mixed seating during his 1895 visit to Shearith Israel, showing a reverence for tradition.[285] Moreover, Cardozo always took pride in his Orthodox Sephardic forebears, who had served as officers in the American Revolution, spoken at a presidential inauguration, and served on the boards of Columbia University and the New York Stock Exchange, as well as nourishing the deep traditions of New York's Spanish and Portuguese Synagogue. As the second Jew to serve on the Supreme Court, Cardozo became the most admired member of New York's Sephardic community and, as such, helped restore its sense of its historically elite position.[286] Cardozo thus became a role model for a generation of aspiring Jewish lawyers and judges from his community and beyond.

Seventy-one years after his death, Cardozo's Sephardic roots unexpectedly returned to public discussion in 2009, when President Barack Obama appointed Sonia Sotomayor, widely considered the first "Hispanic" justice, to the Supreme Court. In the ensuing discussion, several commentators suggested Cardozo had in fact been the first Hispanic high court justice.[287] While most Hispanic organizations and the U.S. Census Bureau do not regard people of Portuguese descent as Hispanic, some still argued that Cardozo deserved the distinction.[288] Two years before Sotomayor's nomination, for example, *The Dictionary of Latino Civil History* listed Cardozo as "the first Hispanic named to the Supreme Court of the United States."[289] In response to such claims, Cardozo's authorized biographer, Andrew Kaufman, while noting that the jurist "regarded himself as a Sephardic Jew whose ancestors came from the Iberian Peninsula," pointed out that "the term 'Hispanic' was not commonly used during Cardozo's lifetime and would probably have been unfamiliar to him when President Herbert Hoover named him to the court."[290]

Following the precedent set by Brandeis, Cardozo made a practice of hiring Jewish law clerks, giving these high achievers access to virtually limitless career potential. As during Brandeis's tenure, Jewish law school graduates labored under the shadow of antisemitism and otherwise would have had limited opportunities of such prestige. In hiring these clerks, Cardozo, like Brandeis, did much to promote the advancement of Jews within the American legal profession. Following their example, non-Jewish high court justices, beginning with William O. Douglas in his 1938 hiring of David Ginsburg, started hiring Jewish clerks as well.

Cardozo's legacy was also furthered significantly with the establishment of Yeshiva University's Cardozo School of Law, which opened its doors in 1976 and graduated its first class in 1979. Cardozo is one of the few Supreme Court justices to have a law school named in his honor. The premier issue of the law school's journal—the *Cardozo Law Review*—was devoted to the jurist's career.

Finally, the court's "Jewish seat" is integral to Cardozo's story. After Cardozo's death, Franklin Roosevelt appointed Felix Frankfurter, the third Jew to serve on the court, to succeed him. As we saw in the previous chapter, Cardozo and Brandeis served together from 1932 to 1938, predating the precedent of a single Jewish seat. Not until Bill Clinton's appointment of Ruth Bader Ginsburg and Stephen Breyer would two Jewish justices serve together for as long, and President Obama made it three for the first time with his 2010 appointment of Elena Kagan.[291] The emergence of an informally designated Jewish seat, occupied in succession by Cardozo, Frankfurter, Goldberg, and Fortas, thus began in 1939 with FDR's appointment of Frankfurter. Roosevelt "felt it appropriate that Frankfurter should replace a fellow Jew," a tradition Presidents Kennedy and Johnson would follow with their respective appointments.[292]

Louis D. Brandeis at age fifteen, living with his parents in Louisville, three years before beginning his legal studies at Harvard Law School. Collection of the Supreme Court of the United States

Brandeis when he coauthored with his law partner, Sam Warren, the famous 1891 *Harvard Law Review* article "The Right to Privacy." Collection of the Supreme Court of the United States

Justices Brandeis and Oliver Wendell Holmes Jr., walking outside the U.S. Capitol building. Collection of the Supreme Court of the United States

Brandeis, in his Supreme Court robes, holding one of his judicial opinions. Collection of the Supreme Court of the United States

The Supreme Court as it was composed from 1916 to 1921, during Brandeis's first five years on the court. The justices are arranged by seniority, with five seated and four standing. Standing from left are Brandeis, Mahlon Pitney, James McReynolds, and John Hessin Clarke. Collection of the Supreme Court of the United States

Brandeis (*center*) with the Jewish philanthropist and Macy's co-owner Nathan Straus (*left*) and Rabbi Stephen S. Wise (*right*), aboard a ship to sail June 12, 1920, for London, where Brandeis and Straus spoke at the World Zionist Congress. Library of Congress

Brandeis and his wife, Alice, riding in a horse-drawn buggy in Washington, D.C., 1921. Library of Congress

Horatio Alger Jr. (*right*), who authored some 130 "rags to riches" novels and was also a Unitarian minister. He tutored Benjamin Cardozo for his entry into Columbia College. Library of Congress

Justice Cardozo in his
judicial robes. Collection
of the Supreme Court
of the United States

The Hughes court, 1937–1938, on which Justices Brandeis and Cardozo
served together. Chief Justice Charles Evans Hughes (front row, middle) sits
next to Brandeis (at left). Cardozo is the far-left figure in the back row.
Collection of the Supreme Court of the United States

Harvard Law School student Felix Frankfurter in his dormitory, 1905.
Historical and Special Collections at Harvard Law School Library

Harvard Law School faculty, 1936–1937, including Professor Frankfurter
(middle row, fourth from left), who had taught there since 1914 and was
the school's first-ever Jewish faculty member. Historical and
Special Collections at Harvard Law School Library

Frankfurter's wife, Marion, at the
Frankfurters' new home in Washington,
D.C., on February 11, 1939, three days after
the Senate confirmed his nomination to
the Supreme Court. Collection of the
Supreme Court of the United States

Justice Frankfurter in his judicial robes.
Collection of the Supreme Court
of the United States

Then labor secretary Arthur Goldberg (*center*), together with Nelson
Glueck (*right*), president of the Hebrew Union College and Jewish Institute
of Religion, and Professor Jacob Rader Marcus (*left*), at the seminary's June 3,
1961, rabbinic ordination ceremonies, held at Cincinnati's Plum Street Temple.
Goldberg received an honorary doctorate of humane letters at the event.
The Jacob Rader Marcus Center of the American Jewish Archives, Cincinnati

Justice Goldberg following his October 1, 1962, appointment to the Supreme Court. Collection of the Supreme Court of the United States

Alan M. Dershowitz—the Felix Frankfurter Professor of Law Emeritus at Harvard Law School and Justice Goldberg's former law clerk—with Goldberg shortly after the latter resigned from the court to become U.S. ambassador to the UN. Private photo collection of Alan Dershowitz. Used with his permission

The Warren court during Arthur Goldberg's tenure as a justice. Here, Chief Justice Earl Warren sits in the middle of the front row; Goldberg stands in the second row, at far right. Collection of the Supreme Court of the United States

Supreme Court of the United States

Memorandum

March 23d, 1964

Charoces recipe.
take 3 or 4 apples.
1/4 cup of raisins
1/2 cup chopped walnuts
cinnamon to taste
Brown sugar to Taste
add Manishewitz wine.

Chopp everything to a
soft mess, taste it
and add if needed
more or less to taste

The Goldberg family Passover Seders were popular events in Jewish Washington, attended by government officials and other luminaries, Jewish and non-Jewish alike. Here, in preparation for the 1964 Seder, Goldberg writes on his Supreme Court letterhead the family recipe for *charoses*, a traditional Passover dish. Library of Congress

On October 31, 1970, Goldberg shakes hands with political supporters in Levittown during his unsuccessful campaign for governor against incumbent Nelson Rockefeller. Collection of the Supreme Court of the United States

In 1939, Interior Secretary Harold Ickes appointed Abe Fortas general counsel of the Public Works Administration. In this May 1 photo, Ickes presents Fortas with his commission at his WPA swearing-in ceremony. Library of Congress

President Lyndon B. Johnson laughs with Justice Fortas in the White House on July 29, 1965, the day after Fortas's Supreme Court appointment. Lyndon Baines Johnson Presidential Library, Austin, Texas

Fortas and his wife, Carolyn Agger, and Lyndon and Lady Bird were close friends who often socialized in Washington, D.C., and at the LBJ Ranch in Texas. This 1960s photo of Fortas and the first lady at the LBJ Ranch is inscribed to Fortas from Lady Bird. White House Photo

The Warren Court, on which Fortas served from 1965 to 1969, with Chief Justice Warren seated in the front row, at center; Fortas stands in the second row, at far right. Collection of the Supreme Court of the United States

President Johnson meeting with his foreign policy advisers, a role Fortas continued to play after his Supreme Court appointment, in the White House Cabinet Room on November 2, 1967. From far left and moving clockwise: former ambassador Robert Murphy (gesturing), former ambassador Averell Harriman, former secretary of state Dean Acheson, General Omar Bradley, General Maxwell Taylor, Fortas, Intelligence Advisory Board chairman Clark Clifford, Secretary of State Dean Rusk, Johnson, Secretary of Defense Robert McNamara, former treasury secretary C. Douglas Dillon, and former national security adviser McGeorge Bundy. Lyndon Baines Johnson Presidential Library, Austin, Texas

Best Wishes to Abe Fortas,
Rosalynn Carter

Fortas, a passionate musician who had played violin since childhood,
organized a chamber music group consisting of amateur and professional violinists
and cellists that often performed at White House social functions. In September 1979,
the Fortas Quintet performed in the East Room for First Lady Rosalynn Carter,
whose inscription appears in the photo's bottom margin. The White House

Fifteen-year-old Ruth Bader
speaking in the summer of 1948 at
Camp Che-Na-Wah, in the Adirondacks,
where she was "camp rabbi." Collection
of the Supreme Court of the United States

Ruth Bader Ginsburg, the first tenured
woman professor at Columbia Law School,
in the spring of 1980, just after President
Jimmy Carter nominated her to serve on
the U.S. Court of Appeals for the District
of Columbia Circuit. Collection of the
Supreme Court of the United States

Ginsburg at her Supreme Court swearing-in ceremony on August 10, 1993, when she became the first Jewish woman to serve on the court. Standing from left to right are President Bill Clinton, Ginsburg, her husband, Martin Ginsburg, and Chief Justice William Rehnquist. Collection of the Supreme Court of the United States

Justices Ginsburg and Antonin Scalia, with their spouses (not pictured), on vacation in 1994, riding an elephant in India. Collection of the Supreme Court of the United States

Sharing a passion for opera, Justices Ginsburg and Scalia appeared in period costume in a Washington National Opera opening-night production of Richard Strauss's *Ariadne auf Naxos*, held at the Kennedy Center in Washington, D.C., in January 1994. Collection of the Supreme Court of the United States

Ginsburg hugging her husband, Martin, at a ten-year reunion for her Supreme Court clerks. Collection of the Supreme Court of the United States

Class of 1955 yearbook photo for Stephen Breyer, who was voted "most likely to succeed" in his graduating class at San Francisco's Lowell High School. Breyer was the debate team star and, in intercity debates, often competed with future four-time California governor Jerry Brown. Lowell High School Alumni Association, San Francisco

In a photo dated November 23, 2004, ten years after his appointment to the Supreme Court, Justice Breyer appears in his judicial robes. Collection of the Supreme Court of the United States

Justice Stephen G. Breyer and his brother Federal Judge Charles R. Breyer at a joint public appearance of the Northern District Court Historical Society program in San Francisco. U.S. Courts for the Ninth District

On October 1, 2010, President Barack Obama, Chief Justice John Roberts, and other justices greet Elena Kagan in the Justices' Conference Room just before her courtroom swearing-in ceremony. Collection of the Supreme Court of the United States

The day of Justice Kagan's swearing-in ceremony, October 1, 2010, the four women who have served as Supreme Court justices appear in the Justices' Conference Room: (*left to right*) Sandra Day O'Connor, retired, along with current justices Sonia Sotomayor, Ruth Bader Ginsburg, and Elena Kagan. Collection of the Supreme Court of the United States

The two Jewish women justices on the Supreme Court, Ginsburg and Kagan,
in the Justices' Conference Room on October 1, 2010, the day of Kagan's swearing-in.
Collection of the Supreme Court of the United States

The Roberts court, pictured in 2010, shortly after Kagan became its third woman, second Jewish woman, and third Jewish justice. Chief Justice Roberts is seated in the front row, middle, with Justice Ginsburg seated at the far right and Justice Kagan standing behind her. In the back row, Justice Breyer stands second from left.
Steve Petteway, curator of the Photo Collection of the
Supreme Court of the United States

5

FELIX FRANKFURTER

City College to the New Deal

ON A SPRING DAY in 1906, two New Yorkers, Franklin Roosevelt and Felix Frankfurter, both recent law school graduates and twenty-four years old, met for lunch at the city's Harvard Club. Two more different luncheon companions could hardly have been imagined. While both were young, ambitious lawyers hoping to get a start in politics, they had little else in common. An independently wealthy aristocrat educated at Groton, Harvard College, and Columbia Law School, Roosevelt descended from a Dutch family that had settled before 1650 in what was then New Amsterdam.[1] Franklin's great-grandfather Isaac Roosevelt had been a delegate to the 1787 Constitutional Convention in Philadelphia. The Delano ancestors of Franklin's mother, Sara, had come over on the *Mayflower*. Franklin had been working in an elite Wall Street law firm, intended merely as a prelude to a political candidacy. The previous year, he had married his distant cousin Eleanor, the favorite niece of President Theodore Roosevelt. Eleanor's pedigree was, if anything, even more aristocratic than Franklin's. With ancestors including Philip Livingston, a Declaration of Independence signer, Eleanor had grown up as part of her uncle Theodore's Oyster Bay branch of the Roosevelt dynasty.[2] After their March 1905 wedding, Eleanor and Franklin took their inherited place as pillars of early twentieth-century New York's patrician society.

By contrast, Frankfurter was a relatively new immigrant to America, a child of Vienna's Jewish ghetto descended from six generations of Austrian rabbis, worlds away from FDR's Hudson Valley aristocracy. Frankfurter's family had arrived in New York in 1894 aboard the *Marsala* passenger liner, having traveled, like most Jewish immigrants of the era, in steerage. Arriving at age twelve without knowing a word of English, Frankfurter was educated in the city's Lower East Side public schools.[3] After graduating from City College in 1902, and working for a year to cover his law school tuition, he enrolled at Harvard Law School in 1903, just as Roosevelt was beginning his senior year at Harvard College.

The Frankfurter-Roosevelt lunch at the Harvard Club was arranged by a mutual friend, Grenville Clark, a college classmate of Roosevelt's, a law classmate of Frankfurter's, and now FDR's colleague at the Carter, Ledyard, and Milburn law firm.[4] Clark, like Roosevelt an heir to social eminence and wealth, would later serve as chairman of the American Bar Association's Committee on the Bill of Rights and would remain one of Frankfurter's lifelong friends.

For both Roosevelt and Frankfurter, according to the future jurist's biographer, their Harvard Club meeting "had no more meaning than two young lawyers sharing a table and pleasant conversation. They became casual acquaintances, nothing more, neither suspecting that their acquaintanceship would grow much later into intimate personal friendship and that their mutual public philosophies would one day affect the policies of the entire nation." Indeed, in the years ahead, Frankfurter would assiduously cultivate this relationship, which developed during their mutual years in Washington during the later Wilson administration and continued intermittently in the decade after World War I.[5] Upon FDR's 1928 election as New York governor, Frankfurter would emerge as one of his closest advisors, a role he continued to hold after Roosevelt's 1933 move to the White House.

Frankfurter's Early Years

Frankfurter was the only Jewish Supreme Court justice not born in the United States. The third of six children, he was born November 15, 1882, in Vienna. His father, Leopold, hailed from Pressburg (now Bratislava, Slovakia), then a center of Austro-Hungarian Jewish life. When anti-Jewish riots broke out in Pressburg following the 1848 revolution, the young Leopold and his family moved to Vienna.[6] Leopold had entered rabbinical seminary in Vienna, but he found Viennese opera and theater much more interesting than his Talmud lessons. By his final year in seminary, he understood he was not cut out to follow in his family's rabbinic tradition. While his brother Solomon pursued what would become a distinguished career as a Jewish communal leader and scholar, Leopold gave up his seminary studies a year before ordination to marry and go into business.[7]

The city of Felix Frankfurter's childhood has been described as "the Vienna of Emperor Francis Joseph, a city of bright cafés in a nation of peasants, that nourished the genius of Sigmund Freud, Gustav Mahler, Hugo von Hofmannsthal and Arnold Schonberg."[8] Its Imperial Opera was the envy of all Europe. Frankfurter's immediate contemporaries included the literary critic Georg Lukacs, the Protestant theologian Paul Tillich, and the philosopher Ludwig Wittgenstein, although their paths—and those of their families —would never have crossed. To be sure, Frankfurter's experience of Vienna was vastly different from that of Tillich and Wittgenstein. When Felix was born, the Frankfurter family lived in the Jewish ghetto, or second district, which contained about half the city's Jews. This district was far away from the café society of the fin de siècle Habsburg capital. Although not poverty-stricken compared to many of his Jewish neighbors, Leopold Frankfurter was never a business success, eking out a living as "a *Handelsagent,* which was not far above a door-to-door salesman."[9]

While Leopold Frankfurter's own business career was forever faltering, his brother Solomon achieved spectacular academic success at the universities of Vienna and Berlin and was appointed to a post at the Vienna state library in 1884, two years after Felix's birth. He became the library's director in 1919 and authored numerous scholarly articles in philology, archaeology, and bibliography. His nephews, especially the young Felix, worshiped Solomon Frankfurter "as a model of learning, culture and successful assimilation, especially when he became a spokesman for the Jewish interests in the city and a *shtadlan* with the gentile power structure."[10]

When Leopold Frankfurter left Vienna in 1893 to visit the United States and attend the Chicago World's Fair, as Felix would recount years later, his father "fell in love with this country."[11] Telling his family they would find greater opportunities as immigrants to America, and hoping he might earn a more secure living in New York than in Vienna, he sent for them. When his family joined him, Leopold settled them initially in the Lower East Side, "in a German- and Yiddish-speaking part of the neighborhood that real estate agents would later rename the East Village." There, he sold linens, silks, and furs, "sometimes out of their apartment, sometimes door-to-door, and never to much profit."[12]

Felix began his education at P.S. 25, where he quickly became fluent in English and began reading extensively about politics and current affairs. During his two years at the school, "Frankfurter's real education came from the public libraries and that downtown institution to which many an immigrant owed his education: Cooper Union." There, he spent at least four afternoons a week devouring "books on literature, politics and history, and he spent hours reading the periodicals from all over the world."[13] Although Frankfurter was still in his early teens, "the Cooper Union became Frankfurter's university."[14] He audited classes in history, geography, and the natural sciences by day, and in the evening attended free lectures by renowned speakers from across the nation. Frankfurter tracked new books coming into the Cooper Union library "as closely as he later kept track of Supreme Court opinions, and he read them as avidly."[15]

Following his 1897 graduation from P.S. 25, Frankfurter enrolled at the City College of New York, "where the ambitious children of immigrants combined high school and college in a five-year program" and "could get a first-rate education without paying tuition."[16] Despite a heavy course load, Frankfurter edited the college newspaper and served as vice president of his senior class. He was best remembered, however, "for his skills as a debater representing one of the college's prestigious literary clubs, the Clionia Society."[17] While at City College, he also belonged to the ZBT Society, the predecessor of the Zeta Beta Tau Jewish fraternity, which was founded in 1898 and whose acronym stood for the Zionist, Hebrew motto "Zion shall in judgment be redeemed."[18] In 1902, at age nineteen, Frankfurter graduated third in his class of 775, a class that was three-quarters Jewish.[19]

Frankfurter at Harvard Law

After working for a year as a civil servant in New York City's Tenement House Department, Frankfurter was accepted to Harvard Law School, where he began his studies in fall 1903.[20] Of Harvard Law during Frankfurter's days, the most important benefits purportedly were found not inside the classroom but outside it, where students could form "social contacts with those who were already powerful and those who aspired to become so." As Louis Brandeis had advised a young lawyer ten years before, "Cultivate the society of men of affairs. . . . Lose no opportunity of becoming acquainted with men of learning to feel instinctively their inclinations. . . . Knowledge of decisions and power of logic are mere handmaidens — they are servants not masters. . . . No hermit can be a great lawyer. . . ."[21]

Much like the youthful Brandeis, who threw himself into Cambridge society in the 1870s, Frankfurter was no hermit. Frankfurter flourished in this environment, where his brilliance and his remarkable facility for building friendships helped him gain acceptance from his more socially elevated classmates, such as Elihu Root Jr., Grenville Clark, and Ogden Mills. These men, constituting the school's social elite, became Frankfurter's lifelong friends. One such friend, his roommate, Thomas Thacher, would later become U.S. solicitor general. Another, Emory Buckner, was the son of a Methodist preacher from Nebraska, "a superb trial lawyer . . . government prosecutor and Wall Street power broker"[22] who would later serve as the U.S. attorney for the Southern District of New York, where he would earn a reputation as one of America's top prosecutors. While at Harvard, Frankfurter also socialized with several Jewish students, including the journalist Walter Lippmann, the philosopher and Zionist theoretician Horace Kallen, and Morris Raphael Cohen, who was Frankfurter's roommate on Cambridge Street from 1904 to 1906. Frankfurter and Cohen, whose family had settled on the Lower East Side after immigrating from Minsk in 1892, had become friends at City College, where Cohen was already recognized as "a promising young philosophy student, with an encyclopedic mind and dazzling vocabulary."[23] After receiving his PhD from Harvard, having studied with Josiah Royce and William James, Cohen would return to New York to teach for decades at City College. There, he attained fame as "the Socrates of CCNY" and one of America's foremost philosophers. Cohen named his first-born son after Frankfurter, and in later years Felix Cohen would speak of Frankfurter as his father's best friend during his most creative years as a philosopher. There was little Morris Raphael Cohen wrote, "especially in the field of legal philosophy, that he did not discuss with Frankfurter."[24]

Frankfurter and the Protestant Elite

Throughout his career, most of Frankfurter's close friends and mentors belonged to New York and New England's Protestant establishment.[25] They included, among others, Henry Stimson, Oliver Wendell Holmes Jr., Franklin Roosevelt, Dean Acheson, Elihu Root Jr., Grenville Clark, Learned Hand, and Harvey Hollister Bundy. After graduating from Harvard Law, Frankfurter passionately strove to be accepted into their world.

However, Frankfurter's way into this world did not come easily. Along with graduating atop his class, he was an editor of the *Harvard Law Review* and boasted enthusiastic recommendation letters from James Barr Ames, the law school's dean. Yet he was turned down by several prestigious Manhattan law firms before receiving an offer from Hornblower, Byrne, Miller, and Potter, a Wall Street outlet that had previously never hired a Jew. Although many Jewish firms were then well established in New York, such as Guggenheimer, Untermeyer, and Marshall, Frankfurter did not apply to any of them. Instead, reflecting his broader aspirations, he applied only to the gentile firms.

Although pleased by the opportunity, Frankfurter found private law practice uninspiring. As fortune would have it, he soon received an offer to work for Henry Stimson, a Harvard Law alumnus who had been appointed by President Theodore Roosevelt as U.S. attorney for the Second District of New York. Stimson introduced Frankfurter to members of America's social elite, opening doors to the power corridors and doyens of Washington society. These doors would otherwise have been closed to Frankfurter, the ambitious and brilliant immigrant Jew. Stimson, a distinguished Republican and close political ally of Theodore Roosevelt, planned to reform the U.S. Attorney's office. In Stimson, "Frankfurter discovered a lifelong mentor, a member of the upper class who embraced the idea of merit."[26] Joining him on Stimson's staff were two of Frankfurter's Harvard Law classmates, Thomas Thacher and Emory Buckner.[27]

Frankfurter's Mentor—Henry Stimson

Henry Stimson, the only person ever to serve in four U.S. presidents' cabinets, would be Frankfurter's most influential political mentor. Of Stimson's social status, it was said that "if America had an aristocracy, he would have been a baron."[28] Stimson's ancestors had fought in the French and Indian War, the American Revolution, and the Civil War. His father, Lewis Atterbury Stimson, a New York surgeon who gave up a New York Stock Exchange seat to practice medicine, had lived in Berlin, Zurich, and Paris while he "perfected his surgical skills, at one time studying with Louis Pasteur."[29] The younger Stimson was educated at Phillips Academy at Andover, Yale College, and, as noted, Harvard Law. Following his Harvard graduation, he was offered a job in the blue-chip Wall Street firm of Root and Clark. Upon the recommendation of Theodore Roosevelt's friend Elihu Root, who had served as TR's secretary of war and state, Roosevelt tapped Stimson to become U.S. Attorney for New York's Second District.

Frankfurter worked for Stimson in the U.S. Attorney's office for close to three years, quickly becoming his most trusted assistant. When Roosevelt "did not seek another presidential term in 1908, Stimson returned to private practice in New York, taking Frankfurter with him."[30] When Stimson, with Roosevelt's "encouragement and support, decided to run for the New York governorship in 1910, he chose Frankfurter to manage his campaign."[31] While doing so, Frankfurter, only twenty-eight years old, became Stimson's chief political strategist and speechwriter.[32] In the same 1910 election in which

Franklin Roosevelt was first elected to public office, as a New York state senator, "Frankfurter made his first political foray as a Republican operative" and "had the exciting experience of riding in a car with the former President Roosevelt. . . ."[33]

Although Stimson lost his governor's race, "even in defeat, the Republican connection served Frankfurter well."[34] Appointed secretary of war by President Taft in 1911, "Stimson took Frankfurter with him to Washington as what today would be called his special assistant." The official job did not exist then, so Frankfurter was officially made solicitor, or legal adviser, in the Bureau of Insular Affairs, "a political appointment to the executive branch, one focused on America's recently acquired empire in the Philippines."[35] In urging Frankfurter to join him in Washington, Stimson wrote: "If you should accept the position I would rely on you for a good deal more than that work alone, as you doubtless realize from your past experience with me. . . ."[36] Frankfurter accepted, and on July 4, 1911, the *New York Times* reported that "Assistant United States Attorney Felix Frankfurter has been appointed [to] one of the most important posts in the War Department. . . . Mr. Frankfurter is the youngest man to hold a corresponding post in the Federal administration in Washington."[37]

After taking the job, Frankfurter "immediately set off with Stimson on a tour of American overseas possessions, a trip that included the opening of the Panama Canal."[38] When they returned to Washington, Frankfurter took up his position as Stimson's all-around aide: "He wanted me to be his special assistant on all sorts of things," Frankfurter later recalled. "The Bureau of Insular Affairs . . . had charge of Puerto Rico . . . the Philippines, San Domingo . . . and the like. That was the nominal shell into which I fitted, but I worked with him mostly on water power because the War Department also had charge of water power on navigable streams. . . ."[39] In his role as Bureau of Insular Affairs counsel, Frankfurter "dealt with the broad legal issues arising within the United States possessions, from Puerto Rico to the Philippines," as well as questions of U.S. treaty obligations and the "constitutional issues arising from the governance of nine million people living in the insular possessions."[40] Frankfurter often wrote speeches for Stimson, and "in his capacity as legal adviser Frankfurter argued several cases in the Supreme Court, making a good impression there."[41]

Justice Holmes, Frankfurter, and the "House of Truth"

When Frankfurter left New York for Washington in 1911, he carried with him an introduction letter to Supreme Court justice Oliver Wendell Holmes Jr. written by his former professor and Holmes's old friend John Chipman Gray.[42] Holmes and Frankfurter soon became close friends themselves, often socializing together and initiating a voluminous correspondence that continued until Holmes's death in 1934. Frankfurter cherished his friendship with Holmes. For Frankfurter, Holmes represented "the best of everything: the Brahmin establishment, achievement in the law, culture, learning."[43] Justice and Mrs. Holmes began inviting Frankfurter to their home on Monday afternoons. Frankfurter would later remember their "quiet evenings by the fire in Holmes's living room or his study, quiet conversation exciting in its quality —philosophy, law, life—very exhilarating for a young man."[44] The Holmeses also visited Frankfurter and his lively friends at their bachelor residence, located at 1727 Nineteenth Street, which they called the "House of Truth."

During his years in Stimson's War Department, the House of Truth, which Frankfurter had founded in 1911 "together with a number of other young men who were intellectually minded and on the threshold of notable public careers,"[45] became known as the city's most famous bachelor quarters. The fashionable residence was owned by Robert Grosvenor Valentine, a bright and wealthy New Englander whom President Taft had appointed commissioner of Indian affairs and Frankfurter had met shortly after arriving in Washington.[46] Valentine invited Frankfurter, who had been living in a rooming house, and Frankfurter's friend Wilfred Dennison to share his home as boarders. Dennison, a Harvard Law alumnus who had worked with Frankfurter on Stimson's staff in the U.S. Attorney's office, was then making his name as an assistant U.S. attorney general. Frankfurter and Dennison would soon be joined by Walter Lippmann and "other brilliant contemporaries . . . who shared a passion for politics and a love of entertaining."[47] Although Frankfurter left Washington in fall 1914 to teach at Harvard Law School, he lived again at the House of Truth during his later two-year wartime stint in the Wilson administration. The House of Truth was actually "so named by Justice Holmes, somewhat facetiously, for the allegedly high-minded conversation that regularly took place around its large dinner table."[48] U.S. government officials, diplomats, philosophers, and artists such as the sculptor Gutzon Borglum, "who one night drew his plans for Mount Rushmore on the dining room table," were frequent guests at the house, where discussion centered on politics, law, art, journalism, and European diplomacy.[49] Holmes found the hosts "enchanting."[50] In an early letter to Frankfurter, he wrote: "It will be many years before you have the occasion to know the happiness and encouragement that comes to an old man from the sympathy of the young."[51] Louis Brandeis, on his trips from Boston to Washington to advise Woodrow Wilson, also often stopped at the House of Truth for lunch or dinner, as did Arthur Willert, the Washington correspondent for the *London Times*, and Stanley King, the future president of Amherst College.

"Almost everybody who was interesting in Washington," said Frankfurter, "sooner or later passed through the house."[52] Playing host to the city's elite, Frankfurter and his friends "shook cocktails and carved roast beef for Supreme Court Justices, writers, Cabinet officials."[53] On one occasion, Justice Horace Lurton, a Democrat from Tennessee whom Taft had appointed to the Supreme Court in 1909, visited the house on a night when Frankfurter was shaking cocktails. Lurton had been impressed with Frankfurter when the young lawyer had appeared before the high court as a War Department lawyer. As Frankfurter poured his drink, the justice reportedly quipped, "I hope you mix drinks as well as you argue cases."[54] While Frankfurter "beamed with pride," Lurton savored his cocktail and answered his own question: "You mix drinks even better than you argue cases."[55]

The lasting friendship between Frankfurter and Brandeis was also fostered during the latter's visits to the House of Truth. As noted in the Brandeis section, the two men first met during a 1905 lecture by Brandeis in Cambridge and became better acquainted in 1908 when Frankfurter was working as Stimson's assistant U.S. attorney in New York. Brandeis's visits to the House of Truth came between 1911 and 1914, when he frequently traveled to Washington to argue cases before the Supreme Court, work for progressive political causes, and advise Wilson. After a lunch with Brandeis, Frankfurter wrote the following reflection in his diary, dated October 20, 1911: "Brandeis has depth and an intellectual sweep that are tonical. He has great force. . . . Brandeis is a very big man, one of the most penetrating minds I know; I should like to see him Attorney General of the United States."[56] Brandeis soon became one of Frankfurter's most important mentors.

Alongside Dennison, Frankfurter's fellow bachelors living at or frequently visiting the House of Truth included Loring Christie, a Canadian Harvard Law graduate working with Dennison in the Justice Department—and later Canada's ambassador to the United States—Lord Eustace Percy, the seventh son of the seventh Duke of Northumberland, then serving as an aide on the

British ambassador's staff, and Walter Lippmann, "who was then writing two of the most remarkable books of the era—*Preface to Politics* and *Drift and Mastery*."[57] Together with Herbert Croly, the Progressive movement editor and political philosopher who often dined at the house, Lippmann in 1914 would cofound the *New Republic*, the liberal opinion journal for which Frankfurter would write frequently over the years, many of his contributions being unsigned editorials on constitutional issues as well as pieces written by Justice Brandeis but appearing under Frankfurter's name.[58] Throughout the 1920s, Frankfurter would be a contributing editor and the legal affairs correspondent for the magazine.

Another house resident, who would become Frankfurter's close friend, was Harvey Hollister Bundy, a Yale and Harvard Law graduate then serving as a law clerk for Justice Holmes and who had recently married the heiress Katherine Lawrence Putnam. With a Boston family lineage dating to 1639, Putnam was related to the Cabots, Lawrences, and Lowells. The niece of Harvard president A. Lawrence Lowell and the poet Amy Lowell, Katherine Putnam was also related to Holmes, whom she referred to affectionately as "Cousin Wendell."[59] Harvey Bundy, whose sons McGeorge and William Bundy would have influential public careers, later served as assistant secretary of state under President Hoover and, during World War II, as special assistant to Secretary of War Henry Stimson.

One visitor to the house, and another lifelong friend of Frankfurter's, was Harold Laski, the British scholar whom Frankfurter had first met when Laski was lecturing at McGill University in 1916. Having heard about Laski through a friend, Frankfurter had arranged to meet him while visiting Canada and was immediately impressed by his erudition. After returning to Harvard to teach at the Law School, Frankfurter recommended that Laski be offered an appointment at Harvard's graduate school, where Laski would teach for four years before accepting a professorship at the London School of Economics in 1920.[60]

Because Frankfurter and the other house residents were considered among Washington's most eligible bachelors, many attractive women often showed up for dinner.[61] One was Marion Denman, whom Frankfurter first met in spring 1913 when she was visiting friends in Washington while vacationing from her job as assistant head of New York's fashionable Spence School for girls. Beautiful yet frail, Denman was the daughter of a Congregational minister from Longmeadow, Massachusetts. She had recently graduated with honors from Smith College, where she had been junior class president and a Phi Beta Kappa member, and had briefly attended the New York School of Social Work. "Sharp-tongued, intelligent, coquettish, and a trifle vain . . . with her shimmering auburn hair and hazel eyes," according to one writer, Marion quickly and "easily won Frankfurter's heart."[62] In addition, she was, like Frankfurter, an agnostic. "As Yankee as Yankee could be," Marion's family had come to America before the Revolution, a fact that enhanced her appeal for Frankfurter.[63] Well bred and genteel, albeit without inherited wealth, she came from the New England Protestant world of which Frankfurter had always aspired to be a part. In this respect, she was, for him, irresistible.

After Marion returned to New York, Frankfurter courted her "in person and by means of amorous letters filled with poetry and politics."[64] Frankfurter and Denman saw more of each other during World War I, when she moved to Washington to work for the War Camp Activities Bureau and Frankfurter served as the secretary of war's assistant. They became engaged five years after first meeting, in May 1918, just before Denman sailed to England "across a sea infested with German submarines" to survey war organizations run by Englishwomen. The night before she departed, Frankfurter proposed to her as they rode together around Central Park in a hansom cab. It was "the traditional romantic setting—moonlight, the steady beating of horses' hooves, the pleasant muffled sounds of a still-friendly city."[65]

The couple were married December 20, 1919, with Frankfurter's friend Judge Benjamin Cardozo, then on the New York Court of Appeals, officiating. Cardozo followed the bride and groom's instructions to perform the civil ceremony "with the minimum number of words that your sense of the significant ones and the law allows."[66]

The wedding party of just seven included Harold Laski and Judge Learned Hand. Conspicuously absent was Frankfurter's mother, Emma, who opposed her son's marriage, offended that "Felix had chosen a *shiksa* as his bride."[67] Frankfurter's father had already died.

Frankfurter had never seriously dated a Jewish woman and now, estranged from his religious community, was marrying the daughter of a Protestant minister. Frankfurter was not surprised by his mother's reaction. He had written to Justice Holmes, while he and Denman were dating, "You know how deeply rooted the feeling against intermarriage is in us Jews"—and he had anticipated correctly that his mother would never come around to accepting his choice of a bride.[68]

The relationship itself, however, was often tumultuous. Temperamentally, the two were opposites: "she was sensitive, high-strung and brittle, while he was awesomely energetic, confident and competent."[69] Throughout their courtship, the independent Denman expressed concern that she would be overwhelmed by Frankfurter's dominating personality. "You threaten the securities of a person whose securities are only in the making, and will never be better than slow . . . and painful," she wrote Felix.[70] In response to an especially pessimistic letter from Denman, Frankfurter tried to reassure her that he was sensitive to her needs and wished to accommodate them.[71]

Although he was at such times reassuring, at another time during their courtship, in 1917, Frankfurter told Marion he could not marry her because she was not Jewish: "I suppose it resolved itself into a choice between you and mother. . . . To understand you will remember all that clusters around the traditions of thousands of years."[72] Of course, Frankfurter eventually changed his mind.

The couple's friends at the House of Truth, however, largely thought Denman and Frankfurter *were* an ideal match. Holmes and Laski named her "Luina," believing she resembled the beauty portrayed by the Renaissance artist Bernardino Luini.[73] Laski evinced happiness that his friend was "safe" with a woman who was "wise and grown-up and good to look upon—a real companion."[74] For Laski, who like Frankfurter was completely estranged from the Judaism of his youth and would marry a non-Jewish woman eight years his senior, Marion's non-Jewishness appeared to be an issue of neither sadness nor concern.

Despite Laski's "characteristically romantic view of things, the personality conflicts that had plagued their courtship and engagement continued to take their toll on Mrs. Frankfurter throughout their marriage."[75] In 1923, she suffered the first of two serious nervous breakdowns and over the years required extensive psychiatric care. Despite her continuously fragile mental state and their marital disharmony, Frankfurter "nevertheless remained devoted to his wife, and proud of her intelligence and beauty." From their first meeting in 1913 until his death in 1965, "she remained the one woman in his life."[76]

Professor Frankfurter

In 1913, after two years in Washington, Frankfurter was forced once again to rethink his future. After Woodrow Wilson's election, Frankfurter's mentor Henry Stimson was leaving Washington along with the defeated Taft administration. One option for Frankfurter was to go into private practice. His Harvard friends, "firmly settled in their careers even years after graduation, chided him on his professional indecision."[77] His friend Emory Buckner, "who had decided to go into private practice and make some money, had tried to persuade Frankfurter to join him." If he ever did practice law, he wanted to do it with "Buck," he assured his friend, "but his interest in private practice was 'pretty tepid.'"[78]

Then, in June 1913, unbeknownst to Frankfurter, Wilfred Dennison wrote to their mutual friend Professor Edward Warren at Harvard Law School, recommending Frankfurter for an appointment to the law school's faculty.[79] The letter went like this: "If you see any reasonable opening in your faculty for Frankfurter I wish you would let me know about it. The administration here appears willing and anxious to have him stay and he is content to do so but ... I think it might be a good thing for him to settle down permanently in your faculty. . . . He has made a tremendous impression with the Supreme Court. The Chief Justice and two of the other Justices have spoken to me with great enthusiasm of his work and I understand their views are shared by the other members of the Court. . . ."[80]

At the same time, Brandeis had been working behind the scenes to secure Frankfurter a Harvard teaching post. Brandeis wrote to Law School dean Ezra Thayer, and to future dean Roscoe Pound, recommending that Frankfurter be hired and suggesting possibilities for funding an endowed administrative law chair for Frankfurter.[81]

As contrasted with Brandeis, both Holmes and Stimson advised Frankfurter against accepting the Harvard position, "the latter pointing out that he was best fitted for public life."[82] Herbert Croly, the *New Republic* editor, "thought Boston would be stultifying after New York and Washington."[83] Stimson remained unenthusiastic about Frankfurter taking the Harvard post until Brandeis finally convinced him "that the law school needed Frankfurter" and Frankfurter had "a great desire to go there."[84]

Encouraged by Brandeis, Thayer then approached Stimson, who had close ties to New York's wealthy German Jews such as Henry Morgenthau Sr., Otto Kahn, and Jacob Schiff with a plan to raise "new money" to hire Frankfurter. "It seems to me," Thayer wrote Stimson, "that with the spirit which is abroad nowadays it ought to be possible to find someone who is enough interested in the things that Frankfurter stands for to meet this difficulty."[85] In this same letter, Thayer told Stimson of Brandeis's interest in working with Roscoe Pound to raise money for an endowment for Frankfurter's professorship, and of Brandeis's readiness to approach Jacob Schiff to contribute to such an endowment.[86]

As it turned out, creating an initial endowment proved unnecessary because of an "unexpected resignation," enabling Thayer to offer Frankfurter an appointment on January 12, 1914. That September, the thirty-one-year-old Frankfurter began teaching at Harvard Law School.[87] He was, as noted in an earlier chapter, the first Jew appointed to the law school's faculty, and continued teaching there for twenty-five years.

Frankfurter left Washington for Cambridge in summer 1914 and began preparing for his new career as a law professor. One of the first visitors to the Frankfurters' new Brattle Street home was Brandeis. The Brandeises and Frankfurters would meet for occasional dinners, and the Frankfurters would be among the guests at Alice Brandeis's frequent afternoon teas. For the next two years, living as virtual neighbors in Cambridge, Brandeis and Frankfurter talked almost daily, strengthening the foundation for their friendship.

In 1917, as the United States entered World War I, Frankfurter was invited back to Washington, where he had made many Democratic friends in the Wilson administration, and was asked to serve as Secretary of War Newton Baker's special assistant, as well as chairman of the War Labor Policies Board, which was tasked with "handling labor relations for the production of munitions and other material during World War I."[88] In his new War Department position, for which he took leave from Harvard, he renewed his acquaintance with Franklin Roosevelt, who, after serving only two years in the New York State Senate, had been appointed assistant Navy secretary. In his role, Roosevelt served on the War Labor Policies Board with Frankfurter.

Frankfurter and Roosevelt's offices "were near each other in the grand, high-ceilinged State, War, and Navy Building, which still stands next to the White House," and the two "saw each other professionally with some frequency."[89] Frankfurter's "command of labor statistics, administrative finesse, and his charm" greatly impressed Roosevelt, who invited Frankfurter home to lunch regularly, "much to his wife's annoyance."[90] Eleanor Roosevelt, who was less accepting of Jews than was her husband, and who "was still a long way from the broad-minded humanitarian she would later become," described Frankfurter in a letter to her snobbish mother-in-law, Sara Delano, "as an interesting little man but very jew."[91] After reluctantly attending a British-embassy-sponsored party to honor the Jewish financier Bernard Baruch, who then headed the War Industries Board, she complained to her mother-in-law: "The Jew party was appalling. I never wish to hear money, jewels, and sables mentioned again."[92] Later Eleanor would refuse to read Maurice Low's interpretive biography of Woodrow Wilson because the author was "such a loathsome little Jew."[93] As Eleanor's biographer Blanche Wiesen Cook has noted, "ER's caustic comments concerning Jews remained a routine part of her social observation for many years," diminishing only as her friendship with Frankfurter, Baruch, and other Jews "flourished."[94] Meanwhile, when Frankfurter returned to Harvard after the war, he and Roosevelt remained in close touch, corresponding frequently during the 1920s, and Frankfurter emerged as one of FDR's close political confidants in the years approaching his 1928 election as New York governor.

Frankfurter, Judaism, and the Zionist Movement

Unlike Brandeis, Frankfurter was raised as a practicing Jew. "As a boy," Frankfurter would later recount, "I was religiously observant. I wouldn't eat breakfast until I had done the religious devotions in the morning. As time went on . . . I was more and more confirmed in my own slow feelings of disharmony between myself and Jewish rituals and the synagogue," which later "ceased to have inner meaning" for me.[95] He first fully realized his disaffection at a Yom Kippur service while a junior at City College and thereupon "left the service in the middle of it, never to return."[96] Frankfurter later confessed that he had "a quasi-religious" feeling about Harvard Law School, "nurtured to full strength during his three years there as a law student and sustained for the rest of his life."[97] For much of his early career, Frankfurter "explicitly rejected Judaism and regarded it only as a barrier to be overcome."[98] His application to exclusively non-Jewish firms after graduating from Harvard Law confirms such an approach. On Hornblower, Byrne, Miller, and Potter, which would ultimately hire him, he would later recall: "Lots of Harvard people were there. I'd heard that they had never taken a Jew and wouldn't take a Jew. . . . I decided that that was the office I wanted to get into not for any reason of truculence, but I was very early infused with, had inculcated in me, a very profoundly wise attitude toward the whole fact that I was a Jew, the essence of which is that you should be a biped and walk on the two legs that man has. . . . You should take that ultimate fact that you were born of some parents instead of these other parents as much for granted as the fact that you've got green-brown eyes instead of blue eyes."[99] Frankfurter regarded his Jewish religion "as a mere accident of birth" and was determined to succeed in the world of upper-crust Bostonians and Wall Street lawyers.[100] Yet even as he would be "a self-described agnostic" for the rest of his life, Frankfurter claimed he did not "cease to be a Jew or cease to be concerned with whatever affects the fate of the Jews."[101]

Although he "seldom set foot in a synagogue or temple after adolescence," Frankfurter's admiration for Brandeis brought him into the American Zionist movement's leadership, and after 1915, together with Julian Mack, he participated in Zionist activities as one of his mentor's most trusted lieutenants.[102] For example, Frankfurter played an important role in the negotiations with President Wilson over U.S. support for the 1917 Balfour Declaration, which expressed British support for "the establishment in Palestine of a national home for the Jewish people." During the talks between Whitehall and Washington over the document's precise wording, Frankfurter "orchestrated the response of American Zionists, most of whom wished to bring immediate pressure upon Wilson to endorse the British proposal."[103] Frankfurter advised delay, arguing "against bringing direct pressure on the President for all-out approval, since Wilson would just dig in his heels and refuse to budge."[104] As it turned out, Frankfurter was correct. While the president notified Brandeis, Frankfurter, Mack, and Stephen Wise that he supported the declaration, he "refused to endorse the document openly until 1918, when British and Arab forces had gained the upper hand militarily against the Turks."[105]

Also, as we saw earlier, in spring of 1919, Frankfurter attended the Versailles Peace Conference as legal adviser to the Zionist delegation, and as a liaison for Brandeis, who remained in Washington. In Paris, Frankfurter was part of an impressive delegation that included Mack, Wise, and Benjamin Cohen, a gifted young lawyer and legal craftsman. The delegation members were hopeful that the Balfour Declaration's promise of a Jewish national home "would be realized in the peace treaty that would emerge from the hubbub and hullabaloo that characterized the Paris Peace Conference. . . . It was to help secure that that Frankfurter went to Paris."[106]

Frankfurter stood out within the Zionist delegation for his negotiating skills, legal acumen, and easy access to the "key figures" in the official British and U.S. delegations, who would ultimately determine international acceptance of the Balfour Declaration and "the fate of Palestine."[107] These key figures included British delegation members such as Philip Kerr, the personal secretary to Prime Minister David Lloyd George. Also at Versailles were Frankfurter's old friends from the House of Truth, Loring Christie, now "the right hand man of the Canadian Prime Minister Robert Borden,"[108] and Sir Eustace Percy, "who in the early months of 1919 was Lord Robert Cecil's assistant in drafting the Covenant of the League of Nations."[109] Kerr and Percy were two of the "many young British officials whose friendships Frankfurter, the Anglophile, had cultivated" in both Washington and London.[110] At one point, Kerr invited Frankfurter to lunch with "that wonderful, charming creature," British foreign secretary Arthur Balfour himself, and arranged for Frankfurter to spend "a British weekend" with the declaration's author at the Cliveden estate of Lady Nancy Astor.[111] Frankfurter also met frequently with Colonel Edward M. House, President Wilson's top adviser—"occasionally to the annoyance of House," who wrote in his diary two months after Frankfurter's arrival in Paris: ". . . Frankfurter came again about his old trouble 'Palestine for the Jews.'"[112]

From Paris's Hotel Meurice, where the Zionist delegation had set up its headquarters, Frankfurter "played a small but meaningful role" at the peace conference, a "unique gathering of princes, presidents and kings-in-waiting, sitting down face-to-face with Emir Feisal ibn Husayn, who would briefly be king of Syria and then of Iraq."[113] One of the "improbable meetings in history" thus took place at the Arabian prince's sumptuous Paris villa in the Bois de Boulogne.[114] Sitting next to the prince was Feisal's translator and adviser, the flamboyant T. E. Lawrence, "fresh from the exploits in insurgency that earned him the nickname Lawrence of Arabia."[115] At the conference, the Zionists "had been carefully cultivating a friendship with Feisal, the third son of Husayn, Sharif of Mecca and the recognized spokesman of the Arab people."[116] Frankfurter, at Brandeis's request, was to make clear to Feisal "that as much as American Zionists wanted a Jewish homeland in Palestine, they were also committed to Arab rights in the region." In exchange for this assurance, Frankfurter was supposed to secure an endorsement of the Balfour Declaration from Feisal, who, American Zionist leaders felt, could "speak authoritatively on behalf of the Arab people."[117] Over coffee in late morning, then, Frankfurter assured the Arab leader that "the Jews did not wish to restore Jewish civilization in Palestine at the expense of the Arab people and culture." As Frankfurter rose to leave, "confident that the meeting had been productive," he and Feisal "exchanged assurances, and it was agreed that each would put his remarks on paper." When Frankfurter returned to the Hotel Meurice, where T. E. Lawrence was also staying, he immediately began composing his letter, as did the prince, "and then they were duly signed."

In his historic letter to Frankfurter, dated March 31, 1919, Prince Feisal actually endorsed the Balfour Declaration:

> We Arabs, especially the educated among us, look with the deepest sympathy on the Zionist movement. Our deputation here in Paris is fully acquainted with the proposals submitted by the Zionist Organization to the Peace Conference, and we regard them as moderate and proper. We

will do our best, insofar as we are concerned, to help them through; we will wish the Jews a most hearty welcome home.

In a letter to Brandeis, Frankfurter expressed his confidence that the then-rising Arab leader Feisal, at least, would not hamper Zionist aims:

The locus of trouble from the Arabs is Palestine and not Paris. . . . I think we can regard Prince Feisal as a genuine friend. At all events, at the least, we must deal with him on the basis that we are his genuine friends and the friends of his people. I do not think the Arab question is out of the way; I do not even say that it is easy of solution; I do insist, however, that it can be solved by cooperative effort. Feisal's letter states the matter as I see it and should be our governing outlook.[118]

A few days after receiving Feisal's letter, Frankfurter wrote back on behalf of the Zionist Organization, reflecting the prince's tone: ". . . We knew the aspirations of the Arab and the Jewish peoples were parallel, that each aspired to reestablish its nationality in its own homeland. . . . The Arabs and Jews are neighbors in territory; we cannot but live side by side as friends."[119]

In Paris and Versailles, in spring of 1919, Frankfurter "appeared everywhere," meeting with foreign ministers and presidential confidants such as Balfour, Colonel House, and others in his efforts to secure the Balfour Declaration and a British mandate over Palestine. More than anything else, Frankfurter's justly famous Paris meeting with Feisal, and his role in facilitating the letter exchange in which the prince endorsed the declaration, was Frankfurter's greatest contribution to Zionist diplomacy and the Zionist movement. The negotiation was "a singular triumph for Frankfurter. He had sat down with royalty, Arab royalty, to explore common ground for agreement. And the prince and he had done so civilly, rationally, gracefully."[120]

Although the Palestine question was hardly settled in Paris, the Balfour Declaration's initial promise was realized when Great Britain was awarded the Mandate for Palestine at the San Remo conference on April 26, 1920.[121] That summer, Brandeis, Frankfurter, and Jacob de Haas sailed for London to meet with English Zionists to settle the "family quarrels" that had divided them. These meetings, however, led to the final, irreparable rupture between Brandeis and Chaim Weizmann, leader of the English Zionists, at the Cleveland Zionist convention the following year, "with Brandeis and his aides, including Frankfurter, severing their official relationship with the Zionist movement."[122]

Frankfurter's brief but extraordinary part in the Paris Zionist delegation, and his meaningful participation the next year, presaged his comparably large role at the Cleveland convention. In Cleveland, Weizmann and his supporters rejected Brandeis and Mack's leadership, "despite a four-hour speech by Frankfurter, the floor leader of the Brandeis-Mack group, that brought the audience to its feet cheering."[123] When, after the conference, Brandeis resigned his leadership position—handing over the reins to Weizmann, later the state of Israel's first president—Frankfurter did so as well. Although Frankfurter later reconciled with Weizmann, his involvement with the Zionists would diminish in the next two decades.

Frankfurter during the 1920s

On returning to Cambridge after the World War, Frankfurter resumed teaching at Harvard and became involved in several controversial projects that transformed him into a national figure.[124] Frankfurter was already identified as a friend of organized labor through his chairing of the War Labor Policy Board. He had also been counsel to the President's Mediation Committee, "a body designed to quell some of the labor troubles that had developed as the war progressed."[125] At Wilson's direction, Frankfurter had participated in two high-profile investigations of wartime labor disputes, and in each case had issued public reports sympathetic to the workers. In one, in which Frankfurter investigated strikes that had crippled the Bisbee, Arizona, copper mines, his report "detailed the way that copper-mine owners in Bisbee, Arizona, had deported a thousand striking workers to New Mexico and left them in the desert without water or supplies."[126]

In another, Frankfurter had recommended a controversial pardon for Tom Mooney, a California labor organizer and member of the radical International Workers of the World (iww) union, who had been tried and convicted on questionable evidence for the July 1916 Preparedness Day Bombing in San Francisco, which had killed ten and wounded fifty.[127]

Frankfurter's reputation as both a political leftist and an outspoken civil libertarian was enhanced especially by his vocal opposition to the numerous arrests of anarchists and socialist agitators made by Attorney General A. Mitchell Palmer during the Red Scare of 1919–1920, and by Frankfurter's subsequent defense of the Italian-American anarchists Nicola Sacco and Bartolomeo Vanzetti during the 1920s.

The Red Scare began June 2, 1919, when a few minutes after 11 p.m. an

Italian-American anarchist, dressed in a suit and carrying a leather briefcase, walked up to 2132 R Street, the home of Attorney General Palmer, located in Washington's upscale Georgetown neighborhood, where the city's political elite resided. He was carrying a Colt automatic and a Smith & Wesson revolver, and the briefcase contained twenty pounds of dynamite. He aimed to blow up Palmer's house and kill all its occupants. As he climbed the front steps, however, the fuse went off prematurely, and the anarchist became an unwitting suicide bomber. The explosion blew up the front of the Palmer house, shattered windows a hundred yards around, and scattered the assailant's body parts over a fifty-foot radius. Living across the street were Franklin Roosevelt, then the Navy secretary, and his wife, Eleanor, who were "just returning home from a night out when they heard a blast so loud that their cook screamed that the world was coming to an end." After ensuring his family was safe, Roosevelt rushed across the street to see if anyone needed help. The next morning, Roosevelt's son James found a piece of the bomber's collarbone on his family's front steps.[128]

Also dispersed by the explosion were fifty copies of the anarchist leaflet *Plain Words*. The leaflet's message was plain indeed: "There will have to be bloodshed . . . there will have to be murder; we will kill because it is necessary; there will have to be destruction; we will kill to rid the world of your tyrannical institutions."[129]

Within the hour, other bombs, also placed by Italian anarchists, exploded in cities throughout the United States, including New York, Boston, Philadelphia, Paterson (New Jersey), Pittsburgh, and Cleveland, each targeting government officials who had played a role in suppressing anarchism. Taken together, these bombings would be by far the most serious terrorist attack in U.S. history until September 11, 2001.[130]

Palmer and other government officials reacted with tremendous force.[131] In the six months following the bombing, Palmer and his special assistant, J. Edgar Hoover, arrested thousands of suspected radicals, anarchists, socialists, and communists alike with alleged connections to the bombings and held them without trial. The great majority of those arrested were immigrants, both Italian and Jewish, many of whom were summarily deported or scheduled for eventual deportation."[132] (Among the Jewish anarchists deported were Emma Goldman and Alexander Berkman.) In part because such acts of political terrorism stirred great public fear, Palmer received significant support for his actions, including from respected legal scholars. John H. Wigmore, for example, the dean of Northwestern University Law School and an authority on criminal evidence, argued that Palmer "had acted entirely within the limits" of both law and reason. "Prompt measures were vital," Wigmore maintained. "Mr. Palmer saved the country, in my opinion."[133]

Frankfurter did not agree with either Wigmore or the attorney general. Quite the contrary: deploring what he considered "the indiscriminate nature of the Palmer raids and arrests," Frankfurter and his Harvard Law colleague Zechariah Chafee filed a brief in Boston's federal court on behalf of nineteen communists who had been arrested and held for deportation, condemning "Palmer's Justice Department for denying the detainees access to lawyers and for obtaining evidence through illegal searches."[134] Together with Chafee and ten other academics and attorneys, Frankfurter also formed a Committee of Twelve aimed at exposing the Red Scare tactics as xenophobic and illegal. In their *Report upon the Illegal Practices of the United States Department of Justice*, Frankfurter and his colleagues argued "that the Attorney General had infringed upon their civil liberties by using rampant and warrantless arrests, searches and seizures."[135]

In the years that followed, Frankfurter also took a public stand on the most publicized civil liberties case of the time, that of Sacco and Vanzetti. In April 1920, the two Italian immigrant anarchists were accused of stealing $15,000 from a shoe company in the Boston suburb of South Braintree and killing the company's paymaster and guard. The evidence against the anarchists was substantial: at the time of their arrest, Sacco and Vanzetti carried weapons —a .32 Colt automatic and a .38 Harrington revolver—"that the prosecution later linked with the bullets found in the bodies of the murdered men." And multiple eyewitnesses placed the defendants at the crime scene, testifying "to the guilt of the accused."[136] At a trial at which the presiding judge Webster Thayer did not hide his contempt for the defendants, referring to them as "those anarchist bastards," and the prosecutor and "at least one of the jurors displayed considerable prejudice against the pair," Sacco and Vanzetti were convicted of robbery and murder and sentenced to die in the electric chair. For their part, many political leftists were convinced that the defendants had been unjustly convicted solely because they were Italians and anarchists.[137] Appeals of their conviction, and motions for their retrial, prolonged the case for almost seven years.

What brought Frankfurter to advocate for the Sacco-Vanzetti defense was an argument raised on appeal in 1925 by the defendants' new lawyer, William G. Thompson, a Harvard Law graduate whom Frankfurter greatly respected. As grounds for a new trial, Thompson presented the affidavit of a ballistics expert,

William Proctor, a major prosecution witness who had given testimony that left the distinct impression that the bullet found in one of the victims had come from Sacco's gun. In his affidavit, however, Proctor claimed that the prosecutor, Frederick Katzmann, "had coached him in his testimony in a way that gave the jury the *mistaken* impression that Proctor believed the bullet found in the victim's body had come from Sacco's gun [emphasis added]." In his affidavit, Proctor also blamed the prosecutor for presenting misleading testimony at the trial and for pressuring Proctor to testify in a way that both the prosecutor and he knew were misleading. When Katzmann "did not issue a flat denial of Proctor's accusation, Frankfurter became convinced that Katzmann had acted unethically and strongly suspected that other perversions of justice would be found in the trial record."[138] After reading through all six thousand pages of the trial record, Frankfurter's "suspicions turned to rage," and in a scathing March 1927 article in the *Atlantic Monthly*, titled "The Portentous Case of Sacco and Vanzetti," he denounced the entire legal proceeding.[139] Later that year, Frankfurter expanded his *Atlantic Monthly* piece into a book-length exposition, *The Case of Sacco and Vanzetti*, that became a national best seller.

In the 1920s, Frankfurter also bitterly opposed the effort by Harvard president A. Lawrence Lowell to impose a quota on Jewish student admissions. Frankfurter had earlier come "to verbal blows" with Lowell, a national officer in the antisemitic Immigration Restriction League, after he had publicly opposed Brandeis's Senate confirmation to the Supreme Court in 1916.[140] At Harvard, the Jewish student population had grown from 7 percent at the beginning of the century to 21 percent in 1922, when Lowell proposed restricting Jewish admissions to 10 percent. Lowell appointed a thirteen-member Committee of Admissions "to examine the issue and make recommendations," of which three members were to be Jews.[141] Julian Mack, a member of the Harvard Board of Overseers who helped lead opposition to Lowell's plan, tried to get his friend Frankfurter appointed to the committee. Lowell's response to Mack came quickly: "I do not myself feel . . . that Professor Frankfurter has the quality of solid judgment that would make him a good member of the committee."[142] A heated exchange of letters, "almost of a name-calling level," ensued between Lowell and Frankfurter.[143] The imbroglio ended in a stalemate: Frankfurter was not appointed to the admissions committee, but neither did Lowell succeed in imposing his quota system.[144] On April 9, 1923, Harvard's admissions committee issued a report that repudiated Lowell's proposed system "as running counter to Harvard's tradition of equal opportunity to all regardless of religion."[145]

For those opposing Lowell's proposed 10 percent quota, however, any celebration was premature. The admissions committee soon developed a new formula "that turned out to be an equally effective alternative to a flat Jewish quota."[146] Henceforth, the committee announced, "the number of students in Harvard's freshman class would be capped at one thousand," and students would be admitted according to a complex policy of "geographic distribution," wherein fewer students from the Boston area and more students from the rural South and Midwest, which had fewer Jewish applicants, would be admitted.[147] By 1928, under this new system, Harvard's official Jewish enrollment had fallen to precisely 10 percent.[148]

During the 1920s, from his academic perch, Frankfurter established himself as one of the country's leading progressive reformers and civil libertarians. While he wrote academic books and articles and taught immensely popular courses, "his horizon extended far beyond Cambridge."[149] As both a public intellectual and a legal scholar, he "invented the job of publicly engaged law professor."[150] Sharing the reformist politics of his friends Herbert Croly and Walter Lippmann, Frankfurter frequently wrote unsigned pieces for their *New Republic* and in 1924 penned a passionately argued—and signed—article, "Why I Shall Vote for La Follette," explaining his decision to back the Progressive Party's presidential candidate.[151] His defense of Sacco and Vanzetti further bolstered his national credentials as a progressive activist.[152] Likewise, Frankfurter served on the national committee of the American Civil Liberties Union, which he had helped establish in 1920. The ACLU's founding president, Roger Baldwin, would later say that Frankfurter was "our constant advisor and critic, from whom we received endless useful suggestions for lawyers, law points and tactics."[153] Frankfurter also advised the NAACP and served on its national board.

The journalist Joseph Alsop is reported to have said that "Justice Frankfurter is a frustrated journalist," an assertion with more than some truth.[154] Throughout his lengthy Harvard tenure, he was most prolific writing for popular journals, including lengthy letters to the editor and opinion pieces —especially in the *New Republic*, but also in publications such as the *Nation*, *Atlantic Monthly*, and *Fortune*. He was less productive as a legal scholar. While Frankfurter wrote a series of notable law review articles during the 1920s, his scholarly publication record was not impressive. His appointment as the James Byrne Professor of Administrative Law in 1921 was made "on the basis of four published articles, two of which could be charitably described as mediocre."[155] This lack of scholarly productivity disappointed many of

Frankfurter's friends and academic colleagues, but his popular output impressed others.

Frankfurter and Roosevelt

Felix Frankfurter and Franklin Roosevelt neither spoke nor corresponded between 1919 and FDR's campaign for New York governor in 1928. While Frankfurter was gaining recognition during the 1920s as a public intellectual, and notoriety among conservatives as Sacco and Vanzetti's defender, Roosevelt struggled against great odds, namely his 1921 affliction with polio, to resurrect his once-promising political career.

In 1920, having completed his service as Wilson's assistant Navy secretary, Roosevelt was chosen as Ohio governor James Cox's vice presidential running mate. With the popular Teddy Roosevelt having died suddenly the previous year, the Democrats jumped at the opportunity to place a Roosevelt on the ticket. While they "were trounced by Republicans Warren G. Harding and Calvin Coolidge . . . with his eloquent and vigorous campaigning, Franklin had further advanced his claim to be the heir apparent to the Roosevelt name and progressive political legacy."[156] At just thirty-eight, Roosevelt had become a national political figure and was positioned to work toward his own future presidential candidacy.[157]

But in August 1921, less than a year after the electoral defeat, Roosevelt rode his yacht to his family's Maine summer home, Campobello, for their annual family vacation.[158] While sailing nearby, he fell into the freezing water, experienced a chill, and soon ached everywhere with a fever. In the next few days, "he suffered delirium, acute pain all over his body, temporary paralysis of his hands, and lasting paralysis of his legs."[159] These were the symptoms of infantile paralysis, or polio. Most observers assumed FDR's political career was over and that he might have to retire from public life.

Confronted with this enormous challenge, Roosevelt began an intense regimen of exercise and physical therapy. Over the next several years, with tremendous determination, he also experimented with every possible cure for polio "and exercised constantly. He used two-thirds of his personal money to purchase a run-down spa at Warm Springs, Georgia, so that he and others could take its bubbling waters which buoyed him into walking movement."[160] Against such stiff odds, he rehabilitated himself until he had the strength to run for governor in 1928.[161]

Frankfurter and Roosevelt had not been close enough for Frankfurter to be in touch during his rehabilitation. However, when Roosevelt was nominated to run for governor, he received a congratulatory letter from Frankfurter praising Roosevelt's "pure-mindedness and real public zeal."[162] When Roosevelt won the election, Frankfurter sent another letter—this time addressed "Dear Franklin"—encouraging Roosevelt to meet with Justice Brandeis to discuss matters of importance regarding his forthcoming gubernatorial duties. Roosevelt wrote back to Frankfurter ("Dear Felix"), thanking him for his note and inviting Brandeis to meet with him in New York. By the following summer, when FDR wrote to Frankfurter asking him to meet with a member of his new Public Service Commission, it was "Dear Felix" and "Dear Frank," as it remained in their correspondence until Roosevelt's death in 1945.[163] In the months following Roosevelt's election, increasing telephone calls were also made from Albany to Cambridge, as well as frequent visits by Frankfurter to Roosevelt's Hyde Park estate.[164] In their communications, Frankfurter advised the governor on utility regulation, public power companies, prison reform, and judicial appointments.[165] He sent FDR a copy of the Dodge Lectures he had delivered at Yale Law School, titled *The Public and Its Government*, which summed up his philosophy of government, including his ideas about "the crucial role that could be played in modern government by trained experts recruited from the nation's universities and professional schools."[166] Roosevelt, in turn, sought Frankfurter's advice on a host of political and legal issues. "Felix has more ideas per minute than any man of my acquaintance," Roosevelt marveled to an assistant. "He has a brilliant mind. . . . I find him tremendously interesting and stimulating."[167]

In cultivating Roosevelt anew, Frankfurter assumed the role of an admiring yet independent academic, "eager to give advice and to recommend policies and personnel, and always quick to offer a flattering comment on Roosevelt's latest speech or decision"—no matter how small.[168] Roosevelt came to appreciate "the practical value of Frankfurter's advice, the quality of the people he recommended, and the value of Frankfurter as a conduit to the world of liberal ideas."[169] After FDR's election as president in 1932, Frankfurter remained one of his most intimate associates. In the history of presidential political friendships, that between Roosevelt and Frankfurter "was destined to become as important as Jackson's with Roger Taney, Lincoln's with Billy Herndon, and Wilson's with Colonel House."[170]

Frankfurter and the New Deal

A major career decision for Frankfurter came in June 1932, when he declined Massachusetts governor Joseph Ely's offer of an appointment to the state's highest court, the Supreme Judicial Court, on which Oliver Wendell Holmes Jr. had once served for twenty years. Holmes encouraged Frankfurter to accept the offer. Brandeis, however, advised Frankfurter strongly to decline. At age fifty, suggested Brandeis, Frankfurter was too young to abandon law school teaching for a judgeship and could make a greater contribution to the law by remaining at Harvard.[171] Years later, Frankfurter would joke that, in weighing whether to accept the appointment, he had been tempted by the fact that all the members of the court went "in lock step . . . to lunch at the Union Club in formal dress and top hat. I thought that would be an interesting thing — to go in lock step in top hat to the Union Club for lunch."[172]

Although most of his friends, except Brandeis, had advised him to accept, Frankfurter "after much anguish of mind" wrote Governor Ely of his decision to decline.[173] Political considerations, as well as his desire to continue teaching at Harvard, helped guide his decision.[174] Frankfurter had received Ely's offer "at about the same time that the Democrats in Chicago had nominated the man likely to be the next President, Franklin Delano Roosevelt."[175] Ely, a supporter of Al Smith for the 1932 Democratic nomination, had frequently attacked Roosevelt, the front-runner.[176] As noted, during Roosevelt's four years in Albany, Frankfurter had assiduously, and successfully, cultivated the governor's trust and friendship.[177] By declining Ely's offer, Frankfurter signaled "his loyalty to FDR and a willingness to play a larger role in the presidential campaign," as he soon would do.[178] Following the Democratic Convention, Frankfurter met with Roosevelt at Hyde Park and talked with him into the night about economic recovery and reform, thus beginning his new role as campaign adviser.[179]

Roosevelt attracted dozens of able people to his new administration — Rexford Tugwell, Raymond Moley, Samuel Rosenman, Harold Ickes, Frances Perkins, Harry Hopkins, Henry Wallace, and Henry Morgenthau Jr., among others. Although he never held an official position in Roosevelt's presidential administration, Frankfurter "sparked more debate than some cabinet officers, White House assistants, and congressional leaders."[180] His impact was great on the president's New Deal policies. General Hugh Jackson, the first director of the New Deal's National Recovery Administration, claimed Frankfurter was "the most influential single individual in the United States." Some newspapers compared his role as an FDR adviser to the careers of Cardinal Richelieu or Rasputin. According to the journalist John Franklin Carter, Frankfurter "more than any other person" was "the legal master-mind of the New Deal."[181]

Frankfurter's own description of his role in the New Deal was much more modest. While admitting to a special relationship with Roosevelt, he later claimed never to have made a suggestion or proposed an appointment to FDR without an invitation from the president first. In fact, Frankfurter's level of influence probably fell somewhere between his understatement and his enemies' vilification. Although he visited the White House more than occasionally, "he nonetheless exercised less sway over Roosevelt's day-to-day thinking than Morgenthau, Hopkins, Rosenman and several others, largely because he refused to leave Harvard in 1933 and join the administration on a full-time basis."[182] His refusal to do so surprised many, including the new president.

Almost from the moment of FDR's election, speculation was widespread that the president would offer Frankfurter a post.[183] A potential role that received much attention was that of solicitor general, a top Justice Department post considered a stepping-stone to the Supreme Court. The incumbent solicitor general was Thomas D. Thacher, Frankfurter's classmate at Harvard Law and sometime roommate at the House of Truth. "I hear you are to succeed me in this office," he wrote Frankfurter on February 25, 1933, the week before Roosevelt's inauguration.[184] Indeed, shortly after entering office, "Roosevelt offered Frankfurter the post of solicitor general, intimidating [sic] that this would pave the way to a seat on the Supreme Court."[185]

Much has been written about the offer of the solicitor generalship and Frankfurter's refusal. On March 8, Frankfurter was having a birthday lunch with Oliver Wendell Holmes Jr., who was turning ninety-two, when a message reached him that he was expected at the White House. Late that afternoon, only three days after Roosevelt had taken office, FDR offered him the job. In turning it down, Frankfurter explained to the president that "it is my genuine conviction . . . that I can do much more . . . of use to you by staying in Cambridge than by becoming Solicitor General." Elaborating, he said he felt he could be more effective as an "outsider-insider," commuting to the White House to offer his counsel, "than as an official member of the administration, with all the constraints such employment would involve."[186] Perhaps contradictorily, the Anglophile Frankfurter told Roosevelt that he had accepted the Eastman Visiting Professorship at Oxford University for the academic year beginning in fall 1933 and did not want to miss out on this opportunity.[187] For the next year, as he told a chagrined FDR, his heart would be in Oxford.

After listening to Frankfurter's arguments, which he did not dispute, Roosevelt told him that "you ought to be on the Supreme Court, and I want you there." Yet Roosevelt hinted to Frankfurter "that it would be much easier to put a solicitor general on the Supreme Court than a Harvard professor."[188] As FDR reminded his confidant, the only person "ever appointed to the Supreme Court from a professor's chair had been William Howard Taft," and his résumé had included experience as a federal judge, not to mention president of the United States.[189]

Prior to his White House meeting, Frankfurter had discussed the possible appointment with both Brandeis and Holmes, who agreed that accepting such a job would be "absurd." However, Frankfurter's old friend Benjamin Cardozo, now serving on the high court, disagreed. Cardozo wanted Frankfurter to accept "not merely because of the arguments that the Court would have from you, but because of the importance of just having you down here these days." In urging him thus, Cardozo "complained that there were few in Washington capable of thinking on 'socio-economic matters' except Brandeis and Frankfurter."[190] For the ambitious Frankfurter, the appointment must have been difficult to turn down. Roosevelt, not used to being told no, called his friend "an independent pig" but added, "I guess that's one reason I like you."[191] Despite his refusal, Frankfurter continued to be perceived "as someone whose closeness and influence with the president continued."[192]

Better than any other law professor in the nation, Frankfurter "knew how to place his students in important jobs," especially Supreme Court clerkships, which often led to top New Deal positions. As we saw in earlier chapters, Frankfurter "had a virtual monopoly when it came to clerk appointments at the Supreme Court."[193] When Justice McReynolds selected a Harvard alumnus "who was not a Frankfurter protégé as his clerk," Brandeis spoke bluntly when asking the clerk how he got the job: "There isn't one chance in a thousand for any graduate of Harvard Law School to come to the Court these days without Professor Frankfurter's approval."[194]

During the 1930s, working closely with Brandeis, Frankfurter sent the best and the brightest of his Harvard Law students—Felix's "Happy Hotdogs," as they came to be called—to Washington to work in New Deal agencies, where they drafted legislation. According to some, Frankfurter and his recruits were running the government.[195] Perhaps the most notable placements of Frankfurter on this front, as discussed in the Brandeis section, were Thomas Corcoran and Benjamin Cohen, the purported "greatest legislative drafting team in history."[196]

By way of further background on Corcoran, he was an Irish Catholic from Pawtucket, Rhode Island, who was valedictorian of his Brown University graduating class. He had stayed at Brown for an extra year to earn a master's degree, with a special emphasis on Greek and Latin, before beginning his law studies at Harvard. There, he "became notes editor of the *Law Review*, won the coveted Sears Prize in his final year, worked as Frankfurter's research assistant, and coauthored with him 'Petty Offenses and the Constitutional Guaranty of Trial by Jury,' an article that appeared in the *Harvard Law Review*."[197] After a year as Justice Holmes's clerk, Corcoran became general counsel of the Reconstruction Finance Corporation, chaired by Brandeis's old friend Eugene Mayer, the publisher of the *Washington Post*. Despite his formal service with the Reconstruction Finance Corporation, the brilliant, witty, and charismatic Corcoran was, in the words of Arthur Schlesinger Jr., "operating all over Washington. Soon introduced into the White House circles, he made an instant impression."[198] In 1934, he became part of FDR's inner circle itself, when the president, "having heard stories of Corcoran's facility on the piano and the accordion, invited him to the White House for an informal musicale." Soon thereafter, Roosevelt gave him the nickname Tommy the Cork, which would stick to him the rest of his life, and like those of FDR's speechwriter Sam Rosenman (Sammy the Rose) and treasury secretary Henry Morgenthau Jr. (Henry the Morgue), "formalized Corcoran's admission into the office club of White House courtiers."[199] Through Corcoran's regular reports, the Cambridge-based Frankfurter kept abreast of Washington gossip and politics.[200]

As for Cohen, the youngest son of Polish Jewish immigrants, he graduated cum laude from the University of Chicago Law School in 1915 and also earned a doctorate in law, studying with Frankfurter, at Harvard.[201] On Frankfurter's recommendation, he clerked for the federal judge Julian Mack and then served as Frankfurter's deputy counsel to the American Zionist delegation to the Versailles Peace Conference. After working first on Wall Street and then for the National Consumers League on minimum-wage legislation, Cohen was brought to Washington by Frankfurter to become the Public Works Administration's general counsel in 1933.[202] By temperamental contrast to his drafting partner, Corcoran was "painfully shy, reclusive, and given to bouts of depression and volcanic anger," but he "inspired awe and reverence among the younger Frankfurter disciples, most of whom considered him the most astute legal mind" in the New Deal government.[203] Working together, Cohen and Corcoran drafted the Public Securities Act of 1933, the Security and Exchange Act of 1934, the Public Utility Holding Act, the Tennessee Valley Authority

Act, the Wagner Act, and the Social Security Act of 1935—all legislation that reflected Frankfurter and Brandeis's reform proposals and programs. Passed over for the most prestigious legal posts in the Roosevelt administration, "Cohen frequently threatened to quit the New Deal, but remained on duty because of loyalty to Frankfurter and the cause of social reform."[204]

Throughout the 1930s, FDR's labor secretary Frances Perkins, interior secretary Harold Ickes, and other New Deal officials sought Frankfurter and Brandeis's advice on policy issues and government appointments. The "Brandeis-Frankfurter placement bureau" was especially successful in placing Frankfurter's students in the Labor, Interior, and Agriculture Departments. Upon their recommendation, Ickes appointed Nathan Margold, an NAACP lawyer who had been one of Frankfurter's Jewish students, as the department's solicitor. Margold, in turn, enlisted Frankfurter in helping staff his office. Charles E. Wyzanski Jr., another Jewish student and one of Frankfurter's favorites, first came to Washington as the Labor Department's solicitor before moving to the Justice Department, where, in 1935, with Frankfurter's help, he was appointed special assistant to the U.S. attorney general. Three of Frankfurter's students, Lee Pressman, Nathan Witt, and Alger Hiss, were named to important Agriculture Department posts, while another, David Lilienthal, became a top TVA official. Yet another Frankfurter student, James Landis, a Presbyterian missionary's son who had served as Brandeis's law clerk in 1925–1926 and had coauthored a book with Frankfurter on the Supreme Court, was instrumental in drafting the Securities Act of 1933 and was named chairman of the Securities and Exchange Commission following the resignation of Joseph P. Kennedy.[205] All in all, as one of Frankfurter's biographers put it, "the list of former Frankfurter students staffing the Roosevelt administration is staggering."[206] Frankfurter also succeeded in securing New Deal posts for some promising non-Harvard lawyers. Among them was the Columbia graduate Felix A. Cohen, the son of Frankfurter's Harvard roommate Morris Raphael Cohen and Frankfurter's namesake. On Frankfurter's recommendation, Cohen would serve as an attorney in the solicitor's office of the Interior Department, where he became known as "the architect of New Deal policy toward Native Americans."[207] Also, in part thanks to Frankfurter and Brandeis, Abe Fortas, a Yale graduate, in 1933 was hired in the general counsel's office of the Agricultural Adjustment Administration, where he began his rapid career ascent as a New Deal lawyer and government official.

One writer has described Frankfurter as "the proprietor of an organization for filling government positions of every kind, from a Cabinet page to a clerkship," while *Fortune* magazine termed Frankfurter "the most famous legal employment service in America."[208] Frankfurter's former House of Truth roommate Harvey Bundy, a Boston attorney who had served as assistant secretary of state under Hoover, would say that "Felix was the greatest placer of men who ever lived."[209] In 1936, *Fortune* went a big step further, describing Frankfurter as "the single most influential individual in America."[210]

Nevertheless, Frankfurter did not succeed in all his placement efforts. After turning down the solicitor general's position himself, Frankfurter tried but failed to secure the appointment for one of his favorite pupils, the former Brandeis law clerk Dean Acheson. Much to Frankfurter's disappointment, FDR's new attorney general Homer Cummings vetoed the appointment, expressing "immediate, violent and adverse" opinions about Acheson.[211] "No, it's not all right," Cummings told Roosevelt. Only later did Acheson and Frankfurter learn the true cause of Cummings's opposition. Acheson's father, the Episcopal bishop of Connecticut, "had taken a dim view of the attorney general's multiple marriages" and had "refused church sanction to his latest, and Cummings had had to look elsewhere for ecclesiastic blessing."[212] Subsequently, however, Acheson was appointed undersecretary of the treasury, and thus launched a distinguished government career that would culminate in his 1948 appointment as President Truman's secretary of state.

Debonair, self-assured, and always impeccably dressed, Acheson—like Henry Stimson, President Roosevelt, Justice Holmes, Harvey Bundy, and so many other of Frankfurter's associates—was part of twentieth-century America's Protestant elite. (Acheson's daughter Mary would later marry Harvey Bundy's son William, a Harvard Law graduate who Frankfurter had hoped would work as his law clerk.) Although Acheson was nine years Frankfurter's junior, the two had, by the late 1930s, become close friends who socialized often. During Acheson's four years as secretary of state, he still sought out his former teacher's advice. According to one account, "Frankfurter and Acheson would walk together from Georgetown to the State Department at Foggy Bottom, where a car (usually driven by a law clerk) would pick up Frankfurter to bring him to the Court."[213] A few years later, Acheson would tell Frankfurter's clerk Richard N. Goodwin that "the Justice is probably the closest friend I have."[214] Several months after Frankfurter's death, Acheson would dedicate his memoir, *Morning and Noon*, to the justice's memory.[215]

6

MR. JUSTICE FRANKFURTER
The Court Years

FOR A FEW DAYS in March 1938, following Adolf Hitler's Anschluss in Austria, Vienna's new Nazi rulers imprisoned one of the city's most distinguished Jewish scholars, Solomon Frankfurter.[1] Ten months later, U.S. president Franklin Roosevelt nominated Frankfurter's nephew, also a Vienna-born Jew, to the U.S. Supreme Court.

Felix Frankfurter was Roosevelt's third Supreme Court appointee of nine, the most named by any president. He followed Hugo Black and Stanley Reed and preceded Frank Murphy and William O. Douglas, FDR's first round of five, nominated between 1937 and 1940. Fifty-seven years old at his appointment, Frankfurter is one of only three foreign-born Americans to ever sit on the high court.

Frankfurter's status as a Jew and an Easterner, not to mention an outspoken liberal, almost kept him off the court. His Jewishness, especially, was assumed to count against him. With two Jewish justices, Louis Brandeis and Benjamin Cardozo, already on the court, many observers believed there wasn't much hope for Frankfurter. When the vacancies created by the 1938 resignations of Justices Willis Van Devanter and George Sutherland were both filled by Southerners—Hugo Black, of Alabama, and Stanley Reed, of Kentucky—Westerners were underrepresented on the court. Even with Cardozo's death in summer of 1938, Roosevelt felt he couldn't appoint his longtime confidant. After an awkward lunch at Hyde Park, "a nervous and embarrassed president" broke the bad news to Frankfurter that the "Holmes seat," occupied by Cardozo since 1932, "would have to go to a Westerner" and that "I could not appoint another Jew."[2] Roosevelt's expressed intention to balance the court geographically produced "a veritable groundswell for Frankfurter that was reminiscent of the events surrounding Hoover's nomination of Cardozo." Unlike Cardozo, however, "Frankfurter actively promoted his own candidacy," with FDR's advisers and Frankfurter's former students Benjamin Cohen and Thomas Corcoran serving as Frankfurter's "almost daily advocates with the president."[3]

The pressure on Roosevelt to nominate Frankfurter eventually became intense, with several of the president's closest advisers—including his new solicitor general, Robert H. Jackson, Interior Secretary Harold L. Ickes, Senator George Norris of Nebraska, a key Westerner, and Supreme Court justice Harlan Fiske Stone—imploring the president "to place excellence over geography" and arguing "that Roosevelt might forever lose the opportunity to put his friend on the Court unless he did it now."[4] The strong support of Norris, a close Roosevelt ally, was especially important. FDR finally yielded to their entreaties and telephoned Frankfurter to tell him of his decision.

Frankfurter himself later recorded in his *Reminiscences* that at 7 p.m. on January 4, 1939, "while he was in his BVDs, late to receive a dinner guest," the phone rang in his study, "and there was the ebullient, the exuberant, resilient, warmth-enveloping voice of the President of the United States, saying 'Hello. How are you?'" Then, after asking about Frankfurter's wife, Marion, FDR told him not once but several times: "You know, I told you I don't want to appoint you to the Supreme Court of the United States . . . I mean it . . . I can't . . . I mean this. I mean this . . . I told you I can't name you." Frankfurter, eager to go down to dinner, "agreed again and again with his caller, becoming more and more exasperated," and was completely unprepared for what the president said next: "But wherever I turn, wherever and to whomever I talk that matters to me, I am made to realize that you are the only person fit to succeed Holmes and Cardozo. But unless you give me an insurmountable objection I'm going to send your name in for the Court tomorrow at twelve o'clock." The overwhelmed Frankfurter replied softly, "All I can say is that I wish my mother were alive."[5]

On January 30, Roosevelt received his first note from Frankfurter—a birthday greeting—written on Supreme Court stationery: "Dear Frank," wrote the new justice, "In the mysterious ways of Fate, the Dutchess County American and the Viennese American have for decades pursued the same directions of devotion to our beloved country. And now, on your blessed birthday I am given the gift of opportunity for service to the Nation which, in any circumstances would be owing, but which I would rather have had at your hands than at those of any other President barring Lincoln."[6]

The January 5 announcement of Frankfurter's appointment had been widely applauded, with newspaper editorials offering praise and friends, political allies, and other Supreme Court justices sending their congratulations. Harold Laski, who was now teaching at the London School of Economics, wrote Roosevelt congratulating him on the appointment. "I think Felix's nomination has pleased me more than anybody else in the whole country," FDR replied.[7] The *New Republic*, to which Frankfurter had been a longtime contributor, noted the nominee's "abhorrence of the second rate in thought or action" and concluded that he was "the ideal choice" to succeed Cardozo and Holmes. Among the numerous congratulatory messages Frankfurter received, the one from Justice Brandeis was especially important. "F.D.'s action is grand—for several reasons. Hope you will join us soon." The note was signed "L.D.B."[8]

Much to Frankfurter's surprise, even his old nemesis, A. Lawrence Lowell, now retired as president of Harvard, sent a congratulatory message indicating his support of the nomination. Lowell had vociferously opposed Brandeis's Supreme Court nomination in 1916, testifying to his detriment in the Senate confirmation hearings, and had confronted Frankfurter over Jewish quotas at Harvard and the Sacco and Vanzetti case. But Lowell apparently meant what he said to Frankfurter in his congratulatory note, telling others he considered the appointment "first rate."[9]

Frankfurter's good friend Dean Acheson served as Frankfurter's personal attorney and confidant during the Senate Judiciary subcommittee confirmation hearings. Within days of his nomination, and the formation of the subcommittee, a campaign was mobilized in opposition to the appointment. Among the opponents was Roosevelt's attorney general Homer Cummings, a longtime Frankfurter adversary who had opposed Acheson's nomination as solicitor general in 1933. Generally, the opposition differed from that to Brandeis's appointment in one significant fashion: it tended to come less from antisemites than from fellow Jews. Prior to his announcement, Roosevelt had asked Henry Morgenthau Jr., his treasury secretary, Dutchess County neighbor, and closest friend and advisor in his cabinet, whether he should choose Frankfurter or James Landis, a former Frankfurter student who had recently been named Harvard Law School dean. Morgenthau, who was on unfriendly terms with Frankfurter, advised picking Landis.[10] Frankfurter, perhaps jealous of Morgenthau's closeness with Roosevelt, "dismissed Morgenthau as a 'stupid bootlick' who did not deserve his high post."[11] The Morgenthau family "knew how Frankfurter felt, and reciprocated his dislike."[12]

Morgenthau's opposition to Frankfurter's appointment was also predicated on his concern that Roosevelt might precipitate antisemitism by appointing a second Jew to the court.[13] Other prominent Jews shared this concern, led by Arthur Hays Sulzberger, the *New York Times* publisher, who organized what Benjamin Cohen called the "Jewish protest against Felix's appointment" and met with Roosevelt at the White House specifically to argue against the appointment.[14]

This faction of the anti-Frankfurter camp held that he "should neither accept nor be given the appointment . . . because this would only intensify charges that Roosevelt's New Deal was actually the 'Jew Deal' and that, as Nazi propaganda would have it, Jews were seeking to control the world by dominating FDR's administration." Responding to this argument, Harold Riegelman, a lawyer and Jewish communal leader who would run in 1953 as a Republican for New York's mayoralty, felt compelled to speak out sharply against Sulzberger, Morgenthau, and their ilk. "Is it bad business in these unsettled times for a Jew to make himself conspicuous by serving the government?" he demanded. "Is it not worse business for a Jew to refuse a service which any government has a right to expect of every citizen?"[15]

Frankfurter had not, according to custom, planned to attend the Senate confirmation hearings, which began January 7. Despite occasional exceptions, nominees typically asked a lawyer, often a friend, to serve as a representative, as Brandeis had done with his law partner Edward McClennen in 1916.[16] Frankfurter thus asked his former law student Dean Acheson to attend the Senate hearings for him. Acheson, by 1939 one of Washington's most influential corporate lawyers, enjoyed the friendship of Senate Judiciary chairman Henry Ashurst of Arizona and of West Virginia senator Matthew M. Neely, who chaired the subcommittee that would conduct the hearings. These ties made Acheson an ideal representative, and one well positioned to answer the subcommittee's inquiries.

After two days of hearings, however, Frankfurter and Acheson changed course, believing that the nominee himself would have to respond personally to outrageous claims from the likes of Nevada senator Patrick McCarran, who "feared Frankfurter was the kind of dangerous radical from whom McCarran should save the nation." On January 12, Frankfurter and Acheson made their way to the Caucus Room of the Old Senate Office Building, which was "so crowded that the Capitol police had to clear a path for Frankfurter and Acheson to the witness table."[17]

Throughout most of the morning, Senator McCarran belligerently questioned Frankfurter about his views on communism. After holding up the book *Communism*, written by Frankfurter's friend Harold Laski, McCarran asked Frankfurter whether he agreed with the doctrine of Marxism, which the senator alleged the volume advocated.[18] Frankfurter cogently answered in the negative. During the hearing, following this exchange, the subcommittee chairman, Senator Neely, a Frankfurter supporter, told Acheson that he believed "the best thing to do was to bring the matter into the open and ask the witness directly whether or not he was or had ever been a Communist." A few moments later, when Neely asked whether Frankfurter had ever formally belonged to the Communist Party, the witness responded: "I have never been enrolled, and have never been qualified to be enrolled, because that does not represent my view of life, nor my view of government."[19] This response was followed by a roar of approval from the Senate Conference Room, after which the subcommittee chairman, banging his gavel, tried to restore order. Later in the day, the subcommittee voted in favor of Frankfurter's nomination.[20]

The same afternoon, Frankfurter and Acheson ate lunch with Senator Ashhurst, who, after offering them a brandy, predicted Frankfurter would be easily confirmed by the Senate. Frankfurter then returned to Harvard to await confirmation. On January 16, the Judiciary Committee "reported unanimously" its approval of Frankfurter's appointment. The following day, the full Senate confirmed his appointment with a voice vote: "No Nay was audible."[21]

Three days after the Senate confirmed Frankfurter's appointment, the Frankfurters left Cambridge for Washington, where they would live for the rest of their lives.[22] After the couple's arrival by train, they were assisted in getting settled by Olie Rauh, the wife of Frankfurter's student Joseph Rauh Jr., who had served as Cardozo's last law clerk and would soon begin his duties as Frankfurter's first. Olie found them a spacious house to rent in Georgetown, near the Achesons, and hired a housekeeper and cook who would remain with the Frankfurters throughout their Washington years.[23]

Frankfurter's Extensive Extrajudicial Activities

During his twenty-three years on the Supreme Court, as we saw earlier, Justice Brandeis secretly engaged in a level of extrajudicial political activity that, by current ethical standards, would be entirely impermissible. Almost from the moment Frankfurter began serving, and for several years thereafter, he followed Brandeis's precedent and also engaged in extrajudicial activity that blatantly violated judicial ethics and propriety and would today not be tolerated for a justice.

Frankfurter, like Brandeis, was not "the first sitting justice to dabble behind the scenes in the affairs of the legislature and the executive branch,"[24] a practice that went back to the republic's early years. Chief Justice John Jay advised President George Washington on his State of the Union Address and served as commissioner of the mint, while "Joseph Story [1812–1845] drafted federal bankruptcy legislation and encouraged friends in Congress to sponsor it" and "Roger Taney [1836–1864] helped pen [Andrew] Jackson's message vetoing the recharter of the Second Bank of the United States."[25] Later in the nineteenth century, as discussed in chapter 3, examples abound of high court justices engaging in flagrant extrajudicial political activity.

Much of Frankfurter's extrajudicial activity between 1939 and 1945 was devoted to advising, and at times actively lobbying, Roosevelt on federal court appointments. Frankfurter's role in influencing such appointments was especially apparent in his successful promotion of Charles Wyzanski Jr., his former student, for the Federal District Court for the District of Massachusetts. A native Bostonian, Wyzanski was one of Frankfurter's most illustrious "Happy Hotdogs," whose future New Deal career Frankfurter helped boost. Frankfurter had first recommended Wyzanski for clerkships with two Federal Court of Appeals Judges, Augustus N. Hand and Learned Hand, and then lobbied successfully for his appointment as solicitor to the Department of Labor in 1933, enthusiastically recommending the candidate to both FDR and Secretary of Labor Frances Perkins, and to New York senator Robert Wagner, who helped push for Wyzanski's Senate confirmation.[26] Wyzanski established a close relationship with Justice and Mrs. Brandeis, who frequently hosted him at their Washington apartment as well as their Chatham, Massachusetts, summer home.[27]

Frankfurter continued to assist Wyzanski throughout the 1930s, helping him secure his 1935 appointment as a special assistant to the attorney general in the Office of the Solicitor General. In response to a private letter from Judge Learned Hand suggesting Wyzanski for a judicial appointment, Frankfurter had written on February 16, 1939: "It has long been my ambition to see him on the Bench, and I shall leave no opportunity unavailed of to express my conviction regarding his pre-eminent judicial qualifications."[28] Frankfurter's opportunity to fulfill this ambition came in 1941, with the retirement of U.S. District Court judge Hugh D. McLellan. Using his customary techniques, Frankfurter immediately "mobilized allies for a campaign that would create the appearance of a ground swell of opinion in favor of Wyzanski."[29] He went out of his way to personally lobby his friend Francis Biddle, FDR's newly appointed attorney general, on Wyzanski's behalf. At a dinner party, Frankfurter and Judge

Hand both approached Biddle to tell him that appointing the thirty-five-year-old Wyzanski would mark an excellent start to his tenure. Soon thereafter, Biddle forwarded Wyzanski's name to the White House, and on December 1, 1941, Wyzanski's nomination was announced.[30] He would serve on the Federal District Court bench for forty-five years, until his death in 1986.

Despite his best efforts, however, Frankfurter failed to secure a Supreme Court spot for Learned Hand.[31] Frankfurter and Hand had first met in 1909, when Frankfurter was working as an assistant U.S. Attorney to Henry Stimson and Hand was a newly appointed district court judge for the Southern District of New York. The Albany-born Hand—Billings Learned Hand, in full—hailed from the American elite, his father tracing his U.S. roots to 1639.[32] The son and grandson of lawyers, Hand had studied philosophy as an undergraduate at Harvard and graduated atop his Harvard Law School class in 1896, several years before Frankfurter began his studies there. Although a lifelong Republican, while practicing law first in Albany and then in New York City he had become active in reform politics and "good government" circles, connections that "would prove useful when an additional federal judgeship was created in 1909, and the Taft administration, eager to promote its reformist credentials, resolved to make a good government appointment."[33] Charles C. Burlingham, a New York attorney and power broker who was a friend of both Hand and Frankfurter, recommended Hand's appointment to Attorney General George Wickersham and to President Taft, who nominated him in April 1909.[34] In 1924, President Coolidge appointed Hand to the U.S. Court of Appeals for the Second District, where he served until his retirement in 1961, earning a reputation as the most eminent American judge and legal scholar never to sit on the Supreme Court. The close Frankfurter-Hand friendship, and their voluminous correspondence, would continue for more than fifty years.

Several presidents, including Wilson, Harding, Coolidge, Hoover, and Franklin Roosevelt, each had the opportunity to appoint Hand to the Supreme Court but for various reasons decided not to. Commenting on the resignation of Justice John Hessin Clarke in 1922, Harold Laski wrote to Justice Holmes, "If God is good you will have Learned Hand." God, however, "was not making the appointment; Warren Harding was, and the President chose to nominate former Senator George Sutherland."[35] Although Harding appointed four men to the Supreme Court during his less than three years in the White House, and although Hand was a Republican like Harding, the president opted for nominees who were more conservative, given Hand's progressive reputation.[36] Supreme Court scholars have suggested that Hoover was prepared twice to nominate Hand but was persuaded to appoint Charles Evans Hughes and Benjamin Cardozo instead. Although when Cardozo died in 1938 some speculated FDR might appoint Hand, the president opted for his closer associate Frankfurter rather than Hand, whom he did not know personally.[37]

As one of FDR's chief advisers on judicial appointments, Frankfurter was increasingly determined to promote his friend Hand's candidacy for the Supreme Court. When Justice James Byrnes resigned from the court in October 1942 to become director of economic stabilization, FDR's "assistant president for domestic affairs," Frankfurter wrote to FDR strongly urging him to appoint Hand as his replacement.[38]

Frankfurter was a forceful and persistent advocate on Hand's behalf, literally bombarding the president with letters attesting to the judge's fine character and well-deserved reputation. Frankfurter also made several personal visits to the president and repeated phone calls on Hand's behalf.[39] In one of his most powerful letters, Frankfurter wrote the president that "you again have a chance to do something for Court and Country comparable to what you did when you made Stone the Chief Justice." In another letter, Frankfurter told Roosevelt that Hand ranked in the same category as exemplary Supreme Court justices such as Holmes, Brandeis, and Cardozo and that Hand's appointment would "bring distinction to the Court and new lustre to the President who made it possible."[40] In closing this letter, Frankfurter even drafted a version of FDR's nomination announcement of Hand for the Senate, an obvious breach of judicial propriety if there ever was one.[41]

Roosevelt at first seemed favorably disposed toward Hand's appointment, but he saw two major obstacles: first, Hand was a New Yorker, and with two New Yorkers already on the court, FDR wanted to create geographical balance by naming a Westerner; second was Hand's age, seventy-one. Each of Roosevelt's previous court appointees was in his fifties or early sixties. After the bitter court-packing fight of 1937, during which FDR had publicly expressed concern about the justices' advanced age and the need for younger nominees, he was very reluctant to appoint someone as old as Hand. Despite these hurdles, Frankfurter, in another letter to Roosevelt, demonstrated his acute awareness of the political benefits of the appointment he was advocating: "Especially on the score of politics, L. Hand is the only lad who will create no headaches for you—or, if you will, break no eggs. He is the one choice who will arouse universal acclaim in the Press—and the only one who won't make the adherents of other aspirants say, "Why in the hell was X chosen and not my man who is as good as X?" . . . Every other person would divide and opinion [*sic*] not to speak of other considerations, I never was more sure of anything—as a matter of Politics."[42]

Needless to say, Roosevelt instead nominated a younger man, Federal Court of Appeals judge Wiley Rutledge, from Iowa. Rutledge may have been chosen, in part, because Roosevelt was upset by Frankfurter's overpersistent lobbying. In fact, Justice William O. Douglas, one of Frankfurter's court rivals, would later suggest that the president had made his decision because "this time Felix overplayed his hand."[43] Frankfurter's vigorous campaign may thus have backfired, "although Hand was extremely grateful for his friend's efforts."[44]

Frankfurter's extrajudicial activities extended beyond advising and lobbying the White House on court appointments. The justice counseled FDR on appointments to other important government posts as well. In 1939, within months of his own confirmation, for example, Frankfurter helped persuade Roosevelt to appoint Archibald MacLeish, Frankfurter's former law student and friend, and a poet who had already won the first of his three Pulitzer Prizes, as the librarian of Congress, a position MacLeish would hold for five years.

While a justice, Frankfurter also assisted White House lawyers "with the drafting of the executive agreement that transferred American destroyers to England in exchange for leases on British naval bases . . . authored sections of the Lend-Lease Act and suggested to congressional allies that it bear the title of H.R. 1776."[45]

Even more controversial in terms of judicial propriety was Frankfurter's role in the famous case of the Nazi saboteurs, in which legal issues touching on the case came before the court's justices. In the summer of 1942, the German government landed eight saboteurs at locations in Long Island and Florida with instructions to blow up bridges, factories, and other military installations. The scheme failed. The saboteurs and their American collaborators were quickly arrested by the local police, the FBI, and military intelligence. After their arrest, Roosevelt ordered they be tried by a special military tribunal. Seeking advice on the tribunal's composition, Secretary of War Henry Stimson consulted Frankfurter, who recommended that it consist of only regular officers and exclude any civilian leaders from the War Department. Frankfurter also took Stimson's side when the war secretary argued against allowing press coverage for the trial, whereas Attorney General Francis Biddle favored it.[46]

Justice Frankfurter also regularly discussed the Nazi saboteur case with Assistant Secretary of War John McCloy, his newest confidant in the War Department and a former student at Harvard, who lived near Frankfurter and often took evening walks with him. Having helped the Roosevelt government structure its judicial proceedings against the Nazi spies, Frankfurter then became the administration's staunchest defender when the accused appealed their arrest and trial in the federal courts. He also was pivotal in shaping and supporting Chief Justice Stone's Supreme Court opinion that rejected their habeas corpus plea and sealed their fates.[47]

Frankfurter's extrajudicial activities ended abruptly with Roosevelt's death in 1945 and the conclusion of World War II. He enjoyed no such access to the Truman administration.[48] During the Eisenhower years, his advising and lobbying would resume "briefly but significantly during the long struggle over school desegregation . . . when he regularly advised his former law clerk, Philip Elman, then in the office of the Solicitor General, about the administration's strategy" in the landmark civil rights case *Brown v. Board of Education of Topeka*.[49] Also, in the 1950s, Frankfurter would successfully promote the candidacy of his former law student and former Brandeis law clerk Henry Friendly, then general counsel for Pan American Airways, for the U.S. Court of Appeals for the Second Circuit.[50] When Friendly was appointed to this judgeship by Eisenhower in 1959, after vigorously lobbying by Frankfurter, he became the second of the jurist's Jewish law students to be seated on the federal bench.

Frankfurter, Nazi Germany, and the Holocaust

Since Adolf Hitler's rise to power in Germany in 1933, Felix Frankfurter had been increasingly concerned about the fate of European Jews. When one of Hitler's first moves had been to oust Jews from teaching positions in German universities, Frankfurter helped organize funds for the University in Exile, a graduate school established in New York City to employ Jewish and other professors dismissed from German universities. He urged Harvard to take in these exiled German Jewish scholars, "and when many American universities were slow or recalcitrant, he publicly criticized them, Harvard included."[51]

At Harvard, Frankfurter was especially vociferous, urging the university and particularly the law school faculty to protest Nazi dismissals and persecution of German Jewish professors. When Harvard was invited to attend university celebrations in Germany, at Gottingen and Heidelberg, Frankfurter urged the school to decline because "they had become political propaganda agencies and, as such, could no longer pretend to the ideal of freed scholarship," and he argued that American universities such as Harvard "had an obligation not to approve the Nazi regime by attendance."[52]

Along with such stances, Frankfurter frequently sought to remind Roosevelt "of the threat to civilization Nazism and its manifestations posed."[53] During the late 1930s, Frankfurter likewise urged Roosevelt to help German Jewish refugees immigrate to the United States, and to persuade Great Britain, through its mandatory government, to open Palestine to increased Jewish immigration from Nazi-occupied Europe.[54] In both areas, however, Frankfurter did not pressure the president unduly, and his requests for White House action on behalf of European Jewish refugees, while well intentioned, were notably unsuccessful. Always loyal to FDR, Frankfurter would not blame his friend the president for his inaction.

Which brings us back to this chapter's opening scene, wherein Nazi storm troopers broke into the Vienna home of Frankfurter's eighty-two-year-old uncle, Solomon, and imprisoned him.[55] Solomon Frankfurter's high stature within the city included service as director of the University of Vienna Library. As a Jewish scholar and communal leader, he had been president of the Society for the Collection and Investigation of Jewish Historic Monuments and director of the Vienna Jewish Museum.[56]

Felix Frankfurter had an especially close and admiring relationship with his uncle Solomon, with whom he had lived in Vienna as a child. But the news of Solomon's arrest, surprisingly, did not prompt him to approach the president to intervene. In such an emergency, "Felix Frankfurter was as close to the President of the United States as he was to the telephone," and yet "he did not believe that he should impose on that friendship for a personal matter, no matter how extreme the emergency."[57] Instead, he called upon an English friend, Lady Nancy Astor, "doyenne of the Cliveden set," who was known for her sympathy with Nazi Germany, and its antisemitism, to use her contacts with the German ambassador in London to seek his uncle's release.[58] The resulting intervention was indeed successful.[59]

Viewed in retrospect, it is difficult to understand why Frankfurter did not personally meet with the president on this matter. He was always more than ready to test his friendship with Roosevelt by advocating for judicial appointments. In campaigning for Learned Hand's high court appointment, for example, Frankfurter had "bombarded" the president with letters and phone calls and made several visits to the White House. Frankfurter's seeming unwillingness to similarly appeal to FDR on his uncle's behalf, whose very life was at stake, seems especially inexplicable.

Throughout the Holocaust years of 1941 to 1945, Henry Stimson served as secretary of war. By 1942 and early 1943, reports had reached the United States that the Nazis were systematically murdering European Jews. Officials in Stimson's War Department, especially his trusted assistant secretary John McCloy, had read the published accounts of Hitler's extermination policies with some skepticism, believing "the reports coming out of Europe were just too horrible to be entirely credible."[60] One of those doubting the reports was McCloy's Georgetown neighbor Frankfurter.

During late summer 1943, Frankfurter had listened to a detailed briefing on what was happening inside the Poland-based extermination camps by Jan Karski, a twenty-eight-year-old liaison sent by the Polish government-in-exile in London to alert political leaders in London and Washington to the dire plight of European Jews and convince them of the veracity of Hitler's extermination plan. Disguised as an Estonian prison guard, Karski, "who had seen firsthand the Warsaw ghetto," had been smuggled into the Belzec death camp and had secretly crossed Nazi-occupied Europe to gather eyewitness accounts of the Nazi atrocities perpetrated against the Jews, especially in Poland.[61] Karski's report told of the mass killing of 1.8 million Polish Jews, describing the entire process from the ghetto roundups to the gas chambers.[62]

By the time Karski, a Polish Catholic, met with Justice Frankfurter, he had already personally briefed Roosevelt, Stimson, and Office of Strategic Services chief William Donovan, none of whom seemed shaken by the revelations. The president apparently listened intently, but when Karski implored Roosevelt to get the Allies to intervene, all the president could say was a noncommittal, "Tell your people that we shall win the war."[63]

Karski hoped to get a more profound reaction from Frankfurter, "who after all was a prominent Jewish figure and a Zionist."[64] On meeting Karski at the Polish embassy in Washington, Frankfurter said, "Please tell me exactly what you have seen."[65] For the next half hour or so, Frankfurter listened as Karski graphically described his observations from inside the Warsaw Ghetto and the Belzec death camp, after which the justice rose from his chair and paced back and forth in silence. Taking his seat again, Frankfurter finally said, "A man like me talking to a man like you must be totally frank. So, I say that I am unable to believe you."[66] Startled, the Polish ambassador, Jan Ciechanowski, a friend of Frankfurter's, exclaimed, "Felix, you don't mean it! How can you call him a liar to his face? The authority of my country is behind him. You know who he is!"[67]

Frankfurter replied: "Mr. Ambassador, I did not say that this young man is lying. I said that I am unable to believe him. There is a difference." He then waved his hands "as if to make the unbelievable news disappear," murmured, "No, no," turned, and abruptly left the room.[68] After thus rudely dismissing Karski, Frankfurter never met with Roosevelt, Stimson, or McCloy to discuss the Karski report or to seek help in requesting Allied intervention to stop the Nazi extermination of Europe's Jews. Nor did Frankfurter ever weigh in on the Roosevelt administration's 1944 proposal to bomb the Auschwitz death camp with FDR, Stimson, or McCoy, the War Department official who ultimately cast the deciding veto of this proposal.

Indeed, one of the most serious indictments leveled against the Roosevelt administration involves its failure to bomb the Auschwitz gas chambers and crematoria and the railroads leading to the death camp. Holocaust scholars have demonstrated conclusively that by spring 1944 the Roosevelt administration could have feasibly bombed Auschwitz.[69] In 1944, however, the War Department rejected out of hand several appeals to bomb Auschwitz and the railroads leading to it, claiming that such actions would divert airpower from operations elsewhere. In rejecting one such request from the World Jewish Congress, McCloy callously noted: "After a study it became apparent that such an operation could be executed only by diversion of considerable air support essential to the success of our forces now engaged in decisive operations elsewhere and would in any case be of such doubtful efficacy that it would not warrant the use of our resources. There has been considerable opinion to the effect that such an effort, even if practicable, might provoke more vindictive action by the Germans."[70]

What "more vindictive action" than Auschwitz was possible remained McCloy and his War Department's secret. McCloy's failure to consider the request "to bomb the crematoria because it would be of 'doubtful efficacy' was especially tragic," for doing so "might have gone far to alert world opinion to the mass murder operation as well as disrupting the delicate strands which made it possible."[71] During spring and summer of 1944, the very months the War Department was turning down such requests, American bombers were already striking industrial targets within the Auschwitz complex itself, only five miles from the gas chambers. Had they been permitted to bomb the railroads and the camp's death apparatus, the lives of tens of thousands of Hungarian and Slovakian Jews deported the same year might possibly have been saved.[72]

The McCloy and Frankfurter families were close and frequently dined at each other's homes. The wives shopped together. Although Frankfurter and the assistant secretary of war took regular evening walks together, "discussing the day's events," and the justice "wrote McCloy brief notes and on occasion lengthy memos on everything from administration appointments to comments on the European war"—and although McCloy had become "Frankfurter's eyes and ears within the War Department"—no record exists, as suggested already, of any entreaty by Frankfurter to McCloy on the rejected Auschwitz bombing proposal his neighbor had so callously vetoed.[73] Nor, as also suggested, is there any record of Frankfurter ever urging Stimson to override McCloy's veto of the bombing proposal, which Stimson had the authority to do. Frankfurter's failure to do so is particularly notable, as with McCloy, given that, throughout World War II, Frankfurter regularly dined with his friend the secretary of war at Woodley, Stimson's Washington estate, and frequently spoke with him at his War Department office.

Frankfurter, Judicial Restraint, and the Flag Salute Cases

When Frankfurter was appointed to the Supreme Court, his supporters expected he would be a champion of civil liberties, as he had been previously, and an outspoken liberal voice. Instead, during his twenty-three years on the bench, Frankfurter would be the court's most eloquent spokesman for judicial restraint and its foremost judicial conservative.

Frankfurter's emerging reputation as a judicial conservative, whose name symbolized a reluctance to rule in favor of civil liberties, originated with his vote in *Minersville School District v. Gobitis*, the so-called flag salute case, decided in June 1940. In its ruling, the court held, by an 8–1 vote, that expelling children of the Jehovah's Witnesses faith from public school for refusing to salute the American flag was constitutionally permissible.[74] Justice Frankfurter wrote the majority opinion upholding the Minersville, Pennsylvania, school board requirement that all students recite the Pledge of Allegiance, even if so doing violated their religious beliefs. This majority opinion, in the first civil liberties case decided during World War II, and written just over a year after his appointment, "would indelibly mark Frankfurter's judicial career."[75] Frankfurter's reasoning in the *Gobitis* case, said Louis Henkin, his former law clerk, a legal scholar highly sympathetic with Frankfurter's position, reduced itself to the following: "This is the flag of the United States. Is it wrong for the State to teach people patriotism, especially in wartime?"[76]

The *Gobitis* case began in November 1935, when two Jehovah's Witnesses, twelve-year-old Lillian Gobitis and her ten-year-old brother, William, were expelled from their public school for refusing to salute the American flag on religious grounds. Jehovah's Witnesses "objected to the flag salute because of their literal reading of *Exodus* 20:4–5, and equated the salute with bowing down to graven images."[77] In other words, saluting the flag was a form of idol worship and thus forbidden by God.[78] The children's father went to court asking that the Minersville School Board desist from punishing his children for adhering to their religious beliefs.[79] In his ruling upholding Gobitis's claim, U.S. District Court judge Albert Maris wrote, "Our beloved flag, the emblem of religious liberty apparently has been used as an instrument to impose a religious test as a condition of receiving the benefits of public education."[80] In siding with the family, Maris further contended that "the children were justified in their objections if they conscientiously believed that freedom of religion was being abridged by saluting the flag."[81] The Third Circuit U.S. Court of Appeals unanimously upheld Maris's opinion, and the Minersville School Board appealed the decision to the U.S. Supreme Court.

By the time the case reached the Supreme Court, the Gobitis family could count among its supporters prominent attorneys and academics, many of whom had worked with Frankfurter on civil liberties issues during the 1920s and 1930s. Grenville Clark, Frankfurter's Harvard Law classmate and long-time friend, who chaired the American Bar Association Committee on the Bill of Rights, worked on the Supreme Court brief for the Gobitis family, as did Harvard professor Zechariah Chafee, a leading civil libertarian who had worked with Frankfurter on several civil liberties cases during the twenties.[82] Roger Baldwin, with whom Frankfurter had helped found the ACLU in 1920, was also a passionate advocate of the Gobitis family's position.

After the *Gobitis* decision, Frankfurter received a torrent of angry letters from former liberal associates who viewed his decision as a betrayal of the causes he had once championed. Some of Frankfurter's most devoted friends were so stunned by his opinion that they did not call him or send congratulations, as they often did after his court opinions. Rather, they felt a need to communicate with Justice Stone, who wrote the court's lone dissenting opinion. "I want to tell you," Frankfurter's friend Harold Laski wrote Stone from England, "how right I think you are in that educational case from Pennsylvania and to my deep regret, how wrong I think Felix is."[83]

Indeed, against his strong civil libertarian beliefs, Frankfurter had "struggled with his equally firm conviction that the judicial branch of government should exercise restraint in reviewing the acts of the popularly elected branches."[84] And despite the expectation by liberals that Frankfurter would actively promote civil liberties while on the bench, many conservatives had applauded his appointment, perceiving much in his philosophy that was appealing. As it turned out, these conservatives "were more prescient in their forecast" than his liberal enthusiasts, "for Frankfurter's philosophy of judicial restraint proved to be his pervasive guide, and his record on civil liberties, so exemplary as a private citizen, would be less impressive as a Justice."[85] Throughout his years on the high court, beginning with his *Gobitis* opinion, his decisions were governed more by judicial restraint than by liberal activism. And for all his liberal stances in the 1920s and 1930s, such as in the Sacco and Vanzetti case, his commitment to restraint had been shaped years earlier—by his studies with James Bradley Thayer at Harvard Law. Some considered his fealty to judicial restraint "his most important intellectual accomplishment [even] during his years as a professor" and the single most important "constitutional contribution" to guide his judicial career.[86] As Justice Frankfurter became an increasingly "articulate and persuasive advocate of judicial abnegation in favor of legislative action," he showed such dedication to the principle that the liberal Yale Law School professor Fred Rodell referred to him sarcastically "as the Supreme Court's Emily Post."[87]

Frankfurter's deep-seated patriotism also informed his decision to uphold the Minersville School Board's expulsion of the Gobitis children. As an immigrant Jew who knew no English when he arrived at Ellis Island in 1894, Frankfurter "was a patriot first and last, and no amount of sophisticated judicial philosophizing could cover up the deep debt that he owed to his adopted country."[88]

Attesting anecdotally to his patriotism, Frankfurter seems to have been the only justice to regularly whistle "Stars and Stripes Forever" as he walked the Supreme Court building's corridors. Shortly before his death, he asked his chosen biographer to tell readers "how much I love my country." Only in the United States, believed Frankfurter, could an immigrant Jew and an outsider like himself reach the heights of influence he had reached. For this, Frankfurter was always grateful. Other outsiders, like Jehovah's Witnesses, "he seemed to reason, should learn the lessons of Americanism as well."[89]

The challenge posed by the Jehovah's Witnesses to compulsory salute of the flag "pitted a tiny religious minority, claiming the protection of the First Amendment for the free exercise of religious beliefs, against the cherished symbol of the United States," the American flag. "We live by symbols," Frankfurter wrote, quoting Justice Holmes in his *Gobitis* opinion. "The flag is the symbol of our national unity, transcending all internal differences, however large, within the framework of the Constitution."[90] He expected Jehovah's Witnesses to choose American patriotism over religious conviction, the very same choice Frankfurter had made for himself. To an immigrant Jew like Frankfurter, and a sitting Supreme Court justice, no claim was evidently more important than that symbolized by flag and constitution.[91]

In 1943, however, in the *West Virginia Board of Education v. Barnette* case, the Supreme Court overruled its *Gobitis* decision by upholding the Jehovah's Witnesses' claim that saluting the flag violated their First Amendment right to freedom of religious expression.[92] Frankfurter felt betrayed by his liberal colleagues William Douglas, Hugo Black, Frank Murphy, and Wiley Rutledge, who had supported him in *Gobitis* but now voted with Chief Justice Stone to reverse the earlier ruling. This sense of betrayal led to an irrevocable split with his more liberal colleagues, especially Douglas and Black, with whom Frankfurter feuded incessantly in the years ahead.

Frankfurter's Judaism, which he always viewed as a "mere accident of birth," did not lead him to sympathize with other religious minorities, such as the Jehovah's Witnesses, in his flag salute rulings. In his dissenting opinion in *West Virginia Board of Education v. Barnette*, Frankfurter wrote: "One who belongs to the most vilified and persecuted minority in history is not likely to be insensible to the freedom guaranteed in our Constitution. Were my purely personal attitude relevant, I should wholeheartedly associate myself with the general libertarian views in the Court's opinion, representing as they do the thought and action of a lifetime. But as judges, we are neither Jew nor gentile, neither Catholic nor agnostic."[93]

Frankfurter's majority opinion in *Gobitis* "involved his dearly held belief that the Court should defer to majority judgment, even when that judgment was intolerant or repressive. It called forth his ardent patriotism, just as World War II was getting underway." It also, as we saw, involved his deeply held belief in national symbols, such as the flag. Moreover, Frankfurter's *Gobitis* opinion reflected his personal belief in the irrelevance of religious faith or affiliation. Frankfurter had chosen to be a secular rather than a religious Jew. In his decisions in both cases, Frankfurter was, "in a very real sense, asking the Jehovah's Witnesses to . . . accept the secular over the religious."[94]

Frankfurter's belief that religious minorities should accept the secular over the religious similarly, and profoundly, shaped his views later in landmark church-state cases, namely *Braunfeld v. Brown* and *McGowan v. Maryland*. In these two cases, both decided May 29, 1961, Frankfurter and his colleagues responded to new legal challenges to the Sunday laws, or blue laws, which had been a source of concern to nineteenth-century Jews and remained a controversial church-state issue well into the twentieth century.[95] The Sunday laws were state regulations requiring everyone to close down their businesses on the Christian Sabbath, thereby making it economically difficult for Jews to rest on their own Sabbath, observed on Saturday. In nineteenth- and early twentieth-century America, religious Jews, as well as Seventh Day Baptists, suffered harshly under these laws. While most Americans worked six days a week, they could only work five. In effect, "on Saturday they rested to uphold the demands of the Lord and on Sunday they rested to uphold the demands of the state."[96]

Indeed, with the twentieth-century advent of the five-day workweek, Sunday laws became less significant for most American Jews. Under pressure from large-scale merchants, such laws in most states were either cut back or repealed. So long as they stood, however, blue laws affected Jews more injuriously than did any other church-state issue. They served as a weekly reminder that, religious liberty notwithstanding, members of a religious minority still paid a stiff price to uphold the tenets of their faith.[97]

Supreme Court rulings redefining separation of church and state, such as *Gobitis* and *Barnette*, spawned a series of legal challenges to the Sunday laws during the 1950s, including the *McGowan* and *Braunfeld* cases. *McGowan v. Maryland* represented a challenge to state laws banning the sale of various forms of merchandise on Sunday as the "establishment of religion." *Braunfeld v. Brown* centered on the contention that Orthodox Jews were precluded by the Sunday laws from freely exercising their religion, since closing down on both Saturday and Sunday saddled them with great economic hardship. With their challenges to the Sunday laws turned down, and the state regulations upheld, their cases went to the Supreme Court.

In *Gobitis*, Frankfurter had affirmed local school officials' power "to compel children to salute the flag against the claims of a religious minority that such coerced participation violated the free exercise of their faith."[98] Twenty-one years later, in upholding state Sunday laws in the *Braunfeld* and *McGowan* cases, Frankfurter, then the only Jewish Supreme Court member, rejected claims that "Sunday closing" laws, which were anathema to Orthodox Jews, "were both a forbidden establishment of religion and an interference with religious liberty."[99] Neither Jehovah's Witnesses nor Orthodox Jews, Frankfurter contended, "could escape the common burdens and shared responsibilities of American citizenship."[100] In his opinion, Frankfurter, who had abandoned Jewish Orthodoxy for secularism, was in a real sense asking Orthodox Jews to make the same choice he had made.

The *Schneiderman* Case

Frankfurter's growing reputation as a judicial conservative was furthered by his vote in a major 1942 case dealing with a Communist Party member's individual liberties during wartime. In the 1920s, during the Red Scare, Frankfurter had been an outspoken defender of the civil liberties of the anarchists, socialists, and communists arrested by Attorney General A. Mitchell Palmer and his Justice Department. While on the court during wartime, in the *Schneiderman v. United States* case, however, he joined with the court's conservative minority in arguing for the revoked citizenship of a high-profile Communist Party member. During World War II, Frankfurter was the court's only foreign-born member, and its only representative from the torrent of turn-of-the-century immigration.[101] This status was reflected, as we will see, in his decision in the case of William Schneiderman, a Jewish immigrant from Russia and a naturalized American citizen who had been a Communist Party member since his youth and in 1932 had run for governor of Minnesota on the Communist ticket. In 1939, the government moved to strip Schneiderman, then thirty-five, of his citizenship because of his party affiliation, arguing "that his Communist activities in the five years prior to the naturalization process showed that he had not been truly 'attached' to the principles of the U.S. Constitution." Schneiderman, in turn, argued "that he did not believe in using force or violence and that in fact he had been a good citizen: he had never been arrested and had used his rights as a citizen to advocate change and greater social justice."[102]

By the time the *Schneiderman* case came before the Supreme Court, the United States had entered the war and publicly acknowledged the Soviet Union as an ally. Politically, "the case was a hot potato" because Communist Russia "was at the time allied with the democracies against Germany."[103] Although the court's majority opinion "protested that there was no connection [between its decision to allow Schneiderman to keep his citizenship and the shared fight with the Soviets], it was not an opportune time for the country to be stripping Communists of their citizenship."[104] Adding to the case's widespread coverage, Wendell Willkie, the Republican candidate for president in 1940, represented Schneiderman before the court, which ruled 5–3 in his favor. "Under our traditions," the ruling said, "beliefs are personal." Frankfurter did not agree.

Given his admiration for Justices Holmes and Brandeis and his liberal record, Frankfurter might have been expected to side with Schneiderman, "as

Holmes had done so eloquently for another immigrant who held unpopular views, Rosa Schwimmer, a Quaker who had been denied citizenship because she refused to bear arms."[105] As a law professor, Frankfurter had applauded Holmes's defense of Rosa Schwimmer and Holmes's famous rationale: "If there is any principle of the Constitution that more imperatively calls for attachment than any other," Holmes had written in a defense joined by Brandeis, "it is the principle of free thought—not free thought for those who agree with us but freedom for the thought we hate."[106]

In the *Schneiderman* case, however, Frankfurter's patriotism apparently trumped his commitment to protecting wartime civil liberties. Frankfurter joined with the court's minority, led by Chief Justice Stone, in seeking to strip Schneiderman of his citizenship. For the Jewish immigrant Frankfurter, Schneiderman was "a fundamentally disloyal immigrant—one who subscribed fully to the beliefs of the Communist Party, and took the oath of naturalization in bad faith, in the hopes of undermining the country that had welcomed him to its shores . . . a dangerous traitor, whose citizenship should be revoked."[107]

Frankfurter was especially entitled to speak on this subject, he maintained, because he too was an immigrant. The *Schneiderman* case brought to the fore Frankfurter's "deep love of the Constitution." He spoke of his own naturalization as a conversion. "Loyalty to the Constitution," he said, "was his religion," and "it is well known that a convert is more zealous than one born to the faith."[108] His faith, as we saw earlier, was a "Constitutional faith" that had effectively replaced Judaism. "As one who has no ties with any formal religion," Frankfurter noted in his diary, "perhaps the feelings that underlie religious forms for me run into intensification of my feelings about American citizenship."[109] Thus, with his dissent in the *Schneiderman* case, Frankfurter, who had been one of Roosevelt's most liberal court appointees, added to his reputation for conservatism.

Brown v. Board of Education

Frankfurter did not take exclusively conservative stands, however. This was especially evident in 1954, in the landmark *Brown v. Board of Education of Topeka* case, in which the Supreme Court overturned the 1896 *Plessy v. Ferguson* decision, which had established the separate-but-equal doctrine, "the legal cornerstone for segregated public schools."[110] In what was perhaps "his greatest contribution to American Law," Frankfurter helped Chief Justice Earl

Warren "forge a unanimous Court to strike down segregated public schools in *Brown v. Board of Education*," a decision that "changed the constitutional universe."[111] According to Frankfurter's former law clerk Philip Elman, who during the two years before the *Brown* decision worked on the segregation issue in the Justice Department and was in continuous touch with Frankfurter, "the historic, unanimous judgment in *Brown v. Board of Education* . . . was the result largely of Frankfurter's efforts."[112]

When Frankfurter was appointed to the Supreme Court, he already was well known as a supporter of black civil rights.[113] He had served on the NAACP's national legal advisory committee throughout the 1930s and mentored Charles Houston, an early black civil rights lawyer who served as special counsel and chief legal strategist for the NAACP and whom Frankfurter had recommended for appointment to the District of Columbia Municipal Court.[114] He had promoted the careers of other African American lawyers as well, such as William Hastie, a former student at Harvard who would become the first African American appointed by FDR to the federal bench and later dean of the Howard University Law School. Hastie "in turn served as a mentor to future Supreme Court Justice Thurgood Marshall."[115] When Hastie became a federal judge in 1938, Frankfurter, who had lobbied FDR for the appointment, had "sought Harlan Fiske Stone's help in having Amherst College, from which both Hastie and Stone had graduated, award Hastie an honorary degree."[116]

Frankfurter abhorred segregation. "The cost of segregation to America's reputation abroad," in the justice's view, was yet another reason to gather unanimous court backing in *Brown v. Board of Education*.[117] His friend Secretary of State Dean Acheson, too, was convinced that segregation seriously harmed American foreign policy interests, and expressed his opinion in a letter later included—"possibly at Frankfurter's suggestion"—in the government's brief in the *Brown* case:

> During the past six years, the damage to our foreign relations attributable to [segregation] has become progressively greater. The United States is under constant attack in the foreign press, over the foreign radio, and in such international bodies as the United Nations because of various practices of discrimination against minority groups in this country. . . . Soviet spokesmen regularly exploit the situation in propaganda against the United States. . . . The continuance of racial discrimination in the United States remains a source of constant embarrassment to this government in the day-to-day conduct of its foreign relations.[118]

Frankfurter understood politics well enough to realize that Congress might never act on its own to end segregation and that "any steps to improve America's reputation by counteracting segregation would have to come from the Court." However, judicial intervention to outlaw segregation was, "in principle, anathema to Frankfurter. A Supreme Court ruling that segregation was unconstitutional would be the most aggressive piece of judicial activism in American history. It was almost impossible to imagine how it could sit comfortably with the philosophy of judicial restraint. . . . This quandary was the most difficult one that Frankfurter faced in his judicial career. Segregation had to go. But voting against it would betray his essential judicial philosophy."[119] Confronted with this conflict, Frankfurter arrived at a compromise: "Judicial activism, if it must be undertaken, should at least be adopted through judicial consensus." This underlined his belief in the need for court unanimity on *Brown* and explained the tenacity of his campaign to achieve it.

To Frankfurter's admirers, his opinion and the court's unanimous ruling in *Brown* "struck precisely the right balance. It was a decision rooted not in expediency but in principle, in light of the constitutional text, national experience, and present conditions." Moreover, while the court's decision was controversial, especially in the South, "it accorded with the nation's trajectory toward racial equality and thus would probably secure consent in the relatively near future (as subsequent history eventually confirmed)."[120]

After *Brown*, "Frankfurter had just one more great opinion left in him, one of the more controversial dissents of his career."[121] It came in a landmark 1962 case about reapportionment and voting rights, *Baker v. Carr*, "a precursor to the Supreme Court's eventual holding that the Constitution guaranteed 'one man, one vote.'"[122] In *Baker v. Carr*, the justices "were confronted with the politically sensitive issue of whether or not the courts should intervene to correct the distortions in representation in Tennessee's malapportioned state legislature," wherein the state's rural voters "had benefited at the expense of the state's urban residents in their representation in the state legislature."[123] The state legislature had not been reapportioned since 1901, "although the population in the districts had shifted."[124] While "redistricting had long been a political matter, decided by the state legislature," the legislature "had not hurried to reapportion to reflect the increasingly urban population in the state, even though the state constitution required it."[125]

At issue in essence was whether the Supreme Court should do the job elected state representatives refused to do. Frankfurter's answer, in this, his most famous dissent, was an emphatic no. For Frankfurter, *Baker v. Carr* "provided the perfect and indeed crowning example of where judicial restraint was appropriate. It was not only that legislatures had always been in charge of redistricting, but rather that the act of designing districts was the most inherently political act possible." By involving the court in the redistricting process, and thus permitting it to enter what he called the "political thicket,"[126] the very legitimacy of the Court would be undermined, according to Frankfurter.[127] "There is not under our Constitution a judicial remedy for every political mischief," he argued. "In a democratic society like ours, relief must come through an aroused popular conscience that sears the conscience of the people's representatives."[128] The Supreme Court did not have the right, in his view, to get involved in political questions such as how state governments should apportion their legislatures. These were questions to be decided by the states' elected political representatives.

Frankfurter's dissent in *Baker v. Carr* helped consolidate his reputation as a judicial conservative. The dissent was also the last opinion Frankfurter would ever write. A few days after the court's ruling, in April 1962, Frankfurter suffered the debilitating stroke that would ultimately lead to his resignation.

Justice Frankfurter and His Law Clerks

In 1948, the year after the Brooklyn Dodgers executive Branch Rickey broke Major League Baseball's color line by signing Jackie Robinson, Felix Frankfurter broke a Supreme Court color line by hiring its first African American law clerk, William T. Coleman Jr. A magna cum laude 1946 graduate of Harvard Law School who had clerked for Herbert F. Goodrich of the U.S. Court of Appeals, Coleman would work closely with Thurgood Marshall as a co-author of the NAACP's *Brown v. Board of Education* legal brief. Coleman, a Republican, would later serve on President Dwight D. Eisenhower's Committee on Government Employment Policy and as a consultant to the U.S. Arms Control and Disarmament Agency before being appointed transportation secretary by President Gerald Ford in 1975.

Following Justice Brandeis's precedent, Frankfurter also hired a number of Jewish law clerks—eighteen during his twenty-three-year tenure, to be precise, ten more than Brandeis had hired during his judgeship of the same length. Many of Frankfurter's clerks "were overachieving Jewish boys who resembled their boss in their biographies, but none came closer to matching Frankfurter's background and experience than the brilliant Alexander M. Bickel," a favorite of Frankfurter's who served in 1952–1953.[129] Bickel had immigrated to America with his parents from Romania at age fourteen (whereas Frankfurter had been twelve). Like Frankfurter, Bickel, "who spoke Yiddish, German, Romanian and Hebrew before ever speaking English," had arrived in America with no English at all.[130] He had excelled at the City College of New York, Frankfurter's alma mater, where he was elected to Phi Beta Kappa and had graduated from Harvard Law School with a brilliant record in 1949.[131] Prior to clerking for Frankfurter, Bickel clerked for U.S. appellate judge Calvert Magruder, who years earlier had been Frankfurter's student at Harvard and later was one of Brandeis's clerks.

In clerking for Frankfurter when *Brown v. Board of Education* was pending, Bickel "was no detached spectator—in fact, he played a crucial role in the case."[132] Frankfurter had assigned him to do the research, and prepare the first draft, for what would become Frankfurter's opinion in the case. In doing so, Frankfurter had asked Bickel "to delve deeply into the question of segregation and the Fourteenth Amendment, and to review the debates in Congress and the states" on the constitutionality of segregation as they evolved over time. Bickel took a full year to fulfill this task, completing his memo in August 1953. The document was so thorough that Frankfurter had it typeset and printed by the court's print shop for distribution to the other justices.[133] In his long section on the Fourteenth Amendment's position on segregation, Bickel concluded that "the legislative history of the Amendment is, in a word, inconclusive."[134] His verdict, incorporated into Frankfurter's 1954 opinion, was adopted by the unanimous court. Indeed, "the Constitution's ambiguous requirement freed the Court to decide the case in terms of broader social principle," that of prohibiting segregation in public schools.[135] In 1955, "after *Brown* had been decided, the Bickel memorandum, now revised, was published as a freestanding article in the *Harvard Law Review*."[136] At least partly on the piece's strength, Bickel was hired to teach at Yale Law School, where he would remain for the rest of his career.[137]

Over the next eighteen years, until his untimely death in 1974 at age forty-nine, Bickel would achieve renown as a legal scholar and one of Frankfurter's most prolific protégés. As the author of such notable books as *Politics and the Warren Court* and *The Supreme Court and the Idea of Progress*, and numerous articles in *Commentary*, the *New Republic*, and the *Public Interest*, he would become arguably the Warren court's most eloquent and thoughtful public critic. Years later, Supreme Court justice Samuel Alito "would credit these writings with inspiring him to attend Bickel's Yale Law School."[138] More than fifty years after its publication, his seminal 1962 book on the Supreme Court,

The Least Dangerous Branch, is still considered a classic of conservative legal scholarship.

Another favorite of Frankfurter's, and his only Orthodox Jewish clerk, was Louis Henkin, the first graduate of Yeshiva University to both study at Harvard Law and then serve as a Supreme Court clerk. Following his clerkship, Henkin, who would be a legal adviser to the State Department and a Columbia Law School professor for more than forty years, specialized in international law, human rights, and U.S. foreign policy. The author of *Foreign Affairs and the Constitution*, *How Nations Behave*, and *The Rights of Man Today*, among other works, Henkin served as president of the American Society of International Law and, until his death in 2010, as chairman of Columbia University Center for the Study of Human Rights.

Like Frankfurter and Bickel, Henkin was an immigrant who knew no English when he moved from Belarus to New York City's Lower East Side. The son of Rabbi Yosef Eliyahu Henkin, who in the United States became known as an authority on Jewish law, Henkin grew up speaking Yiddish and learned English through helping his father mail letters to other rabbinic scholars throughout the country. After graduating from Yeshiva College in 1937, and Harvard Law in 1940, he clerked for Learned Hand and then enlisted in the Army during World War II.

Henkin began his clerkship with Frankfurter in 1946. The justices held their weekly conference with their respective clerks on Saturday, and Henkin "would on Friday nights secretly sleep on Frankfurter's office couch because he couldn't travel home on the Sabbath."[139] At the Saturday meetings, "Henkin was careful not to write."[140] Henkin's religious observance was so subtle — "he wore a yarmulke only in the synagogue" — that the unobservant Frankfurter at first may not have "even have noticed that his clerk was keeping the religious laws."[141] But over time, Frankfurter came to admire the religious devotion of his clerk, who would remain a close friend throughout his life.

Another of Frankfurter's Jewish clerks, Richard Goodwin, would attain renown at an especially young age in John F. Kennedy's White House and State Department. A Boston native who had graduated first in his class at both Tufts University and Harvard Law School, and who had clerked for Frankfurter in 1958, Goodwin became special counsel to the House's Legislative Oversight Committee, leading its much-publicized investigation of the quiz show scandals in 1959. These "television quiz shows — the *$64,000 Question* and *Twenty-One* especially — achieved cult status akin to shows like *American Idol* today."[142] Winners became national celebrities, with Columbia

University professor Charles Van Doren making the cover of *Time* magazine and becoming a "cultural correspondent" on NBC's *Today Show*.[143] As the special counsel to the House committee, "Goodwin . . . pieced together the quiz shows' dark secret: that the big winners like Van Doren were given the questions and (mostly) the answers ahead of time."[144]

Amid this investigation, Goodwin was invited by Kennedy's chief aide, Ted Sorensen, to join the then-senator's speechwriting staff. Goodwin had met Kennedy in Washington during his clerkship with Justice Frankfurter. Combining "a sharp intellect with sound political instincts and a sure prose style," Goodwin soon became the "number-two speechwriter," after Sorensen, on Kennedy's campaign staff.[145] Although he had no special knowledge of Latin American affairs—a big issue in the 1960 presidential campaign, after Fidel Castro's success in Cuba—Goodwin "found himself writing speeches on Latin America" and in September 1960 coined the term "Alliance for Progress" for JFK's eventual Latin America policy.[146] For several months after Kennedy entered the White House in January 1961, Goodwin "was increasingly the man Kennedy counted on" to devise a Latin America program "to fit the phrase."[147] Before the inauguration, Goodwin organized a high-level task force on Latin America and, in February 1961, "headed a White House review of hemispheric policy in preparation for a major presidential speech on the area."[148] Later in 1961, at age twenty-nine, Goodwin was named deputy assistant secretary of state for Inter-American Affairs and given a substantial role in formulating Latin America policy. His tenure, however, was cut short because of his rivalry with Sorensen. Since joining the Kennedy campaign staff, Goodwin had been "the only speechwriter Kennedy ever found who could rival Sorensen, a fact that did nothing to endear him to Sorensen," with whom Goodwin continuously feuded and who eventually undermined Goodwin. Lasting only eight months in the State Department, Goodwin combined "considerable brashness" with his considerable brilliance, rendering "a fate unique in White House history: at the age of twenty-nine he was a key Administration policy-maker; at thirty, as far as White House power was concerned, he was a has-been."[149] Nevertheless, in 1964, Goodwin returned to White House prominence during the Johnson administration and, into the 1960s, was a key speechwriter "for, successively, Sargent Shriver, Lyndon Johnson, Robert Kennedy, and Eugene McCarthy."[150] By 1968, Goodwin was regarded as "probably the best speechwriter in America today."[151]

A few of Frankfurter's law clerks also came from Brahmin families, including Elliot Richardson, possibly the clerk to whom he was closest next to

Alexander Bickel. Descended from Pilgrim settlers, Richardson had clerked for Learned Hand before joining Frankfurter in 1948. He had impressed the justice "with his insistence on taking an hour each morning during his Supreme Court clerkship to read Shakespeare." The following year, with Frankfurter's enthusiastic recommendation, Richardson was offered a job as special assistant to the new secretary of state, Dean Acheson. Frankfurter would subsequently endorse Richardson for the presidency of Harvard University when he was just thirty-three, although he would not be ultimately chosen.[152] Richardson would later become the only presidential appointee in American history, other than Henry Stimson, to serve in four separate cabinet posts — as secretary of health, education, and welfare; defense; commerce; and as attorney general.

Two brothers to turn down clerkship offers with Frankfurter were McGeorge and William Bundy, the sons of Frankfurter's friend Harvey Hollister Bundy. What made the offer to McGeorge Bundy both unique and surprising was that the future Harvard dean and special assistant on national security affairs to Presidents Kennedy and Johnson — one of the "best and the brightest" policymakers in Washington during the 1960s and, for better or worse, an architect of the Vietnam War — had never attended law school.

The stories of McGeorge Bundy's brilliance were legendary. Learned Hand considered him "the brightest man in America."[153] After entering the elite Dexter School, one class behind John Kennedy, and prepping at Groton, he graduated first in his class and became the first freshman ever at Yale to have received three perfect scores on his college entrance exams.[154] At Yale, where he majored in mathematics, wrote a column for the *Yale Daily News*, and graduated Phi Beta Kappa, he was secretary of the Yale Political Union and elected to the school's prestigious Skull and Bones secret society, as had been his father and Henry Stimson before him. After declining an offer to attend Harvard Law School, Bundy joined Harvard's Society of Junior Fellows, "the elite Harvard institution, modeled after Oxford's All Soul Society," that had been founded in 1933 by his great-uncle A. Lawrence Lowell, who endowed it with $1.5 million of his considerable fortune.[155] While stationed in London as a U.S. Army officer during World War II, he was a regular guest at Harold Laski's salon, where British intellectuals gathered to debate politics and discuss war news. Frankfurter's friend Laski, along with being a London School of Economics professor, was a socialist and leader of England's Labor Party who also often wrote speeches for the U.S ambassador.[156] While in Britain, Bundy was an occasional dinner guest at the Cliveden estate of the American-born Lady Nancy Astor, the first woman to serve in the British House of Commons. Bundy's brother, William, would later joke that McGeorge, while stationed in London, "went to Harold Laski's soirees on Tuesday night and Lady Astor's on the weekend. It was a balanced ticket."[157]

In 1946, at age twenty-seven and once again a Harvard junior fellow, Bundy began helping Henry Stimson write his memoirs, *On Active Service in Peace and War*, which acknowledged Bundy as a coauthor. For close to two years, as Bundy often corresponded with Frankfurter concerning the Stimson memoirs, and Frankfurter read and edited portions of the manuscript, Frankfurter began to consult Bundy on all sorts of issues, including some of the cases before his court. In September 1947, with the Stimson memoirs completed, Frankfurter made Bundy the "unexpected offer" to serve as his clerk.[158] At first enticed, including by the opportunity to follow in the footsteps of his father, who had clerked for Justice Holmes in 1915, Bundy declined after weeks of hesitation. Following nearly two years as Stimson's assistant, Bundy wrote, "It would be wrong for me to take another job as personal assistant to anyone. By next Spring it will be time for me to go to work on my own, awhile at least."[159]

In 1948, with Frankfurter's recommendation, Bundy was appointed to a junior faculty position in Harvard's Government Department. From there, his rise was meteoric. In 1951, he was given tenure as an associate professor—not only lacking a PhD but also having never taken a single undergraduate- or graduate-level course in government. In 1953, having narrowly missed becoming Harvard's president, he was appointed dean of faculty, the school's number-two position, which he held until 1961, when he became President Kennedy's special assistant for national security affairs.

Disappointed that McGeorge had declined his offer, Frankfurter was "determined" to get at least one Bundy to clerk for him, so he offered a post to McGeorge's older brother, William, a Harvard Law graduate about to begin working at the Washington law firm Covington and Burling. Married to Dean Acheson's daughter Mary, he was encouraged by Acheson and Harvey Bundy to accept the offer but turned it down, later offering the excuse that "I was thirty years old, and I decided it was time for me to make a living."[160]

McGeorge and William Bundy were among the very few ambitious young men to turn down a Frankfurter clerkship offer. It is perhaps ironic that years later, Frankfurter refused to hire as his clerk an especially well-credentialed Harvard Law School graduate and law review editor, Ruth Bader Ginsburg. In 1960, the Harvard Law professor Albert Sacks, who had clerked for Frankfurter during the 1940s and proposed the lion's share of the jurist's Harvard-educated clerks,[161] proposed that Frankfurter hire Ginsburg, "one of his star pupils."[162] Frankfurter refused to even interview her because, as he acknowledged, "he was not yet prepared to hire a woman."[163] Indeed, women had not yet been admitted as students during Frankfurter's years at Harvard, an issue that had "deeply divided" the faculty and administration for decades.[164] On October 11, 1949, Dean Erwin Griswold finally announced the decision to admit women to the law school. But while women began arriving on campus in the early 1950s, "during the era of Dean Griswold, who ruled Harvard Law School with an iron grip from 1946 to 1967, when he left for Washington to become President Lyndon Johnson's Solicitor General, women were accepted . . . in token numbers."[165] When Ginsburg entered Harvard in 1956, she was one of only nine women in a class of more than five hundred.[166] No doubt, when Albert Sacks asked Frankfurter to interview Ginsburg for a clerk position, the justice recognized her accomplishments, including her number-one rank in her law school class.

A few years later, on April 5, 1962, while working at his Supreme Court desk, Frankfurter had a stroke. Several others followed, leaving his speech impaired and his left arm and leg paralyzed. On July 26, two weeks after Frankfurter left the hospital,[167] Dean Acheson arranged for President Kennedy to visit the justice in the garden of his Georgetown home. Kennedy had come, he told the justice, "to seek Felix Frankfurter's advice on the general trend of affairs."[168] And for forty-five minutes, as Kennedy listened, "the ailing, aged Felix Frankfurter was once again advisor to presidents."[169] On August 22, Frankfurter wrote to a friend: "You will want to know that I have never worked harder at anything in my life than I have at the task of recovery."[170] With his general health worsening, though, such work was insufficient. Despite physical therapy, he was not improving. Reluctantly, on August 28, 1962, Frankfurter wrote to Kennedy notifying him of his retirement from the Supreme Court. His letter explained, "To retain my seat on the basis of a diminished work schedule would not comport with my own philosophy or with the demands of the business of the Court."[171]

The following day, Kennedy announced that he was appointing his secretary of labor, Arthur J. Goldberg, to succeed Frankfurter and fill the Holmes-Cardozo-Frankfurter court seat. Frankfurter was disappointed in Kennedy's choice, as he confided to Alexander Bickel, having hoped the president would appoint his former student Paul Freund, a Harvard legal scholar who, unlike Arthur Goldberg, was also committed to Frankfurter's philosophy of judicial restraint.[172] When the liberal Goldberg took Frankfurter's seat, he ensured Chief Justice Warren "a dependable fifth vote" on civil liberties and other cases dear to the Warren court's liberal agenda.

The following year, Kennedy notified Frankfurter that he was to receive the Medal of Freedom, the most prestigious U.S. civilian honor. Frankfurter replied to the president that it is "only by trying to convey to you my feelings about America and how they came to be almost religious feelings in their nature that I can tell you how deeply I feel about the honor that you have bestowed on me."[173]

During his remaining three years, both Frankfurter and his wife, Marion, were confined to wheelchairs, and Frankfurter "spent more time with Marion than had been possible for many years."[174] Despite his physical limitations, Frankfurter "remained an animated conversationalist, always eager to hear the latest political or legal gossip."[175] Acheson visited frequently, as did many of his former clerks. When Kennedy was assassinated, Frankfurter attended the funeral in his wheelchair.

On February 21, 1965, at age eighty-two, Justice Frankfurter was stricken again and taken to George Washington University Hospital. A few minutes after five o'clock the next afternoon, which was George Washington's birthday, "Frankfurter turned to an aide who had worked for him since he joined the Court and said: 'I hope I don't spoil your Washington's birthday.'"[176] Felix Frankfurter then turned his head and died.

A simple and private memorial service was held in the Frankfurters' Washington apartment.[177] The one hundred attendees included all the sitting Supreme Court justices, except William Douglas, and President Lyndon Johnson. Paul Freund, a Frankfurter protégé and close friend who had also been Brandeis's law clerk, read the same passage from Paul Bunyan's *The Pilgrim's Progress* that Frankfurter had read at Brandeis's funeral service, on the death of Mr. Valiant-for-truth: "My sword I give to him that shall succeed me in my pilgrimage, and my courage and skill to him that can get it. My marks and scars I carry with me, to be a witness for me that I have fought his battles who now will be my rewarder."[178]

The last person to speak was Frankfurter's former law clerk Louis Henkin, who recited in Hebrew the traditional mourner's Kaddish.[179] Frankfurter, "who had left the synagogue at fifteen and never returned," had not wanted a rabbi to officiate but had specifically requested that Henkin speak.[180] "Do you know why I want him"? Frankfurter had asked his close friend the playwright Garson Kanin, whom Frankfurter had asked to make the arrangements for the memorial service. "No," Kanin replied. "Because he is my only close personal friend who is also a practicing, Orthodox Jew. He knows Hebrew perfectly and will know exactly what to say. I came into this world a Jew and although I did not live my life entirely as a Jew, I think it is fitting that I should leave as a Jew."[181] When Henkin rose to recite the Kaddish, which begins "May His great Name be blessed forever and to all eternity," he explained to those assembled that "it is not a lamentation but a *magnificat* which has bound generations of Jews to each other."[182]

Frankfurter's Enigmatic Legacy

Felix Frankfurter was one of the twentieth century's most influential jurists. As a Harvard law professor for twenty-five years, he trained a generation of lawyers, judges, legal scholars, and public servants—Dean Acheson, Henry Friendly, Paul Freund, Louis Henkin, Charles Wyzanski Jr., James Landis, Benjamin Cohen, Joseph Rauh Jr., David Riesman, Fred Graham, Richard Goodwin, Elliot Richardson, Archibald MacLeish, Charles Houston, William Hastie, Louis Jaffe, Thomas Corcoran, and Harry Shulman among them —who would make enduring contributions to academia and American public life. As a Supreme Court justice for twenty-three years—the third longest tenure of the FDR appointees, behind Justices Black (1937–1971) and Douglas (1939–1975)—he mentored an extraordinary group of law clerks, who, in their later academic, judicial, and government positions, would continue "to spread his influence so that it remains almost as potent today as it did in his lifetime."[183] His clerks included a future *Washington Post* publisher, a librarian of Congress, a touted presidential speechwriter, a Securities and Exchange Commission chairman, the attorney general and lieutenant governor of Massachusetts, an ambassador to England, cabinet members in the Nixon and Ford administrations during the 1970s, and deans of Harvard, Yale, and Columbia Law Schools during the 1980s.

Despite occupying the "scholar's seat" on the court previously held by Holmes and Cardozo, Frankfurter, as we saw, while at Harvard achieved more success in his popular than his academic writings. To be sure, he lectured frequently at academic institutions, with these lectures published, most notably, as *The Public and Its Government*, based on his Dodge Lectures at Yale Law School, *The Commerce Clause under Marshall, Taney and Waite*, and *Mr. Justice Holmes and the Supreme Court*, with the last based on three Harvard lectures he delivered in 1938. He also published *The Business of the Supreme*

Court: A Study in the Federal Judicial System, coauthored with his student James Landis. His best known book remains undoubtedly *The Case of Sacco and Vanzetti*, the expanded version of his *Atlantic Monthly* defense of the convicted anarchists. However, Frankfurter never produced an enduring classic of legal scholarship comparable to Holmes's *The Common Law* or Cardozo's *The Judicial Process*. Nor did he achieve the "scholar on the bench" stature enjoyed by Holmes and Cardozo. In his legal scholarship, Frankfurter did, however, exceed the accomplishments of Brandeis, whose only lasting work of legal scholarship was his 1891 *Harvard Law Review* article "The Right to Privacy," coauthored with his law partner Samuel Warren.

Yet Frankfurter contributed to legal scholarship in other ways, such as by inspiring his former students and clerks to write judicial biographies as well as studies of the Supreme Court. Even when he was old and ill, just before retiring, Frankfurter "was occupied about what history would record about him and . . . his legacy" and sought also to choose biographers to chronicle the lives of the great jurists he had known.[184] He selected Andrew Kaufman for Cardozo, Philip Kurland for Robert Jackson, Mark de Wolfe Howe for Holmes, and Alexander Bickel for himself, although Bickel's untimely death prevented him from writing the great judicial biography of his mentor that Frankfurter had hoped for. During the 1960s, as we saw, Bickel became, at Frankfurter's urging, one of the Warren court's most thoughtful critics, writing several books on the topic. Another former student, Paul Freund, also wrote scholarly studies of the Supreme Court inspired by Frankfurter. When Andrew Kaufman, who had clerked for Frankfurter during the 1955 and 1956 court terms, published his biography of Cardozo in 1998, he recalled that Frankfurter had first "suggested in the Winter of 1957 that I write this book." Forty-one years after the suggestion, he noted gratefully that "this must surely be the last book that owes its beginning to Felix Frankfurter."[185] Kaufman's book on Cardozo, one of our era's great judicial biographies, might thus be considered a part of Frankfurter's legacy.

On January 5, 1939, the day following the announcement of Frankfurter's Supreme Court appointment, a group of New Dealers had met in the office of Interior Secretary Harold Ickes to toast the occasion.[186] Attorney General Frank Murphy came, as did Harry Hopkins from the White House and then Securities and Exchange Commission chairman William O. Douglas. Tommy Corcoran, then the president's special assistant, brought champagne, and all of them agreed with Ickes's characterization of the nomination as "the most significant and worthwhile thing the President had done."[187]

Demonstrating the gleeful sentiments on the left, the *Nation* exulted, "Frankfurter's whole life has been a preparation for the Supreme Court. No other appointee in our history has gone to the Court so fully prepared for its great tasks."[188] The poet and nominee's friend Archibald MacLeish proclaimed that "Frankfurter's great devotion to civil liberties, as evidenced over the previous twenty years, would be the hallmark of his tenure on the bench."[189] Frankfurter's liberal admirers concurred happily with this prediction, believing the jurist's Supreme Court decisions and legacy would reflect this devotion to civil liberties.

An entire book has been written about the "enigma" of Felix Frankfurter, and today, more than fifty years after his retirement, much of the enigma remains.[190] As this chapter has shown, his longtime commitment to civil liberties did not translate into a liberal judicial philosophy on the high court.[191] Instead, the Sacco and Vanzetti champion became the court's most persistent proponent of judicial restraint, and its most conservative justice, during the 1940s and 1950s. His opinions in the flag salute and *Schneiderman* cases, in the early 1940s, began his transformation, one that made many of his former allies into opponents and sometimes villifiers. Into the 1950s and beyond, he "became the liberals' target rather than their hero."[192] Frankfurter's famous dissent urging judicial restraint in the voting rights case of *Baker v. Carr*— written shortly before his retirement—"helped consolidate his reputation" as a judicial conservative.[193] The succeeding generation of liberals who clerked in the Warren court, as well as the liberal generation after it, would view Frankfurter's passionate advocacy of judicial restraint, as reflected in his *Baker v. Carr* position, as anathema. This may explain the diminishing attention given over time to such dissents, as compared to those of Holmes and Brandeis.[194] Indeed, today some of Frankfurter's more conservative opinions "are all but ignored by both the courts and academia."[195] This may also explain why, as Joseph P. Lash has noted, "there are Frankfurter admirers who believe that Frankfurter's influence on constitutional law was greater before he went on the Bench than after," and that his legal writings culminating in his 1938 book, *Mr. Justice Holmes and the Supreme Court*, "are of more lasting interest than the aggregate of his judicial opinions."[196] "History," as one of his biographers has noted, "has not been kind to Felix Frankfurter."[197]

Frankfurter's critics "accused him of betraying an earlier progressive faith and capitulating to the forces of reaction."[198] Some called him "an intellectual whore" who cultivated those in power while ignoring the weak; "or a hypocrite, who referred to the Court as 'a monastery,' but continued his political machinations off the bench."[199] His admirers, some of them long-standing, some newfound, praised Frankfurter's "devotion to judicial restraint" and his willingness to stand against the prevailing fashions of the liberal legal academy.[200] "No judge, not even Brandeis," wrote Alexander Bickel, "has faced the essential judicial task with greater valor or . . . greater rectitude."[201] On Frankfurter's retirement, Judge Learned Hand called him "the most important single figure in our whole judicial system."[202] Reinhold Niebuhr, during the 1960s as earlier, thought of Frankfurter "as the most intelligent person he had ever met."[203] On the day after he nominated Warren E. Burger to be the Supreme Court's chief justice, President Richard Nixon "asserted that in filling vacancies on the high court he would look for those who could follow in the judicial tradition of the late Mr. Justice Felix Frankfurter," a tradition still revered by many conservative jurists, legal scholars, and politicians.[204] Even some liberal scholars and jurists, such as Ronald Dworkin, who disagreed with Frankfurter on a host of issues, continued to admire Frankfurter's Supreme Court legacy. Indeed, Dworkin, who had clerked for Learned Hand before beginning his distinguished academic career at Oxford, Yale, and NYU, and who authored such liberal tomes as *Taking Rights Seriously* and *Law's Empire*, would later cite one of his main regrets as having turned down a clerkship offer with Frankfurter.[205] A former Frankfurter clerk, Philip Kurland, who taught at the University of Chicago Law School, remarked: "Whether one likes what Frankfurter did as a Justice of the Supreme Court or not—and there are many on both sides of that question—the fact remains that he was the latest of the great keepers of the legend: a legend of a nonpartisan Supreme Court dedicated to the maintenance of a government of laws founded on reason and based on a faith in democracy."[206]

Moreover, as both his admirers and most vocal liberal critics would agree, one of Frankfurter's greatest achievements on the Supreme Court was in bringing together unanimous backing in *Brown v. Board of Education* to overturn the fifty-eight-year school segregation precedent set by *Plessy v. Ferguson*.[207] This role in changing "the constitutional universe" is one of his foremost contributions to U.S. constitutional law and a central part of his judicial legacy.[208]

As for Frankfurter's acrimonious relationship with most of his judicial colleagues, throughout much of the 1940s and 1950s, as noted, he feuded with liberals such as Hugo Black and William Douglas, whose jurisprudence he attacked as "shoddy," "result-oriented," and "demagogic."[209] He reserved his greatest animosity for Douglas, "whose putative political ambitions during the forties"—Douglas actively pursued a possible Democratic candidacy for vice president in 1944 and for vice president *and* president in 1948—"became an obsessive concern."[210] Frankfurter's diaries and correspondence are replete with comments critical of Douglas's political "ambitions."[211] While Frankfurter blatantly engaged in his own extensive extrajudicial activities regarding presidential appointments, he "always strongly disapproved of extrajudicial ambitions" by judges using the court as a stepping-stone to elective political office.[212] Indeed, no one denounced more fervently than Frankfurter "the extrajudicial activities of his colleagues," especially Douglas, "while engaging furiously in off-the-bench politics and policy-making."[213] To his clerk Philip Elman, Frankfurter condemned Douglas as "an absolute cynic who didn't believe in anything" and who was using the court as "a political launching pad."[214] He referred derisively to Black, Douglas, and Frank Murphy as "the Axis" and once counted Douglas as one of the "two completely evil men I have ever met."[215] Douglas, "needless to say, cared just as little for Frankfurter," as demonstrated by his nonattendance at his funeral.[216]

The liberal justices who allied themselves with Black and Douglas—first Murphy and, eventually, Earl Warren and William Brennan in the 1950s —"were subjected by Frankfurter to the same harsh judgment and treatment."[217] By the late 1950s and early 1960s, Frankfurter was likewise referring to Brennan as "shoddy." Although initially Frankfurter had high expectations for Earl Warren, who was nominated by Eisenhower in 1953, "the Chief Justice's liberalism proved a major disappointment and, by 1957, Frankfurter was referring to Warren's work as 'dishonest nonsense.'"[218] The lone close associate of Frankfurter was Robert Jackson, with whom he shared "a common ideological outlook, and a common antipathy toward Douglas."[219]

Enigma also characterized Frankfurter's discord with other justices. Frankfurter was "a person of paradox and contradiction, someone who frequently acted . . . in ways that were not always consistent."[220] To those he did not perceive as enemies, Frankfurter "was a warm and charming companion, a helpful and devoted friend," to whom he further endeared himself through the "generous application of flattery."[221] Prior to his high court appointment, he was always adept at flattering those in power, as well as family, friends, and colleagues who relished his devotion. He flattered Henry Morgenthau Sr. on their trip to Turkey, although he personally disliked him; he flattered Stimson, Holmes, and Brandeis; he flattered his wife, Marion, when she suffered bouts of depression; he flattered his colleagues at Harvard, even when he disagreed with them; and, above all, he incessantly flattered FDR.[222] As Max Freedman, the editor of the Roosevelt-Frankfurter correspondence, has concluded, Frankfurter was "an artist in adulation" who "laid on the flattery with a trowel." He engaged in sycophancy with Roosevelt just as he had done with Justice Holmes, whose "awing majesty and wonder" had captivated Frankfurter years earlier.[223] Yet he seemed unable or unwilling to similarly flatter his liberal judicial colleagues, when doing so would have helped further collegiality on the court. While he was "warm, charming, and supportive with his law clerks, he could be rude, abrasive, and petty with his brethren on the Court."[224] The publication of his court diaries and correspondence in the 1970s "revealed a man of enormous insecurities, one frequently consumed and crippled by anger, vanity and self-pity"[225] and "an obsessive concern with the motives of his judicial opponents mixed with high pitched anger at their behavior and doctrines."[226] Apart from Justice James McReynolds, an antisemite and a racist, "it is difficult to recollect a member of the Court who had worse personal relations with his colleagues."[227] It may well be that "one of the great tragedies of Frankfurter's career is that a man renowned for his talents in personal relations, who knew so well the high value the Justices placed on careful collegiality," could fail to establish cordial interpersonal relationships with his colleagues on the court.[228]

Enigmatic also was Frankfurter's relationship with Harvard's President A. Lawrence Lowell, "a descendent of two of Boston's first families, [who] was the archetypical Brahmin [and] represented to Frankfurter the snobbery of the Boston aristocracy—an aristocracy to which Frankfurter knew he could never really belong."[229] The antipathy Frankfurter felt toward Lowell, an antisemite who had opposed Brandeis's Supreme Court appointment and tried to impose a Jewish admissions quota at Harvard, highlighted his ultimate ambivalence about the Protestant establishment.[230] While Frankfurter openly courted select members of the Protestant elite, such as Stimson, Holmes, FDR, Acheson, and Harvey Bundy, he "lashed out at others, like Lowell, on issues that clearly marked him as an outsider."[231] Lowell's support for Frankfurter's high court nomination marked an interesting twist in the narrative.

His Jewish legacy, both before and after his Supreme Court tenure, is enigmatic as well. Fresh out of Harvard Law, he applied only to Protestant firms, most of which rejected him, while eschewing Jewish firms that would have happily hired him. Soon after joining Hornblower, Byrne, Miller, and Potter, when "a senior partner suggested that he might rise faster there if he anglicized his Jewish-sounding name," Frankfurter "politely but firmly refused," recalling his mother's admonition to "always hold yourself dear."[232] Although no longer a practicing Jew, "Frankfurter refused to deny his Jewishness at Hornblower or anywhere else."[233] As a high court justice, Frankfurter "expressed anger when told that one of his former Jewish students, faced with the same decision, had chosen to do otherwise."[234] To the surprise of many, Frankfurter, a self-described agnostic married to a Protestant minister's daughter, and someone who never worshiped in a synagogue as an adult, asked that the Kaddish be recited at his funeral. For the former justice, this recitation "was Frankfurter's link with the heritage of his birth."[235]

On reflection, Frankfurter's short-lived leadership in the Zionist movement, from 1917 to 1921, had puzzling components too. Frankfurter was never really an ardent Zionist, as were Judge Julian Mack and Rabbi Stephen Wise.[236] He visited Palestine only once, "reluctantly, in 1934, while spending a sabbatical year in Oxford, and so was already halfway there."[237] The Arab riots of 1929, "which prompted the first in a series of British efforts to undercut the Balfour Declaration by restricting Jewish immigration and land purchases in Palestine, momentarily rekindled Frankfurter's interest."[238] But he remained reluctant to publicly defend Zionism, and for the most part confined his later movement-related work to defending the disputed authenticity of Emir Feisal's 1919 letter to him welcoming the Zionists to Palestine.[239] Frankfurter had followed Brandeis into the Zionist leadership more out of fealty to Brandeis than devotion to the Zionist cause.[240] As David Ben-Gurion noted, Zionism "was only a desultory, secondary undertaking, not his heart's core."[241] What has been said of Benjamin Cohen, Frankfurter's deputy legal adviser to the Zionist delegation in Paris, could be said of Frankfurter as well: "Zionism was less a cause than an assignment, and while he pursued that assignment with characteristic effort and energy, his involvement was more often in the service of other people's dreams than of his own."[242]

More remarkable insofar as his Jewish legacy is concerned was his virtual silence on saving Jewish lives during World War II, as compared to his intense pressuring of FDR about judicial appointments such as those of Learned Hand and Charles Wyzanski Jr. Frankfurter's failure to intercede personally with Roosevelt to rescue his dear uncle Solomon in Vienna is similarly perplexing. Troubling and seemingly inexplicable, finally, was his rude dismissal of Jan Karski after their 1943 meeting in Washington, and his subsequent failure to discuss the horrific details of the Final Solution disclosed in Karski's report with White House or War Department officials.

Tens of thousands of Jewish lives might have been saved had U.S. fighters bombed the Auschwitz killing infrastructure or rail lines, yet Frankfurter did not exert his influence to override Assistant War Secretary John McCloy's veto of the proposal. Unlike Treasury Secretary Henry Morgenthau Jr., whom Frankfurter jealously dismissed as a "stupid bootlick" undeserving of his high post, Frankfurter never once urged FDR to attack the death camp, a claim lamentably reinforced by the lack of any evidence of a letter or conversation with McCloy or War Secretary Stimson on the subject. Frankfurter was the only one of FDR's Jewish advisers or appointees who enjoyed Stimson and McCloy's complete trust and friendship. Frankfurter's Jewish legacy must be based, at least in part, on this failing—which should stand as a serious moral indictment. Frankfurter must share part of McCloy and Stimson's blame in the matter.

Frankfurter hired more Jewish clerks than any previous Supreme Court justice, continuing the precedent begun by Brandeis. In hiring eighteen Jewish clerks, and helping them find prestigious employment in an era when Jewish lawyers still faced widespread discrimination, Frankfurter did much to promote Jewish advancement within the American legal profession. He also set a precedent by becoming the first Supreme Court justice to appoint an African American clerk. The fact that Frankfurter refused to consider appointing the first Jewish woman clerk, Ruth Bader Ginsburg, must regrettably remain on the minus side of his ledger. Hiring Ginsburg, as a side bonus, would have made Frankfurter the first Jewish Supreme Court justice for whom a law clerk went on to serve on the high court.

At Harvard Law School, an endowed chair was named in Frankfurter's honor, making him the first Jewish justice to enjoy this distinction—although it was surely a lesser one than the university and law school named for Brandeis and the law school named for Cardozo. Occupants of this chair have included such high-profile attorneys as Alan Dershowitz and Cass Sunstein, who served most recently as a top adviser in the Obama White House. A chapter of the Jewish teen group Aleph Zadik Aleph (AZA) is also named for Frankfurter.

As for Frankfurter's extrajudicial activities, which extended even beyond those of Brandeis, these have garnered recent attention from scholars and journalists. Despite previous high court justices engaging in such political activities, "Frankfurter's extrajudicial efforts were unusual in scope and volume."[243] This, too, must remain a part of the jurist's legacy. Nor can it be ignored that, by engaging in such extrajudicial activity, Frankfurter continued a precedent that future Jewish Supreme Court justices, most notably Abe Fortas, would follow.

7

ARTHUR J. GOLDBERG

A Promising Tenure Cut Short

AT AN OCTOBER 1969 White House reception for Israeli prime minister Golda Meir, Arthur Goldberg, then a former Supreme Court justice, told a reporter, "I believe I can beat Goodell next year." He was referring to the liberal New York Republican senator Charles E. Goodell, who had been appointed to serve out Robert F. Kennedy's Senate term following his assassination. "Did I hear you correctly, Mr. Justice," asked the reporter. "Are you running for the Senate in New York next year?" "Well," Goldberg said, smiling, "when I make that decision, I will announce it to the press."[1] Goodell, however, was a vocal Vietnam War critic, as was Goldberg, who the previous year had resigned his post as Lyndon Johnson's ambassador to the UN over his war opposition. While contemplating a candidacy, Goldberg came to realize that not enough separated his political views from those of Goodell to justify running, and that an attempt would likely result in defeat.

Although deciding against the Senate challenge, Goldberg was generally understood to have a career in New York Democratic politics if he wanted one. Shortly after resigning his UN ambassadorship, Goldberg had accepted a lucrative senior partnership in the Park Avenue law firm Paul, Weiss, Rifkind, Wharton, and Garrison, whose managing partner, former Federal District Court judge Simon H. Rifkind, was a New York Democratic Party leader with close ties to every president since FDR. Goldberg thus joined a firm that included many prominent Democrats, including former JFK speechwriter Ted Sorensen, former LBJ attorney general Ramsey Clark, and Morris B. Abram, the Georgia-born Rhodes Scholar who had recently served as president of Brandeis University and had also contemplated a race for Goodell's New York Senate seat. At various times during Goldberg's tenure at the firm, at least one and up to four of its members—Goldberg, Sorensen, Abram, and

Clark—were either running for elective office or making known their possible interest in doing so. No other New York law firm in recent years, not even President Richard Nixon's former Wall Street firm, "could match Judge Rifkind's collection of political availables."[2]

On March 19, 1970, Arthur Goldberg announced his candidacy for governor of New York against Nelson Rockefeller, a popular liberal Republican who was seeking an unprecedented fourth term.[3] To the surprise of Goldberg's many admirers, his campaign was a disaster. From the day of his announcement, he was viewed—and portrayed by the press—as a carpetbagger who had come to New York City following his UN ambassadorial appointment in 1965 but had little understanding of the Empire State and its many problems. Unlike the charismatic Rockefeller, Goldberg was noticeably unaccustomed to the rough-and-tumble world of electoral politics. He lacked Rockefeller's personal warmth and informality and seemed ill at ease on the campaign trail. Also lacking Rockefeller's oratorical skills, the long-winded Goldberg spoke in a nasal monotone that left his audiences uninspired. As his former Supreme Court law clerk Alan Dershowitz, who helped Goldberg in his campaign, would recall, Goldberg was stiff as a campaigner, "and not particularly knowledgeable about New York. Once while eating a knish at Yonah Schimmel's on Houston Street on the Lower East Side of Manhattan, he told the assembled press how pleased he was to be in Brooklyn."[4] Moreover, Goldberg's "judicial" demeanor put off voters: always mindful of his former Supreme Court office, "Mr. Justice Goldberg," as he was all-too-often introduced, came across to many voters as pompous, vain, and dull.[5]

Goldberg's landslide defeat in November by 700,000 votes was therefore no surprise. The margin of victory was the largest of Rockefeller's four elections. More dispiriting for Goldberg, the loss marked an inglorious departure from public life for one of twentieth-century America's great success stories.

Goldberg had pulled himself up from the poverty of Chicago's immigrant West Side, becoming the country's preeminent labor lawyer and the AFL-CIO labor organization's chief counsel. He also served as a much-respected labor secretary in the Kennedy administration, Felix Frankfurter's successor as the fourth Jewish justice on the Supreme Court, and briefly, thereafter, as President Johnson's UN ambassador.

From Maxwell Street to Camelot: Goldberg's Rise

The youngest of eleven children, Arthur Joseph Goldberg was born on August 8, 1908, in a tenement in Chicago's Maxwell Street slum, which was populated mostly by Irish and Jewish immigrants. Other Jewish luminaries, and contemporaries of Goldberg, to come out of the neighborhood included the clarinetist Benny Goodman; the heavyweight boxer "Kingfish" Levinsky, whose family owned Maxwell Street's biggest fishmonger and who once lost a bout to heavyweight champion Joe Louis; and the Chicago political boss Jacob Arvey, whose Russian-immigrant father had been a peddler.[6] A childhood friend of Goldberg's, also born in 1908, was the boxer Jackie Fields (formerly Finkelstein), whose father owned a kosher butcher shop on Maxwell Street and who, in the 1924 Paris Olympics, made history as the youngest boxer, at age sixteen, to win an Olympic gold medal.[7]

Not far from the Goldberg family home was Hull House, the pioneering social settlement center founded by Jane Addams, which was central in educating and Americanizing the East European Jewish immigrant children of Maxwell Street. The young Goldberg himself attended classes and lectures at Hull House, as did his childhood friend Benny Goodman.[8]

An educated man who had served as town clerk in the Russian village of Zhinkov, near Kiev, before immigrating to America in the 1890s, Joseph Goldberg, Arthur's father, eked out a living delivering produce to the shops and hotels on Chicago's West Side. Arthur would later remember riding with his father as a boy as he delivered fruit and vegetables by horse-and-cart to Maxwell Street's open-air pushcart market.[9]

When his father died at age fifty-one, Arthur, then just eight, began working part-time jobs, while attending school, to help support his family. These jobs included wrapping fish, selling shoes, and working as a library page. But a favorite job was at the Chicago Cubs' Wrigley Field, where during the Prohibition years, Goldberg "carried a large coffee urn strapped to his back and sold cups of it, rather than the traditional beer, to fans."[10] While working at Wrigley, Goldberg developed a lifelong love for baseball, and especially for his hometown Cubs.

Goldberg completed his high school studies at age fifteen, the first member of his family to graduate from high school, and then took night classes at a junior college and DePaul University. During his last year in high school, he attended the sensational Chicago murder trial of the two wealthy Chicagoans Nathan Leopold and Richard Loeb, and was so impressed with their passionate defense by the illustrious Clarence Darrow, who managed to spare his young clients the death penalty, that he became determined to be a lawyer himself.[11]

In 1926, Goldberg began his legal studies at Northwestern University. While working part-time at construction jobs to support himself, Goldberg still managed to graduate first in his class in 1929 and was elected editor-in-chief of the *Northwestern Law Review*. In his brilliant law school career, Goldberg followed in the footsteps of Louis Brandeis, one of his judicial heroes. Whereas fifty years earlier Brandeis had graduated with the highest academic record ever at Harvard Law School, Goldberg did the same at Northwestern. The law school's dean, John Henry Wigmore, who with Julian Mack had, years earlier, helped found the *Harvard Law Review*, was so impressed with Goldberg that he selected him as his assistant in preparing the third edition of Wigmore's classic treatise on evidence, which still remains the preeminent legal textbook in that field.[12]

Upon graduation, Goldberg began practicing law with the Chicago Jewish firm Pritzker and Pritzker, founded by the German-Jewish family that would later own the Hyatt hotel chain. Despite his standout law school record, Goldberg was automatically barred from Chicago's blue chip firms, dominated by the city's Protestant elite, which would not open their doors to Jewish attorneys until the 1950s. Because of the prevailing antisemitism in the legal profession in Chicago, as in other cities, Goldberg could not hope to gain employment at a firm such as Cutting, Moore and Sidley, where three years earlier Adlai Stevenson had begun work after graduating from Northwestern.[13] Goldberg's experience here echoed that of Felix Frankfurter, who was turned away from Wall Street's big gentile firms. Goldberg, unlike Frankfurter, however, was willing to cut his teeth at a Jewish firm. During the 1930s, two of the firm's partners, Abraham and Jack Pritzker, would leave law practice to devote themselves to real estate, with the resulting empire including not only the Hyatt hotel chain but also the Royal Caribbean cruise lines. Abraham Pritzker's granddaughter Penny Pritzker would be appointed commerce secretary by President Barack Obama in 2013.

As it turned out, Goldberg did not stay at Pritzker and Pritzker for very long, despite the promise of high income and a possible future partnership. As the Depression worsened, as Goldberg would later explain, much of his legal work involved mortgage foreclosures and he could not "in good conscience continue to earn his living by foreclosing on other people's property."[14] Leaving the firm in 1933, he opened a small office where, while also working for other attorneys, he began devoting much of his own practice to the new field of labor law. During these Depression years, a sense of mission infused the trade union movement and young, idealistic attorneys such as Goldberg specialized in this field.[15] Goldberg would later credit his junior college English teacher, Lillian Herstein, who was also an executive board member with the American Federation of Labor's Chicago branch, with first awakening his interest in labor issues and the labor movement.[16]

Goldberg was also encouraged in this transition by his wife, Dorothy Kurgans, an artist and educator whom he had married in 1931. A liberal idealist like her husband, she supported his move into this less lucrative field of law. When the Depression closed the Chicago public schools' art departments, where she had worked, Dorothy Goldberg became a social caseworker in the steel mill area of South Chicago. For several years in the 1930s, Arthur and Dorothy struggled to make ends meet.[17]

Goldberg first gained attention in the labor law field as the attorney for the Chicago Newspaper Guild in its much-publicized 1938 strike against the Chicago Hearst papers, the *Evening American* and the *Herald-Examiner*, sparked by a dispute over the firing of several of the newspapers' employees. Shortly after the strike began, the *Evening American*'s city editor and strike leader asked Goldberg to represent the Newspaper Guild. For the next eight months, Goldberg was in court almost daily representing the picketers, eventually persuading William Randolph Hearst and his newspapers' publishers to recognize the union.[18]

During World War II, Goldberg was appointed head of the European Labor Division of the Office of Strategic Services (the predecessor of the CIA) and helped establish secret operations with antifascist labor groups behind Nazi lines. After serving with distinction in OSS posts during the war, Goldberg continued immersing himself in the rapidly growing, and better-paid, field of labor law. During the late 1940s and 1950s, while representing the country's major labor unions and earning a reputation as the country's top labor lawyer, Goldberg himself helped establish labor law as a recognized field of specialization.[19] Goldberg argued some of the most important labor cases before the Supreme Court, including the famous steel-seizure case of 1952, *Youngstown Steel and Tube Co. v. Sawyer*. Here, Goldberg, as general counsel for the United Steelworkers of America, challenged President Truman's authority to take control over the entire steel industry in response to a strike.[20] The Supreme Court upheld Goldberg's argument, ruling that the president lacked the constitutional authority to seize the country's steel mills.

During the early 1950s, Abner Mikva, a recent University of Chicago Law School graduate who had clerked for Supreme Court justice Sherman Minton, joined Goldberg's practice as a partner. Goldberg and Mikva, who would later serve as a Democratic congressman representing Chicago, a federal judge, and President Bill Clinton's White House counsel, would remain close friends and political allies throughout Goldberg's public career.

In 1955, Goldberg helped engineer the historic merger of the American Federation of Labor (AFL) with the Congress of Industrial Organizations (CIO) and served as the AFL-CIO's general counsel until 1961, when President Kennedy named him labor secretary. As AFL-CIO general counsel, Goldberg became the group's ethical conscience, always insisting on strict adherence to due process in his successful, and widely applauded, effort to rid the unions of both communists and corrupt officials. He even drafted ethical guidelines to be followed in ousting these officials from their union leadership positions.[21] It was primarily as architect of the AFL-CIO merger that Goldberg came into the national spotlight.

In Kennedy's Cabinet

Goldberg had first met John Kennedy in 1948, when Kennedy was a freshman congressman and Goldberg was the recently installed CIO general counsel. At first, Goldberg was less than impressed with Kennedy, who, he would recall, "looked like a high school graduate" and had earned a reputation among his congressional colleagues as a lightweight. Their paths crossed occasionally in the following years, when Kennedy served on the House Labor Committee from 1948 to 1952 and, following Kennedy's election to the Senate in 1952, on the Senate Labor Committee. Goldberg's impression of Kennedy improved significantly with the January 1957 formation of a Senate investigating committee, chaired by the antilabor Arkansas senator John McClellan, seeking to expose corruption and racketeering in the trade unions. Despite the senator's antilabor stance, Goldberg and other labor leaders hoped the committee hearings would eventually yield a legislative reform bill that would not harm the labor movement. During McClellan's hearings, Goldberg and Kennedy worked closely on a labor reform measure eventually known as the Kennedy-Ives Bill. Goldberg spent long hours with Kennedy, answering his questions about specific provisions of the proposed legislation and "educating him more generally about the labor movement."[22] As Ted Sorensen, then Kennedy's top legislative assistant, would later write, Kennedy's work on the

Kennedy-Ives Bill was "the first time in his congressional career . . . [in which] he concentrated intensively and almost exclusively for a period of years on a single piece of legislation."[23]

While working closely with Kennedy on the bill, Goldberg "gradually came to the conclusion that here was someone to be reckoned with," and emerged as Kennedy's closest adviser on labor issues as the senator prepared to seek the Democratic Party's 1960 presidential nomination.[24] When Kennedy formally announced his candidacy, Goldberg was the first and most important labor leader to endorse him, and he persuaded AFL-CIO chief George Meany and other labor leaders to support Kennedy as well.

Goldberg's early support for Kennedy earned him a cabinet post. Although Goldberg initially hoped to be appointed attorney general, "the most direct stepping-stone to his cherished goal of a seat on the Supreme Court,"[25] the naming of the president's brother Bobby to the job situated Goldberg as the leading candidate for labor secretary, an appointment Arthur Schlesinger Jr. would later call "almost inevitable."[26] Given his vast experience on labor matters, his role as architect of the AFL-CIO merger, and his reputation as a pioneer in the labor law field, the top position in the Labor Department was his perfect match.

Goldberg was only the third Jew in U.S. history appointed to a presidential cabinet, after Oscar Straus, who served as Theodore Roosevelt's secretary of commerce and labor, and Henry Morgenthau Jr., FDR's secretary of the treasury. No Jewish cabinet members served in the administrations of Harry Truman or Dwight Eisenhower, although Eisenhower nominated the Jewish investment banker Lewis Strauss as secretary of commerce, a nomination the Senate rejected.[27] With Goldberg's appointment as labor secretary in December 1960, and the subsequent naming of Connecticut governor Abraham Ribicoff as secretary of health, education, and welfare, two Jews were serving in a presidential cabinet for the first time.

Goldberg was a singularly popular and effective labor secretary. Although the second oldest member of JFK's cabinet, despite still being in his early fifties, Goldberg was considered the most energetic, "Bobby Kennedy notwithstanding," making 165 speeches during his fifteen-month tenure. One of Kennedy's closest advisers, he seemed "to be everywhere, doing everything," involved in all areas of administration policy making, "making speeches on affecting foreign policy, for example, as well as labor." He became the administration's most celebrated negotiator, settling no fewer than twelve contentious labor strikes, including the high-profile Metropolitan Opera strike of 1961.

Some called him "the Davy Crockett of the New Frontier"; Hubert Humphrey called him "the vitamins of the Administration."[28]

Goldberg's Appointment to the Supreme Court

As noted in the previous chapter, Felix Frankfurter, on retiring from the court in August 1962, had hoped Kennedy would name Paul Freund, an advocate of judicial restraint, to replace him Although Freund, like Goldberg, was on Kennedy's short list for the court, and had the strong support of McGeorge Bundy, Kennedy national security adviser Clark Clifford, and Ted Sorensen, the nomination was not to be.

Two major factors had militated against Freund's appointment. Kennedy respected Freund and, in December 1960, had offered him the solicitor general post, which Freund had declined. Kennedy then nominated Freund's Harvard Law colleague Archibald Cox, who took the job. Freund's refusal had apparently hurt his high court chances among Kennedy's advisers, especially his brother Robert, as contrasted with Goldberg's acceptance of the labor secretary job.[29]

Robert Kennedy, with whom the president was understandably close, also opposed Freund as being too "academic" and remote, urging his brother to appoint Cox for the Supreme Court instead. Cox had been more active than Freund in the 1960 presidential campaign and served ably for fifteen months as solicitor general in Robert Kennedy's Justice Department. The president's brother argued that the better of the Harvard professors for the seat was Cox, who held liberal views admired by RFK.[30] "Archie Cox had come to work for the Administration and had done a fine job while Paul Freund had refused the position of Solicitor General," Robert Kennedy later wrote in further explanation of his preference.[31] Moreover, when President Kennedy had consulted Chief Justice Earl Warren and Justice William O. Douglas about Frankfurter's successor, they had opposed Freund's nomination, fearing his adherence to judicial restraint.[32]

Thus, the day after Frankfurter's retirement, President Kennedy announced his nomination of Goldberg to fill the Holmes-Cardozo-Frankfurter seat on the Supreme Court, widely considered the Jewish seat. JFK, who had told a friend Goldberg was "the smartest man I ever met," and was reluctant to lose Goldberg in his cabinet, had apparently hoped he would turn down the offer.[33] However, Goldberg, who had dreamed of serving on the Supreme Court since law school, quickly accepted. Moreover, in nominating Goldberg rather than Archibald Cox, Kennedy demonstrated recognition of the political importance of appointing a Jewish justice to succeed Frankfurter. Kennedy's White House counsel Myer Feldman had indicated to the president that Jewish communal leaders "would be upset if this appointment did not go to a person of the Jewish faith."[34] Goldberg's nomination was thus applauded throughout the Jewish community and across the partisan divide, drawing praise from voices as diverse as liberal Democratic senators Ralph Yarborough of Texas and Paul Douglas of Illinois and conservative Republicans such as Arizona senator Barry Goldwater. Emanuel Celler, the liberal Jewish Democratic New York congressman who chaired the House Judiciary Committee, called it "a splendid choice."[35] After receiving the unanimous approval of the Senate Judiciary Committee, Goldberg was confirmed in late September by a near-unanimous Senate vote, with only South Carolina senator Strom Thurmond opposing. When Goldberg's mother-in-law was asked, "Wasn't it wonderful about Arthur?" she replied: "Wonderful? Yes, but who cares about Arthur? Everybody knows something like this could happen to him, but that it should happen to *me*, that's more wonderful. That I'm the mother-in-law of a Supreme Court Justice!"[36]

Justice Goldberg and His Law Clerks

During his brief Supreme Court tenure, six of Justice Goldberg's eight law clerks were Jewish. Two of them, Stephen Breyer and Alan Dershowitz, later colleagues at Harvard Law School, would achieve extraordinary prominence in the legal profession.

Breyer, who clerked for Goldberg in 1964–1965, was the fourth of five Supreme Court justices to begin his legal career as a clerk.[37] After graduating from Stanford in 1959, he won a Marshall Scholarship to Oxford University's Magdalen College, where he received a bachelor's degree in philosophy, politics, and economics with first-class honors in 1961. He then attended Harvard Law, where he graduated magna cum laude in 1964 and served as articles editor of the *Harvard Law Review*, before beginning his clerkship with Goldberg.

Following his clerkship, Breyer worked for two years in the Justice Department, serving as special assistant to Donald Turner, the assistant attorney general for the Antitrust Division, a Harvard law professor who significantly influenced the development of antitrust regulation, a field in which Breyer would specialize during his own academic career.[38] In 1967, Breyer began teaching at Harvard Law, where he remained until 1994, also teaching at Harvard's Kennedy School of Government. While at Harvard, Breyer took several leaves for government service: in 1973, he served briefly as assistant special prosecutor on Archibald Cox's Watergate prosecution team, and he later was special counsel and subsequently chief counsel to the Senate Judiciary Committee. In 1980, President Jimmy Carter appointed Breyer to the U.S. Court of Appeals for the First Circuit, where he served as chief judge from 1990 until his 1994 appointment to the Supreme Court.[39]

Dershowitz, who was raised in Borough Park, Brooklyn, received his bachelor's degree from Brooklyn College and, in 1959, entered Yale Law School, where he was elected editor-in-chief of the *Yale Law Journal*. While at Yale, he concentrated in constitutional and criminal law, studying with Alexander Bickel, Frankfurter's former clerk discussed in the section on Frankfurter. Bickel ultimately recommended Dershowitz for both federal and Supreme Court clerkships. Fifty years later, Dershowitz would fondly recall his admiration for Bickel's writings, his seminar on constitutional law, and the later experience of collaborating with Bickel on constitutional law cases.[40] After graduating first in his law school class in 1962, Dershowitz clerked for Chief Judge David L. Bazelon of the U.S. Court of Appeals in Washington, D.C., before serving a one-year Supreme Court clerkship (1963–1964) with Goldberg. During his clerkship, Dershowitz wrote the first draft of Goldberg's famous opinion in the landmark 1964 civil liberties case of *Escobedo v. Illinois*, which outlawed police interrogation of criminal defendants held in custody without access to a lawyer. This decision marked an enduring contribution to constitutional law in the area of criminal law and procedure, and also began his longtime collaboration with Goldberg to abolish the death penalty as unconstitutional.

Dershowitz was appointed to the Harvard Law faculty following his clerkship and, in 1967, at age twenty-eight, became the youngest tenured professor in the law school's history. During five decades at Harvard, much of it as the Felix Frankfurter Professor of Law, he published thirty books, including the national best sellers *Chutzpah*, *The Best Defense*, and *The Case for Israel*. Dershowitz, who retired in 2014, achieved fame as one of America's preeminent appellate attorneys, whose celebrity clients included the Newport socialite Claus von Bulow, the former heavyweight boxing champion Mike Tyson, the financier Michael Milken, the hotel owner Leona Helmsley, and the disgraced former football star O. J. Simpson. Dershowitz's 1986 book about the von Bulow case, *Reversal of Fortune*, was later made into a movie written and directed by Dershowitz's son, Elon.

Dershowitz's deep interest in Soviet Jewry led him also to defend the Soviet dissident, and future Israeli politician, Natan Sharansky, whom the Soviets had accused of being an American spy in 1977 and sentenced to thirteen years in prison. Dershowitz represented Sharansky for nine years, until his release from a Soviet prison in February 1986. During his fifty-year teaching career at Harvard, Dershowitz achieved renown as one of America's most influential Jewish legal scholars and public intellectuals, as well as one of the country's most outspoken liberal defenders of Israel.

Mr. Justice Goldberg

Despite his relatively short tenure, Goldberg had a significant influence on the Warren court. Prior to taking his seat, Goldberg told his wife, Dorothy, that he intended to be an activist justice, and throughout his tenure he remained true to this intention.[41] In case after case, he was a voice for judicial liberalism, frequently providing the critical fifth vote that transformed the Warren court's liberal bloc, consisting of Earl Warren, Hugo Black, William O. Douglas, and William Brennan, into a majority.[42] His 89 percent liberal voting record while on the court was second only to that of Justice Douglas.[43] Thus, Felix Frankfurter's retirement and Goldberg's appointment not only deprived the court of its most forceful proponent of judicial restraint but provided a reliable fifth vote in favor of judicial activism.

Goldberg joined Chief Justice Warren, whom he greatly admired, in taking an activist judicial approach. For the court to substitute judicial restraint when individual liberties were at stake, he argued, "would make the legislature or the executive their ultimate guardian, thereby undermining the purposes of embodying them in a Bill of Rights."[44] Goldberg's activism, and his advocacy for individual liberties, was evident in the majority opinion he wrote in the 1963 landmark case *Kennedy v. Mendoza-Martinez*.[45] Here, the Supreme Court declared unconstitutional portions of the Immigration and Nationality Act of 1952 that revoked the citizenship of those who had left or remained outside the United States in times of war or national emergency to evade military service. In his opinion, Goldberg argued that because the revocation of citizenship had been automatically imposed by Congress as a punishment for draft evasion, the necessary constitutional and judicial safeguards to accompany such punishment had been absent.[46]

Goldberg's activist orientation was also apparent in the 1963 case *Watson v. City of Memphis*, in which the Supreme Court unanimously required the immediate desegregation of all Memphis's public parks and municipal facilities.[47] The city had planned for the slow desegregation of these public facilities over twelve years. In his opinion, Goldberg made clear his understanding of the court's order in *Brown v. Board of Education*, which called for desegregation of public places "with all deliberate speed," accelerated and not delayed.[48] He upheld this view in *Watson*. "The basic guarantees of our Constitution," he argued, "are warrants for the here and now and, unless there is an overwhelmingly compelling reason, they are to be promptly filled."[49]

Goldberg's commitment to Supreme Court activism in defense of individual liberties surfaced again in the case *Escobedo v. Illinois*, often identified as Goldberg's most important opinion.[50] During interrogation in a police station, Danny Escobedo, who was accused of killing a relative, was questioned without his lawyer's presence despite his repeated requests. His attorney, while attempting to advise him on his right to remain silent, was denied access by the police to the interrogation room. Escobedo, meanwhile, had not been advised by the police of his right to remain silent and, after confessing to the murder, was sentenced to twenty years in prison.[51]

In his majority opinion for a divided 5–4 court, which overturned Escobedo's conviction, Goldberg attacked involuntary confessions elicited by law enforcement officers generally, stating: "We have . . . learned the . . . lesson of history that no system of criminal justice can, or should, survive if it comes to depend for its continued effectiveness on the citizens' abdication through unawareness of their constitutional rights. No system worth preserving should have to fear that if an accused is permitted to consult with a lawyer, he will become aware of, and exercise, these rights. If the exercise of constitutional rights will thwart the effectiveness of a system of law enforcement, then there is something very wrong with that system."[52] Goldberg's *Escobedo* opinion, which held that a criminal defendant's Sixth Amendment right to counsel extended to the interrogation phase of the criminal proceeding, changed forever the law relating to forced confessions. This was an important step toward the court's historic 1966 ruling in *Miranda v. Arizona*, which mandated the well-known Miranda warnings ("You have the right to remain silent . . .").[53]

Not everyone was pleased with Goldberg's *Escobedo* opinion. Justice Byron White's strongly worded minority opinion, on behalf of the court's four dissenters, accused Goldberg and his liberal colleagues of having a "deep-seated distrust of law enforcement officers everywhere," and therefore moving to bar all confessions, "whether involuntarily made or not."[54] Police and prosecutors unsurprisingly agreed, interpreting the decision, in the words of Los

Angeles police chief William Parker, as "handcuffing the police" and arguing that it "will do nothing to enhance the security of America against crime." The Goldberg opinion produced considerable partisan debate as well, with liberals applauding the ruling and conservatives attacking it. In denouncing the decision, Republican presidential candidate Barry Goldwater exclaimed that "no wonder our law enforcement officers have been demoralized and rendered ineffective in their jobs."[55] In his 1964 presidential campaign, Goldwater charged that the Warren court's *Escobedo* decision had contributed to the breakdown of law and order in U.S. cities.[56]

Justice Goldberg and the Death Penalty

As noted earlier, one of Goldberg's great causes was ending the death penalty, and he sought persistently to persuade his court brethren to declare it unconstitutional. Until Goldberg's appointment, no Supreme Court justice had ever argued that the death penalty might be categorically unconstitutional.[57] To the surprise of even his most liberal colleagues, Goldberg would make precisely this argument. Indeed, Goldberg came to the court with an agenda —a to-do list of changes he wanted to implement—and as his law clerk Alan Dershowitz would recall, banning the death penalty was atop this list.[58] Goldberg considered the death penalty morally offensive, barbaric, and inhuman, cruel and unusual punishment in violation of the Eighth Amendment.

Although Goldberg realized he had little chance of convincing a majority of his fellow justices to support his view, he hoped to at least begin a dialogue that would eventually lead to the judicial abolition of the death penalty. In pursuit of this goal, in summer 1963, Goldberg took the unusual step of preparing and circulating a lengthy memorandum to the court, drafted by Dershowitz, detailing his legal argument on capital punishment, despite the issue not being before the court.[59] Later in 1963, Goldberg dissented from the Supreme Court's majority refusal to hear the death penalty case *Rudolph v. Alabama*. Goldberg's dissent, once again drafted by Dershowitz, inspired liberal attorneys throughout the country to successfully challenge the constitutionality of capital punishment in other cases on appeal in the federal courts. These challenges culminated in the 1972 case *Furman v. Georgia*, in which the Supreme Court, by a majority 5–4 vote, indeed ruled it unconstitutional.

Even though the death penalty never officially came before the court during his tenure, and Goldberg could never transform his memorandum into a landmark opinion, he stayed active in the national debate on the issue in his postcourt years. In 1970, he coauthored with Dershowitz an influential *Harvard Law Review* article, "Declaring the Death Penalty Unconstitutional," challenging the death penalty on Eighth Amendment grounds.[60] With the 1972 announcement of the *Furman v. Georgia* decision, Goldberg called Dershowitz to exult in the moment, aware of the role their 1963 memo and accompanying campaign had played.[61]

Justice Goldberg Resigns from the Court

On July 14, 1965, Adlai Stevenson, the two-time Democratic presidential candidate who was then serving as U.S. ambassador to the UN, died suddenly, creating a vacancy in Lyndon Johnson's cabinet. Two days later, Johnson called Goldberg to offer him the UN ambassador post. Johnson had long hoped to appoint his friend and adviser Abe Fortas to the Supreme Court, although Fortas himself didn't want the position, and Goldberg's resignation would create just this opportunity. While Goldberg at first declined, saying that he "cherished" his court seat and was uninterested in other jobs either in or out of government, Johnson refused to take no for an answer. For several days, the notoriously tenacious Johnson pressured a reluctant Goldberg, including by inviting the justice and his wife to travel on Air Force One to attend Stevenson's funeral in Illinois. On the flight, Goldberg finally acquiesced. As he would later explain, "Have you ever had your arm twisted by LBJ?" A week later, on July 26, 1965, Goldberg and his family unenthusiastically made their way to the White House Rose Garden to accept LBJ's appointment as Stevenson's successor. Although Dorothy Goldberg would come to support her husband's decision, at first she strongly opposed it, as did the justice's daughter and son.[62]

Arthur Goldberg, who served for less than three years, enjoyed the shortest tenure of the eight Jewish high court justices. He was also the rare justice to resign to accept another government appointment, given that jurists typically consider the Supreme Court a culmination of their public careers. Indeed, prior to Goldberg's resignation, only eight justices in the previous 175 years had left office before their retirement.[63] Only three other twentieth-century justices—Charles Evans Hughes, John Hessin Clarke, and James Byrnes— had done so to accept other government appointments or run for office. For his part, Clarke had resigned in 1922 to become head of the League of Nations Association, informing President Harding that he would "die happier working for world peace than devoting my time to determining whether . . . the digging of a ditch was unconstitutional or not." Byrnes resigned in 1942 to become FDR's director of economic stabilization and "assistant president" and, in time, secretary of state. And Hughes, who resigned in 1916 to run against Woodrow Wilson as the Republican Party's presidential candidate, would return to the court as Hoover's chief justice appointee in 1930.

Even allowing for Johnson's talents of persuasion, scholars and pundits remain perplexed by Goldberg's decision to leave his beloved court post for a job that would end when LBJ left office. Goldberg would later describe his court years as "the culmination of a life's ambition," fueling curiosity on why he didn't stand up to the president.[64]

Although Goldberg never wrote an autobiography and was always reticent when it came to discussing his resignation, several theories have been suggested to explain why he succumbed to pressure from a president who had not appointed him and to whom he was not noticeably close. Goldberg did once concede, "I left because of vanity. I thought that I could influence the President to get out of Vietnam."[65] In trying to induce his resignation, Johnson reportedly offered Goldberg several other posts, including attorney general and secretary of health, education, and welfare. As for Goldberg's ambition to help end the Vietnam War, in his talk with Johnson en route to Adlai Stevenson's funeral, he allegedly told the president he would only consider accepting the UN position if he had LBJ's assurance that he would be a member of the cabinet and major presidential adviser involved in all decision making aimed at forging a negotiated peace in Vietnam. According to Dorothy Goldberg, Johnson responded that he was committed to such a negotiated peace and that one of the main reasons he was offering Goldberg the post was to enlist "America's greatest negotiator" as a cabinet-level adviser to help resolve the Vietnam conflict. Johnson also reportedly assured Goldberg that he would have immediate access to the president.[66]

Some scholars have speculated that LBJ offered Goldberg the possibility of a later reappointment to the court, perhaps even to succeed Earl Warren as chief justice. Indeed, Goldberg's biographer David Stebenne has suggested that Goldberg may have genuinely believed that Johnson, now in his debt, would later feel obligated to reappoint him to the court. Goldberg was also aware that his friend Warren was planning to retire before the 1968 presidential election and that the chief justice would probably ask Johnson to name Goldberg to succeed him. At least one Supreme Court historian has suggested that the prospect of a reappointment by Johnson influenced Goldberg's decision to take the UN job.[67] Charles Evans Hughes's reappointment as chief justice, several years after his having stepped down to run for president, may have struck Goldberg as a precedent. When Goldberg was interviewed in 1983 for an oral history for the Lyndon Johnson Library in Austin, Texas, the first question he was asked was what prompted him to leave the court for the UN.[68] When queried as to whether he had resigned with the understanding, implicit or explicit, of a reappointment, Goldberg replied unequivocally: "No, never. I would never make such a deal."[69]

Goldberg also later denied reports that he had been bored, restless, or dissatisfied while serving on the court and that he had actively sought John-son's proposed cabinet appointments. Indeed, he was later so outraged when he read in Johnson's memoirs the former president's assertion that he had been bored while on the court, and had solicited a different administration appointment, that he called Johnson at his Texas ranch to berate him and demand the return of one of his wife Dorothy's paintings, which she had given to LBJ years before.[70]

In his best-selling biography of Abe Fortas, Bruce Allen Murphy has sug-gested that LBJ's real inducement to Goldberg was a potential vice presidency in Johnson's second full term, which would have made him America's first Jewish vice president. "You're over there on the Court, isolated from the ac-tion," Johnson evidently told Goldberg, "and you can't get to the Vice Presi-dency from the Court." By taking on a more political role as UN ambassador, he insisted, Goldberg would be better positioned to become Johnson's run-ning mate in 1968. To Goldberg, known to possess a sizable ego, the prospect of becoming the first Jewish vice president may have seemed irresistible.[71]

Murphy's argument is certainly plausible. Not long after Goldberg left the court, the *Jewish Press* suggested that Goldberg's move to the UN positioned him for a future appointment as secretary of state, a possible vice presiden-tial candidacy on a ticket with Hubert Humphrey in 1972, or even perhaps to become the first Jewish president. If such possibilities occurred to Jewish journalists at the time, they probably occurred to Arthur Goldberg as well.[72]

According to Goldberg's friend Daniel Patrick Moynihan, who had served as his deputy and speechwriter while Goldberg was labor secretary and who helped draft his Supreme Court resignation and UN ambassadorship accep-tance, the justice simply "did not know how to say no to a President telling him that the highest interests of the American nation were at stake."[73] Recall-ing his family's reaction, Goldberg's daughter would later say, "We all felt that he shouldn't have made that decision, but he felt that it was the best thing to do for the nation. His thinking was, when the president asks you to do some-thing, you respond positively."[74]

Whatever his initial reasoning, there is little question that Goldberg later regretted his resignation from the court. And he would never again find a post remotely comparable to what he described, in his UN appointment acceptance, as the "richest and most satisfying period of my career." During his failed 1970 campaign for New York governor, he would wistfully tell a voter who expressed the wish that he was still on the Supreme Court, "So do I, sometimes." It may well be that Goldberg's disinclination to write his memoirs, or to reminisce candidly at length about his resignation, resulted from a realization that his decision had been a profound mistake.

In a tribute to Goldberg after his death in 1990, National Public Radio correspondent Daniel Schorr noted that in the years following his court resignation, whenever Goldberg's friends would get together (without him), they would play a game of "what-if," predicting what might have happened had Goldberg remained on the court, including the possibility of a "Goldberg court" rather than a Burger court. According to Schorr, this was "a game that any number of Goldberg admirers could play—but did not when he was present. I made the mistake once of teasing Mr. Goldberg by saying I was planning to write a novel starting with his decision not to leave the Court, and calling it, 'The Goldberg Variations.' He didn't think it was funny, and I guess it wasn't."[75]

Goldberg at the United Nations

Compared to his years as labor secretary and Supreme Court justice, Goldberg's tenure as UN ambassador was neither happy nor satisfying. He experienced, to be sure, some notable achievements, the foremost of which was helping negotiate a cease-fire to the 1967 Six Day War between Israel and the Arab states and, thereafter, securing the Johnson administration's support for a carefully worded UN Security Council resolution, which Goldberg himself helped draft, to serve as the potential basis for a comprehensive Middle East peace agreement. UN Security Council Resolution 242, enacted unanimously on November 22, 1967, and for which Goldberg helped obtain support from the Soviet ambassador, has subsequently served as the starting point for the broader Middle East peace process and as the diplomatic centerpiece for peace plans such as the Camp David Accords, the Oslo Accords, and the Roadmap for Peace.[76] The fact that UN Resolution 242 "was largely Goldberg's handiwork" and that it has endured "underscores the importance of this achievement and Goldberg's abilities as a diplomat."[77]

During his three years as UN ambassador, Goldberg achieved at least two other major diplomatic successes. First, when the growing Greek-Turkish tensions over Cyprus brought the two countries to the brink of war in November 1967, Goldberg helped draft a Security Council resolution that helped avert an armed conflict. Shortly thereafter, when North Korean patrol boats seized the USS *Pueblo*, a naval intelligence ship, on January 23, 1968, producing a U.S.-North Korean crisis, Goldberg's influential presentation to the UN Security Council, televised live throughout the United States, helped peacefully resolve this major diplomatic incident, which could have led to a military conflict.[78]

Despite these achievements, Goldberg was often frustrated as UN ambassador. For all Johnson's assurances that his negotiating skills and public prestige would be applied to ending the Vietnam conflict, this was not to be. Johnson, to Goldberg's dismay, flatly reneged on his Vietnam promises. Moreover, Goldberg later realized that Johnson had no intention of seeking a negotiated withdrawal from Vietnam, or of calling upon Goldberg's legendary negotiating skills to effectuate such a withdrawal. Meanwhile, Goldberg found himself excluded from Vietnam-related meetings with other cabinet members and foreign policy advisers. "I was asked," he later confessed, "to participate in a venture to try to extricate our country as a principal adviser and found I was not the principal adviser."[79] Holding increasingly different views from Johnson on how to approach the war, Goldberg's relationship with the president deteriorated. As U.S. military involvement in Vietnam deepened in 1966, Goldberg began openly challenging the Johnson administration's policy.[80] By the end of Goldberg's tenure, Washington insiders reported that Johnson took exception to his UN ambassador's "frequent telephone calls and memoranda calling for American de-escalation of the war."[81]

On April 23, 1968, Goldberg resigned his UN ambassadorship and returned to private practice as a senior partner in Paul, Weiss, Rifkind, Wharton, and Garrison, whose managing partner, Simon Rifkind, a former Federal District Court judge, had long been close friend of Goldberg's. Soon thereafter, Goldberg was elected national president of the American Jewish Committee, a position he held for a little more than a year, before announcing his candidacy for New York governor.

Following his unsuccessful New York gubernatorial race in 1970, Goldberg moved back to Washington, where he practiced law at Caplin and Drysdale. Among his celebrity clients were the Reverend William Sloane Coffin Jr., the controversial Yale University chaplain and anti–Vietnam War activist, and

Curt Flood, the St. Louis Cardinals' African American center fielder who challenged Major League Baseball's reserve clause in an antitrust suit against the league and its commissioner, Bowie Kuhn.[82] In representing Flood in *Flood v. Kuhn*, argued March 20, 1972, Goldberg returned to the Supreme Court for the first time since his 1965 resignation. A lifelong baseball fan, Goldberg agreed to represent Flood without charge. "The case is of tremendous interest to me, and I would regard it as *pro bono* work, a public service."[83]

Goldberg's oral argument in support of Flood's suit, however, was not his finest hour. Rambling and disorganized, it was an embarrassment to his friends as well as his former colleagues, who ruled against Flood, 5–3. "It was one of the worst arguments I'd ever heard—by one of the smartest men I've ever known, in the setting where he should have been a superb advocate," his cocounsel Daniel Levitt would recall. "It was like he choked." Goldberg realized as much and said afterward that he would never again argue a case before the Supreme Court.[84] And he never did.

While practicing law during the 1970s and early 1980s, Goldberg also taught at various colleges and law schools, remained active in Jewish communal life, wrote newspaper columns, served on government commissions, and was frequently called on to advise and mediate in international arbitration cases. In 1971, he published a book, *Equal Justice: The Warren Era of the Supreme Court*, and in the following years wrote law review articles on various constitutional issues. From 1977 to 1978, he served as a U.S. ambassador-at-large to the Belgrade Conference on Human Rights for President Jimmy Carter. In that role, he became an outspoken critic of East European bloc nations for their human rights violations, and an especially vocal advocate for resolving international diplomatic problems through negotiation. For these efforts, Carter awarded him the Presidential Medal of Freedom in 1978.[85]

Goldberg died in Washington of a heart attack on January 19, 1990, at age eighty-one. Three days later, after a memorial service at Washington Hebrew Congregation, he was buried beside his wife, Dorothy, who had died two years earlier, in Arlington National Cemetery, only a short distance from the grave of his Supreme Court colleague Earl Warren.[86]

The Jewishness of Justice Goldberg

Arthur Goldberg was active in Jewish communal and public life. In 1964, while still serving on the Supreme Court, he was elected chairman of the Board of Overseers of the Jewish Theological Seminary of America. In 1965, he was elected an honorary vice president of the AJC, succeeding Herbert Lehman, the former New York governor and U.S. senator. That same year, he received the AJC's American Liberties Medallion, and was honored by the Anti-Defamation League with its America's Democratic Legacy Award in 1966. As noted earlier, he was elected AJC president two years later.

Although Goldberg did not make religious observance central to his daily life, he remained proud of his Jewish heritage throughout his career. When accepting the AJC presidency, he declared that his concern for social justice, human rights, international peace, and enlightenment all stemmed from his Jewish heritage.[87]

His personal religious identity was also evident in his concurring opinion in the 1963 school prayer case *Abington Township School District v. Schempp*, in which the Supreme Court outlawed all devotional reading of the Bible in public schools, including recitation of the Lord's Prayer. Although Goldberg sided with the Warren court's liberal majority in this case, he took the opportunity to remind his fellow justices that "neither government nor this Court can or should ignore the significance of the fact that a vast portion of our people believe in and worship God and that many of our legal, political and personal values derive historically from religious teachings." In this same opinion, Goldberg expressed his concern that the First Amendment's Establishment Clause not be allowed to overshadow the Free Exercise Clause, warning that "untutored devotion to the concept of neutrality could lead to . . . a brooding and pervasive devotion to the secular and a passive, or even active, hostility to the religious."[88]

A labor Zionist in his youth who had attended Chicago's Zionist-oriented Theodore Herzl Elementary School, Goldberg's first visit to Palestine while working for the OSS during World War II reinforced his youthful commitment to Zionism, a commitment that became central to Goldberg's Jewish identity. As he would later put it, he had been "a Zionist for a long time, since I was a kid . . . because I was Jewish. I didn't see how you could be a really Jewish person, proud of your ancestry, and not be a Zionist. It's not possible, logically. . . . It's like asking an Irishman . . . Do you believe in home rule?"[89] Goldberg and his wife, Dorothy, remained lifelong Zionists and counted future Israeli prime minister Golda Meir, whom they had known since their early Zionist days in Chicago and whom they always called Goldie, as one of their closest friends. During the early 1960s, when one of Goldberg's law clerks was visiting Israel, the Goldbergs asked him "to smuggle a carton of unfiltered Chesterfields past her security guards" so that Golda could enjoy a few puffs of her favorite cigarette, which her physician had forbidden her to indulge in.[90]

Like his Jewish predecessor, Felix Frankfurter, Goldberg, who had grown up in an Orthodox home, gave up strict Orthodox religious observance as a young man. When he started working for the Pritzker and Pritzker firm, founded by religiously Reform German-American Jews, he adopted a more liberal Jewish lifestyle, joining a Reform temple and eventually eating ham, which he had never done in his youth.[91] Unlike Frankfurter, however, who was married to the daughter of a Protestant minister, Goldberg married a Jewish woman and maintained a liberal Jewish religious identity, including temple membership, throughout his public career. Goldberg also retained a sentimental connection to his Judaism. On an official visit to Scandinavia while labor secretary, he stopped in Amsterdam to visit the home of Anne Frank, where he laid a wreath.[92] On a trip to Russia in 1969, he and his wife visited Goldberg's parents' hometown of Zhinkov, where the mayor showed him around as if he were a long-lost hometown boy made good. "The town was like something out of *Fiddler on the Roof*," Goldberg would later recall. "But it was hard to place my father here. Because as I went around the town, I realized that there were no Jews left. At one time over half the town was Jewish. It was incredible to think that the entire community had vanished. They all had gone either to America or Auschwitz."[93]

In the early 1960s, Goldberg, who often spoke at synagogues, told Honolulu's Temple Emanu-El a story about his recent visit to his elderly mother, who had become active in several Jewish organizations. While he was sleeping late one morning, the telephone rang for him and his mother answered. "Who's this?" she asked. The caller replied, "This is the President." Goldberg, barely awake, heard his mother inquire, "*Nu*, president from which shul?"[94]

Unlike Justices Brandeis, Cardozo, and Frankfurter, Goldberg held a Passover Seder every year. Throughout his time in Washington, D.C., the Goldberg family Seders were popular events, attended by government officials and other luminaries Jewish and non-Jewish alike. The labor leader George Meany would sing Irish ballads; Hubert Humphrey would regale the guests with stories; and Dorothy Goldberg would sing Yiddish labor union songs.[95] The Seders also reflected Goldberg's deep commitment to social justice and civil rights. A friend of Goldberg's once noted that his Seders recounted the ancient Israelites' story in terms of the 1960s civil rights struggle, and always included denunciations of such contemporary evils as poverty, segregation, and inadequate housing. He made the entire Seder, this friend noted, "the story of all the oppressed and outcast of the world, as if he were presenting a brief before the Supreme Court of history that will forever put Pharaoh in outer darkness."[96] Goldberg's opposition to the death penalty was also guided by this liberal Jewish outlook.

During his three years on the Supreme Court, Goldberg's law clerks were always invited to the family Seders. Although Goldberg did not personally observe the Jewish dietary laws, he was always sensitive to those guests who did. Thus, when he invited Alan Dershowitz, then an Orthodox Jew who kept strictly kosher, Goldberg arranged for the entire Seder dinner to be provided by a kosher caterer. Vice President Humphrey, several Supreme Court justices, cabinet members, and foreign diplomats had also been invited. As Dershowitz would later recall, Arthur and Dorothy Goldberg "firmly believed that people who kept kosher should not be treated as second-class citizens, with 'special kosher' meals. If there was one kosher person, the entire affair would be kosher."[97]

Goldberg's Legacy

Justice Goldberg is alone among the eight Jewish jurists to have served in a president's cabinet prior to his Supreme Court appointment. He enjoys other distinctions as well. He was the first labor lawyer appointed to the court; the last justice to have also served in a presidential cabinet; and the only justice to have served in two presidential cabinet-level positions. He is also one of only two former justices—Charles Evans Hughes being the other—to run for major elective office following his resignation from the court. Goldberg is finally the only Jewish justice to have hired a Jewish law clerk—Stephen Breyer—who himself would be appointed to the high court.

Goldberg's resignation, too, was unique in the modern history of the Supreme Court, and may well be the most compelling element of his legacy. Although we can speculate on the reasons for his acceptance of the UN ambassadorship—that the justice saw it as a stepping-stone to elective office; couldn't turn down a sitting president's offer; or, as he himself claimed, had a prideful desire to negotiate an end to the Vietnam War—his full reasoning will likely never be known. While Justice Goldberg wrote a few important judicial opinions, he wrote far fewer important opinions than did his three Jewish predecessors on the court, and his tenure was far too brief for him to have achieved judicial "greatness." This short tenure has contributed significantly to his enduring legacy as an "average," rather than "great" or "near great," justice. Of the first four Jewish justices, Goldberg is the only one not to be ranked, by judicial scholars, in the "great" or "near great" category.

Nevertheless, according to one writer, "the brevity of his tenure is not an accurate measure of his impact, which was arguably greater than many Justices who served more than twice as long."[98] His judicial opinions made enduring contributions to constitutional law in criminal law and procedure and in civil liberties. Most notable here was Goldberg's majority opinion in *Escobedo v. Illinois*, which expanded constitutional protections for criminal defendants and laid the foundation for the Warren court's historic 1966 ruling in *Miranda v. Arizona*, which mandated that before a criminal defendant could be interrogated by police, he must be notified of his right to remain silent.

Goldberg was also the first Supreme Court justice to argue that the death penalty was unconstitutional based on the Constitution's cruel and unusual punishment and due process clauses, an argument that would be affirmed in 1972, when the high court declared capital punishment unconstitutional in *Furman v. Georgia*. Even though an actual case on the death penalty's constitutionality never came before the court during his tenure, his 1963 memorandum on the subject began a legal dialogue and public debate culminating in the *Furman* ruling almost a decade later. Had Goldberg not resigned when he did, he probably would have authored the court's landmark majority opinion in *Furman*. His absence from the court during this decision, one may surmise, may well have been one of Goldberg's enduring regrets.

Indeed, had he remained on the court, Goldberg's legacy as a justice would undoubtedly have been far greater. Given that he lived twenty-five years after his resignation, he might well have served longer than his more famous Jewish predecessors, Brandeis and Frankfurter, and he surely would have authored many more landmark opinions. Many Supreme Court scholars also believe that had Goldberg remained on the court after 1965, he might well have succeeded Earl Warren as chief justice, thus becoming the only Jewish chief justice in the court's history.

Viewed in retrospect, Goldberg's legacy as labor secretary in the Kennedy administration was far greater than his Supreme Court legacy. Although "the best and the brightest" has become a pejorative label for the Kennedy-Johnson foreign policy advisers, who were architects of the Vietnam imbroglio, the term can also apply, without taint, to Kennedy's domestic team, especially Goldberg, "the smartest man I ever met," in Kennedy's words.[99] In particular, Goldberg was known for his extraordinary negotiating acumen and for his close advisory relationship with the president. When he left Kennedy's cabinet to join the court in 1962, Goldberg "could point to a legacy of strike settlements, civil rights advocacy, and economic policy initiatives." In his brief time as labor secretary, he had chaired the President's Committee on Equal Employment Opportunity, been among the cabinet's strongest civil rights supporters, helped create the first Presidential Commission on the Status of Women, drafted the legislative bill establishing the Manpower Development and Training Program, and, "under the pressure of emergency," successfully mediated twelve national labor disputes.[100] As his former clerk Alan Dershowitz would later suggest, Goldberg "was perhaps the most successful secretary of labor in history, settling one strike after another and being recognized as a legendary mediator."[101]

Goldberg's Jewish legacy was also significant. Following the precedent set by Brandeis and Frankfurter, Goldberg hired a number of Jewish law clerks. Indeed, during an era when most prestigious big city law firms were still discriminating against Jews, 75 percent of his clerks were Jewish. In terms of religious affiliation, involvement in Jewish communal affairs, and identification with the state of Israel, Goldberg was perhaps the most engaged of all the Jewish justices. Whereas, for example, Frankfurter visited Israel on only one brief occasion, Goldberg visited Israel many times and also encouraged his law clerks to do so. A lifelong Zionist, Goldberg was a strong public advocate for the safety and security of Israel while UN ambassador during the Six Day War. Other than Brandeis, Goldberg is the only Jewish justice to have served as national president of a major Jewish organization, having been elected AJC president in 1968. In accepting this role, he succeeded Morris Abram, his law partner at Paul, Weiss, Rifkind, who had served as president from 1964 to 1968 and had resigned to become president of Brandeis University.

A synagogue member throughout his public life, Goldberg was also the first Jewish Supreme Court justice to hold an annual Passover Seder. Moreover, his Jewish religious commitments transcended denominational lines. Although a Reform Jew by synagogue affiliation, he took time from a busy public career to serve on the Board of Overseers of the Jewish Theological Seminary, where America's Conservative rabbis are trained. And, in 1964, as a high court justice, he was elected president of this board, the only justice to hold such a prominent lay leadership position in an American Jewish seminary.

While serving on the court, Goldberg was always sensitive to the religious observance of Orthodox Jews, especially those in the legal profession. Once, while hearing oral arguments before the court, Goldberg asked one of his Jewish clerks whether Jewish law required that an Orthodox woman always wears a hat, even while arguing a case before the Supreme Court. The court, as his clerk knew, had a rule against wearing any head coverings in the courtroom. When his clerk notified Goldberg that such a rule indeed pertained, Goldberg said he was willing to insist to his fellow justices that an exception be made for Orthodox Jewish women arguing before the court.[102]

Illustrative of Goldberg's support for Orthodox Jews in the legal field is a story Alan Dershowitz has recounted more than once. During Goldberg's court years, some predominantly Jewish firms had a policy against hiring Orthodox Jews, in the correct assumption that their Sabbath observance would make them unavailable on Friday nights and Saturdays. When Dershowitz was first offered his clerkship with Goldberg, he said to the justice, "I hope you won't withdraw your kind offer when I tell you that I'm Sabbath observant—that means I can't—." Goldberg cut him off, saying: "I know what that means, and I'm insulted that you would even suggest that it might cause me to withdraw my offer. I know how it feels to be discriminated against. How could I possibly discriminate against anyone on account of their religion?" Dershowitz apologized for asking the question, and explained to Goldberg that while at Yale Law School he had been offered a job at Paul, Weiss, Rifkind, Wharton, and Garrison, an offer that was quickly withdrawn when the partners learned of Dershowitz's Sabbath observance. The firm, Dershowitz told Goldberg, had a policy of wanting its attorneys to be available seven days a week, twenty-four hours a day. Goldberg never forgot Dershowitz's story. In 1968, after his resignation as UN ambassador, when he was being courted by several New York law firms, Goldberg brought up the issue of discrimination against Orthodox Jews in his meetings with the partners at Paul, Weiss, Rifkind, where he was offered a senior partnership. Before accepting, however, he insisted on being assured that this anti-Orthodox policy would end. Much to Goldberg's abiding credit, it did end, and in recent years the Paul, Weiss, Rifkind firm has had a kosher kitchen, a daily Talmud class, and many Orthodox Jewish lawyers and paralegals.[103] Goldberg's public support for the religious rights of Orthodox Jews in the legal profession, which began during his Supreme Court tenure, is certainly one of the enduring legacies of his legal career.

8

ABE FORTAS
A Tale of Achievement and Scandal

PERHAPS NO INDIVIDUAL was more responsible for Lyndon Johnson's rise to political power than Abe Fortas, who first met the future president in 1937, soon after Johnson arrived in Washington as a newly elected Texas congressman. At the time, Fortas was serving as special assistant and legal counsel to William O. Douglas, the recently appointed chairman of the Securities and Exchange Commission. From 1942 to 1946, while undersecretary of the interior, Fortas had worked closely with Johnson while the latter chaired the House's Naval Affairs subcommittee investigating waste in the conduct of the naval war. President Roosevelt was impressed with Johnson's handling of the assignment, as was Fortas.

Fortas and Johnson also worked together on one of Johnson's pet projects, the development of the Lower Colorado River near Austin, Texas, "which promised rich benefits in electric power and flood control to Johnson's constituents." The project was directly supervised by the Public Works Administration, for which Fortas was general counsel.[1] In little time, Johnson and Fortas became close, with their friendship continuing after Fortas's 1946 departure from the Interior Department to become a partner in the Washington, D.C., law firm Arnold, Fortas, and Porter. They had several mutual friends, including Arthur Goldschmidt, a Texas political ally of Johnson's and Fortas's SEC colleague, who had introduced them, and Alvin Wirtz, a Texas lawyer who had promoted Johnson's early political career and been one of Fortas's Interior Department colleagues. Fortas, Johnson, and their wives socialized regularly. Their frequent dinners, backyard cookouts, and informal Sunday afternoon cocktail receptions would often include other New Deal notables such as Justice William O. Douglas (appointed by FDR to the Supreme Court in 1938), Justice Hugo Black, Thomas Corcoran, Benjamin Cohen, Attorney General Francis Biddle, Interior Department secretary Harold Ickes, and

Judge Thurman Arnold, one of Fortas's former Yale Law School professors and now his law partner.

In 1948, two years after Fortas entered private practice, Fortas helped guide Johnson to victory in his second U.S. Senate race, the most crucial campaign of his political career. Almost from the day he set foot in Washington, Johnson's all-consuming ambition had been to win a Senate seat. Reelected to the House six times, he had lost a bitterly contested Senate race in 1941. In 1948, when Johnson challenged Texas's popular governor Coke Stevenson in the Democratic Senate primary, with the winner virtually assured of a general election victory, he defeated Stevenson by just eighty-seven votes out of almost a million cast, earning him the nickname Landslide Lyndon. After Stevenson contested the outcome, Johnson called on Fortas to represent him in his legal appeal, which eventually went to the Supreme Court. Fortas was victorious, but allegations would persist for years that Landslide Lyndon, and his legal team, had stolen the election. The fact that 202 votes appeared at the last moment from a single ballot box in a precinct controlled by Johnson's crony George Parr, the political boss of Duval County, and "were all cast for Lyndon Johnson in the same handwriting and ink," seemed to give credence to the charge of voter fraud. Such allegations notwithstanding, Johnson's slim margin has often been characterized "as the eighty-seven votes that changed history."[2] Johnson had been required to give up his safe congressional seat to run for the Senate, and had he lost the 1948 Senate race, his political career would have been over at age forty and Lyndon Johnson would have been but a footnote in American political history.[3] In developing the legal strategy that brought Johnson victory, Fortas "had won Johnson's everlasting gratitude by singlehandedly helping him to save his political career."[4] Johnson would thus remain in Fortas's debt.

Over the next fifteen years, as LBJ rose from junior senator to Senate majority leader to vice president, Fortas was one of his closest confidants, enjoying a reputation as one of Washington, D.C.'s most influential political insiders. The day after Johnson became president, on November 23, 1963, Fortas met him privately in the Oval Office and soon emerged as the new president's most important adviser.

The Rise of Abe Fortas

The son of Orthodox Jewish immigrants from England, Fortas grew up in a poor section of Memphis, Tennessee. His rise to prominence, like that of

Brandeis and Frankfurter before him, was later portrayed as the embodiment of the American dream. Fortas's parents, Woolfe and Rachel, arrived in Memphis in 1905 from Leeds, England, where they had owned a china shop. Abe, the youngest of their five children, was born on June 19, 1910. In Memphis, Woolfe Fortas at various times managed a furniture factory, owned a men's clothing and jewelry store, and worked as a pawnbroker and cabinetmaker, "drifting from one trade to another, mastering none."[5]

While his father did not prove to be a successful breadwinner, Abe Fortas inherited a love of music from his father, who encouraged his son to study violin. By his early teenage years, Fiddlin Abe, as Fortas came to be called, gained a reputation as a local violin prodigy, earning extra money by giving violin lessons and forming his own jazz dance band, which took in $8 an evening playing at high school and college dances.[6] His success as a violinist helped pay for his college and law school education and, much later, would make him a musical and cultural fixture in the nation's capital, where he would befriend the violinist Isaac Stern and the cellist Pablo Casals. Other than the law, Fortas's love for the violin would remain his life's great passion.

As a Jew, the young Abe Fortas always felt himself an outsider in Protestant Memphis. For Fortas, as for Frankfurter before him, the Judaism of his parents would always remain as "an obstacle to overcome, rather than as a heritage to be celebrated."[7] By his college years, Fortas had abandoned Orthodoxy, no longer attending synagogue or eating only kosher food. Yet ironically perhaps, his religion helped him escape a career in carpentry or retail, which his father had hoped he would pursue given that he could not afford college tuition. A scholarship established by Memphis's most prominent rabbi, Hardwig Peres, enabled Fortas to attend Southwestern College, a small Presbyterian school in the city. After beginning his undergraduate studies there in fall 1926, Fortas never quite fit in at the school, which counted just six Jews in a student body of five hundred, and at which daily attendance at chapel services was required. Despite his sense of being an outsider, Fortas excelled academically, graduating first in his class at age nineteen, with highest honors in both English and economics. During these years, Fortas also decided on pursuing a career in law.

Having been accepted at both Harvard and Yale Law Schools, Fortas chose Yale, in part thanks to the $50 extra per month in scholarship money the school offered. When Fortas began at Yale Law in fall 1930, he was among his class's minority in being a Southerner, in having not graduated from an elite college, and in being a Jew.[8] He was also the youngest member of the class. Akin to

Brandeis's illustrious career at Harvard Law, Fortas's equally illustrious career at Yale Law, serving as editor-in-chief of the *Yale Law Journal* and graduating atop his class in 1933, would later have about it the aura of legend. "He was the golden boy," a colleague would later say. "He was perhaps the most brilliant legal mind ever to come out of Yale Law School."[9]

Upon graduation from Yale at just age twenty-two, Fortas was offered a teaching position at the school. Generally speaking, the appointment of Jews to such positions had been encouraged by Brandeis's Supreme Court appointment in 1916, and Frankfurter's teaching appointment at Harvard Law the year before. Beginning in the 1920s and 1930s, Yale became one of the country's first elite law schools to appoint Jews to its faculty, led by three open-minded deans, Thomas W. Swan, Robert M. Hutchins, and Charles E. Clark, who had "set the pattern for a long tradition of meritocracy at the law school."[10] Among the early Jewish faculty at Yale Law was Leon Tulin, a 1922 graduate of Yale College and 1925 graduate of the law school, who taught there from 1926 until his untimely death in 1929. During his short tenure, Tulin, the son-in-law of Rabbi Stephen Wise, invited several Jewish leaders, including Wise, the Zionist leader Chaim Weizmann, and the federal judge Julian Mack, the first Jew to serve as an overseer of Harvard University, to speak to the school's students. In 1930, the year Fortas began his law studies, Harry Shulman, a Russian-born protégé of Felix Frankfurter who had just completed a Supreme Court clerkship with Brandeis, was appointed to the Yale Law faculty and would later be the first of several Jewish deans at the school. Eugene V. Rostow, who would graduate from Yale College in 1933 and from its law school in 1937, and would remain close to Fortas for much of their lives, would be on the Yale Law faculty for several decades, while later serving two terms as Yale Law dean, as an undersecretary of state for President Johnson, and briefly as President Reagan's director of arms control and disarmament.

While a student at Yale, Fortas studied under William O. Douglas, who would do much to shape Fortas's early career. Douglas's personal story had a Horatio Alger–like aura to it. Having grown up in poverty in Yakima, Washington, Douglas had overcome childhood polio to become a noted athlete, outdoorsman, and mountain climber. Following his graduation from Whitman College, with six cents in his pocket, he had traveled east employed feeding sheep on a freight car from Washington to New York, where he worked his way through Columbia Law School, graduating second in his class in 1925. Joining the Yale Law faculty in 1929, he soon gained recognition as an authority on corporate finance and bankruptcy, and in 1934 was recruited by

Joseph Kennedy to direct a study of corporate bankruptcy and reorganization for the newly formed Securities and Exchange Commission. With Kennedy's patronage, he rose within the New Deal, becoming an SEC commissioner in 1936. The following year, at age thirty-eight, he was appointed by President Roosevelt as the commission's chairman. With his wit and immense personal charm, Douglas became part of FDR's inner circle and was a guest at the president's Saturday night poker parties, held at the home of Interior Secretary Harold Ickes or Treasury Secretary Henry Morgenthau Jr.[11] In 1939, Douglas was appointed to the Supreme Court by FDR, at forty the youngest appointee in more than a century. Douglas would remain on the court for thirty-six years, longer than any justice in American history.

For Fortas, the Yale faculty offer was especially welcome, among other reasons, because antisemitism still made it difficult, if not impossible, for Jews to secure jobs at elite law firms. Despite his stellar record and recommendations, Fortas got no offers from any of the top New York City firms to which he applied. When such firms wrote Douglas or Thurmon Arnold, another Fortas Yale Law mentor, seeking to fill job openings, their letters invariably included some form of the following antisemitic disclaimer: "We have no prejudices but have found from experience that Jews are so unlikely to click with our clients that we employ them only in very extraordinary circumstances."[12] Despite these obstacles, Douglas wrote Emory Buckner, the former U.S. attorney who was now a partner in the Wall Street firm Root, Clark, headed by former secretary of state Elihu Root, recommending Fortas as "not quite as old" as some recent graduates but "in every respect as mature and able." He continued, "There have been few men graduating from here since I have known the place who would receive such wholehearted support and recommendation as Mr. Fortas." To Wall Street's Colonel William J. Donovan, who would lead the OSS during World War II, Douglas wrote that Fortas was "not merely a good man, but an outstanding man in every respect. In my seven or eight years of teaching I have seen but few men equal to him. He is an extraordinary person." Yet neither this nor other letters sent by Douglas yielded a job offer. Within much of the legal profession, as one of Fortas's biographers has noted, the 1920s and early 1930s were "an era of profound, if genteel, anti-Semitism, a time when a Jew's religiosity, or lack thereof, meant nothing. What mattered was that the world considered him a Jew."[13] When Fortas graduated from Yale, only two of the many Wall Street law firms had a Jewish partner.[14]

Before Fortas began teaching at Yale, however, he received an offer to come to Washington, D.C., to work on the legal staff of the Agricultural Adjustment

Administration (AAA), one of the New Deal agencies created during Roosevelt's historic first hundred days in office. This offer, which Thurman Arnold had helped arrange, was too enticing to refuse. Although Fortas had already accepted his Yale faculty position, his classes would not begin until fall. Thus, open to working for the New Deal only for the summer if necessary, Fortas moved to Washington in July 1933 to join the AAA's Office of the General Counsel. During the next five years, while teaching part-time at Yale, Abe Fortas commuted between New Haven and Washington, where he was known as one of the New Deal's Whiz Kids. Asked about the role of young lawyers in government, one New Dealer replied that "the symbol of the whole thing is Abe Fortas."[15]

The staff of AAA general counsel Jerome Frank, who was himself Jewish, also included the up-and-comers Adlai Stevenson, the future Illinois governor and presidential candidate, and Alger Hiss, a former Harvard student of Frankfurter and clerk of Oliver Wendell Holmes Jr. Unlike in the top Wall Street firms, a candidate's Jewish faith was no barrier to government employment. The New Deal created exhilarating and plentiful opportunities for Jewish law review editors such as Fortas, who had tried unsuccessfully to seek employment on Wall Street but found almost unlimited job opportunities in the government's New Deal agencies. In New Deal Washington, as at Yale Law, a commitment to meritocracy was evident. "We never knew who was Jewish and who was Christian," one of Fortas's Protestant friends recalled. "It absolutely made no impression. We would find out somebody was Jewish because their parents would come and all of a sudden they'd be setting up a kosher kitchen."[16]

During FDR's first months in office, America's devastated agricultural sector was recognized as a top crisis facing the administration.[17] Jerome Frank was unconcerned that most of his legal staff, including Fortas, Hiss, and Stevenson, had no previous experience in the agricultural field. "What we need," he told his associates, "are brilliant young men with keen legal minds and imagination."[18] In later years, however, some of Fortas's colleagues on Frank's legal staff, including Hiss, Lee Pressman, and Nathan Witt, were accused of having organized a Communist Party cell at the AAA during this period. In the late 1940s, at the height of this controversy, which centered on Hiss and his alleged espionage for the Soviet Union, generated by the much-publicized allegations of Whittaker Chambers, some would accuse Fortas of having been a member of this Communist cell, a charge Fortas would always staunchly deny.[19]

Meanwhile, shortly after returning to Washington in summer 1934, following his spring semester at Yale, Fortas left the AAA to join the legal staff of his mentor William O. Douglas, who was now working for the SEC under its first chairman, Joseph Kennedy. Fortas remained at the SEC for four years while he continued supplementing his government salary at Yale, where he was first an instructor and then an assistant professor of law.

On the personal front, in July 1935, Fortas married Carolyn Agger, a petite, attractive blonde whom he had met when both worked at the AAA. The daughter of a Rutgers University economics professor, Carolyn had graduated from Barnard College and had earned a master's degree in economics from the University of Wisconsin before moving to Washington. Carolyn's Protestant background did not bother the religiously unobservant Fortas. Shortly after their wedding, Carolyn enrolled at Yale Law, to which she commuted from Washington weekly. Like her husband, Carolyn accumulated a brilliant law school record, graduating second in her class of 125 in 1938.[20]

With William O. Douglas as his mentor, Fortas rose swiftly in the New Deal hierarchy. At age twenty-three—ten years younger than colleague Adlai Stevenson—he was the wunderkind of the AAA's legendary legal staff, traveling throughout the country organizing agricultural-production hearings for agricultural leaders more than twice his age, formulating legal regulations for the Department of Agriculture, and shaping farm policy for the Roosevelt administration.[21] In his early twenties, Fortas was the right-hand man to now SEC chairman Douglas, a close FDR adviser. Before taking his Supreme Court seat in 1939, Douglas arranged for Fortas to take an even more important position, as general counsel of the Public Works Administration, on the staff of Interior Secretary Harold Ickes. Four years later Fortas, who had become Ickes's chief assistant, was appointed undersecretary of the interior, the number-two position in the Interior Department. At age thirty-two, Fortas was the youngest subcabinet official to date in American history. A further distinction was that he stood just behind Oscar Straus, Teddy Roosevelt's secretary of commerce and labor, and Henry Morgenthau Jr., FDR's treasury secretary, in the early pantheon of Jewish cabinet appointments. When Ickes first asked FDR to appoint Fortas his undersecretary, he asked the president, "You know him, don't you?" FDR's reply was, "Yes. He is a Hebrew, isn't he?" Ickes replied that he was but that "he was one of the quiet, unobtrusive types and pointed out that he was one of the ablest lawyers in Washington."[22]

Law Practice in Washington

In 1946, after having been undersecretary of the interior for four years, Fortas left government service to enter private law practice. He had first considered returning to New Haven, where Yale had offered him a full law professorship and relative financial security. There was, however, Fortas and his wife, Carolyn, recognized, much greater financial remuneration to come from private practice in the nation's capital than from a law school professorship, even at a prestigious school like Yale. The prospect of more money was especially appealing given that the couple had developed expensive tastes. Moreover, after graduating from Yale Law, Carolyn had become a tax specialist and, following a job with the Justice Department's tax division, had gone into private practice with Randolph Paul, probably the day's foremost tax attorney. Soon, she would become a partner in the D.C. office of the New York firm Paul, Weiss, Rifkind, Wharton, and Garrison, of which Randolph Paul was a senior partner—ironically, the same firm Arthur Goldberg would join after leaving his UN ambassadorship in 1968. Given her strong professional position, Carolyn was reluctant to begin her career anew and possibly solo in New Haven. Years later, after Randolph Paul's death, Carolyn would join her husband as a partner in Arnold, Fortas, and Porter, where she would be a senior partner and head of its tax department.

Thurman Arnold also helped persuade his former student Fortas to turn down Yale's offer and go into private practice. As head of the Justice Department's Antitrust Division during the late 1930s, Arnold had spearheaded the New Deal's attack against monopolies, and in 1943, Roosevelt had appointed him to the U.S. Court of Appeals in Washington, D.C., the country's second most influential court. Energetic by nature, with an activist temperament more suited to litigating, Arnold found his judicial work boring and resigned from the Appeals Court in 1945 to open a private practice.[23] Fortas accepted Arnold's invitation to join this practice and, in January 1946, the new Washington law firm of Arnold and Fortas began to accept clients. The following year, Paul Porter joined the practice as a third partner. A former New Deal official like Arnold and Fortas, Porter had served with Fortas on the AAA legal staff, as chairman of the Federal Communications Commission, as head of the Office of Price Administration, as publicity director for the Democratic National Committee, and as ambassador to Greece.[24] Over the next two decades, Arnold, Fortas, and Porter would become a legal powerhouse in Washington.

While Fortas quickly gained a reputation as one of the country's preeminent appellate lawyers, arguing several cases before the Supreme Court, his most important work as an attorney "took place not in courtrooms but in the offices of corporations," advising business executives "on how to enlarge their market power and their profits while staying within the myriad rules laid down by government," flying around the country "to attend meetings, to handle negotiations, to discuss finances and corporate structure as much as the law."[25] Fortas represented major national corporations including Coca-Cola, Lever Brothers, Western Union, the American Broadcasting Company, Philip Morris, Cyrus Eaton, Pan American Airways, and the commonwealth of Puerto Rico. Aided by his close relationship with the Spanish cellist Pablo Casals, Fortas also represented the Casals Festival and arranged for Casals's 1962 performance at the White House. His corporate clients, whom he served as both attorney and adviser, frequently invited Fortas to serve on their boards, roles that garnered him generous financial retainers. By 1965, when he left private practice to take his Supreme Court seat, he had served as a director of Federated Department Stores, Braniff Airlines, Franklin Life Insurance Company, and Madison National Bank.[26]

For Fortas, a particularly lucrative client was the commonwealth of Puerto Rico, which he represented for close to twenty years. As undersecretary of the interior, Fortas had been greatly involved in Puerto Rican affairs and had developed a close friendship with the island's popular politician Luis Munoz Marin. Shortly after leaving his government post, Fortas was given an annual $12,000 retainer to represent Puerto Rico "in all future proceedings before the United States Supreme Court, the United States Circuit Court in Boston, and agencies of the Federal Government."[27] In 1948, when the United States granted Puerto Rico the elective governorship for which Fortas had lobbied as interior undersecretary, and Munoz took office as the island's first democratically elected governor, Fortas began spending increasing time on legal matters relating to Puerto Rico, advising Munoz and his administration, helping draft the new Puerto Rican Constitution, and lobbying on behalf of Puerto Rico in Congress.[28]

During his almost two decades of private practice, Abe Fortas would live lavishly with Carolyn Agger, who kept her maiden name, as one of Washington, D.C.'s notable power couples. Their combined annual salary of more than $300,000 allowed for many indulgences. They drove a Rolls-Royce, owned an elegantly furnished Georgetown home and a summer house in Westport, Connecticut, and took pride in their collection of antique furniture and Chinese art, their three French poodles, and Carolyn's 150 pairs of shoes.

In their elegant Georgetown home, they hosted expensive dinner parties, attended by senators, Supreme Court justices, and foreign diplomats, in honor of Pablo Casals, the violinists Isaac Stern and Alexander Schneider, the pianist Rudolf Serkin, and other celebrity friends. Lyndon and Lady Bird Johnson, with whom the Fortases socialized regularly during LBJ's years as Senate majority leader and vice president, and William O. Douglas were among the Fortases' most frequent dinner guests. Despite Fortas's love for children, his wife, according to friends, "had made it clear to Fortas at the time of their marriage that she wanted no children." [29]

At his Georgetown home, Fortas, a gifted musician, hosted a Sunday evening chamber music group of amateur and professional violinists and cellists that he came to call "the 3025 N Street Strictly No Refund String Quartet." Isaac Stern, a frequent attendee who bought Fortas a new Italian violin to play on these evenings, would later remember his friend as "one of the most fanatically devoted amateur musicians I've ever known" and as having had "a passionate and wholly unambiguous, unashamed love affair with music." [30] Alexander Schneider was not the only one of Fortas's friends to suspect music meant more to Fortas than law. "Abe Fortas—I'm a violinist," he would often introduce himself at White House social functions during the 1960s. It was rumored that Fortas played his violin while being chauffeured around Washington in the backseat of his Rolls-Royce. [31]

Throughout his years as a partner at Arnold, Fortas, and Porter, Fortas's most important client would be Lyndon Johnson, who remained devoted to Fortas after his invaluable legal assistance in securing the contested Texas Senate seat for Johnson in 1948. Throughout the 1950s, Fortas continually praised his friend, the increasingly powerful U.S. Senate majority leader. "You did a superb—an unparalleled—job, during the last session of Congress," he complimented Johnson in a letter of August 9, 1956. When Johnson helped engineer passage of the Civil Rights Bill of 1957, Fortas lauded him again, writing that "you have made another magnificent contribution to the nation in your extraordinary management of the civil rights bill." [32] Johnson, for his part, always appreciated such praise and encouragement. "I am deeply grateful for your friendship and believe me there have been many times in the past months when I would have been helpless had I not had the privilege of tapping your rich store of wisdom," Johnson wrote Fortas after receiving the August 9 letter, mailed just prior to the 1956 Democratic presidential nominating convention. "Your remarks about the present session of Congress," Johnson added, "touched a deep chord in my heart. . . . As you know, I tried to do my best—and the fact that you think my best was adequate for the task is one of the most soul-satisfying pieces of information I have had in a long time. Praise from others I take with a grain of salt but praise from a man of your judgment is heartwarming, indeed."[33] During Johnson's tenure as majority leader, Fortas came to be viewed by many in Washington as LBJ's legal counsel and adviser par excellence.

In the late 1950s, before LBJ's election to the vice presidency, Fortas often took the initiative to offer his friend political advice. In 1958 alone, he advised Johnson on issues such as antitrust legislation, manpower in the armed forces, air transportation problems, and the Senate's Humane Slaughter Bill, in which he took a special interest as an animal lover. Indeed, pro bono, he advised the Animal Welfare Institute, which advocated for the bill. The *Washington Post* would later credit Fortas with playing a major role in getting it enacted.[34]

Over the years, Fortas would be steadfast in his representation of Johnson's financial interests and those of his political allies as well. In such endeavors, ethical considerations were not always paramount. When, for example, Johnson's old political crony George Parr, the notoriously corrupt Democratic political boss of Duval County, Texas, who had helped "produce" Johnson's extra votes to secure his Senate victory, was later convicted of mail fraud, Johnson engaged Fortas on Parr's behalf. It was fall of 1959 and Johnson, who was beginning his campaign for the 1960 Democratic presidential nomination, worried that unless Parr's mail fraud conviction was overturned, Parr might go public about the voter fraud in LBJ's 1948 Senate campaign and jeopardize Johnson's national political future. Fortas, a master legal technician, took Parr's appeal, pro bono, to the Supreme Court, where he won a reversal of the conviction on a technicality.[35] In winning this appeal, Fortas thus helped ensure Parr's continuing loyalty to Johnson.

With Johnson's election as vice president in November 1960, Fortas took on new assignments as his chief legal counsel and political adviser. Soon after entering the White House, President Kennedy named Johnson chairman of the President's Equal Employment Opportunity Commission, with the mandate to curb discrimination by government contractors. Johnson called on Fortas to draft a tough executive order that would give the EEOC the authority to cancel government contracts with businesses that discriminated in the hiring of blacks. Having done so, Fortas became an ex officio adviser to the presidential commission. EEOC staff members with decisions to make or problems to solve were told to "check it with Abe."[36]

Fortas also helped bolster Johnson's declining stature within the Kennedy White House, and with First Lady Jackie Kennedy, by arranging for his usually reclusive friend, the cellist Pablo Casals, to perform at a White House dinner on November 13, 1961. Fortas had first met Casals in 1957, when, as legal adviser to the commonwealth of Puerto Rico, he had persuaded Casals to hold his annual festival in Puerto Rico rather than France, its previous location. Thereafter, as director of the annual Puerto Rico–based event, Fortas developed his friendship with the cellist. So close was their relationship that when Casals's cello broke at the last rehearsal prior to the 1958 Casals Festival, Fortas bought first-class airplane tickets for himself and the instrument, and personally flew Casals's precious cello to New York for repair. Although not an excessive drinker, Fortas bought martinis for the occupants of both seats and downed each. In recounting why he had been so anxious, Fortas explained, "Carrying a man's cello is like carrying his wife."[37] Casals's much-celebrated White House appearance, meanwhile, came to symbolize the Kennedy presidency's commitment to high culture and its Camelot legacy. The arrangements for the White House concert, however, were so complicated that Fortas told Isaac Stern that he would never again get involved in organizing such an activity, even "if Jesus Christ were available for a Jew's Harp concert."[38]

Fortas further sought to enhance Vice President Johnson's reputation by arranging for Isaac Stern, Alexander Schneider, Rudolf Serkin, and other virtuoso friends to perform at official White House functions.[39]

Throughout Johnson's thousand days as vice president, Fortas reinforced his reputation as a top Washington insider, and this reputation only increased after President Kennedy's assassination in Dallas. On November 23, 1963, the day after Johnson became president, Fortas's chauffeur quietly drove his Rolls-Royce into the parking lot of the Executive Office Building near the White House. A little before noon, Fortas met privately with his old friend in the Oval Office, and the conversation resumed through much of the afternoon. Fortas soon emerged as the new president's most trusted adviser. "Check it with Abe" became the watchword of the Johnson White House.[40]

Prior to his Supreme Court appointment, Fortas's influence as a presidential adviser took a variety of forms. During the first several days of the Johnson presidency, Fortas was by Johnson's side continuously, reportedly advising LBJ on the establishment and staffing of the Warren Commission, charged with investigating Kennedy's assassination, and helping him draft the president's first nationally televised address to a joint session of Congress, "which would set the overall course of the Johnson administration."[41]

Moreover, in 1964, Fortas worked together with Isaac Stern and Johnson's press secretary, Pierre Salinger, to create the National Council on the Arts, a federal program. Stern would later recall his White House meeting with Fortas and LBJ, and Johnson saying, "Isaac, I don't know from beans about the arts, but you and Abe tell me this is a very important thing to do, and so I think it's important, and I will back it. And I promise you I will keep my cotton-pickin' hands off it."[42] Fortas then successfully promoted his friend Roger Stevens, a well-known impresario and chairman of the newly planned Kennedy Center for the Arts, to be appointed as the first chairman of the new National Council on the Arts. Fortas also advised Johnson on the composition of the first group of presidential appointees to the National Council, which included, in addition to Stern, Leonard Bernstein, Richard Rodgers, Agnes de Mille, Ralph Ellison, David Brinkley, and Gregory Peck. At a White House–sponsored party for the new council, Fortas entertained guests by playing a violin duet with Stern.[43]

During the first eighteen months of the Johnson presidency, the close Johnson-Fortas family friendship was a Washington social fixture. Soon after the Johnsons were settled in the White House, Fortas and his wife, Carolyn, were among the first Washingtonians to host a private social event for the new president and first lady, a dinner dance attended by more than one hundred guests. Fortas was a frequent White House visitor, and Georgetown neighbors noted that the presidential limousine was often parked outside the Fortas home on evenings, while LBJ stopped by for dinner, drinks or just to talk.[44]

Gideon v. Wainwright

The case that made Fortas a legal legend, and his most famous Supreme Court case, was decided in 1963, two years before he was appointed to the court. This was the landmark case of *Gideon v. Wainwright*, involving legal counsel for indigent defendants. In June 1962, Fortas, one of the few eminent Washington attorneys with a serious interest in criminal law and criminal defendants' civil rights, was selected by Chief Justice Warren to represent an impoverished prisoner whose appeal for a new trial had raised a fundamental constitutional issue. Like other lawyers appointed by the Supreme Court to represent indigent prisoners, Fortas took the case pro bono. Fortas's client, Clarence Earl Gideon, was a fifty-one-year-old ne'er-do-well who had been accused of breaking into and entering a Florida pool hall with the intent to commit a crime, a felony in that state. He had subsequently been tried and convicted without an attorney, over his objection that the Constitution guaranteed every defendant in a criminal trial the right to free legal counsel.[45] From his prison cell, Gideon had handwritten in pencil an appeal asking the court to provide him with legal counsel. When the case came up for argument in January 1963, Fortas spoke before the Supreme Court for more than an hour, passionately insisting that it was impossible for a criminal defendant to have a fair trial without an attorney speaking on his behalf. Fortas won the case, convincing a unanimous Warren court that Clarence Gideon could not adequately defend himself, and the justices ruled in *Gideon v. Wainwright* that every indigent criminal defendant must be given free legal counsel.

The Fortas Appointment to the Court

On July 28, 1965, the same day he announced Arthur Goldberg's appointment as UN ambassador, President Johnson announced that Fortas would fill Goldberg's previous seat on the Supreme Court. This was not an appointment Fortas had sought or wanted. Quite the contrary: both Fortas and his wife, Carolyn, were adamantly against his accepting such a post, just as they had opposed his taking an earlier-offered cabinet position under Johnson. This was in part because a government post would considerably dampen the couple's earnings and opulent lifestyle. The Supreme Court appointment would lower Fortas's annual salary by more than $150,000. In the longer term, the appointment would be as disastrous for Fortas's career as it had been for Goldberg's, likely more so.

When Robert Kennedy had resigned as attorney general in August 1964, Johnson, according to a report by the newspaper columnist Drew Pearson, had "moved heaven and earth" to persuade Fortas to succeed Kennedy as attorney general. Much to Johnson's disappointment, Fortas had declined, telling the president he had no interest in leaving his lucrative law practice.[46] In 1964, notably, the attorney general post paid $35,000 a year, a significant drop from Fortas's $200,000 salary at his law firm.[47]

Also in 1964, Johnson had approached Fortas's wife, Carolyn, by then a partner at Arnold, Fortas, and Porter as well, to offer her an appointment to the U.S. Court of Appeals for the District of Columbia.[48] Similarly uninterested in taking a big salary cut, she declined LBJ's prestigious offer.

Although, as the previous chapter detailed, Justice Goldberg did not notify Johnson that he would resign from the Supreme Court and accept the UN ambassadorship until July 20, the president had reportedly offered Fortas the seat before then. In fact, on July 19, after receiving LBJ's phone call offering him Goldberg's seat, Fortas had sent a handwritten letter to the White House declining the offer. "Again, my dear friend, I am obligated and honored by your confidence and generosity. . . . But after painful searching, I've decided to decline—with a heart full of gratitude," wrote Fortas. "This has been a hard decision. . . . I shall always be grateful." Johnson was so moved by his friend's penned rejection "that he kept it in his coat pocket and read it aloud to his entire family at the dinner table." But while moved, Johnson was not convinced that Fortas, if subjected to further pressure, would absolutely refuse a court appointment.[49]

In the days that followed, after further appeals from LBJ, Fortas wrote the president again refusing in no uncertain terms the Supreme Court offer. The famously persistent Johnson, however, continued pressuring Fortas to reconsider and finally succeeded in wearing him down through a trick. "I'm going to make a statement about Vietnam," he told Fortas of a televised July 28 press conference to which he invited Fortas. When Fortas arrived at the Oval Office, Johnson told him that he was about to announce the fateful commitment of fifty thousand more American troops to Vietnam and had wanted his adviser at the televised press conference. While walking to the East Room of the White House, where the press conference would be held, the president told Fortas that he would be announcing Fortas's Supreme Court nomination as well. While Fortas continued to protest that he would not accept, LBJ made one final and irrefutable argument: "I'm sending all these boys to Vietnam," he said. "They're giving their life to their country and you can do no less. If your president asks you to do something for your country, can you run out on him?"[50] As Fortas later told the story, Johnson did not notify him of his appointment until "we were half way down the hall to the press conference." Fortas, "overwhelmed by the persuasive magic of Lyndon Johnson," walked with him to the East Room, where he sat in the front row and awaited the announcement of his Supreme Court nomination. Fortas would later recall that "to the best of my knowledge and belief, I never said yes. . . . I so strongly felt that I did not want to do it."[51]

Thus, shortly after 1 p.m. on July 28, President Johnson announced Fortas's appointment to the Supreme Court. In apparent "deference to his old friend's reluctance to go on the Court," Johnson told those reporters covering the press conference that "Mr. Fortas has, as you know, told me on numerous occasions in the last twenty months that he would not be an applicant or a candidate, or would not accept any appointment to any public office.

This is, I guess, as it should be, for in this instance the job has sought the man."[52] Johnson had accomplished yet another of his dreams: his old friend Abe Fortas was finally going where he belonged—to the U.S. Supreme Court. Fortas had succumbed to Johnson's legendary arm twisting, and against his better judgment, Fortas had accepted LBJ's appointment. When the cartoonist Herblock depicted Fortas's investiture on the court, the new justice's right arm was twisted.[53]

In the days before Fortas's nomination was officially announced, Johnson asked his attorney general, Nicholas Katzenbach, to prepare a short list of other potential appointees in the unlikely event that Fortas persisted in his refusal. Each of the three men on the list were Jewish, thus continuing the tradition of a Jewish seat on the Supreme Court. Before this decision was made, however, Johnson had instructed Katzenbach to prepare a Justice Department memo on whether the Jewish seat should be reconsidered. In his long memo to the president, Katzenbach wrote that

> the question of whether or not this appointee should be Jewish concerns me. I think most Jews share with me the feeling that you should not seek a Jewish appointment for the "Jewish Seat" on the Court. It is somewhat offensive to think of religion as a qualification, and you will recall that after Mr. Justice Murphy's death there was not a Catholic on the Court for a period of eight years. At the same time, I think it undesirable for there to be no Jew on the Court for too long a period and I think it would be desirable if a Jew were appointed to the Court before 1968.
> . . . On balance, I think if you appoint a Jew he should be so outstanding as to be selected clearly on his own merits as an individual.

Fortunately, the attorney general concluded in his memo, such an ideal Jewish candidate, Abe Fortas, existed and was presumably available. Katzenbach then prefaced his recommendation of the three other Jewish candidates with the following evaluation of his top pick: "Before making these recommendations I think I should say that from a completely objective viewpoint Abe Fortas has every qualification for the Court. If you did not know him he would be my first recommendation—and still is."[54]

As for the three short-listed candidates, all legal scholars, they were Harvard law professor Paul Freund, University of Chicago provost Edward Levi, and Federal Court of Appeals judge Henry Friendly. Freund and Friendly, previously mentioned as possible nominees for the Jewish seat, had both studied under Felix Frankfurter at Harvard and clerked for Justice Brandeis.

In fact, as Bruce Allen Murphy has documented, it was the second time in two days that a high Johnson administration official had recommended the appointment of Freund, "the man who had so narrowly lost out to Byron White and Arthur Goldberg for the last two court vacancies, as a top candidate for the post. But Freund was doomed to become the bridesmaid again."[55]

So, too, was Edward Levi, who would become the first Jewish president of the University of Chicago in 1968 and the first Jewish U.S. attorney general several years later. This was the first of many times his name would be mentioned as a Supreme Court candidate. Both Lyndon Johnson and Richard Nixon would consider Levi to succeed Fortas, and to succeed Earl Warren as chief justice, and Gerald Ford would consider him to succeed Justice William O. Douglas. The descendant of one of America's most distinguished Reform rabbinic families, Levi was the son, grandson, and great-grandson of rabbis, as well as the grand-nephew of Rabbi Kaufmann Kohler, the second president of Cincinnati's Hebrew Union College. After receiving his undergraduate and law degrees from the University of Chicago, and a doctorate in jurisprudence from Yale Law School in 1938, where Fortas had been one of his teachers, Levi was appointed to the University of Chicago Law School faculty, becoming dean in 1950. When Levi was later named attorney general by President Ford in 1975, helped by his reputation for integrity and nonpartisanship, his appointment restored public confidence in the Justice Department, which had been shaken by the Watergate scandal and the personal involvement of Attorneys General John Mitchell and Richard Kleindienst. When Justice Douglas retired in November 1975, Ford asked Levi to compile a list of potential appointees and relied heavily on Levi's counsel in eventually selecting John Paul Stevens for the job.[56] Although three presidents—Johnson, Nixon, and Ford—seriously considered Levi for the high court, Levi, like Freund, was never offered an actual seat.

Meanwhile, in announcing Fortas's nomination on July 28, Johnson intoned that "the distinguished American who was my first choice for the position now vacant on the Supreme Court has agreed to accept this call to his vital duty." He described Fortas as "a scholar, a profound thinker, a lawyer of superior ability and a man of humane and deeply compassionate feelings toward his fellow man." Remarking on the future justice's hesitancy, he explained, "Mr. Fortas agrees that the duty and the opportunity of service on the highest court of this great country is not a call that any citizen can reject." In responding to reporters' questions, Fortas confessed that he felt "a little overwhelmed" and that while the Supreme Court appointment had indeed been offered to him before, "I had reminded the President that I was not seeking any government post, judicial or otherwise. The President was kind enough to say it was a place where I would perform superior service."[57]

No one was more surprised at the announcement than the nominee's wife, Carolyn, who had not been invited to the White House press conference to share in the moment. At the very moment Johnson was announcing her husband's nomination, Carolyn Agger was in a meeting at the Internal Revenue Service. She was outraged when she heard the news, having previously shared her views on the matter with both her husband and the president. She felt betrayed by Johnson, whom she had heretofore considered a close friend. "You don't treat friends that way," a law partner heard her say when Johnson later phoned her at her office. Livid, she hung up on the president. When LBJ called back the following day to invite the Fortases and some of their friends to dinner on his yacht, Carolyn refused to go and, true to her warning to the president, none of their friends went either. Abe Fortas later confided to his law partner Paul Porter that he had "never heard anybody talk to the President like Carol did." For the next two months, Carolyn refused to talk to Johnson, and it took her considerable time to forgive her husband for accepting the court appointment.[58]

Outside the Fortas home, however, Johnson's appointment was widely applauded. An unusual variety of individuals, from Elvis Presley's manager to FBI officials, sent congratulatory telegrams. In Fortas's home state of Tennessee, the *Chattanooga Times* noted approvingly the nominee's "deep commitment to the rule of law in the affairs of free men." The *New York Times* praised the appointment, predicting "a significantly useful career on the Supreme Court," while the *Washington Post* expressed "every reason to believe" that the nominee would serve the court "with great distinction."[59] News of the Fortas appointment especially delighted old New Dealers with whom Fortas had remained close. Florence Frank, the widow of Jerome Frank, Fortas's boss at the AAA, wrote telling Fortas "of how gratified Jerome would be if he were here. You were one of his most treasured persons." When his New Deal colleague and FDR confidant Benjamin Cohen congratulated Fortas on "the opportunity to apply the great talents of your mind and heart in meeting the critical and significant problems which challenge the powerful development of the Great Society," Fortas graciously replied, "The only man I know of who is supremely qualified for the Court is you."[60]

For Carolyn Agger's part, she complained privately about the "dirty trick LBJ played" by appointing her husband and confided to friends that the couple could not afford for Fortas to leave his lucrative private law practice for the court seat. "It's the goddamnest thing," an angry Agger told the Johnson aide Douglass Cater and his wife after they had offered congratulations at a White House reception days later. "Now I'll have to make all the money in the family and support him."[61]

Around the same time, while dining at the home of Supreme Court justice Hugo Black, Agger lamented to the judge's wife, Elizabeth, that the financial sacrifice might force them to give up their new house and several other recent undertakings. After living for more than twenty years in their elegant N Street home, the Fortases had decided they needed more land and purchased a palatial Georgetown property, then valued at $250,000, with room for an ample garden and swimming pool. They now had a $100,000 mortgage to pay off and ambitious plans for redecorating. As they made these plans, the selling price represented only the first of their increasing expenditures.[62]

Mr. Justice Fortas

After taking his Supreme Court seat, Abe Fortas, like his predecessor, Arthur Goldberg, provided a reliable fifth liberal vote on civil rights and civil liberties issues for the Warren court. During his less than four years on the bench, Fortas was a great supporter of judicial decisions that broadened the constitutional rights of criminal defendants. He notably provided the decisive fifth vote for Chief Justice Warren's majority opinion in the 1966 case *Miranda v. Arizona*, which as discussed in the Goldberg chapter required law enforcement officers to inform criminal suspects of their constitutional rights prior to questioning. In the *Miranda* case, which has been called the Supreme Court's most controversial decision in the area of criminal law, a laborer in his early twenties named Ernesto Miranda had been convicted of kidnapping and rape after confessing to these crimes while in police custody. However, at no time while being held in custody at the Phoenix Police Department station had Miranda been told of his right to counsel, or of his right to remain silent without an attorney present. In the court's 5–4 decision, Fortas joined Warren along with Justices Black, Douglas, and Brennan in voting to overturn Miranda's conviction, ruling that the Fifth Amendment protection against self-incrimination required the police to warn an arrested suspect of his rights to remain silent and legal counsel, and that any statements he made during interrogation might be used against him in a court of law. Following the court's decision, Miranda was released because, during his interrogation, he had not been told of his right to remain silent and to have an attorney present when questioned, or that his statements while in police custody might be used against him in court.[63]

During his court tenure, Fortas was especially concerned with protecting and expanding the legal rights of juveniles. In the aftermath of the *Miranda* decision, Fortas led the Warren court into a new area of criminal law previously ignored by the federal courts—the constitutional rights and treatment of juvenile criminal defendants. In Fortas's second year on the court, the justices debated the appeal of a fifteen-year-old Arizona boy named Gerald Gault, who was already on probation for purse snatching and had been accused of making an obscene telephone call to a neighbor. Without notifying Gault's parents, police officers arrested him and took him to a children's detention home, where probation officers questioned him and kept him in custody for several days without advising him of his right to an attorney and his right to remain silent while being questioned. Based on his statements while in custody and at a subsequent juvenile court hearing, without a lawyer present, Gault had been committed to a state industrial school for six years for making lewd comments over the phone, a crime for which an adult would have been imprisoned for only two months. Writing the court's majority opinion in the 1967 case *In re Gault*, Fortas held, in what would be his most celebrated ruling, that the Fifth Amendment privilege against self-incrimination, the right to legal counsel, and the right to confront and cross-examine opposing witnesses extended to juvenile court proceedings. In so doing, he was credited with having created a "Bill of Rights" for juvenile criminal defendants.[64] Juvenile defendants, maintained Fortas, were entitled to the same constitutional protections as were adults. "Neither the Fourteenth Amendment nor the Bill of Rights is for adults only," Fortas wrote. "Under the Constitution the condition of being a boy does not justify a kangaroo court."[65]

While Fortas's majority opinion was widely praised in liberal circles for having created a Bill of Rights for juvenile criminal defendants, and Chief Justice Warren predicted that it would become known "as the Magna Carta for juveniles," conservative critics of the court attacked it for promoting crime by granting juvenile defendants the same rights that the Warren court had too capriciously given adult criminal defendants. "The Supreme Court is the criminal's best friend," a cartoon mailed to Fortas alleged.[66]

Fortas's Extrajudicial Political Activity

During his Supreme Court tenure, Fortas engaged in a level of extrajudicial political activity far greater than that of even Justices Brandeis and Frankfurter. His extraordinary role as a presidential adviser to the Johnson White House actually increased while Fortas was on the bench. The ethical questions raised about the judicial propriety of such activity would lead to Fortas's disgraced resignation from the Supreme Court.

At various times while on the court, Fortas served the president as a political adviser, legal counsel, speechwriter, and crisis manager, often spending more hours of the day conferring with Lyndon Johnson than with his Supreme Court colleagues.[67] Fortas counseled not only the president but also his cabinet members on issues such as civil rights policy, fiscal policy, the setting of steel industry price increases, the sending of federal troops to Detroit during race rioting, and arbitrating transportation strikes. He attended high-level White House meetings on labor legislation, fiscal policy, election reform, and campaign financing, often giving advice on issues that would later come before the federal courts. One senator remembered calling the White House to ascertain President Johnson's position on pending Senate legislation and being told, "Well, the President is away, but Mr. Justice Fortas is here and he's managing the bill for the White House." As one of LBJ's most trusted speechwriters, Fortas helped write and edit the president's speeches on civil rights and criminal justice reform, rewrite parts of Johnson's 1966 State of the Union address, and draft an amendment to a congressional appropriations bill providing Secret Service protection for all presidential candidates. Fortas also advised LBJ on appointments for attorney general and to federal judgeships.[68]

On foreign policy, between 1965 and 1969, Justice Fortas continued to serve the president by participating in top White House diplomatic and military strategy meetings relating to the Vietnam War and the June 1967 Six Day War in the Middle East. Indeed, Fortas attended more cabinet and national security meetings relating to the Vietnam War than did UN ambassador Arthur Goldberg, one of the few doves in the Johnson administration. In a November 2, 1967, debate among LBJ's foreign policy advisers on whether to halt or continue the bombing of North Vietnam, Fortas, a Vietnam hawk, advised Johnson to continue escalating, advice the president followed. Early in 1968, after the Communist Viet Cong's Tet Offensive into Hanoi had practically destroyed hopes for a U.S. military victory in Vietnam, Fortas helped LBJ draft the defiant presidential address in which Johnson declared: "Make no mistake about it—I don't want a man here to go back thinking otherwise —we are going to win." When in a March 1968 meeting of Johnson's foreign policy advisers, with public protest against the war growing, Arthur Goldberg advocated direct talks with Hanoi and a "cessation of the bombing" of North Vietnam, while Fortas opposed any such halt.[69]

Fortas's hawkish role in Vietnam policy discussions was later said to be a source of great anger and resentment to Goldberg. According to one Johnson administration official, Goldberg "felt the deepest irony and anger" at Fortas's much greater influence on Vietnam policy making, while occupying the very Supreme Court seat from which Johnson had persuaded Goldberg to step down.[70] Goldberg, who had expected his UN ambassadorship to give him a major voice in winding down the war, found this voice eclipsed by his Supreme Court replacement, who held views on the war diametrically opposed to his.

Fortas, a strong supporter of Israel, played an especially prominent foreign policy role as an informal liaison between Avraham Harman, Israel's ambassador to the United States, and the Johnson White House. Fortas had become friendly with Harman after the Israeli ambassador's fall 1959 arrival in Washington. When Israeli prime minister David Ben-Gurion visited the United States in 1960, Fortas had hosted a breakfast meeting at his house for Ben-Gurion, Harman, and Johnson. In 1966, when Johnson had invited Israeli president Zalman Shazar to meet with him and Ambassador Harman at the White House, Fortas had attended as well. So, too, would Fortas often join when Israeli prime minister Levi Eshkol and foreign minister Abba Eban would meet with Johnson or Harman during their Washington visits. In late spring 1967, as tensions grew in the run-up to war between Israel and the Arab states, Fortas served as the intermediary between Ambassador Harman and other Israeli diplomats in their talks with both the White House and the State Department. Fortas, who never had a warm relationship with Secretary of State Dean Rusk, conveyed his concern to Harman that Israel should not count on support from the secretary, who had opposed U.S. recognition of the new state of Israel in 1948 and who invariably endorsed the anti-Israel policies favored by the Middle East specialists and Arabists on his State Department staff, a concern Fortas also conveyed to the White House.[71] With war on the horizon in late May 1967, Fortas's concerns about Rusk were vindicated: after Egyptian president Gamal Abdel Nasser closed the Straits of Tiran to Israeli shipping on May 22, and signed military pacts with Jordan, Syria, and Iraq, and close to 500,000 Arab soldiers were converging on Israel's borders, Rusk announced: "If Israel fires first, it'll have to forget the U.S." Shortly thereafter, Fortas warned Harman, as the ambassador left the justice's Supreme Court office, "Rusk will fiddle while Israel burns."[72] Rusk, for his part, considered Fortas "ill-informed" about foreign policy and believed that a Supreme Court justice should not be advising a president.[73] Many administration officials agreed, believing that in his extensive extrajudicial political activity, especially regarding the Vietnam War and Six Day War, Fortas had far exceeded the bounds of judicial propriety.[74]

Prior to his appointment to the high court, Abe Fortas, who had a private telephone line to the White House in his law office, was always available to answer Johnson's numerous calls for political and policy advice. Following his appointment, Fortas is widely known to have maintained a private phone line to the White House in his Supreme Court chambers. "Everyone talked about it around town," one of his court colleagues said of a practice that made some justices "uncomfortable."[75] While rumors were rife in Washington that Fortas talked by phone with LBJ almost daily, the Fortas biographer Bruce Allen Murphy has documented a total of 254 contacts between Fortas and the president between October 1966 and December 1968, most of them personal phone calls. During this two-year period, Fortas met personally with Johnson at the White House at least once a month. Another presidential scholar has reported that LBJ and Fortas met "at least eighty-seven times to discuss everything from Vietnam policy and the Detroit race riots to the drafting of presidential speeches and President Johnson's re-election strategy."[76] To some Supreme Court justices and law clerks, Fortas seemed to be devoting more time to advising LBJ on such policy matters than to discussing judicial issues, and writing judicial opinions, on cases before the court. Indeed, one law clerk who would later recall Fortas's greater attention to advising the president than to his judicial duties said he felt comfortable napping in Fortas's court chambers given the unlikelihood Fortas would show up.[77]

The close relationship between President Johnson and Justice Fortas fueled increasing media attention and speculation. "Few important Presidential problems are settled without an opinion from Mr. Justice Fortas," reported *Newsweek*, quoting "a well placed insider" who said that "the first person the President consults on anything is Abe Fortas." *Time* magazine opined in 1968 that "Fortas is the true *éminence grise* of the Johnson administration. No one outside knows exactly how many times Abe Fortas has come through the back door of the White House, but any figure would probably be too low."[78]

Even before Fortas was nominated to succeed Earl Warren as chief justice in 1968, increasing ethical questions had been raised, both in the press and in the Senate, about the propriety of Fortas's extensive advisory role in the White House. And rumors circulated that Fortas occasionally used his influence with the president to recommend close friends for government and judicial positions. The *New York Times*, for example, reported that Fortas had pushed to get his friend Bill Moyers appointed undersecretary of state. While Fortas denied such rumors, they contributed to increasing public criticism that Fortas's extrajudicial political activity violated standards of judicial ethics and propriety.[79]

The Fortas Nomination for Chief Justice

On March 31, 1968, Lyndon Johnson announced his decision not to run for reelection. On June 13, as the presidential campaign was gaining momentum, Chief Justice Earl Warren informed Johnson that he planned to resign from the Supreme Court. Warren's resignation plans were contingent, however, on the confirmation of his successor to ensure the Democrat Johnson would fill his seat before the November presidential election. Warren, a politically astute former Republican governor of California, feared that the Republican candidate, Richard Nixon, whose "law and order" campaign had included attacks on the Warren court and promises to appoint judges committed to reversing the court's liberal decisions, would win in November.[80]

Less than two weeks after being notified of Warren's decision, Johnson announced that he was nominating Associate Justice Abe Fortas to succeed Warren as chief justice. In seeking to promote Fortas, Johnson set in motion one of the most contentious Senate confirmation battles over a Supreme Court appointment since the 1916 nomination of Louis Brandeis.

In nominating Fortas to replace Warren, Johnson had sadly miscalculated his political support in the Senate as a lame-duck president. After five years of battles over Vietnam and civil rights, and especially since his March 31 announcement that he would not run again, Johnson's support on Capitol Hill had declined significantly, even among his former Democratic Senate colleagues from the South. With LBJ not seeking reelection, and with his vice president Hubert Humphrey trailing Nixon in the polls, Senate Republicans, together with Southern Democrats who opposed Justice Fortas's liberal positions on civil rights and the civil liberties of criminal defendants, joined forces to oppose the Fortas nomination.

Senate opposition to the Fortas nomination coalesced almost immediately.

Eighteen Senate Republicans, led by Michigan senator Robert P. Griffin, announced that they would fight the nomination and might use a filibuster to do so. Arguing that Johnson was a lame duck and that the appointment of a new chief justice should be made by the new president, they also attacked him for "cronyism" in nominating Fortas as chief justice and another old friend, Federal Court of Appeals judge Homer Thornberry, to take Fortas's seat. Indeed, Thornberry's nomination seemed to further fuel an unfriendly climate that adversely affected the Fortas nomination as well. Thornberry, a onetime mayor of Austin who had held LBJ's former congressional seat for eight terms and been one of his closest Texas political allies, had been a Johnson-appointed federal district and appellate court judge prior to his Supreme Court nomination. Members of the Senate Judiciary Committee wondered out loud whether it was ethically permissible for a president to appoint friends such as Fortas and Thornberry to the Supreme Court, irrespective of their qualifications.[81] One powerful Southern Democrat on the Judiciary Committee, Senator John McClellan of Arkansas, who would staunchly oppose the appointments, was especially angry about not having been consulted about the president's decision prior to LBJ's public announcement of their nominations. "I'm only the second ranking man on the Judiciary Committee," McClellan told a White House aide, "yet no one bothered to consult me." Had Johnson even briefly consulted McClellan before making his announcement, the conservative Democrat's aggressive opposition to the nominations might have been lessened.[82]

Fortas departed from precedent and became the first chief justice nominee to testify before the Senate Judiciary Committee, where he faced hostile questioning about the propriety of his activity as a presidential adviser while serving as a justice. Senator James Eastland of Mississippi, voicing the concerns of several Judiciary Committee colleagues, stated: "The judge's role is not known to the public. The nature and scope of his activities are kept secret and are not, therefore, subject to public scrutiny. . . . For instance, a litigant challenging the constitutionality of our involvement in Vietnam might not realize that one of the Justices acted as an adviser to the President on that matter. And when acts hidden from public view are made known, suspicion of wrongdoing may be the natural consequence, damaging public confidence in the Court."[83]

Responding to the especially harsh questions of Eastland and other Southern senators, Fortas admitted that he had taken part in White House strategy sessions relating to the Vietnam War, civil rights policy, and the riots in

Detroit and other cities. He claimed, however, that he had been careful never to advise Johnson on any case before the Supreme Court, or on issues that might possibly come before the court. Fortas was offended by the suggestion that the truth was otherwise, as it indeed was. He also claimed that as a citizen he had the right and duty to advise the president, even while serving on the court. These were disingenuous claims that most of his Judiciary Committee interrogators found difficult to accept.

While testifying, Fortas also lied about his role as a presidential speechwriter for LBJ, as the drafter of legislation while serving on the court, and as a presidential adviser who recommended political and judicial appointments. "I have never, since I became a Justice," Fortas told the committee, "initiated any suggestions or any proposal to the President of the United States." But, of course, as his biographer Bruce Allen Murphy has written, Fortas knew this was not true. "Forgive me for suggesting persons for appointment," he had written to Johnson in October 1967. Earlier, he had written that former governor Pat Brown of California, who had been defeated by Ronald Reagan in the 1966 gubernatorial election, "would be a good man to have somewhere in your administration. . . ." Shortly after joining the court in 1965, Fortas began making recommendations for appointments to the White House staffers Jack Valenti and Harry McPherson, as well as to Civil Service Commission chairman John Macy. In May 1966, Fortas offered the White House his own unsolicited list of candidates for appointments to ambassadorships and judgeships. In 1967, he recommended Pat Brown's defeated lieutenant governor, Glenn Anderson, for the ambassadorship to Chile.[84]

When Senator Eastland questioned Fortas about his efforts to lobby for the appointment of Bill Moyers as assistant secretary of state, Fortas replied that this is "completely, absolutely, totally without foundation in fact. I . . . did not make any recommendation for Mr. Moyers in connection with any position." As Bruce Allen Murphy has concluded, "Once more Fortas knew that the truth was otherwise."[85]

Still, Fortas's confirmation might have survived the controversy over his friendship with LBJ and his role as his presidential adviser. As pointed out by the pro-confirmation forces led by Republican senator Everett Dirksen of Illinois, Felix Frankfurter had continued to advise Franklin Roosevelt on political matters and judicial appointments while serving on the court. Moreover, Dirksen noted that earlier presidents had frequently appointed "cronies" to the Supreme Court, citing Abraham Lincoln's appointment of his campaign manager David Davis, Harry Truman's appointment as chief justice of his private attorney Fred Vinson, who often advised Truman on political questions while serving on the court, and President Kennedy's appointment of his campaign adviser Byron White.[86] Like Frankfurter, Davis, Vincent, and White, Fortas's relationship with the president predated his court years. Dirksen's observation notwithstanding, the well-documented allegations of judicial impropriety stemming from Fortas's advising of LBJ seemed to predispose most Senate Judiciary Committee members to oppose Fortas's confirmation. This was the case even as few appeared to know that he was not the only Supreme Court justice to "moonlight" as a Johnson adviser. In 1965, for example, Justice William O. Douglas had prepared a legal memo for the president at Fortas's urging. And although Fortas "often crossed the separation of powers line drawn by the Constitution, he had scrupulously avoided sitting on legal cases that involved his former law firm, Arnold and Porter."[87]

Indeed, the most damaging allegation against Fortas had nothing to do with his role as an LBJ adviser. Shortly after the first round of Senate Judiciary Committee hearings had concluded, it was disclosed that in summer 1968 Fortas had received a $15,000 honorarium for teaching a nine-week seminar at the American University Law School. While earning outside income from university teaching had not been unusual for a Supreme Court justice, the relatively large amount and the source of the Fortas honorarium generated further ethical questions. When the Judiciary Committee hearings resumed, it was revealed that Fortas's former law partner, Paul Porter, had approached five wealthy associates to raise $30,000, with half going to the American University Law School and the other half being paid to Fortas. Although Porter claimed Fortas had not been aware of this financial arrangement, the Judiciary Committee members charged it was improper for Fortas to have accepted this $15,000 fee, which was 40 percent of a Supreme Court justice's salary at the time. Fortas's Judiciary Committee opponents thus claimed that he lacked the "sense of propriety" a chief justice should have.[88] Such perceived ethical failings turned the tide decisively against him in his Senate confirmation hearings.

When the Fortas nomination subsequently came to the Senate floor, Republican senators launched a historic filibuster, the very first against a Supreme Court nomination. On October 1, 1968, after four days of Senate debate, the Senate fell fourteen votes short of the two-thirds majority necessary to end the filibuster. President Herbert Hoover's 1930 Supreme Court nominee, the federal judge John J. Parker, had been the most recent court nominee rejected by the Senate. Realizing his nomination was doomed, Fortas asked Johnson to withdraw it. Johnson reluctantly agreed, stating that Fortas was the most qualified person for the job and calling the Senate's refusal to end the filibuster and actually vote on the nomination "historically and constitutionally tragic."[89] Following his failure to be confirmed as chief justice, Fortas returned to his seat as an associate justice.

As Fortas's biographer has documented, considerable evidence suggests that Fortas's religion played a role in his Senate confirmation battle for chief justice. Fortas's attitude toward Judaism and the Jewish community had changed after he became a Supreme Court justice. Because he was the only Jewish justice, he felt he should try to be more publicly Jewish. Although he was religiously unobservant and rarely, if ever, had attended synagogue as an adult, he now worried about giving a public speech on the first night of Rosh Hashanah, the Jewish New Year. He passed requests from Jewish groups to the White House, such as sending a March 10, 1966, letter to Johnson advising him to accept an AJC speaking invitation, and Fortas himself began speaking more frequently before Jewish groups. He cultivated the friendship of Jewish leaders such as Rabbi Louis Finkelstein, the chancellor of the Jewish Theological Seminary, who, he told the Johnson White House, was regarded by American Jews as "the nearest thing to Jesus in the United States."[90]

He also cultivated relationships with influential Jewish politicians such as New York's Republican senator Jacob Javits, who Fortas hoped might be of help to his career. In the early days of his confirmation battle for chief justice, knowing that Senator Javits had promised to "help in any way he can," Fortas asked his former law partner Paul Porter to mobilize various Jewish groups and leaders on behalf of his nomination. Within a few days, B'nai B'rith groups and 150 major American Zionist leaders were informed that antisemitic opposition to the Fortas nomination was emerging. The White House began alerting the White House press corps to this fact, and the president's aides started briefing Jewish leaders about the alleged anti-Jewish bias held by some Senate Judiciary Committee members. As Murphy has noted, "There was no doubt that religious and racial bigotry existed and motivated some very powerful players in the Senate." The Judiciary Committee chairman himself, James Eastland, was heard to admonish a Senate colleague: "You're not going to vote for that Jew to be Chief Justice, are you?"[91]

The White House, with Fortas's approval, launched a campaign to further alert the Washington media of growing antisemitic opposition to his nomination, and began to question the motivations of any Fortas opponent in the Senate. Johnson, who was convinced that antisemitism was behind much of the Senate opposition to the Fortas nomination, and predicted that the campaign against Fortas would precipitate increased antisemitism throughout the country, reportedly reminded Senate minority leader Everett Dirksen that if he didn't actively support the Fortas nomination, he risked antagonizing Jewish voters and campaign contributors in a presidential election year.[92] When Senator Javits was subsequently put in the awkward position of having to defend some Senate colleagues against related allegations of antisemitism, Fortas himself suggested that the antisemitism card be played up to bolster the support of Javits and other liberal Republican senators on Fortas's behalf. Taking a behind-the-scenes role in his own defense, Fortas enlisted Paul Porter to "get telegrams to the [Judiciary] Committee and individual members, of the Committee and the Senate, from Jews and Jewish groups." The Senate fight against his nomination, Fortas claimed, "is anti-Negro, anti-liberal, anti-civil rights, [and] anti-Semitic." When Senate opposition mounted against the Fortas nomination in August, Javits met with the Republican presidential candidate, Richard Nixon, who had not yet commented publicly about the Fortas nomination, to warn him that he risked losing Jewish votes in November unless he spoke out about the nomination and could persuade some Senate Republicans to support it. Other Republican senators, such as Thruston Morton, a liberal Republican from Kentucky, came to share the Fortas and Javits view that Nixon's continued silence about the nomination would be linked to antisemitism and bigotry.[93]

In an August 22, 1968, letter, Paul Porter warned William P. Rogers, a close adviser to Nixon and later his secretary of state, that a failure to win Fortas's Senate confirmation would raise "possible ugly undertones of bigotry." Shortly thereafter, the Johnson White House asked other liberal Republicans and various Republican Jewish leaders to meet with Nixon and seek his support. Nixon finally made a public statement, telling the press, "The nomination is in the hands of the Senate. I don't oppose Fortas. I don't support him. I oppose a filibuster [against him]. I oppose any filibuster."[94] For the White House, for Javits, and for the Fortas nomination, Nixon's statement and opposition to a Republican filibuster was too little, too late. Javits, Morton, and other liberal Senate Republicans, as we saw, could not muster the two-thirds majority vote necessary to defeat the filibuster.

When Fortas's financial arrangement with American University first came to light in September 1968, his Senate supporters had asked him whether anything else in his past might cause similar or greater embarrassment. Fortas had assured them nothing would. Again, though, Fortas was wrong—whether owing to forgetfulness or willful nondisclosure.[95]

Several months after resuming his associate justiceship, on May 5, 1969, *Life* magazine "dropped a bombshell" in the form of an article titled "The Justice . . . and the Stock Manipulator." The article, by a Pulitzer Prize-winning reporter, which became front-page news nationwide, claimed that while Fortas was a justice, he had received a $20,000 retainer from the family foundation of Louis E. Wolfson, a shady investor then under SEC investigation who had since gone to prison for stock manipulation and fraud. The article further alleged that Fortas had visited Wolfson, a friend and former client, at his Florida farm in June 1966, shortly before Wolfson's indictment and that Wolfson had boasted to important Washingtonians that Fortas would help him stay out of prison.[96] There was evidence to support these and more damaging allegations. Although Fortas had, presumably under pressure, returned the $20,000 retainer to the Wolfson Foundation eleven months after receiving it, the *Life* article confirmed Justice Department rumors that Fortas, while sitting on the Supreme Court, had given informal advice to Wolfson about his legal problems. At the urging of Attorney General John Mitchell and Assistant Attorney General William Rehnquist, the Nixon administration Justice Department began a preliminary investigation of the Fortas-Wolfson relationship. (Rehnquist, who would lead this investigation, would in 1971 be appointed by Nixon to the Supreme Court.) This Justice Department investigation uncovered the revelation that Fortas had asked for and agreed to more than a onetime $20,000 payment from Wolfson: the Wolfson Foundation had promised to pay Fortas $20,000 a year for life and, should Fortas predecease his wife, would continue to pay her $20,000 annually. After initially denying any details of his relationship with Wolfson, on May 14, 1969, Fortas resigned from the court in the face of growing public condemnation and congressional talk of impeachment. In a letter to Chief Justice Warren, Fortas denied any wrongdoing but said he wanted to let the court "proceed with its vital work free from extraneous stress."[97]

After his resignation, Fortas returned to private law practice in Washington, but not with his old firm. Several of the younger partners in what was now called Arnold and Porter, embarrassed by the Wolfson scandal and the public disgrace of Fortas's resignation, shunned the former justice and strongly opposed his return. The firm, much to Fortas's anger and disappointment, decided not to take him back. Although some thought it unusual that Fortas's wife, Carolyn, remained at Arnold and Porter, Fortas supported her decision to do so. Certainly, her six-figure salary was an inducement for her to stay. The couple had kept up their expensive lifestyle and needed her salary, especially now that Fortas didn't have full-time work. Having rejected a publisher's invitation to write his memoirs, and the substantial advance to go with it, Fortas had approached former Oregon senator Wayne Morse and other prominent Washington and New York attorneys about going into private practice with him. They all turned him down.[98]

Fortas eventually formed a small but highly lucrative D.C. law practice with Howard Koven, a partner in the big Chicago law firm Friedman and Koven. In 1970, Fortas registered as a lobbyist on behalf of his former client John Loeb's investment banking firm. Between 1974 and 1981, while specializing in antitrust and securities matters, and advising wealthy clients and other lawyers on litigation strategies, Fortas's annual salary, although lower than during his best years at Arnold, Fortas, and Porter, exceeded $390,000. At the same time, Fortas retained three prominent nonpaying clients, Lyndon Johnson, Pablo Casals, and Isaac Stern, and often gave free legal advice to his aging mentor Justice William O. Douglas. In 1975, when Douglas resigned from the Supreme Court, Fortas helped him and his wife, Cathleen, draft his formal letter of resignation to President Ford.[99]

During the 1970s, Fortas also donated considerable free legal work to cultural institutions such the Kennedy Center, on whose board of directors he had long served, and Carnegie Hall. Fortas had served on the board of directors of Carnegie Hall while on the Supreme Court and became a very influential member of its executive board during the 1970s, when Isaac Stern was serving as Carnegie Hall's president.[100]

Although Fortas frequently smoked cigarettes and suffered from a worsening gall bladder condition, he continued practicing law until his death at age seventy-one, on April 5, 1982, from a ruptured aorta.[101]

Fortas's memorial service, held at the Kennedy Center, was attended by Supreme Court justices, members of Congress and the diplomatic corps, former first lady Lady Bird Johnson, and Isaac Stern, along with other musicians who cherished the former justice's friendship. Roger Stevens, the Kennedy Center's chairman, spoke first, praising Fortas's passionate arts advocacy. The television news anchor Eric Sevareid then paid tribute to his friend Fortas as a lawyer and jurist. Stern followed, recalling Fortas as a violinist and music lover who played in quartets with his friends every Sunday evening. "What can we musicians say?" he concluded. "How many ways can we say 'I love you' to Abe Fortas?"[102]

In his will, Fortas bequeathed to Isaac Stern the Italian violin that Stern had once given Fortas as a gift, with the personal request that Stern give it to a promising young violin student. He also left Stern his cherished desk, "a beautiful piece of furniture made out of an old square fortepiano," which Fortas had arranged to have sent to Carnegie Hall for Stern's use in his capacity as its president.[103]

Fortas's Legacy

Although Abe Fortas served on the Supreme Court for only three-and-a-half years, just a year longer than his predecessor, Arthur Goldberg, court scholars have rated him a "near great" justice, an entire category above Goldberg, who generally receives an "average" rating. In view of his brief tenure, this rating is probably overgenerous, although the scholarly and poignant literary style of his opinions and his additional year of court service may explain his "near great" status. Also prompting the sympathetic evaluation may be Fortas's strong support for the Warren court's judicial decisions that broadened the constitutional rights of criminal defendants, such as in *Miranda v. Arizona*. Most notably perhaps, Fortas's justly celebrated opinion in the 1967 *Gault* case, "which wrought a revolution in constitutional law by extending most of the Bill of Rights safeguards to juvenile offenders," is part of his enduring legacy.[104]

Part of Fortas's legacy, even though it predated his court tenure, was his passionate defense of Clarence Gideon in the landmark 1963 Supreme Court case *Gideon v. Wainwright*. Fortas is perhaps better remembered for his celebrated role in this case than for any of his judicial opinions while on the court —and it garnered him enduring fame. Justice William O. Douglas praised Fortas's presentation as "the best single legal argument" he had heard in all his court years.[105] With Fortas's cooperation, Anthony Lewis, the legal affairs columnist for the *New York Times*, wrote a best-selling book about the case, *Gideon's Trumpet*, which was later adapted into a movie of the same name, starring Henry Fonda as Gideon and the Puerto Rican actor José Ferrer as Fortas. When Fortas died, Linda Greenhouse's obituary in the *New York Times* described the *Gideon* case and Fortas's role before the Supreme Court more prominently than any of Fortas's later opinions as a justice.[106]

Today, however, Fortas is most often remembered not for these accomplishments but rather for the scandal that prompted him to resign from the Supreme Court. Sadly, Fortas's judicial career was cut short, and his legacy irrevocably tarnished, by his personal greed and highly questionable judgment. The only Jewish high court justice to have resigned in disgrace from the court, Fortas's story remains a symbol of avarice, greed, and judicial impropriety.

A few days following his resignation, the American Bar Association's Committee on Professional Ethics had announced that Fortas's financial relationship with Louis Wolfson violated a judge's obligation to engage in conduct free of any appearance of impropriety. One additional legacy of Fortas's brief court tenure, and the events surrounding his resignation, was thus that the ABA eventually completely revised its code of judicial ethics in an effort to prevent future judges from accepting outside income as Fortas had done. Ironically, although Fortas was appointed to the Supreme Court by Lyndon Johnson "to change the face of constitutional law by his analytical brilliance and eloquence," he is better remembered in American judicial history "as the man who spurred the American Bar Association to change its code of judicial ethics."[107]

For Justice Fortas, as for Justice Frankfurter, his Jewish religious legacy was negligible. Fortas, like Frankfurter, while raised in a religiously Jewish home, abandoned the Orthodoxy of his youth, married a non-Jew, and, throughout his adult life, was never active in Jewish communal life and never belonged to a synagogue. For Fortas, as for Frankfurter, his parents' Judaism would always remain "an obstacle to be overcome, rather than a heritage to be celebrated."[108] Although, as noted earlier, Fortas's attitude toward Judaism changed somewhat after he became a Supreme Court justice, the sincerity of Fortas's religious involvement remained questionable, given his continued nonattendance at synagogue, even for High Holy Day services. While he stayed home from the Supreme Court on Yom Kippur, the holiest day on the Jewish calendar, he did so because his secretary insisted on this, not because of his personal sense of its religious significance. Because he was the court's only Jewish justice, he felt he should try to seem more publicly observant.[109]

Fortas's Kennedy Center memorial service, like the service for Justice Brandeis, was completely devoid of Jewish religious content, with no rabbi officiating. Whereas Isaac Stern had joined Fortas's chamber music group in playing their friend's favorite piece, from Mozart's string quartet in C, and other musicians had played from Brahms, Rachmaninoff, and Schubert, no Kaddish was recited. Since Fortas had not been religiously observant, one of his friends recalled, it seemed appropriate to take "religion out [of the service] and [make] music fill its place."[110] Fortas did not live his life as a religious Jew, and as reflected in this secular service, he did not die as one.

While the sincerity of Fortas's religious involvement remained questionable, his staunch support for Israel was most sincere and remains an enduring, if sometimes forgotten, legacy of his public career. One of his important achievements as Lyndon Johnson's adviser, both before and during his presidency, was his strong political advocacy on behalf of Israel, his friendship with Israeli ambassador Avraham Harman and other Israeli diplomats in Washington, and his role in helping promote a pro-Israel Johnson foreign policy. In the weeks leading up to the 1967 Six Day War, as noted earlier, Fortas, who also counted Jerusalem mayor Teddy Kollek as a friend, served as an invaluable go-between for the Israeli embassy in its negotiations with the Johnson White House and the State Department. In the days following Egyptian president Nasser's May 22 closing of the Straits of Tiran to Israeli shipping, with war increasingly imminent, Ambassador Harmon was in close touch with Fortas, regularly visiting the justice at his Supreme Court chambers or his house, and apprising him of political developments and information on which Fortas might then advise President Johnson. On the evening of June 4, Johnson had dinner at the Fortas home, and Fortas advised the president that war in the Middle East was near. Fortas's advice proved prescient: at 4:30 a.m. the next morning, Israel attacked Egypt, launching a war in which Israel more than tripled its size by routing the alliance of Arab military forces, and winning control of the entire Sinai Peninsula, the West Bank of the Jordan River, the Golan Heights, and the Old City of Jerusalem, from which the Jews had been expelled in 1948.[111] Fortas, who remained one of LBJ's most influential pro-Israel advisers before, during, and after the war, was delighted by Israel's victory. After Isaac Stern visited the territories Israel had captured from Syria, Jordan, and Egypt, he wrote to Fortas: "Your inner self would smile."[112]

Had Fortas been confirmed by the Senate to succeed Earl Warren in 1968, he would have made history as the first Jewish chief justice of the Supreme Court. Part of Fortas's legacy is the lamentable fact that in his resignation, he made history by abruptly ending the tradition of the Jewish Supreme Court seat to which he had been appointed. Both of President Nixon's unsuccessful nominees to fill the Fortas vacancy, Clement Haynsworth and G. Harrold Carswell, were Protestants, as was Nixon's successful nominee, Harry Blackmun, who was ultimately confirmed by the Senate in April 1970. The *New York Times* story about Blackmun's appointment pointed out that he was the fourth Protestant nominated to the court by Nixon, since Warren Burger, also a Protestant, had already been appointed chief justice to succeed Earl Warren in 1969. Nixon's next two court appointees, Lewis F. Powell Jr. and William Rehnquist, who took their seats in January 1972, were Protestants as well.

The Jewish seat had held continuously for fifty-three years, from Brandeis's appointment in 1916 to Fortas's resignation in 1969. Presidents from Wilson and FDR to Kennedy and Johnson came to view the appointment of a Jewish justice, and the continuity of a Jewish seat, as recognition of Jewish representation and acceptance in American government and public life as well as a significant factor in their appeal for Jewish votes.

Nixon, in breaking with this tradition, explicitly announced that he would not seek religious or racial balance or representation in making his Supreme Court appointments. Since he had received only 17 percent of the Jewish vote in the 1968 election, down from 18 percent in his 1960 presidential campaign against JFK, and since throughout his political career he had never been notably close with the Jewish community, he did not feel obligated to reward Jewish voters when filling Supreme Court vacancies.[113] Nixon's appointment of Justice Blackmun, rather than a Jew, to succeed Fortas did generate some controversy. Nixon's speechwriter Pat Buchanan, a Catholic not known for his closeness to the Jewish community, told Nixon that he was "right in ending the Jewish seat" and argued for the appointment of an Italian-American justice, because Italians "have never had one of their own" on the Supreme Court. "Politically, the elevation of a Catholic Italian-American to the Jewish seat on the Court would mean ten million Italians would light candles in their homes for the President," Buchanan contended, and remove "some of the hurt Italian-Americans constantly feel as a result of Italian-Sicilian control of organized crime in the United States." Nixon, however, did not follow Buchanan's advice, and an Italian-American justice would have to wait until Ronald Reagan's appointment of Antonin Scalia in 1986. Nor did Nixon follow the advice of his Jewish speechwriter William Safire, who argued for a Jewish appointment. "If the President is not going to appoint a Jew," Safire wrote White House chief of staff H. R. Haldeman, "nothing he says beforehand is going to placate that community."[114] Frank Mankiewicz, an aide to Robert Kennedy and George McGovern's campaign manager in 1972, was more emphatic in his criticism of Nixon for not appointing a Jewish justice to the Fortas seat: "He's the guy who's taken the Jew off the Supreme Court."[115]

After the Fortas resignation in 1969, it would be twenty-four years until President Bill Clinton's appointment of Ruth Bader Ginsburg would place another Jewish justice on the Supreme Court.

9

THREE JEWISH JUSTICES

Ginsburg, Breyer, and Kagan
Join the Court

DURING HIS EIGHT YEARS in the White House, President Bill Clinton appointed more Jews to high-level administration positions than had any other president. Of special historic significance, Clinton was the first president to appoint two Jews to the Supreme Court, Ruth Bader Ginsburg and Stephen G. Breyer. The first court vacancy came within six weeks after Clinton's inauguration, on March 3, 1993, with the surprise retirement of Justice Byron White, who had served for thirty-one years. White's resignation made Clinton the first Democratic president since Lyndon Johnson to appoint a justice to the Supreme Court.[1]

Determined to "hit a home run" in making his appointment, Clinton asked his White House counsel, Bernard Nussbaum, to put together a comprehensive list of potential candidates. Working together with Ron Klain, Clinton's deputy White House counsel, who had clerked for Justice White in the late 1980s, Nussbaum compiled an initial list of forty-two names, supported with some ten pages of biographical profiles for each. This list included jurists such as Eighth Circuit Court of Appeals judge Richard Arnold, a Clinton friend and political ally from Arkansas; Chief Judge Judith Kaye of New York state's highest tribunal, occupying the position Benjamin Cardozo had once held; Stephen Breyer, then on the First U.S. Court of Appeals; and Ruth Bader Ginsburg, on the U.S. District of Columbia Court of Appeals. The list also included a few law professors and Democratic politicians including New York's liberal governor Mario Cuomo, former South Carolina governor (and Clinton's new secretary of education) Richard Riley, former Arizona governor (and Clinton's secretary of the interior) Bruce Babbitt, and George Mitchell, the Senate majority leader and a former federal district judge in Maine.[2]

Clinton's first choice was Cuomo, then midway through his third term as governor. Cuomo's nomination was also being pushed by several members of Clinton's White House staff, including George Stephanopoulos and economic adviser Gene Sperling, who had once worked for Cuomo. On March 30, Stephanopoulos phoned Cuomo, whose first response was noncommittal. When Clinton himself called Cuomo from Air Force One a few days later, Cuomo reiterated his ambivalence, saying that while he was predisposed not to accept, he would nonetheless continue considering the offer. On April 7, after Clinton had returned from a summit with Russian leader Boris Yeltsin, and Cuomo had still not given the White House a definitive answer, Stephanopoulos pressured Andrew Cuomo, the governor's son and chief political adviser. "We need an answer," he told Andrew Cuomo by phone. According to Stephanopoulos, Andrew Cuomo assured him that he had talked to his father for more than two hours that day, and that the governor had told his son, "If you want me to, I'll call Clinton and take it." Word quickly spread around the White House that the Cuomo appointment was a done deal and that the nomination would be announced the following day. An hour later, however, Mario Cuomo officially took himself out of the running, faxing the president that he was withdrawing his name from consideration and stating that duty to New Yorkers took precedence over his desire to sit on the Supreme Court.[3]

After Richard Riley and George Mitchell subsequently also withdrew their names, and Clinton ultimately decided not to offer Bruce Babbitt the nomination, the president turned his attention from politicians to federal judges. Since the announcement of Justice Byron White's resignation the previous month, Senator Edward Kennedy of Massachusetts had been lobbying the White House on behalf of Stephen Breyer, a former Harvard Law School professor and Kennedy staffer on the Senate Judiciary Committee. Now, he was the highly respected chief judge of the Federal Court of Appeals based in Boston. While on leave from Harvard and working for Kennedy on the Senate Judiciary Committee in the 1970s, Breyer, a Democrat, had won the admiration of several prominent Republican senators, including Orrin Hatch of Utah, who, at Kennedy's request, called Clinton to recommend Breyer's appointment.[4] Breyer's bipartisan popularity impressed Clinton, who instructed Ron Klain and another White House attorney, Vince Foster, to first interview Breyer in Boston and then invite him for a personal interview with Clinton in Washington.

Unfortunately for Breyer, his interview with Clinton was scheduled days after he had broken ribs and punctured a lung in a bicycle accident near his home in Cambridge. Although his initial interview with Klain and Foster, held at Mount Auburn Hospital, had gone well, Breyer's injuries were serious enough that he was not permitted to subsequently fly to Washington for his White House interview. Following a "bone-jarring" Amtrak train ride to Washington's Union Station, where Foster met him and drove him to the Oval Office, Breyer's relatively brief meeting with the president did not go well. "Normally a friendly and almost garrulous man," Breyer was short of breath from his injuries and writhing in pain.[5] Judge Breyer and President Clinton simply did not click, in notable contrast to the candidate Clinton ultimately nominated, Ruth Bader Ginsburg, with whom Clinton made a rapid "emotional connection."[6]

In filling Byron White's seat, Clinton had announced he was seeking a nominee with "a fine mind, good judgment, and wide experience in the law and in the problems of real people, and somebody with a big heart." Ginsburg seemed to perfectly fit the bill: she was the first woman to receive tenure at Columbia Law School, and she had enjoyed a distinguished thirteen-year judicial career on the prestigious U.S. Court of Appeals for the District of Columbia. During his ninety-minute meeting with Ginsburg, the president reportedly "fell in love" with her life story and "big heart," while empathizing with her long personal and professional struggles against gender discrimination. In announcing her appointment, Clinton praised her historic achievements on behalf of legal rights for women, noting that she had won several landmark sex discrimination cases before the Supreme Court during the 1970s. He called Ginsburg "the Thurgood Marshall of gender equality law," who was "to the women's movement what Thurgood Marshall was to the rights of African Americans." Clinton also praised her demonstrated ability, while a federal judge, to serve as a consensus builder, a healer, and a "moderate liberal."[7]

Ginsburg's nomination was widely applauded throughout the legal community and by senators from both parties. New York's Daniel Patrick Moynihan, the influential chairman of the Senate Finance Committee, which had the power to approve or defeat Clinton's proposed health plan, had been especially persistent in his support. "Pat Moynihan has been calling me every day to say that we should nominate her," Clinton said.[8]

Given her unquestionable qualifications and bipartisan support, Ginsburg's Senate confirmation hearings, from July 20 to 23, 1993, were uncontroversial. The Judiciary Committee, which now included two women, Dianne Feinstein of California and Carol Moseley-Braun of Illinois, quickly approved the nomination by a unanimous 18–0 vote. Soon thereafter, the full Senate confirmed her nomination by a vote of 97–3, and on August 10, 1993, she took the oath of office as the 107th justice, the second woman, and the first Jewish high court justice in twenty-four years.

In early April 1994, a little more than a year after Justice White's retirement, Justice Harry Blackmun, now eighty-four years old and in declining health, announced his plans to retire after twenty-four years on the court. Once again, Clinton had initially hoped to appoint a politician rather than a judge, and his first choice was Senate majority leader George Mitchell, who had turned down the president's offer for the same post the previous year. Once again, however, Mitchell disappointed the president. When Interior Secretary Bruce Babbitt also withdrew his name from consideration, Ted Kennedy resumed his lobbying for Stephen Breyer. On May 10, 1994, Kennedy, Judge Breyer's most persistent advocate, met with Clinton at the White House to once again make his case. Acknowledging that Breyer had not made a favorable impression the year before, Kennedy argued that the president had perhaps unfairly misjudged Breyer's personality as lacking warmth and being "personally distant." Breyer, Kennedy reminded Clinton, had traveled with much discomfort to the White House that day, directly from his hospital bed in Boston. Kennedy also reminded the president that Breyer enjoyed strong bipartisan support on the Senate Judiciary Committee, for which Breyer had earlier served as chief committee counsel. He would thus enjoy an easy, noncontentious confirmation hearing. Demonstrating the judge's bipartisan backing, Senator Orrin Hatch, the ranking Republican member of the Senate Judiciary Committee, again called the White House on Breyer's behalf. Further strengthening the Breyer case was the fact that Bernard Nussbaum had been replaced as White House counsel by Lloyd Cutler, a Washington corporate attorney who was a close friend and supporter of Breyer.[9]

On July 19, the Senate Judiciary Committee voted unanimously, 18–0, as it had for Ginsburg the previous year, to recommend Breyer's confirmation, praising him as "a principled moderate pragmatist." He was subsequently confirmed by a full Senate vote of 87–9 and was sworn in by Chief Justice William Rehnquist as the 108th justice, and the seventh Jewish justice, to serve on the Supreme Court.[10] For the first time since the 1930s, two Jewish justices were serving together.

The Rise of Ruth Bader

Born on March 15, 1933, Ruth Bader grew up in a working-class part of Brooklyn's Flatbush neighborhood. Like the parents of Justices Frankfurter,

Goldberg, and Fortas, her parents were impoverished immigrants, her mother, Celia, from Austria and her father, Nathan, from Russia. When she was only two, Ruth's older sister, Marilyn, died of meningitis. Perhaps because of this early tragedy, Ruth, now an only child, became very close to her parents, especially her mother. While her father was busy eking out a meager living as a furrier and later as a haberdasher, her mother, while working in a garment factory, took charge of Ruth's intellectual development. Encouraging Ruth to read, she frequently took her daughter to the local public library. Because the library was one floor above a Chinese restaurant, Ruth would later recall, "I learned to love the smell of Chinese food in those days."[11]

Ruth Bader was an outstanding student at James Madison High School, a public school whose other distinguished alumni have included U.S. senators Chuck Schumer, Bernie Sanders, and Norm Coleman, the playwright and film producer Garson Kanin, the singer-songwriter Carole King, the actor Martin Landau, four Nobel Prize laureates, and the presidential biographer Robert Dallek. Bader edited the school paper, the *Highway Herald*, and wrote articles about the school's history and the U.S. judicial system. Her interest in the law was already apparent, as demonstrated in an editorial, "Landmarks of Constitutional Freedom," in which she discussed the meaning of the Ten Commandments, England's Magna Carta, the Declaration of Independence, the Bill of Rights, and the UN charter. She was also an officer of the Go-Getters, a pep club for sporting and social events, played cello in the school orchestra, and twirled a baton at football games. During summers, she worked as a camp counselor in the Adirondacks. In 1948, at age fifteen, she served as the camp rabbi, delivering sermons to her fellow campers.

When she graduated from high school in 1950, Bader won several awards and a New York State Scholarship, which helped pay for her tuition at Cornell University. Many years later, shortly after her appointment to the Supreme Court, Madison High dedicated a mock-trial courtroom in her honor. Attending the dedication ceremony, Justice Ginsburg joked that the mock-trial courtroom was more impressive than some of the real courtrooms in which she had practiced. But Ruth's actual high school graduation was infused with tragedy. Her mother, having suffered from cervical cancer, had died the day before. Ruth was grief-stricken on leaving home that fall to begin her Cornell undergraduate studies.[12]

At Cornell, where she majored in government and was elected to Phi Beta Kappa, Bader was her class's top woman graduate. During her freshman year, she met Martin Ginsburg, a sophomore, whom she married soon after her graduation in June 1954. Robert Gordis, one of the most distinguished Conservative rabbis in America, officiated at their wedding. The next July, she gave birth to her first child, Jane, who is today a professor at Columbia Law School.

When Ginsburg began her studies at Harvard Law School the following year, where Martin was a year ahead of her, she was one of only nine women in a class of five hundred. Prior to the 1950s, the contentious issue of whether to admit women to the law school had divided the faculty and administration for almost a century. Although Dean Erwin Griswold, who would later serve as President Lyndon Johnson's solicitor general, had announced the decision to admit women in October 1949, thus opening a door previously closed to Jewish women in the legal profession, Harvard Law was not especially welcoming to Ginsburg and her fellow eight women classmates. During Griswold's twenty-one-year tenure, which lasted until 1967, women were accepted in only token numbers. Moreover, they were not permitted to live in the law school dormitories or study in one of Lamont Library's rooms. Also, there were no women's bathrooms in one of the two buildings in which they attended classes. At a dinner hosted for the women students at his home, Dean Griswold, who like some other faculty colleagues during the 1950s publicly questioned whether women should have the right to enter the legal profession, asked each woman how she could justify taking places that would otherwise have gone to qualified male students. Despite such obstacles, Ginsburg excelled, making history by becoming the first female member of the *Harvard Law Review*.[13]

When Martin graduated from law school in 1958, he accepted a position at a major New York City firm, where he established a reputation as one of the country's top tax attorneys, counting the Texas billionaire oil tycoon and future third-party presidential candidate Ross Perot among his clients.[14] Ruth followed him to New York, transferring to Columbia to complete her legal studies. There, as one of only twelve female students, she was elected to the *Columbia Law Review* and graduated in 1959 as one of the class's top two students. Despite her impressive academic record and service on two prestigious law reviews, she confronted gender discrimination when applying for a Supreme Court clerkship. Ironically, as we saw in chapter 6, the Supreme Court Justice who refused to hire her was Felix Frankfurter. Women had not yet been admitted as students during Frankfurter's twenty-five years as a Harvard Law professor, and he had never taught women or employed them as research assistants. In 1960, Albert Sacks, the Harvard Law professor who selected most of Frankfurter's law clerks, proposed hiring Ginsburg, but Frankfurter refused to even interview her. The reason, he acknowledged, was that "he was not yet prepared to hire a woman."[15] As the Frankfurter chapter discussed, the justice had been ready to break the color barrier, by hiring the first African American law clerk, but not to break the glass ceiling that had limited the advancement of women in the American legal profession by hiring the first female law clerk.

After being rejected for the Frankfurter clerkship, Ginsburg continued struggling to secure a job. Not a single New York City firm to which she applied offered her a position. As she would later recall, "In the fifties, the traditional law firms were just beginning to turn around on hiring Jews. In the forties, it was very difficult for a Jew to be hired by one of the well-established law firms. They had just gotten over that form of discrimination. But to be a Jew, a woman and a mother to boot, that combination was a bit much."[16] Aided by her former Columbia law professor Gerald Gunther, she was eventually offered a clerkship with Judge Edmund L. Palmieri, of the Federal District Court of Manhattan. Following this two-year position, Ginsburg was hired as a research associate with and then associate director of Columbia Law School's Comparative Law Project, with the assignment of studying Sweden's judicial system. This work, funded by the Carnegie Foundation, allowed her to learn Swedish, visit Sweden to observe the country's courts, and coauthor, with a Swedish judge, *Civil Procedure in Sweden*, a major text for which she was later awarded an honorary doctorate by the University of Lund. It also furthered her growing interest in pursuing a career as a law professor.[17]

Thus, in 1963, Ginsburg joined the faculty of Rutgers University Law School, where she would teach for the next nine years. The second woman on the school's faculty, and one of only twenty women law professors in the country, Ginsburg rose to eventually become a full professor, and spent 1971 as a visiting professor at Harvard Law School, before accepting a position as the first tenured women professor at Columbia Law School in 1972. While still an assistant professor at Rutgers, Ginsburg became pregnant with her second child. She concealed the news by wearing loose-fitting clothes borrowed from her mother-in-law, fearing that discovery of the pregnancy by the dean or her colleagues might cost her her job.[18]

While still at Rutgers, Ginsburg also cofounded the ACLU Women's Rights Project and began to teach courses on sex discrimination. In her eight years as a Columbia professor, Ginsburg taught courses in civil procedure, constitutional law, and sex discrimination law, and prepared the first legal casebook on gender-based discrimination. Also, throughout the 1970s, as attorney for the Women's Rights Project, Ginsburg led a campaign to persuade the Supreme Court that gender discrimination, like race discrimination, should be prohibited by the Constitution's equal protection clause. Inspired by the gradualist litigation strategy of Thurgood Marshall, who had famously led the NAACP Legal Defense Fund's fight to end racial discrimination, she won several historic cases in the emerging field of sex discrimination law. Most notably perhaps was her landmark victory in the Supreme Court case *Reed v. Reed*, for which she wrote the ACLU's legal brief and in which the court unanimously overturned an Idaho state law that gave legal preference to men over women as administrators of estates of the deceased. Following *Reed v. Reed*, in which the court for the first time struck down legislation on grounds that it constitutionally discriminated against women, Ginsburg, as attorney for the Women's Rights Project, argued six gender-discrimination cases before the Supreme Court. In these cases, including *Frontiero v. Richardson*, *Weinberger v. Wiesenfeld*, and *Craig v. Boren*, Ginsburg sought to achieve legal recognition of women's rights by persuading the court's members that any form of sex-based discrimination was unconstitutional. She won five out of these six cases.

In 1980, Ginsburg, having made her reputation as the country's preeminent litigator for women's legal equality and as the first tenured woman professor at Columbia Law, was appointed by President Jimmy Carter to the U.S. Court of Appeals for the District of Columbia, the nation's second most powerful federal court. This appointment was pathbreaking, given that only eight other women were then serving on America's federal courts. Judge Ginsburg moved to Washington, D.C., with her husband, Martin, who left his New York law practice and endowed chair at Columbia Law School to become a professor at the Georgetown University Law Center.[19]

Although while serving on D.C. Court of Appeals Ginsburg's judicial opinions gave consistent support to liberal issues such as gender equality and the constitutionality of affirmative action, she also developed a conservative record on criminal law issues. Moreover, to the surprise of some liberal and feminist supporters, she voiced public criticism of *Roe v. Wade*, the Supreme Court's landmark 1973 decision that affirmed a constitutional right to abortion, because the court did not ground its decision in the equal protection clause's guarantee against sex discrimination. Although she privately defended a woman's right to abortion on equality grounds, when she was nominated for the Supreme Court in 1993 some women's groups opposed her appointment because she had earlier expressed criticism of the court's

Roe v. Wade ruling. Her views on such issues sometimes allied Ginsburg with conservative colleagues such as Judge Antonin Scalia, her friend and fellow opera lover, who also served on the D.C. court and would later serve with her on the Supreme Court.[20]

Two of the cases on which she voted while sitting on the D.C. Circuit Court of Appeals — *Goldman v. (Secretary of Defense) Weinberger* and *United States v. Pollard* — were of special interest to American Jews.[21] Very significantly, Judge Ginsburg dissented from the Circuit Court's 1984 decision in *Goldman v. Weinberger*, which upheld an Air Force regulation that prohibited an Orthodox Jewish Air Force officer named Simcha Goldman from wearing a yarmulke while on duty. Goldman, an Orthodox Jew and an ordained rabbi serving as a clinical psychologist in an Air Force hospital, normally kept his head covered at all times in accordance with Orthodox practice. When outdoors, he wore the regulation Air Force cap; when indoors, he wore a small cloth skullcap. In May 1981, Goldman's superior officer notified him that wearing a yarmulke indoors while in uniform violated the Air Force dress code and ordered him to remove it or face a court-martial. Goldman's attorneys claimed that this regulation infringed upon his First Amendment right to the free exercise of religion. Judge Ginsburg agreed, arguing in her dissent that for a military commander to prohibit the yarmulke that Goldman had worn without incident through several years of military service reflected "callous indifference to Dr. Goldman's religious faith" and "runs counter to the best of our traditions."[22]

In a quite different case of concern to many American Jews, in March 1992, a three-judge Circuit Court panel upheld, by a 2–1 vote, a lower court denial of the motion of convicted spy Jonathan Pollard to withdraw his guilty plea. Two judges affirmed the life sentence for Pollard, convicted for passing classified information to Israel, rejecting his attorneys' claim that the government had breached a plea bargain agreement that might have resulted in a lesser sentence. One of these two judges was Laurence Silberman, a conservative Republican whom Ronald Reagan had appointed to the D.C. Circuit Court; the other was Ginsburg. Many of Pollard's supporters within the American Jewish community, including a number of liberal Democrats allied ideologically with Ginsburg, were shocked by their ruling, noting the irony that both judges who voted against Pollard were Jewish.[23]

Another Judge Ginsburg

As discussed in the last chapter, several Jews were considered for the Supreme Court between Abe Fortas's resignation in 1969 and Ginsburg's appointment in 1993, including Edward Levi and Paul Freund. Among those mentioned during the 1970s and 1980s were Harvard Law professor Laurence Tribe, one of the country's preeminent constitutional law scholars and Supreme Court litigators whose widely used treatise, *American Constitutional Law*, has been called the most influential book ever published in the constitutional law field;[24] Alan Dershowitz, a Harvard Law professor, prolific author, and celebrated appellate attorney who had served together with Stephen Breyer as one of Arthur Goldberg's clerks; Richard Posner, a University of Chicago Law School professor and Ronald Reagan appointee to a federal judgeship on the U.S. Court of Appeals for the Seventh District in Chicago in 1981 who was the most frequently cited legal scholar serving on the federal bench and had been short-listed for the high court by both Reagan and George H. W. Bush; and Laurence Silberman, whom we met earlier as Ginsburg's U.S. Court of Appeals colleague and who had served as an undersecretary of labor, deputy attorney general, and ambassador to Yugoslavia during the Nixon and Ford administrations before Reagan appointed him to the federal bench in 1985. Silberman, for his part, had been short-listed for Supreme Court nominations in 1987, 1990, and 1991.

The one actual Jewish nominee between 1969 and 1993 was Federal Judge Douglas H. Ginsburg, one of Ruth Bader Ginsburg's colleagues on the U.S. Court of Appeals in D.C. A graduate of Cornell and the University of Chicago Law School, Ginsburg had clerked for Supreme Court justice Thurgood Marshall and taught at Harvard Law from 1975 to 1983, before coming to Washington to serve in the Justice Department's Antitrust Division. In 1987, less than a year after President Reagan had appointed Ginsburg to serve on the D.C. Appeals Court, Reagan nominated him to fill the Supreme Court vacancy created by the retirement of Lewis F. Powell Jr., following the Senate's rejection of Reagan's first nominee, Robert Bork, in one of the most contentious Senate confirmation battles in American history.[25]

Ginsburg's ill-fated nomination, however, collapsed after only nine days amid news reports revealing he had smoked marijuana both as a college student and while a professor at Harvard. Many Senate Democrats were already opposing his nomination because of his staunch record as a market-oriented conservative believed to oppose a strong government role in achieving social equality, and who had once been described as "dancing along this periphery of what can be called conservative economic extremism."[26] For many Senate Republicans, as well as conservatives within the Reagan administration, Ginsburg's admission that he had smoked marijuana while a law professor, including with his students, seemed alarmingly illicit for a Supreme Court aspirant and provided sufficient rationale to vocally oppose his nomination. Officials in the Reagan Justice Department were concerned he would become known as the "marijuana judge." After a number of important Republican senators announced their opposition to his nomination, Secretary of Education William Bennett, a leading conservative spokesman for the administration, met with Ginsburg to urge him to withdraw his nomination to the Supreme Court. Under growing pressure from many, including former supporters, Ginsburg asked Reagan to do just that.[27]

The quick collapse of Douglas Ginsburg's Supreme Court nomination did not adversely affect his tenure as a judge on the U.S. Appeals Court, where he continued to serve until 2011, including a stint as chief judge from 2001 to 2008.

The Rise of Stephen Breyer

Stephen Breyer was born in San Francisco on August 15, 1938, of Romanian- and German-Jewish ancestry. Unlike Justices Cardozo, Frankfurter, Goldberg, and Fortas, who grew up in Orthodox Jewish homes, Breyer's religious upbringing was decidedly Reform. Breyer's grandparents and parents all belonged to San Francisco's Temple Emanu-El, one of California's largest Reform congregations, where Breyer attended Sunday school and celebrated his bar mitzvah. Also, unlike some other Jewish justices, whose childhoods were impoverished, Breyer grew up in a comfortably middle-class family. His father, Irving—a Stanford graduate who was the first in his family to attend college—had a forty-year career as an attorney for the San Francisco Board of Education, and his mother volunteered for the local Democratic Party and the League of Women Voters. Justice Breyer still wears the wristwatch his father received on his retirement, inscribed "Irving G. Breyer, Legal Advisor, San Francisco Unified School District, 1933–1973, from his friends." His younger brother, Charles, who became a partner in a politically influential San Francisco law firm, and served as the city's deputy district attorney in 1979–1980, was appointed a federal district judge by President Clinton in 1997. (Justice Breyer recuses himself in all appeals of his brother's court rulings.[28])

At Lowell High School, San Francisco's most prestigious public high school, known for its competitive admissions, Breyer excelled academically, receiving only one B, and was voted by his classmates the "most likely to succeed." He was a star on the Lowell High debate team, and one rival debater, from the city's Catholic Saint Ignatius High School, was Jerry Brown, the state's future attorney general and four-time governor. Although Breyer had wanted to attend Harvard, where he was accepted for admission, his parents persuaded him to stay closer to home and follow his father at Stanford. Following his 1959 graduation from Stanford, having majored in philosophy and been elected to Phi Beta Kappa, Breyer won a Marshall Scholarship to Oxford University's Magdalen College, where he studied philosophy, politics, and economics, graduating with first-class honors in 1961. After returning to the United States, Breyer began his legal studies at Harvard, where he graduated magna cum laude in 1964 and was an editor of the *Harvard Law Review*.[29]

After his law school graduation, Breyer clerked for Supreme Court justice Arthur Goldberg, drafting the justice's oft-quoted opinion—an expansive interpretation of the right to privacy—in the landmark case *Griswold v. Connecticut*. Following his clerkship, Breyer stayed in Washington, working from 1965 to 1967 as a special assistant to Assistant Attorney General Donald Turner, an authority on antitrust regulation. Around this time, Breyer met his future wife, Joanna Hare, a fellow Oxford graduate and the daughter of Lord John Hare, the First Viscount Blakenham, a British aristocrat and politician who had served as a cabinet minister under Prime Minister Harold Macmillan and as chairman of England's Conservative Party. When Breyer met Joanna, she was working in the Washington office of London's *Sunday Times*. In 1967, the couple were married at a small village church in Suffolk, England, in an Anglican ceremony that was carefully edited to omit any references to Jesus. Breyer may be the only Supreme Court justice in American history, and certainly the only Jewish justice, to have married into the British aristocracy. Joanna Breyer later became a psychologist and worked for many years with pediatric cancer patients at the Dana-Farber Cancer Institute in Boston, of which Justice Breyer is now a trustee.[30]

Shortly after his marriage, Breyer joined the Harvard Law faculty, where he taught federal administrative law and regulation, receiving tenure in 1970 and garnering acclaim as a regulatory law expert. Breyer stayed at Harvard until 1980, with periodic leaves for government work in Washington: in 1973, he commuted to Washington to serve as assistant prosecutor on Archibald Cox's Watergate prosecution team, and he stayed on to serve as special counsel (1974–1975) and later as chief counsel (1979–1980) to the Senate Judiciary Committee. As special counsel, Breyer worked closely with Senator Ted Kennedy, then the Judiciary Committee's chairman. Helping Kennedy organize the Judiciary Committee's public hearings on airline deregulation, Breyer became convinced that government regulations were impeding the growth of the airline industry and subsequently helped draft and win congressional support for legislation that deregulated the industry in 1978. As the Judiciary Committee's chief counsel, Breyer encouraged Kennedy, as well as Republican committee members, to also support deregulation of the trucking and gas industries. His approach to winning support for deregulation was uniquely bipartisan: several mornings a week, Breyer had breakfast with the top staff lawyer for Senator Strom Thurmond, then the committee's senior Republican member, and "together, cordially, the two staffers mapped out plans for the committee." Although the liberal Democrat Kennedy and conservative Republican Thurmond were deep ideological adversaries on a variety of policy issues, they instructed their Senate staffers "to find areas of common ground." Indeed, as the legal analyst Jeffrey Toobin has pointed out, "it turned out to be a remarkably successful legislative partnership," resulting in landmark legislation deregulating the airline, trucking, and natural gas industries. Breyer's support for deregulation, as well as his personable, evenhanded bipartisan approach, won him the admiration of Thurmond and other Republican committee members, most notably, as noted, Utah senator Orrin Hatch.[31]

Breyer's bipartisan popularity proved important in 1980 when President Carter, in the closing months of his administration, nominated Breyer to serve on the U.S. Court of Appeals for the First District in Boston. When Breyer's confirmation hearings began before the Senate Judiciary Committee in mid-November 1980, Ronald Reagan had already been elected president and Strom Thurmond had replaced Ted Kennedy as Judiciary Committee chairman. Although some speculated that Thurmond would not permit Carter, now a lame duck, to have an additional federal judgeship appointment, Kennedy asked his friend Orrin Hatch to urge Thurmond to let the Breyer nomination go through before Reagan's inauguration. With Hatch praising Breyer as "a member of the family" for his work as Senate Judiciary Committee counsel, he and Thurmond convinced the committee's other Republicans to support Breyer. Although Breyer's nomination came only nine days after the Republicans had won both the presidency and the Senate, the latter for the first time in twenty-five years, Breyer, a lifelong Democrat, was confirmed on December 9, 1980. Breyer was the last federal judge to be confirmed before Carter left office in January 1981.[32]

Breyer sat on the U.S. Court of Appeals for fourteen years, serving as its chief judge from 1990 until his appointment to the Supreme Court. In 1985, Breyer was named to the U.S. Sentencing Commission, where he helped formulate federal guidelines to minimize disparities in criminal sentencing for comparable crimes, to be applied by judges nationwide.[33]

While serving on the U.S. Court of Appeals, Breyer also published two major books dealing with regulatory law. In *Regulation and Its Reform*, his experience with airline deregulation helped him identify a set of regulatory programs "in which the regulatory weapon is not well suited to deal with the problem at hand." In *Breaking the Vicious Cycle: Toward Effective Risk Regulation*, he criticized government regulation of health and safety risks, arguing that changed priorities could permit the government to formulate more cost-effective health regulations and save many lives.[34]

The Decline of Antisemitism in the Legal Profession

From the 1960s era, when Arthur Goldberg and Abe Fortas served on the Supreme Court, to the 1990s, when Ginsburg and Breyer took their seats, the decline in antisemitism within the legal profession was dramatic. Whereas Harry Shulman had broken an academic glass ceiling for Jews in 1951 by becoming dean of Yale Law School, by the 1980s the law school deans at Yale, Harvard, Columbia, the University of California, Berkeley, and the University of Pennsylvania were all Jewish. By the 1990s, six Jewish deans had served at Yale Law, with Eugene Rostow having filled the position twice. By the mid-1970s, Edward Levi had risen from being the first Jewish law school dean and president at the University of Chicago to becoming the first Jewish U.S. attorney general, shattering another glass ceiling for Jewish leadership in the legal profession and in American public life. In 1969, Bernard Segal, a prominent Philadelphia attorney and Jewish philanthropist, became the first Jewish president of the American Bar Association.

After 1945, elite law schools such as Harvard and Yale began dropping their discriminatory policies and admitting more Jewish students.[35] At the same time, the elite "white shoe" Protestant Wall Street firms — such as Davis, Polk, and Wardwell; Dewey, Ballantine, which had hired few if any Jews prior to 1945—began afterward to hire Jewish Ivy League law school graduates. By the early 1960s, the white shoe firms, which had earlier blatantly discriminated against Jews, had begun hiring Jewish associates, and by the 1980s each boasted at least a few, and sometimes many, Jewish partners.

Prior to the 1950s, the elite Wall Street firm to hire the most Jewish partners was Sullivan and Cromwell, whose two senior partners for many years were John Foster Dulles and his brother, Allen Dulles—who served, respectively, as secretary of state and CIA director during the Eisenhower administration. During the 1930s and 1940s, when John Foster Dulles was the firm's managing partner, Sullivan and Cromwell was the world's largest law firm. Alfred Jaretzki, who had become the firm's first Jewish partner in the 1890s, had risen from a poor Jewish family to attend Harvard with George Cromwell, the son of the firm's original partner William Nelson Cromwell. During the 1920s, Jaretzki's cousin Edward Green, his son Alfred Jaretzki Jr., and his son-in-law Eustace Seligman all became partners. This was indeed an impressive collection of Jewish partners for the time, although, as another former Sullivan and Cromwell partner pointed out, "they were all relatives." Also, these young Jewish partners were not religiously observant. Eustace Seligman, the son of the Columbia University economist E. R. A. Seligman and grandson of the banker and philanthropist Joseph Seligman, who had declined the treasury secretary post offered by President Ulysses S. Grant, was an active member of the Ethical Culture Society and had no involvement in Jewish religious or communal life. Edward Green belonged to the Protestant Riverside Church. Seligman, whose relatives considered him a self-hating Jew, "divided his active social life, giving Jewish and non-Jewish cocktail parties, both of which his relatives found stuffy and stopped attending."[36] Times have changed at Sullivan and Cromwell too: the current managing partner is a Sabbath-observing Orthodox Jew.[37]

From the time Paul Cravath, an eighth-generation American Protestant, took charge of Cravath, Swaine, and Moore in 1900, a role he held until the 1950s, every attorney promoted to partner was a Protestant.[38] Nonetheless, the law firm is distinguished for having hired several Jewish associates: the pioneering woman attorney Helen Lehman Buttenwieser in 1936, Eugene Rostow in 1937, and Lloyd Cutler in 1940. Edward Nathan Benjamin, who became an associate in 1950, became the firm's first Jewish partner in 1958. By 1962, the firm had employed at least thirty Jewish associates, three of whom became partners in 1965. Since then, at least thirty Jews have become partners.

While Davis, Polk, and Wardwell began to hire "token" Jewish associates after 1945, it did not promote as many to partnership positions as did Cravath. Under the leadership of its founding partner, John W. Davis, the former solicitor general, ambassador to Great Britain, and Democratic presidential candidate in 1924, and a titan of the U.S. legal profession, Davis, Polk, and Wardwell gained a reputation as "the most socially exclusive office on Wall Street," in which only Protestant members of the Social Register would become partners into the 1950s. Late in life, Davis would describe himself as one of those "who resent all immigration in general and that of the Russian Jew in particular." Throughout his long tenure as the firm's senior partner, his presence, including his "genteel anti-Semitism," was "felt everywhere within the firm," and it was well known that Jews were not welcome. Not until 1961, six years after Davis's death, did a Jew become a partner.[39] And, according to the non-Jewish novelist Louis Auchincloss, whose father had been a Davis, Polk partner, the firm during his father's era "would have been shocked that its senior partner would ever be Jewish," though this is just what happened during the 1980s. Equally interesting, in 1971 Lydia Kess, an Orthodox Jewish woman, became a partner at Davis, Polk, making her the first woman partner, and the first Jewish woman partner, in a white shoe law firm.[40]

In their legal ascents, Ginsburg, Breyer, and later Elena Kagan did not face the antisemitism experienced by their Jewish predecessors on the court. By the 1960s–1980s, most of the elite New York, Washington, and Chicago law firms that had been closed to Frankfurter, Goldberg, and Fortas when they began their legal careers were hiring growing numbers of Jews as associates and partners. For her part, Ginsburg did experience discrimination within the legal profession, but as a woman, not as a Jew. Also, by the time Ginsburg, Breyer, and Kagan were rising professionally, the antisemitism that had earlier prevailed in the nation's top law school faculties had significantly declined. By the 1970s and 1980s, a significant proportion, and sometimes a majority, of these faculties were Jewish. Ginsburg, Breyer, and Kagan all served on elite law school faculties—Columbia, Harvard, and Chicago, respectively—together with a substantial number of Jewish colleagues. In 2003, Kagan broke another glass ceiling when she was appointed the first woman, and the first Jewish woman, dean of Harvard Law School. This appointment was a milestone for American Jewish attorneys and an important stepping-stone on her road to appointment as U.S. solicitor general and, subsequently, as the eighth Jewish justice of the Supreme Court.

The Rise of Elena Kagan

Born on April 28, 1960, Elena Kagan grew up in a comfortably middle-class family on Manhattan's Upper West Side. Her mother, Gloria, was a grade-school teacher at the highly selective, public Hunter College Elementary School, which Elena attended. Her father, Robert, was a real estate lawyer whose small firm specialized in converting Upper West Side buildings from rental apartments to cooperatives. At Hunter College High School, Elena was a top student in a school known for its competitive entrance exam and a popular student leader who was elected student government president. She entered high school planning to follow her father into the legal profession. Her high school yearbook photo, in which Kagan is pictured in a judicial robe, holding a gavel, includes a quotation from Supreme Court justice Felix Frankfurter: "Government is itself an art, one of the subtlest of arts."[41]

Even as a teenager, Elena Kagan was shattering glass ceilings for women. For example, her parents belonged to the Lincoln Square Synagogue, a new modern Orthodox congregation on the Upper West Side, whose young, charismatic rabbi, Shlomo Riskin, was attracting hundreds of families and singles to its innovative yet traditional Sabbath and holiday services. A precocious and highly self-confident Hebrew school student, the twelve-year-old Kagan told Rabbi Riskin she wanted to celebrate her bat mitzvah, which at the time was not done at Orthodox synagogues. Her rabbi had never officiated at a bat mitzvah. "Elena Kagan felt very strongly that there should be ritual bat mitzvahs in the synagogue, no less important than the ritual bar mitzvah," Rabbi Riskin said. "This was really the first formal bat mitzvah we had." Because she was not permitted to read from the Torah at a Saturday morning service, as boys did, her bat mitzvah ceremony took place on a Friday night, in May 1973, at which she read from the Book of Ruth and gave a talk analyzing the biblical portion that she read. "We crafted a lovely service, but I don't think I satisfied her completely," recalled Rabbi Riskin, who left the synagogue in 1983 to settle in Israel, where he became chief rabbi of the new West Bank town of Efrat.[42]

Following her high school graduation in 1977, Kagan entered Princeton University, where she was on staff at the *Daily Princetonian*, serving as the newspaper's editorial chair during her senior year. (Kagan would later become the third consecutive Princeton graduate appointed to the Supreme Court, following Samuel Alito, class of 1972, and Sonia Sotomayor, class of 1976.) After graduating summa cum laude with a major in history in 1981, Kagan was awarded Princeton's prestigious Daniel M. Sachs Fellowship for study at Oxford University, where she was awarded a Master of Philosophy at Worcester College in 1983.

After returning from Oxford, Kagan began her legal studies at Harvard, five years before Barack Obama arrived at Harvard Law. There, she was a law review editor and a research assistant for Professor Laurence Tribe, for whom Obama would also later be a research assistant. Tribe was a political confidant and friend of Democratic politicians such as Sargent Shriver and Senators Ted Kennedy and Joseph Biden. He had dedicated the first edition of his famous treatise *American Constitutional Law* to Shriver and seemed to be on everybody's short list for appointment to the Supreme Court once another Democrat reached the White House. But Tribe's impassioned three-hour testimony against Robert Bork's Supreme Court nomination in 1987 doomed his chances. Senate Judiciary Republicans, in reprisal for Tribe's influential role in rejecting Bork, vowed to block his nomination if it ever happened. Even Tribe's most ardent admirers came to realize he would never be confirmed by the Senate, and as a result, President Clinton never seriously considered him for appointment as solicitor general or to the Supreme Court. Although thus frustrated in his ambition to sit on the Supreme Court, Tribe would later serve briefly as a legal adviser to the Obama administration. An important law school mentor to Kagan and Obama, he would continue to serve as their confidant in the years ahead. As Jeffrey Toobin, one of Kagan's law school classmates, would later note, Tribe selected only his best students to work for him, and only those students who shared his liberal politics and political ambition.[43]

After graduating from law school in 1986, Kagan served a one-year clerkship with Abner Mikva, a judge on the Court of Appeals for the District of Columbia, followed by a Supreme Court clerkship with Thurgood Marshall, who nicknamed the five-foot-three Kagan "shorty."[44]

After two years as a litigator with the Washington, D.C., law firm Williams and Connolly, Kagan moved to Chicago to teach at the University of Chicago Law School, where she did some scholarly writing about the First Amendment and won an award for teaching excellence. Not long after receiving tenure in 1995, however, Kagan moved back to Washington when her former boss Judge Mikva, then serving as President Clinton's White House counsel, invited her to join his legal staff. Two years later, Kagan decided to remain in Washington when her former Princeton classmate Bruce Reed, then Clinton's domestic policy adviser, asked her to serve as deputy director of the White House domestic policy staff. These two White House staff positions have been noted as pivotal in Kagan's career. She quickly won the respect of Clinton, who would say that any time Kagan entered the Oval Office the room's average IQ doubled. In her role, Kagan negotiated the resolution of lawsuits, and helped craft legislation involving the cigarette industry and campaign finance reform. More important perhaps, her White House jobs allowed her to impress not only Clinton but also a generation of senior Democratic Party politicians and government officials, many of whom would later play central roles in the Obama administration.[45]

In 1999, Clinton nominated Kagan for a federal judgeship on the Court of Appeals of the District of Columbia Circuit, where she had clerked for Mikva. With Clinton's second term drawing to a close, the Republican-controlled Senate Judiciary Committee postponed voting to confirm her nomination, eventually letting it lapse. In 2001, President George W. Bush nominated John G. Roberts Jr., the Supreme Court's future chief justice, to the D.C. Court of Appeals seat for which Kagan had been nominated but not confirmed. After a lengthy delay, the Senate confirmed Roberts's appointment.[46]

In preparing to leave Washington at the end of the Clinton administration, Kagan had assumed she would be able to return to the University of Chicago Law School, even though the school had a strict rule that faculty could only remain on leave for two years without forfeiting their tenured positions. But the school held to its policy, refusing to make an exception. Kagan, meanwhile, had published very little as a legal scholar, and her former University of Chicago colleagues felt she was more interested in working in government than in law school teaching. Kagan thus was able to secure a visiting professorship at Harvard Law School, where she quickly published a major law review article on administrative law, which was named the year's best scholarly article by the ABA's Section of Administrative Law and Regulatory Practice. After two years of teaching, she was granted tenure. And in 2003, Harvard president Lawrence Summers, who as a former Clinton White House aide and treasury secretary had worked with and befriended Kagan in Washington, named her the first female Harvard Law dean in the school's history. She was also Harvard Law's third Jewish dean, following Albert Sacks (1971–1981) and James Vorenberg (1981–1989).

Kagan's six years as dean of Harvard Law School were a notable success. When she began the position, ideological battles among the faculty were hindering the hiring of new members. Kagan solved this problem by hiring both liberal and conservative faculty and in so doing built bridges between the warring political factions. In her six years as dean, she made forty-three new full-time permanent faculty appointments, recruiting well-known professors from other law schools, including the prolific liberal scholar Cass Sunstein from the University of Chicago and the conservative scholar Jack Goldsmith, who had been assistant attorney general and Defense Department special counsel in the second Bush administration. She was increasingly popular among students, giving them free coffee and access to an ice rink during winter. Her consensus-building leadership style was especially apparent in her handling of the debate over ROTC military recruiting on campus. She maintained the law school's longtime opposition to ROTC and other recruiters who discriminated against gay people, not permitting them to hold official interviews on campus. At the same time, however, she warmly welcomed soldiers and veterans who were law school students, and she introduced an annual Veterans Day dinner for active military students, veterans, and their spouses. Kagan's tenure as dean was so successful that when Lawrence Summers was ousted as president in 2006, Kagan was on the short list to succeed him, although the post eventually went to another woman, the noted Civil War historian Drew Gilpin Faust.[47]

Elena Kagan had first met Barack Obama when they were colleagues at the University of Chicago Law School, where he was a lecturer in constitutional law. During those years in the early 1990s, she had plenty to talk about with Obama, the first African American president of the *Harvard Law Review*, over an occasional coffee or lunch in Hyde Park, including their shared tutelage under Laurence Tribe. Judge Abner Mikva, the politically influential former Democratic congressman from Chicago, was also a shared mentor. Kagan had clerked for him when he was a federal judge, after which Mikva recommended her for her Supreme Court clerkship with Thurgood Marshall, her professorship at the University of Chicago Law School, and when he became President Clinton's White House counsel, invited her to join his legal staff. While a federal judge, Mikva had also offered Obama a judicial clerkship upon his graduation from Harvard, which he declined, preferring to work in public service as a community organizer in Chicago. Mikva remained a mentor to Obama during his years as a young state senator from Chicago and U.S. senator from Illinois. In 2014, President Obama awarded Mikva the Presidential Medal of Freedom, the nation's highest civilian honor. When the former congressman died in July 2016, Obama said, "I've lost a mentor and a friend."[48] University of Chicago Law School professor Cass Sunstein, whom Kagan recruited to join the Harvard Law faculty when she was dean, was another mutual friend—and a future Obama administration member, serving as administrator of the White House Office of Information and Regulatory Affairs. Kagan and Obama's paths crossed in the coming years when Kagan was the Harvard Law School dean and then senator Obama was a rising star in the Democratic Party.

When Obama ran for president in 2008, Kagan let it be known that "she was backing [him and] hoped to join him in Washington." During the transition period following Obama's election, White House counsel designate Gregory Craig met with Kagan in Cambridge to discuss administration positions that might interest her. After ruling out her first choice, deputy attorney general, which had already been promised to someone else, she was offered the post of solicitor general, one of the top Justice Department positions, which had never before been held by a woman.[49] Less than a week after his inauguration, in January 2009, Obama nominated Kagan to the solicitor generalship, a position often considered a stepping-stone to the Supreme Court. William Howard Taft had served as solicitor general before being elected president in 1908 and subsequently appointed Supreme Court chief justice in 1921; FDR appointed two of his solicitors general, Robert Jackson and Stanley Reed, to the court; and Thurgood Marshall, for whom Kagan had clerked, served as Lyndon Johnson's solicitor general before his appointment to the court in 1967. When her appointment was confirmed by the Senate on March 19, Kagan thus became the first woman and third Jewish solicitor general in U.S. history. As solicitor general, the federal government's top appellate lawyer — sometimes known as the "tenth justice" — Kagan was responsible for all government litigation before the Supreme Court. Her appointment was also unique in that she had no previous appellate experience. Indeed, although she had been a junior associate at the Williams and Connolly law firm, she had never actually argued a case on her own in a courtroom.[50]

Kagan, Ginsburg, Breyer, and *Citizens United*

On September 9, 2009, six months after her appointment as solicitor general, Kagan argued her first case before the Supreme Court, *Citizens United v. Federal Election Commission*, in which the court ruled 5–4 against her in a highly controversial landmark decision about political campaign finance and corporate money's role in U.S. politics.[51] In *Citizens United*, the court was asked to decide whether it was unconstitutional, under the First Amendment, to limit corporate free speech, in the form of campaign contributions, during election campaigns. Kagan, arguing on behalf of the Obama administration, maintained that it was unconstitutional and that corporations did not enjoy the same First Amendment rights to free speech as did living people. The court disagreed, ruling against Kagan that corporations did, indeed, have these rights and that corporations such as Citizens United, a conservative nonprofit group, enjoyed a First Amendment right to spend unlimited money to support the election or defeat of political candidates. Justice Anthony Kennedy, speaking for the court's majority, thus ruled that corporate speech in the form of election campaign contributions could not be limited.[52]

Arguing for Citizens United in this case was Theodore Olson, himself a former solicitor general under George W. Bush, who had argued, and won, numerous cases before the Supreme Court. "Mr. Olson," Justice Ginsburg said, effectively representing the views of her liberal dissenting colleagues, Stephen Breyer, Sonia Sotomayor, and John Paul Stevens, "are you taking the position that there is no difference in the First Amendment rights of an individual? A corporation, after all, is not endowed by its creator with inalienable rights. So is there any distinction that Congress could draw between corporations and natural human beings for purposes of campaign finance?" To this, Olson replied, "What the Court has said in the First Amendment context, over and over again, is that corporations are persons entitled to protection under the First Amendment." The court's ruling in *Citizens United*, a setback for liberal campaign finance reform advocates such as Kagan and Justice Ginsburg, was widely criticized by liberal legal scholars and pundits and Democratic politicians, including President Obama. To this day, Ginsburg, who dissented in the case, has referred to the ruling as "the most tragic decision" in her twenty-two-year court tenure.[53]

Although losing her first case before the Supreme Court, Kagan had made a historic debut. Less than a year later, on May 10, 2010, Obama nominated Kagan to the Supreme Court to succeed Justice John Paul Stevens, who had announced he would be retiring that summer. Stevens had served on the court for thirty-five years, longer than any other justice except William O. Douglas. On the first day of her Senate confirmation hearings, Kagan spoke with pride and nostalgia about her parents, expressing her regret that they had not lived to witness her nomination, which she called the "honor of a lifetime." Although the National Rifle Association's announcement of its opposition cost her the votes of several Republican, some of whom were facing strong primary challenges from more conservative opponents for whom support for gun rights was a conservative litmus test, Kagan was confirmed August 5, 2010, by a vote of 63–47. Perhaps the best remembered moment of her confirmation hearings came when Republican senator Lindsey Graham, while questioning Kagan about her views on the war on terrorism, asked her where she had been the previous Christmas Day, when a suspected terrorist attempted to blow up a Northwest Airlines flight en route to Detroit. She replied, to uproarious laughter: "You know, like all Jews, I was probably at a Chinese restaurant."[54]

Once her appointment was confirmed, Elena Kagan became the 112th Supreme Court justice, and the eighth Jewish justice, in American history. Also, for the first time, with the Protestant Stevens's departure, no Protestant justice was sitting on the court. Its composition was now six Catholics and three Jews.

Kagan's appointment made history in several ways. She became the fourth representative of one of the five New York City boroughs on the Roberts court. A Manhattanite, she joined Justice Ginsburg, who came from Brooklyn, Justice Sotomayor, from the Bronx, and Justice Scalia, from Queens.[55] The youngest Supreme Court justice, then age fifty, she also became the only justice on the Roberts court with no previous experience as a judge. Kagan was the first Supreme Court justice since Thurgood Marshall to have previously served as solicitor general, and the first justice since Harlan Fiske Stone with prior experience as a law school dean. The fourth woman, and the second Jewish woman, to serve on the court, she is also the only Supreme Court justice in U.S. history to have celebrated a bat mitzvah.

Breyer, Ginsburg, and Collegiality on the Supreme Court

We have already discussed the extent to which Stephen Breyer's rise to the federal bench, and thus the beginning of his judicial career, owed in part to his reputation for collegiality and bipartisanship as chief counsel for the Senate Judiciary Committee. Throughout his more than twenty years as a Supreme Court justice, Breyer has been known as one of the court's most affable and gregarious members. Breyer has always enjoyed cordial relationships with his colleagues, even ideological adversaries such as Clarence Thomas and Antonin Scalia. Throughout his tenure, Breyer has sat next to Justice Thomas, a colleague he apparently genuinely likes, and they are often seen laughing and whispering together. According to Breyer's former law clerk Neal Katyal, "Lots of times his colleagues will throw barbs at him in opinions, but he'll never say a bad word about them, in public or private."[56]

Breyer is also known for his love of baseball, a sport that "has played a revered role in life at the Court for several decades." Justice Potter Stewart, for example, was known to keep a small television set in his court chambers so that he could track the progress of his hometown Cincinnati Reds. Justice Sotomayor is a diehard Yankees fan, while Justice Alito has reportedly transformed his Supreme Court desk into "a shrine for the Philadelphia Phillies." An avid Boston Red Sox fan, Breyer's passion for baseball was evident when he addressed attorneys in a Supreme Court football antitrust case with detailed questions about the Red Sox. "I know baseball better," he explained to his fellow justices' delight. It was also evident when he told an interviewer that his "favorite thing" in his Supreme Court office was a Red Sox baseball he was given after being invited to throw out the first pitch of a game at Fenway Park. In preparation for his Major League debut, Breyer recalled with enthusiasm, he practiced pitching for several days with his wife, Joanna, and four-year-old granddaughter Clara.[57]

Also, during her twenty-plus years as a justice, amid the often ideologically polarized Rehnquist and Roberts courts, Ginsburg has been a consistent voice for nonpartisanship, collegiality, and civility. She has, for example, enjoyed a warm friendship with the retired justice David Souter, a bachelor, whom she and her husband, Martin, often invited to their home for gourmet dinners and to attend classical musical events.[58]

Her great capacity for friendship, however, is perhaps best exemplified by her three-decade relationship with the late justice Antonin Scalia, one of her conservative adversaries, a friendship that surprised many of Scalia's liberal critics. Ginsburg and Scalia first met in the 1970s when they were both law professors, she at Columbia and he at the University of Chicago, and she heard him speak at a legal conference. While she thoroughly disagreed with Scalia's critique of a recent Washington, D.C., Court of Appeals ruling, she was charmed by him. "I was fascinated by him because he was so intelligent and so amusing," Ginsburg later said. "You could still resist his position, but you just had to like him."[59] Despite their ideological differences, a genuine friendship developed and was reinforced with Scalia's appointment to the D.C. Court of Appeals two years after her 1980 appointment to the same court. Ginsburg, Scalia, and their spouses began celebrating New Year's Eve together, a tradition that would continue even after Martin Ginsburg's death in 2010. Ginsburg has acknowledged that Scalia had a way of upsetting the other justices: "I love him. But sometimes I'd like to strangle him. Still, more than any of my colleagues, he has the ability to make me smile, even laugh, because of his engaging wit."[60] Their friendship has been attributed to both their shared background as law professors who respected each other's scholarly judicial opinions and, especially, to their shared love of opera. Ginsburg and Scalia appeared together in white powdered wigs and eighteenth-century costumes as "extras" in the Washington National Opera's 1994 production of

Richard Strauss's *Ariadne auf Naxos*. To the amazement of many, the Ginsburgs and Scalias never let their political differences affect their friendship. Following Martin Ginsburg's death, as Chief Justice Roberts gave a moving tribute to "the husband of our colleague Ruth Bader Ginsburg," recalling "his sharp wit and engaging charm," Scalia wept.[61]

Another opera fan on the court, although perhaps not as ardent as Scalia, is Breyer, who with Ginsburg played themselves in the Washington Opera production of *Die Fledermaus* on September 6, 2003.[62]

Ginsburg also has enjoyed a very close relationship with Kagan, whom she has informally adopted as a court protégé, with Kagan's appointment more or less coinciding with the death of Ginsburg's husband. Sharing a love for classical music, Kagan like Scalia would frequently be Ginsburg's opera date. In February 2014, Kagan delivered the annual Ruth Bader Ginsburg Distinguished Lecture on Women and the Law in New York City, praising her colleague's influence and legacy as a Supreme Court litigator, federal judge, and Supreme Court justice. In her introduction of Kagan, Ginsburg revealed that they had the same personal trainer and that Kagan "has the best jab-cross-hook-punch combination on the federal bench."[63]

Justice Ginsburg and the Virginia Military Institute Case

Ruth Bader Ginsburg's most notable majority opinion came in 1996, three years after her appointment to the Supreme Court. In her opinion in *United States v. Virginia*, a landmark gender discrimination case, Ginsburg held that the Constitution's equal protection clause does not permit the state of Virginia to finance a military college, the Virginia Military Institute (VMI), open only to male students. As she noted, VMI, which had been founded in 1839, was the only one of Virginia's fifteen public colleges or universities that was not coeducational. VMI's male-only admissions policy, she continued, was in violation of the Fourteenth Amendment's equal protection clause. Therefore, VMI could no longer remain an all-male institution, and the state of Virginia's refusal to admit women to the school was unconstitutional. Writing for the court's 7–1 majority—Justice Thomas, whose son attended VMI, recused himself—Ginsburg stated that "neither federal nor state government acts compatibly with equal protection when a law or official policy denies to women, simply because they are women, full citizenship stature—equal opportunity to aspire, achieve, participate in and contribute to society based on their individual talents and capacities." While conceding that most women, as most men, might not want to meet the rigorous demands of the VMI military-training program, Ginsburg dismissed Virginia's argument that VMI's program was unsuitable for women, calling it "the kind of 'self-fulfilling prophecy' once routinely used to deny rights or opportunities" to women.[64] "The state may not rely on overbroad generalizations about the different talents, capacities, or preferences of males and females," Ginsburg wrote. "Generalizations about 'the way women are,' estimates of what is appropriate for *most women*, no longer justify denying opportunity to women whose talent and capacity place them outside the average description."[65]

When the VMI case reached the Supreme Court, Ginsburg had devoted more effort to litigating the constitutional issues relating to gender discrimination than any other justice. As the cofounder of the ACLU Women's Rights Project during the 1970s, and having litigated major sex discrimination cases before the Supreme Court, Ginsburg had sought to persuade the court "that discrimination on the basis of sex was no less a violation of equal protection than discrimination on the basis of race." The VMI case gave Ginsburg her first opportunity to address gender discrimination as a justice. Her majority opinion in *United States v. Virginia* has correctly been described as a "fitting capstone to her career as an advocate for gender equality."[66]

Justice Stephen Breyer and the Ten Commandments Cases

During their shared tenure, Justices Ginsburg, Breyer, and Kagan have usually formed part of the court's liberal bloc, consistently voting in favor of abortion rights, campaign finance reform, women's rights, gun control, gay rights, and same-sex marriage. Thus, for example, in the July 2013 case *United States v. Windsor*, Breyer, Ginsburg, and Kagan were part of the liberal majority that ruled, 5–4, that the Defense of Marriage Act, which denied all federal marriage benefits to same-sex couples who were married under state law, was unconstitutional. More recently, in the landmark June 2015 case *Obergefell v. Hodges*, in which the Supreme Court declared, 5–4, that the Constitution guarantees a right to same-sex marriage, Breyer, Ginsburg, and Kagan joined Anthony Kennedy in his majority opinion legalizing same-sex marriage nationwide.[67] Earlier, in *Bush v. Gore*, the court's 5–4 ruling that gave the much-disputed 2000 presidential election to George W. Bush, Breyer and Ginsburg were part of the liberal minority that sought unsuccessfully to keep Bush out of the White House.

Justice Breyer, however, has occasionally provided the fifth vote—the so-called swing vote—for a conservative majority. Such a role was notable in one of two cases involving the public display of the Ten Commandments on government property, *Van Orden v. Perry* and *McGreary County v. American Civil Liberties Union of Kentucky*, both of which were decided by the Supreme Court in June 2005. In *Van Orden v. Perry*, civil liberties groups had challenged the constitutionality of the public display of the Ten Commandments on a six-foot red granite monument at the Texas state capitol in Austin, claiming it violated the establishment clause of the First Amendment. Similarly, in the *McGreary County* case, the ACLU had challenged the constitutionality of public displays of framed copies of the Ten Commandments placed on the walls of Kentucky courthouses by local officials, accompanied by a Christian minister, in 1999, causing an immediate public controversy.

When the Supreme Court announced its decisions on both cases on June 27, 2005, each was decided by a 5-4 vote. But whereas in the state capitol in Austin the public display was ruled constitutional, the display in the McGreary County courthouse was ruled unconstitutional. In each case, Justices Ginsburg, Souter, Stevens, and Sandra Day O'Connor argued that the public displays of the Ten Commandments were unconstitutional violations of the First Amendment's establishment clause, while Justices Rehnquist, Scalia, Thomas, and Kennedy supported the constitutionality of these public displays. Justice Breyer provided the decisive swing vote in each case.[68]

By way of background, beginning in the 1990s, numerous lawsuits across the country were filed challenging the constitutionality of the public display of the Ten Commandments on government property. While such displays were just then becoming a contentious issue, the Ten Commandments had been publicly displayed throughout the United States for several decades, with very few instances subject to constitutional challenges or controversy. The original construction and public displays of the Ten Commandments, usually carved into a granite monument, had been funded by the Fraternal Order of Eagles, a private and secular organization, to help publicize the release of Cecil B. DeMille's celebrated 1956 movie, *The Ten Commandments*. (Indeed, in several cities, the film's stars such as Charlton Heston and Yul Brynner attended the dedication of these monuments.)[69]

For the most part, these public displays of the Ten Commandments did not generate national controversy until the early 1990s, when Judge Roy Moore, a justice of the Alabama Supreme Court, and later its chief justice, placed a small wooden plaque of the Ten Commandments in his courtroom, and subsequently had a two-and-a-half-ton Ten Commandments monument placed in the Alabama Supreme Court building's lobby. Judge Moore's actions precipitated widespread litigation nationally, usually sponsored by the ACLU, challenging the constitutionality of Ten Commandments displays. Ironically, the Supreme Court commentator and litigator Jay Sekulow, chief counsel for the conservative American Center for Law and Justice—established by the Rev. Pat Robertson—noted, "The Supreme Court building itself has incorporated artistic pictorials of the Ten Commandments, and more than once, members of the Court have pointed upward to the depiction of Moses and the Ten Commandments in the Court's own courtroom to illustrate acceptable accommodation by government of a religious practice or display."[70] Separately, the marble frieze in the Supreme Court courtroom itself depicts Moses, holding the Ten Commandments, as part of a procession of "great lawgivers of history," including Hammurabi, Confucius, Justinian, Napoleon, and Chief Justice John Marshall. The Ten Commandments, argued Sekulow, have acquired secular as well as religious meaning and have come to be viewed as "uniquely symbolic of law." Attorneys for the Bush administration, which had filed briefs urging the Supreme Court to uphold the Ten Commandment displays in both cases, took Sekulow's position, referring to the Ten Commandments as "a uniquely potent and commonly recognized symbol of the law."[71]

In his opinion in *Van Orden v. Perry*, Breyer sided with his four conservative colleagues, who upheld the constitutionality of the Ten Commandments monument at the state capitol, which indeed had been donated by the Fraternal Order of Eagles in 1961 to recognize DeMille's film. Breyer thus pointed out that "there was no single mechanical formula that can accurately draw the constitutional line in every case."[72] While the government has a constitutional obligation not to promote religion, Breyer concluded in his decisive opinion, not all public displays supporting religion violate the establishment clause of the First Amendment.[73] Thereafter, Breyer contrasted the "40-year history" of the Austin monument with the much shorter history of the McCreary County Courthouse displays. Perhaps most important, Breyer argued, no one had previously complained or attempted litigation targeting the Austin display, which had been situated for several decades together with sixteen other monuments and twenty-one historical markers within a twenty-two-acre area between the Texas state capitol and state Supreme Court building.[74]

By contrast, in his *McCreary County* opinion, Breyer sided with his four liberal colleagues, who ruled that the Kentucky courthouse displays, which had sparked community controversy and divisiveness, were unconstitutional. In so doing, Breyer distinguished the "40-year history" of the conflict-free Texas monument with "the short (and stormy) history of the Kentucky court-house Commandments displays," which, he argued, demonstrated "the substantially religious objectives of those who mounted them." As Breyer noted, the Kentucky courthouse display made clear that the posted Ten Commandments came from the "King James Version" of the Bible, an explicitly Christian reference prohibited by the First Amendment's establishment clause.[75]

Justice Breyer invoked the First Amendment jurisprudence of Justice Arthur Goldberg, for whom he had clerked, in holding "that there is no simple and clear measure which by precise application can readily and invariably demark the permissible" regarding the establishment clause.[76] In response to the strict separationist position of his four liberal colleagues, Breyer did not express the belief that the Texas display was an unconstitutional violation of the "wall of separation" between church and state that the establishment clause had been enacted to prevent. In joining his conservative colleagues in upholding the Texas display's constitutionality, Breyer carefully noted that "the Establishment Clause does not compel the government to purge from the public square all that in any way partakes of the religious." Breyer also warned his liberal colleagues of a "brooding and pervasive devotion to the secular" that can result in an active "hostility to the religious" throughout American government and public life.[77]

As one Supreme Court analyst has correctly suggested, Breyer's swing vote in these two cases, with Breyer alone among his colleagues in the majority in each, has been the "high point" of Justice Breyer's influence on the court.[78]

Moreover, as Harvard Law School professor Michael J. Klarman noted in a *Harvard Law Review* tribute to Breyer, his ruling in *Van Orden v. Perry*, which insulated from further constitutional challenge the thousands of Ten Commandments displays constructed in the 1950s and 1960s by the Fraternal Order of Eagles, "defends an important principle of liberal constitutionalism—a firm separation of church and state." At the same time, with more than seven in ten Americans having no objection to public displays of the Ten Commandments, "it acknowledges political reality and makes a wise concession to the force of public opinion." In so doing, concludes Klarman, Justice Breyer's opinion in *Van Orden* is "a laudable act of judicial statesmanship."[79]

Justice Kagan's Dissent in the
Town of Greece v. Galloway Prayer Case

One of Justice Kagan's most impressive judicial opinions was her dissent in the May 2014 ruling in *Town of Greece v. Galloway*, a case in which the Supreme Court affirmed, in a 5–4 vote, the constitutionality of opening town meetings or state legislative sessions with sectarian prayer.

For many years, the town council of Greece, New York, located just outside Rochester, had opened its monthly meetings with prayers by local religious leaders. While town officials said that clergy and members of all religious faiths, as well as atheists, were welcome to give the opening prayer, in practice an overwhelming majority of these prayers were given by Christian ministers who would invoke "the name of Jesus" with an explicitly Christian prayer.[80]

Justice Kennedy, writing for the court's majority, argued that American traditions beginning with the first Congress supported the constitutionality of ceremonial prayers to open legislative sessions. Both houses of Congress, he noted, had appointed and paid for official chaplains almost continuously since ratification of the Constitution and the beginning of the republic. In reaching its decision, the court's majority built upon the precedent of the Supreme Court's 1983 decision in *Marsh v. Chambers*, which upheld the constitutionality of Christian chaplains paid with tax dollars delivering prayers to open each session of the Nebraska state legislature. Legislative prayer, Kennedy said, is "a practice that was accepted by the framers and has witnessed the critical scrutiny of time and political change."[81]

In her lengthy dissent, Kagan disputed Kennedy's assertion, noting that some of the nation's founders—including George Washington, James Madison, and Thomas Jefferson—sought to keep religion and sectarian prayer separate from public life. "The demand for neutrality among religions is not a product of 21st century 'political correctness,'" wrote Kagan, "but of the 18th century view." Moreover, Kagan asserted, "no one can fairly read the prayer from Greece's town meetings as anything other than explicitly Christian—constantly and exclusively so."[82]

In concluding her spirited dissent, Kagan invoked the American Jewish experience to argue against permitting the town of Greece's prayers, citing the story of George Washington's historic visit to the Jewish community of Newport, Rhode Island: "In 1790," wrote Kagan,

George Washington traveled to Newport, Rhode Island, a longtime bastion of religious liberty and the home of the first community of American Jews. Among the citizens he met there was Moses Seixas, one of the congregation's lay officials. The ensuing exchange between the two conveys, as well as anything I know, the promise this country makes to members of every religion. Seixas wrote first, welcoming Washington to Newport. He spoke of "a deep sense of gratitude" for the new American government, "a Government, which to bigotry gives no sanction, to persecution no assistance—but generously affording to All liberty of conscience, and immunities of Citizenship; deeming every one, of whatever Nation, tongue or language, equal parts of the great governmental Machine." The first phrase there is the more poetic: a government that to "bigotry gives no sanction, to persecution no assistance." But the second is actually the more startling and transformative: a government that, beyond not aiding persecution, grants "immunities of citizenship" to the Christian and Jew alike, and makes them "equal parts" of the whole country. Washington responded the very next day. Like any successful politician, he appreciated a great line when he saw one—and knew to borrow it too. And so he repeated, word for word, Seixas's phrase about neither sanctioning bigotry nor assisting persecution. But he no less embraced the point Seixas had made about equality of citizenship. "It is now no more," Washington said, "that toleration is spoken of, as if it was by the indulgence of one class of people" to another, lesser one. For "all possess alike . . . immunities of citizenship." That is America's promise in the First Amendment: full and equal membership in the polity for members of every religious group, assuming only that they, like anyone "who live[s] under [the Government's] protection[,] should demean themselves as good citizens." For me, that remarkable guarantee means at least this much: When citizens of this country approach their government, they do so only as Americans, not as members of one faith or another. And that means that even in a partly legislative body, they should not confront government-sponsored worship that divides them along religious lines. I believe, for all the reasons I have given, that the Town of Greece betrayed that promise. I therefore respectfully dissent from the Court's decision.[83]

As one commentator noted at the time, a small but significant factual error existed in this concluding section of Kagan's dissent: Newport was not "the home of the first community of American Jews." This historical distinction goes to New Amsterdam (today's New York City), where Jews fleeing persecution in Recife, Brazil, first settled in 1654. This minor error notwithstanding, Justice Kagan's fascinating and uniquely Jewish dissent in *Town of Greece* is the only opinion by one of the Supreme Court's eight Jewish justices to explicitly and eloquently invoke an episode from the American Jewish experience in support of his or her approach to contemporary jurisprudence. Also important to note, within two weeks of the announcement of the court's decision, Kagan's factual mistake was brought to the attention of the Supreme Court clerk's office. Kagan's dissenting opinion has now been revised to read in part: "In 1790, George Washington traveled to Newport, Rhode Island, a longtime bastion of religious liberty and the home of *one of the first communities of American Jews.*"[84]

The Jewishness of the Three Justices

As indicated by her uniquely Jewish dissent in *Town of Greece v. Galloway*, Elena Kagan has a more than casual familiarity with American Jewish history that has, at least this once, helped shape her jurisprudence. Kagan, currently the Supreme Court's youngest Jewish justice, seems to have a stronger Jewish religious identity and involvement than either Justice Breyer or Ginsburg. The product of a serious Jewish religious education who was raised in a religiously Conservative Jewish home, she still considers herself a Conservative Jew and in recent years has attended High Holy Day services at Adas Israel, Washington's largest Conservative synagogue.[85]

Although as a teenager Ruth Bader was the "camp rabbi" in the Adirondacks, and was confirmed in Brooklyn's religiously Conservative East Midwood Jewish Center, where her parents belonged, at age seventeen, when her mother died, she turned away from Jewish religious practice. In the days after her mother's death, she was also excluded from the minyan traditionally required for Jewish communal prayer, and could not recite the Kaddish, the traditional Jewish prayer of mourning, because she was a woman. "The house was filled with women, and only men could participate in the minyan," she later told an interviewer. She further explained, while pointing to the mezuzah on her Supreme Court office door, that she's like other nonobservant Jews who "identify themselves proudly as Jews but don't take part in the rituals."

More recently, after attending a bat mitzvah at a liberal Washington, D.C., synagogue where the rabbi and cantor were both women, and where women were included in the minyan, Ginsburg said she might feel differently about Jewish religious practice if she were young now.[86] Also, in March 2015, Ginsburg coauthored a moving feminist essay titled "The Heroic and Visionary Women of Passover," a tribute to the five heroic women at the center of the Passover story in the Book of Exodus—Moses's mother, Yocheved, his sister, Miriam, the midwives Shifra and Puah, who defied Pharaoh's decree to kill all the Israelite baby boys, and the Pharaoh's daughter, Batya, who also defied her father's decree, saving the baby Moses from the Nile. Ginsburg's coauthor was Rabbi Lauren Holtzblatt, Adas Israel's assistant rabbi and the wife of Ginsburg's former law clerk Ari Holtzblatt.[87]

While Ginsburg does not belong to a synagogue, in recent years she, like Justice Kagan, has attended High Holy Day services at Adas Israel. She has also admitted to having a strong "devotion to Jewish ethical values." Addressing the American Jewish Committee's 1995 annual meeting, Ginsburg spoke proudly of the age-old connection between Judaism and the law and of Judaism's commitment to social justice. "The demand for justice runs through the entirety of the Jewish tradition," she declared. "Jews in large numbers became lawyers, some eventually became judges, and the best of those jurists used the law to secure justice for others." She continued: "[The role of laws] as protectors of the oppressed, the loner, is evident in the work of my Jewish predecessors on the Supreme Court. The biblical command, 'justice, justice thou shalt pursue' is a strand that ties them together. I keep those words on the wall of my Supreme Court chambers, as an ever present reminder of what judges must do 'that they may thrive.'" Quoting her Jewish Supreme Court predecessor, and former AJC president, Arthur Goldberg, who once said that "my concern for justice, for peace, for enlightenment, all stem from my heritage," Ginsburg concluded that "I am fortunate to be connected to that heritage."[88] Although Ginsburg has especially praised Judaism's commitment to social justice, she has interestingly denied that being Jewish has ever directly affected her judicial opinions.[89]

For his part, Justice Breyer may be the least religious of the current Jewish justices—indeed, his British wife is an Anglican Protestant and one of his daughters is an Episcopal priest—but he has nonetheless emerged as a Jewish voice on the court who has spoken with great pride and knowledge about the American Jewish experience and the state of Israel before a variety of Jewish audiences, including the AJC, Jewish Theological Seminary, and

Conference of Presidents of Major American Jewish Organizations. Although not a synagogue member, Breyer does not work on Yom Kippur. In 2003, the Supreme Court, for the first time in its twenty-eight-year tradition of opening its sessions on the first Monday in October, suspended its opening arguments for a day in deference to the public requests of Justices Breyer and Ginsburg, who both planned to be in synagogue for Yom Kippur, the holiest day on the Jewish calendar. When asked about how Judaism has influenced his public career, Breyer responded, "It's a little corny, but I think of what the rabbinic sage Hillel said: 'If I am not for myself, who am I for?' I've always thought of the practical nature of Jewish religious beliefs and the way they're involved in making the world a better place, requiring people to have a sense of justice and to think about other people."[90] For Breyer, as for Ginsburg, the Jewish commitment to social justice, so important to the Jewish faith's legal-religious tradition, has been central to his Jewish identity.

For Breyer, moreover, the Jewish commitment to social justice found expression in the Zionist ideal, to which Breyer remains deeply devoted. In likely one of the most eloquent essays on a Jewish historical topic ever penned by a Jewish Supreme Court justice, Breyer published "Zion's Justice" in the *New Republic*. In this little-known 1998 essay, based on a talk he gave at the Conference of Presidents of Major American Jewish Organizations, Breyer, a proud Israel supporter, evinces his great admiration for the Zionist dream of a Jewish state and for the historic contribution to this goal by his two predecessors Louis Brandeis and Felix Frankfurter through their Zionist leadership. Quoting Brandeis's famous observation "that to be good Americans, we must be better Jews, and to be better Jews we must become Zionists," Breyer notes that Brandeis "used his pen, his pocketbook, and his nationally recognized position as a distinguished member of the legal profession to make perfectly clear to American Jews and to the world that support for the Zionist ideal and American patriotism were perfectly compatible." As Brandeis pointed out, Breyer concludes, the modern Zionist ideal includes the universal aspiration toward "democracy and social justice," an ideal that in 1998 continued to retain "its hold on our imagination and that of the world."[91]

The Question of Retirement

One of the great prerogatives of presidential leadership is to appoint Supreme Court justices who share the president's political views and policy preferences. It is thus commonly assumed that a liberal Democratic president's nominees will have a liberal record while on the court and a conservative Republican's appointees will have a conservative record. History, however, has often proven this assumption incorrect. President Eisenhower famously lamented that his appointment of Earl Warren as chief justice was the biggest mistake of his presidency, and had he lived FDR would presumably have shared this lament about Felix Frankfurter, a staunchly liberal New Dealer who ended his career as the Warren court's most conservative member. The court's most recent retirees, Justices David Souter and John Paul Stevens, both appointed by Republican presidents, moved to the left throughout their respective tenures. George H. W. Bush, on the recommendation of his conservative White House chief of staff, John Sununu, nominated David Souter, a little-known judge whom Sununu had appointed to the New Hampshire Supreme Court while governor, assuming he would be a reliably conservative voice. Indeed, however, Souter proved to be a consistent liberal who invariably voted with the liberal bloc on the court. And the Chicago Republican John Paul Stevens, appointed by President Gerald Ford in 1975, turned out to be a much-admired liberal justice for thirty-five years, until his retirement in 2010, when President Obama appointed Elena Kagan to succeed him. Both Justices Souter and Stevens waited to retire until a Democrat, Barack Obama, was president and could appoint a liberal to succeed them.[92]

Following Stevens's retirement at age ninety-one, many speculated that the seventy-seven-year-old Ginsburg, who had undergone treatment for colon and pancreatic cancer and was the next oldest justice, would soon retire as well. But Ginsburg, who had also just endured the death of her husband of fifty-six years, insisted she had no such plans to retire any time soon, and that she wanted to serve at least as long as Justice Brandeis, who had retired at age eighty-two after twenty-three years on the court. As of mid-2016, Ginsburg has now equaled Brandeis; she will surpass him, and Frankfurter, who also served twenty-three years, thus becoming the longest-serving Jewish justice in American history, by remaining through much of 2017. Her attempts to achieve these milestones have generated much discussion, including criticism.

Some of this criticism came from supporters who felt Ginsburg should have retired before 2012, with Democrats holding the White House and the Senate, allowing Obama to appoint a liberal Democrat as her successor. After all, the argument went, there was no guarantee Obama would be reelected and that the Democrats would continue as the majority in the Senate. Meanwhile, a Republican President Mitt Romney would be highly unlikely to appoint a liberal to the bench. Some liberals, in calling for Ginsburg's retirement, cited the precedent of the liberal justice Thurgood Marshall, who had held his seat in ill health for several years, permitting President George H. W. Bush to appoint the conservative Clarence Thomas to succeed him. In an April 2011 *New Republic* article, "The Case for Early Retirement," the liberal Harvard Law School professor Randall Kennedy also called for the retirement of Breyer, who is five years younger than Ginsburg. Their retirement, argued Kennedy, "would be the responsible thing for them to do. Both have served with distinction on the Supreme Court for a substantial period. . . . Both are unlikely . . . to outlast a two-term Republican presidential administration, should one supersede the Obama administration following the 2012 election." After citing the examples of "liberal leaning" justices such as Harry Blackmun, John Paul Stevens, and David Souter, who retired during the Clinton and Obama presidencies, "while more conservative-leaning justices such as Sandra Day O'Connor, Lewis Powell and Warren Burger retired during the Reagan, Bush I and Bush II presidencies," Kennedy noted that "if Ginsburg or Breyer (or both) announced retirement at the end of this Supreme Court term (pending the confirmation of successors), they could virtually guarantee that President Obama would get to select their replacements." While, technically, Kennedy was directing his retirement advice to both Breyer and Ginsburg, he was more concerned about Ginsburg, who appeared to be following Justice Marshall's inadvisable precedent of resisting retirement for many years, despite failing health. For Kennedy, the belated retirement of Marshall, for whom Kennedy had clerked, offered a "cautionary tale." If Justice Ginsburg retired after 2012, with a Republican in the White House, "it is probable that the female Thurgood Marshall will be replaced by a female Clarence Thomas."[93]

Pressure for Ginsburg to retire did not let up after Obama's reelection. Now eighty-three and with her pancreatic and colon cancer apparently in remission, Ginsburg says she is in excellent health, even lifting weights despite having cracked a pair of ribs and having had a stent placed in one of her coronary arteries. Indeed, she "has vowed to resist any pressure that might come from liberals who want to ensure that Democratic President Barack Obama can pick her successor before the November 2016 presidential election." Ginsburg has articulated her own timetable for knowing when to retire. "When I forget the names of the cases that I once could recite at the drop of a hat," she has said, "I will know."[94]

Appointments to the Supreme Court can reinterpret constitutional law, change American history, and contribute significantly to the historical legacy of the president who makes them. Supreme Court justices, with their lifetime appointments, are often among a president's most enduring legacies. This is certainly true of Bill Clinton, whose naming of Justices Ginsburg and Breyer were among his major presidential achievements, even though Ginsburg was not his first (but rather his seventh!) choice for the court. It should be remembered that if one of Clinton's earlier choices—Mario Cuomo, George Mitchell, or Bruce Babbitt, for example—had accepted his offer, Ginsburg might have remained a judge on the Washington, D.C., Court of Appeals, rather than the high court's first Jewish woman member. And another sixteen years might have had to pass until Obama would appoint the first Jewish woman, Elena Kagan, to the court.

Since the 1920s, only one president, Jimmy Carter, has not had the opportunity to make a Supreme Court appointment. Republican presidents have made twelve of the eighteen appointments during the past half-century. When Chief Justice John Roberts swears in the next president in January 2017, Justice Breyer will be seventy-seven and two of the current justices will be eighty or older: Ginsburg, eighty-three, and Anthony Kennedy, eighty. (When Justice Scalia died in early 2016, he was seventy-nine.) Whether a Democrat or Republican wins the 2016 presidential election, she or he may have the opportunity to make three, or perhaps four, Supreme Court appointments.[95] If the next president hopes to further religious diversity on the court, he or she would be probably be advised to appoint a Protestant—male or female —justice, a call Obama appears to have ignored in naming Merrick Garland, who would be the fourth Jewish justice on the current court. If and when Ginsburg retires, she will likely be replaced by another woman, perhaps African American or Asian American but probably not by another Jewish woman. Kagan, fifty-six years old in 2016, will probably remain the court's one female Jewish justice for several presidential administrations to come. Nonetheless, Ginsburg's unique place in American Jewish history as the court's first Jewish woman, and likely the longest-serving Jewish justice in the history of the court, is all but assured.

Ginsburg has already earned another distinction not shared by any other justice on the court: she will be portrayed in a movie by the Jewish, Harvard-educated, Academy Award–winning actress Natalie Portman. The film's script was written by the nephew of Ginsburg's late husband, Martin, and the movie is scheduled to open in 2017. When asked about the growing interest in her life and legal career, especially by young women, Ginsburg responded, "It's amazing. To think of me, an icon, at 82?" Ginsburg will be only the second

Supreme Court justice portrayed in a full-length movie, the other being Oliver Wendell Holmes Jr., the subject of the 1950 biopic *The Magnificent Yankee.*

The 2015 book *Notorious RBG: The Life and Times of Ruth Bader Ginsburg*, a *New York Times* best seller, testifies to the cult following that has emerged around Ginsburg, who has become a liberal cultural icon, especially for younger women.[96] The book devotes passages to fun facts such as RBG's workout routine, which includes twenty pushups a day, and "RBG's Favorite Marty Ginsburg Recipe," a tribute to her husband, who did all the family's cooking, along with imparting her personal and professional life story. A cottage industry has also sprung from the book, including T-shirts, mugs, stickers, and tote bags.

In the century since Woodrow Wilson's historic appointment of Louis Brandeis to the Supreme Court, American Jews have looked to presidents for political recognition and representation through court appointments, as well as positions as ambassadors, cabinet members, and White House staffers. Bill Clinton's presidency ushered in what might be called a golden era for Jewish participation in American government and public life. Although hardly remarked on, a distinctive Clinton legacy was the extraordinary number of Jewish appointees to positions throughout the executive branch and to the judiciary, the latter most notably with his unprecedented two Jewish appointments to the Supreme Court. Without using religion as a criterion, Clinton brought more Jews into high-level government positions than any other president. Alongside the two court nominees, five Jews headed cabinet departments during Clinton's eight years in office, while six others held cabinet-rank portfolios. Two Jews, Robert Rubin and Lawrence Summers, served as treasury secretary, Robert Reich was labor secretary, and Dan Glickman, a nine-term Kansas congressman, became the first Jewish agriculture secretary. Three Jewish attorneys — Bernard Nussbaum, Lloyd Cutler, and Abner Mikva — served on the White House staff as special counsel, while numerous other Jews got their start in public service in advisory positions at the White House. Notable among them was Elena Kagan, who served as associate White House counsel and deputy director of the White House's Domestic Policy Council, giving her leverage to become Harvard Law School dean and later solicitor general and Supreme Court justice. Through Clinton's Supreme Court appointments, including that of the first Jewish woman, American Jews received political recognition and influence that would have been unimaginable decades earlier, when Brandeis joined the court.

The End of a Jewish Seat

Of the 112 justices who have served on the U.S. Supreme Court since its founding, eight have been Jewish. As the court's first Jewish justice, Brandeis was appointed to the seat vacated by Joseph Lamar and was succeeded by William O. Douglas. Benjamin Cardozo, the second Jewish justice, appointed by President Herbert Hoover in 1932, occupied the seat vacated by Oliver Wendell Holmes Jr. and was succeeded in turn by Felix Frankfurter, Arthur Goldberg, and Abe Fortas. When Cardozo died in 1938, Franklin Roosevelt appointed Frankfurter, the third Jew to serve on the court, to succeed him, with Brandeis resigning three weeks later. No single Jewish seat therefore existed between 1932 and 1938, when two Jews served on the court simultaneously. Both Cardozo's appointment and death occurred during Brandeis's long tenure. The emergence of a single, informally designated Jewish seat, occupied by Justices Cardozo, Frankfurter, Goldberg, and Fortas in direct succession, thus came about after FDR's appointment of Frankfurter to replace Cardozo.

As noted earlier, this fifty-three-year tradition of a Jewish seat, begun with President Wilson's appointment of Brandeis in 1916, was broken in 1969 with the resignation of Abe Fortas and President Nixon's appointment of Harry Blackmun, a Protestant, as Fortas's successor. Although none of the five Nixon and Ford court appointees was Jewish, no evidence suggests that this was a deliberate attempt to keep a Jewish justice off the court.[97]

In their respective appointments of Brandeis and Cardozo, Wilson and Hoover set precedents that later presidents would follow. The emergence of a Jewish seat came to have great symbolic importance for American Jews. Yet during the later twentieth century, as antisemitism declined in American public life, including in the legal profession, as an increasing number of Jews were appointed as presidential advisers and cabinet members, university presidents, deans and faculty at the country's top law schools, and partners in the country's most prestigious historically non-Jewish law firms, the symbolism of a Jewish Supreme Court seat diminished somewhat. Indeed, when President Clinton made history by appointing two Jews to the court in 1993 and 1994, thus filling the only two court vacancies of his presidency, little public attention was devoted to the Jewishness of Justices Ginsburg and Breyer. No antisemitic comments or innuendo was evident in the Senate debates over their confirmation, as there had been in the confirmation hearings for Justices Brandeis, Cardozo, and Frankfurter. As Ginsburg would aptly put it: "Justice Breyer and I are both Jews. In contrast to Frankfurter, Goldberg, and Fortas, however, no one regarded Ginsburg and Breyer as filling a Jewish seat. Both of us take great pride in and draw strength from our heritage, but our religion simply was not relevant to President Clinton's appointments."[98] Breyer was similarly pleased that his Jewishness had not been an issue in his appointment. "Here I am, absolutely Jewish," he said. "I am appointed to the Supreme Court, and there's already another Jewish member, and there's no issue for or against. My parents and grandparents would never have believed it. It's the kind of ideal that many people have aspired to in terms of the place of a Jew in public life. It's neither a qualification nor a disqualification."[99]

So, too, when President Reagan named Federal Judge Douglas Ginsburg to succeed Justice Powell in 1986, the public controversy surrounding Ginsburg's ill-fated nomination had nothing to do with his religion. His Jewishness was rarely mentioned by opponents and backers alike, and antisemitism had absolutely nothing to do with his decision to ask Reagan to withdraw his name from consideration. Nor were Jewish communal leaders noticeably upset when, after the withdrawal occurred, Reagan nominated a Catholic, Anthony Kennedy, in his stead.[100]

The response was similar when, in 2010, President Obama appointed a third Jewish justice, Elena Kagan, to succeed her Protestant predecessor, John Paul Stevens. Although her appointment resulted in the first U.S. Supreme Court with no Protestant, a fact that did generate significant media attention, there was little or no media discussion of Kagan's religion following her nomination or during her Senate hearings. There is no indication that President Obama considered Kagan's Jewishness when nominating her. Most press accounts reported that Obama had a short list of four candidates to succeed Stevens: Kagan; Diane Wood, a Protestant federal judge on the Seventh Circuit Court of Appeals; Sidney Thomas, another Protestant judge, on the Ninth Circuit; and Merrick Garland, a Jewish federal judge on the D.C. Circuit who was later tapped to fill Antonin Scalia's seat. Obama was apparently most impressed by Kagan's six-year tenure as dean of Harvard Law School and, especially, by her service to his administration as solicitor general.[101] As with Clinton's appointments of Ginsburg and Breyer, Kagan's religion appears simply not to have factored into the president's thinking.

President Obama's March 16, 2016, nomination of Judge Merrick Garland, a lifelong Democrat, to succeed the late Justice Antonin Scalia precipitated a major controversy over his nomination and Senate confirmation. Despite his reputation as a judicial moderate admired by many Republicans as well as Democrats, Senate Republicans, led by majority leader Mitch McConnell, refused to consider even meeting with the nominee, much less holding hearings and voting on his confirmation during the 2016 presidential election year. Mc-Connell repeatedly insisted that the opportunity to nominate a new Supreme Court justice should belong to the next president, who was scheduled to be elected on November 8. Garland, the highly respected chief judge of the U.S. Court of Appeals for the District of Columbia Circuit, had been on the short list of potential Supreme Court nominees when Obama nominated Justice Sotomayor in 2009 and Justice Kagan in 2010. It is worth noting that amid all the controversy surrounding his nomination, Judge Garland's Jewish identity seemed to be irrelevant; there was almost no media discussion of it at all. The media did note that, had he been confirmed, Garland would have been the fifth white male on the Roberts Court and, as a Harvard Law graduate, the ninth justice to have attended Harvard or Yale Law School.

For eight months, Judge Garland's nomination by President Obama, as well as his potential for renomination by a President Hillary Clinton, remained a possibility. However, with the victory of Donald Trump in the presidential election of November 8, 2016, Garland's hopes of ever having a seat on the Supreme Court were dashed. During the campaign, Trump had circulated lists of twenty-one potential Supreme Court nominees to succeed Justice Scalia, all of them well-established conservative Republicans; none of them were Jewish.

There were probably not many Jews in the United States yearning to see Merrick Garland confirmed to the Supreme Court so that their coreligionists might hold four of the court's nine seats. For the Senate Republicans, as for most of the country, his religious identity was utterly beside the point. So, too, presumably, the religious identity of President Trump's nominee to succeed Justice Scalia would be irrelevant to the politicians and pundits who would support or oppose the nomination, as well as to most of America's Jews.

Things were very different a century ago when Woodrow Wilson became the first president to nominate a Jew to the Supreme Court. The appointment of Louis Brandeis one hundred years ago introduced a new dimension of religious diversity on the Supreme Court. Before his appointment, a Jewish justice would have been unimaginable to many, as would have been a Supreme Court lacking a Protestant. Today, the once-traditional Jewish seat is no more. Yet, with three Jews serving simultaneously in the centennial year of Brandeis's appointment, it would seem unimaginable to many, within the Jewish community and without, that there could be a Supreme Court without a Jewish justice.

NOTES

1. Before Brandeis: Presidents, Presidential Appointments, and America's Jews, 1813–1912

1. Jonathan D. Sarna, *Jacksonian Jew: The Two Worlds of Mordecai Noah* (New York: Holmes & Meier, 1981), 27.

2. Jonathan D. Sarna and David G. Dalin, *Religion and State in the American Jewish Experience* (Notre Dame, IN: University of Notre Dame Press, 1997), 89.

3. Ibid., 90.

4. Sarna, *Jacksonian Jew*, 28.

5. David G. Dalin, "Presidents, Presidential Appointments and Jews," in *Jews in American Politics*, ed. L. Sandy Maisel and Ira N. Forman (Lanham, MD: Rowman & Littlefield, 2001), 30.

6. Belmont's career in nineteenth-century Democratic politics is discussed in detail in Irving Katz, *August Belmont: A Political Biography* (New York: Columbia University Press, 1968).

7. Jonathan D. Sarna, *When General Grant Expelled the Jews* (New York: Schocken, 2012), 109–16; Esther L. Panitz, *Simon Wolf: Private Conscience and Public Policy* (Cranberry, NJ: Associated Presses, 1987), 43–51; and David G. Dalin and Alfred J. Kolatch, *The Presidents of the United States and the Jews* (Middle Village, NY: Jonathan David Publishers), 89–90.

8. Quoted in Dalin and Kolatch, *The Presidents*, 89.

9. Sarna, *When General Grant Expelled the Jews*, 83.

10. Simon Wolf, *The Presidents I Have Known, from 1860 to 1918* (Washington, DC: Byron S. Adams, 1918); and Sarna, *When General Grant Expelled the Jews*, 86.

11. Sarna, *When General Grant Expelled the Jews*, 89–92; and Lee M. Friedman, *Jewish Pioneers and Patriots* (Philadelphia: Jewish Publication Society, 1948), 353–64.

12. L. Sandy Maisel and Ira N. Forman, ed., *Jews in American Politics* (Lanham, MD: Rowman & Littlefield, 2011), 411; and Sarna, *When General Grant Expelled the Jews*, 87, 89.

13. David G. Dalin, "Jews and the American Presidency," in *Religion, Race, and the American Presidency*, ed. Gaston Espinosa (Lanham, MD: Rowman & Littlefield, 2008), 132.

14. Oscar Straus's life is discussed in: Naomi W. Cohen, *A Dual Heritage: The Public Career of Oscar S. Straus* (Philadelphia: Jewish Publication Society, 1969); and in Straus's memoir, *Under Four Administrations: From Cleveland to Taft* (New York: Houghton Mifflin, 1922). See also my articles "Jews and the American Presidency," 132–35, and "Presidents, Presidential Appointments and Jews," 31–34.

15. Dalin, "Jews and the American Presidency," 132.

16. Dalin and Kolatch, *The Presidents*, 107.

17. Dalin, "Jews and the American Presidency," 132; and Dalin, "Presidents, Presidential Appointments, and Jews," 32.

18. Wolf, *The Presidents I Have Known*, 111.

19. Biographical information on Hirsch can be found in: Robert E. Levinson, "Solomon Hirsch," *Encyclopedia Judaica*, Vol. 8 (Jerusalem: Keter Publishing House, 1971), 516–17; and Donald Altschiller, "Solomon Hirsch," in *Jews in American Politics*, ed. L. Sandy Maisel and Ira N. Forman (Lanham, MD: Rowman & Littlefield, 2011), 354. In 1897, as reported in Altschiller, President William McKinley offered Hirsch the ambassador post in Belgium, which Hirsch declined.

20. Ibid.

21. Kurt F. Stone, *The Jews of Capitol Hill* (Lanham, MD: Rowman & Littlefield, 2011), 54–55.

22. Dalin, "Jews and the American Presidency," 133.

23. Dalin and Kolatch, *The Presidents*, 117–18.

24. Morgenthau's appointment by Wilson and his tenure as U.S. ambassador to Turkey are discussed in: Henry Morgenthau III, *Mostly Morgenthaus: A Family History* (New York: Ticknor and Fields, 1991), 98–172; Barbara W. Tuchman, "The Assimilationist Dilemma: Ambassador Morgenthau's Story," *Practicing History: Selected Essays* (New York: Alfred A. Knopf, 1981), 208–17; and Michael B. Oren, *Power, Faith, and Fantasy: America in the Middle East, 1776 to the Present* (New York: W. W. Norton, 2007), 332–37.

25. Morgenthau, *Mostly Morgenthaus*, 39.

26. Ibid., 99–100.

27. Ruth Bader Ginsburg, introduction to *The Jewish Justices of the Supreme Court Revisited: Brandeis to Fortas*, ed. Jennifer M. Lowe (Washington, DC: Supreme Court Historical Society, 1994), 3.

28. Ibid., 151.

29. Joseph M. Proskauer, *A Segment of My Times* (New York: Farrar, Straus, 1950), 30.

30. Louis M. Hacker and Mark D. Hirsch, *Proskauer: His Life and Times* (Tuscaloosa, AL: University of Alabama Press, 1978), 32.

31. Jerold S. Auerbach, *Unequal Justice: Lawyers and Social Change in Modern America* (New York: Oxford University Press, 1976), 185.

32. Harry Barnard, *The Forging of an American Jew: The Life and Times of Judge Julian W. Mack* (New York: Herzl Press, 1974), 126.

33. Auerbach, *Unequal Justice*, 122.

34. Eli N. Evans, *Judah P. Benjamin: The Jewish Confederate* (New York: Free Press, 1988), 83.

35. Robert A. Burt, *Two Jewish Justices: Outcasts in the Promised Land* (Berkeley: University of California Press, 1988), 4.

36. Arthur L. Goodhart, *Five Jewish Lawyers of the Common Law* (New York: Oxford University Press, 1971), 1–15. Goodhart was the nephew of Irving Lehman, who served as chief judge of the New York Court of Appeals, and of Herbert Lehman, who was New York governor (1932–1942) and later a U.S. senator (1949–1957). These men all came from the family that created the Lehman Brothers investment banking firm.

37. Dan A. Oren. *Joining the Club: A History of Jews and Yale* (New Haven: Yale University Press, 1985), 6.

38. Stone, *The Jews of Capitol Hill*, 16; and Charles A. Madison, *Eminent American Jews, 1776 to the Present* (New York: Frederick Ungar, 1970), 42.

39. Robert Douthat Meade, *Judah P. Benjamin: Confederate Statesman* (Baton Rouge: Louisiana State University Press, 2001), 83.

40. Evans, *Judah P. Benjamin*, 7; and Stone, *The Jews of Capitol Hill*, 17–18.

41. Stone, *The Jews of Capitol Hill*, 18.

42. Ibid.

43. Evans, *Judah P. Benjamin*, 83.

44. Meade, *Judah P. Benjamin*, 85, and Evans, *Judah P. Benjamin*, 83–84. Eli Evans has also suggested that, in turning down the appointment, Benjamin may have been anticipating "the possibility of representing clients before the Supreme Court" (84), which presumably would have been a lucrative additional income source.

45. Evans, *Judah P. Benjamin*, 135, 89.

46. Madison, *Eminent American Jews*, 41.

47. Meade, *Judah P. Benjamin*, 85, and Evans, *Judah P. Benjamin*, 84.

48. Jonathan D. Sarna, "Two Jewish Lawyers Named Louis," *American Jewish History* 94, nos. 1–2 (March–June 2008): 1–2.

49. Ibid., pp. 3–4.

50. Dalin and Kolatch, *The Presidents*, 112–13.

51. Jerold S. Auerbach, *Rabbis and Lawyers: The Journey from Torah to Constitution* (Bloomington: Indiana University Press, 1990), 95.

52. This campaign has been thoroughly analyzed elsewhere. See, for example: Naomi W. Cohen, "The Abrogation of the Russo-American Treaty of 1832," *Jewish Social Studies*, 35 (January 1963): 3–41; Gary Dean Best, *To Free a People: American Jewish Leaders and the Jewish Problem in Eastern Europe, 1890–1914* (Westport, CT: Greenwood Press, 1982), 166–205; and Morton Rosenstock, *Louis Marshall, Defender of Jewish Rights* (Detroit: Wayne State University Press, 1965), 71–79.

53. This point is discussed in more detail in David G. Dalin, "Louis Marshall, the Jewish Vote and the Republican Party," *Jewish Political Studies Review* 4, no. 1 (Spring 1992): 55–83.

54. Lawrence H. Fuchs, *The Political Behavior of American Jews* (Westport, CT: Greenwood Press, 1980); and Ira N. Forman, "The Politics of Minority Consciousness," in *Jews in American Politics*, ed. L. Sandy Maisel and Ira N. Forman (Lanham, MD: Rowman & Littlefield, 2001), 152.

55. Quoted in Dalin, "Louis Marshall, the Jewish Vote, and the Republican Party," 68.

56. Jonathan D. Sarna, "The Jewish Vote in Presidential Elections, 1908–1920, with Special Reference to Boston," unpublished paper, Brandeis University, 1973, 11.

57. Ibid.

58. Louis Marshall, letter to Jacob Schiff, August 5, 1912, Louis Marshall Papers, box 1581, Jacob Rader Marcus Center of the American Jewish Archives, Cincinnati.

59. Ibid.

60. Indeed, the story is not even mentioned, much less discussed, in Jeffrey B. Morris, "The American Jewish Judge: An Appraisal on the Occasion of the Bicentennial," *Jewish Social Studies* XXXVIII (Summer/Fall 1976), or in the standard history of Supreme Court appointments: Henry J. Abraham, *Justices, Presidents, and Senators: A Political History of the Appointments to the Supreme Court* (Lanham, MD: Rowman & Littlefield, 1999). Marshall's Supreme Court candidacy similarly goes unmentioned in the various biographies of William

Howard Taft: e.g., Henry F. Pringle, *The Life and Times of William Howard Taft*, 2 vols. (New York: Farrar & Rinehart, 1939); Donald F. Anderson, *William Howard Taft* (Ithaca, NY: Cornell University Press, 1968)—and in the definitive scholarly study of Taft's role in Supreme Court appointments, Walter F. Murphy, "In His Own Image: Mr. Justice Taft and Supreme Court Appointments," *Supreme Court Review* (1961): 159–93. The Marshall candidacy is likewise unmentioned in the Pulitzer Prize–winning biography of Charles Evans Hughes, who ultimately received the bid Marshall sought: see Merlo J. Pusey, *Charles Evans Hughes*, 2 vols. (New York: Macmillan Company, 1951).

61. Lloyd P. Gartner, "The Correspondence of Mayer Sulzberger and William Howard Taft," *Jubilee Volume of the American Academy of Jewish Research Proceedings* XLVI–XLVII (1979–1980): 131.

62. Jerome C. Rosenthal, "The Public Life of Louis Marshall" (PhD diss., University of Cincinnati, 1983), 697.

63. Auerbach, *Rabbis and Lawyers*, 95–96.

64. Sarna and Dalin, *Religion and State*, 209.

65. Ibid.

66. Auerbach, *Unequal Justice*, 122.

67. Rosenthal, "The Public Life of Louis Marshall," 262.

68. Quoted in Gartner, "The Correspondence of Mayer Sulzberger and William Howard Taft," 130–31.

69. Ibid., 131.

70. Ibid., 131–32.

71. Ibid., 132.

72. Gartner, "The Correspondence of Mayer Sulzberger and William Howard Taft"; Stephen S. Wise, *The Challenging Years* (New York: G. P. Putnam's Sons, 1949), 145–46.

73. Ibid., 132.

74. Abraham, *Justices, Presidents, and Senators*, 166.

75. Wise, *The Challenging Years*, 145–46; and Gartner, "The Correspondence of Mayer Sulzberger and William Howard Taft," 132.

76. Gartner, "The Correspondence of Mayer Sulzberger and William Howard Taft," 139.

77. For a discussion of Sulzberger's achievements as a judge, see Morris, "The American Jewish Judge," 203–4; and Louis E. Levinthal, *Mayer Sulzberger, P.J.* (Philadelphia, 1927). Biographical material on Sulzberger generally can be found in Moshe Davis, *The Emergence of Conservative Judaism* (Philadelphia: Jewish Publication Society of America, 1963), 362–65; David G. Dalin, "Mayer Sulzberger and American Jewish Public Life," in *An Inventory of Promises: Essays on American Jewish History in Honor of Moses Rischin*, ed. Jeffrey S. Gurock and Marc Lee Raphael (Brooklyn: Carlson Publishing, 1995), 31–42; and David G. Dalin, "The Patriarch: The Life and Legacy of Mayer Sulzberger," in *When Philadelphia Was the Capital of Jewish America*, ed. Murray Friedman (Philadelphia: Balch Institute Press and Associated University Presses, 1993), 58–73.

78. Gartner, "The Correspondence of Mayer Sulzberger and William Howard Taft," 130.

79. "Mr. Marshall as a Public Man," Louis Marshall Papers, box 1619, Jacob Marcus Center of the American Jewish Archives, Cincinnati.

80. Barnard, *The Forging of an American Jew*, 19. In 1884, when Julian Mack spoke at his high school commencement at Cincinnati's "celebrated Music Hall," his valedictory oration

on "Municipal Reform" and the special honors he received were "elaborately commented upon" in Isaac Mayer Wise's *American Israelite*. See Barnard, p. 21.

81. Lewis L. Gould, *The William Howard Taft Presidency* (Lawrence: University Press of Kansas, 2009), 132.

82. Dalin and Kolatch, *The Presidents*, 128.

83. Ibid.

84. A brief discussion of the friendship between Isaac Mayer Wise and the Taft family, in my book *The Presidents of the United States and the Jews*, is derived primarily from my discussion at Cincinnati's American Jewish Archives with the late Dr. Sefton Temkin, Wise's most recent biographer, when I was a Loewenstein-Wiener Summer Fellow at the Archives in June 1983. Included in this discussion was the relationship of William Howard Taft, and his father, Alphonso, with Wise and other Cincinnati Jews. According to Temkin, the Wise and Taft families dined together a few times during the late 1870s and early 1880s, when the future president, having completed his undergraduate studies at Yale, was studying at the University of Cincinnati Law School and, thereafter, beginning his law practice in Cincinnati. It is likely, suggested Temkin, that the Macks, who were active congregants and close friends of the Wises, first met the Tafts at one such dinner at Wise's home. Since William Howard Taft lived at home prior to his marriage to Helen Taft in 1886, and the young Julian Mack didn't leave Cincinnati to begin studying law at Harvard until 1884, Mack and Taft likely first met at one of these dinners.

85. Barnard, *The Forging of an American Jew*, 19.

86. Melvin I. Urofsky, *Louis D. Brandeis: A Life* (New York: Pantheon Books, 2009), 82.

87. Ibid.

88. Barnard, *The Forging of an American Jew*, 25, 291.

89. William Lasser, *Benjamin V. Cohen: Architect of the New Deal*, Century Foundation Book (New Haven: Yale University Press, 2002), 17.

90. Barnard, *The Forging of an American Jew*, 56; and Peter M. Ascoli, *Julius Rosenwald: The Man Who Built Sears, Roebuck and Advanced the Cause of Black Education in the American South* (Bloomington: Indiana University Press, 2006), 61.

91. Stephanie Deutsch, *You Need a Schoolhouse: Booker T. Washington, Julius Rosenwald, and the Building of Schools for the Segregated South* (Evanston, IL: Northwestern University Press, 2011), 109.

92. Ibid., 114.

93. Barnard, *The Forging of an American Jew*, 114–15.

94. Lasser, *Benjamin V. Cohen*, 18; and Barnard, *The Forging of an American Jew*, 126.

2. Louis D. Brandeis: "People's Attorney," Presidential Adviser, and Zionist

1. John Milton Cooper Jr., *Woodrow Wilson: A Biography* (New York: Vintage Books, 2009), 162.

2. Melvin I. Urofsky, *Louis D. Brandeis: A Life* (New York: Pantheon Books, 2009), 341; hereafter cited as Urofsky, *Brandeis: A Life*.

3. Cooper, *Woodrow Wilson*, 163.

4. Urofsky, *Brandeis: A Life*, 341.

5. Leonard Baker, *Brandeis and Frankfurter: A Dual Biography* (New York: Harper & Row, 1984), 82.

6. Peri E. Arnold, *Remaking the Presidency: Roosevelt, Taft, and Wilson, 1901–1916* (Lawrence: University Press of Kansas, 2009), 163.

7. Alpheus Thomas Mason, *Brandeis: A Free Man's Life* (New York: Viking Press, 1946), 377.

8. Ibid.

9. Cooper, *Woodrow Wilson*, 162.

10. James Chace, *1912: Wilson, Roosevelt, Taft and Debs—The Election That Changed the Country* (New York: Simon & Schuster, 2004), 192; and Urofsky, *Brandeis: A Life*, 343.

11. Arthur S. Link, *Wilson*, Vol. 2 (Princeton, NJ: Princeton University Press, 1956), 11.

12. Ben Halpern, *A Clash of Heroes: Brandeis, Weizmann, and American Zionism* (New York: Oxford University Press, 1987), 69.

13. Jonathan D. Sarna, "'The Greatest Jew in the World since Jesus Christ': The Jewish Legacy of Louis D. Brandeis," *American Jewish History* 81, nos. 3–4 (Spring/Summer 1994), 347.

14. Melvin I. Urofsky, "Justice Louis Brandeis," in *The Jewish Justices of the Supreme Court Revisited: Brandeis to Fortas*, ed. Jennifer M. Lowe (Washington, DC: Supreme Court Historical Society, 1994), 12–13.

15. Louis D. Brandeis, letter to Elizabeth Brandeis, December 29, 1900, in Melvin I. Urofsky and David W. Levy, eds., *The Family Letters of Louis D. Brandeis* (Norman: University of Oklahoma Press, 2002), p. 85; hereafter cited as *LDB Family Letters*.

16. Louis D. Brandeis, letters to Alfred Brandeis, October 7, 1917, and March 19, 1921, in Melvin I. Urofsky and David W. Levy, eds., *Letters of Louis D. Brandeis*, Vol. 4 (Albany: State University of New York Press), 313, 543, hereafter cited as *LDB Letters*; and Sarna, "'The Greatest Jew in the World,'" 348.

17. Sarna, "'The Greatest Jew in the World.'"

18. Louis D. Brandeis, letter to Felix Frankfurter, August 15, 1925, in Melvin I. Urofsky and David W. Levy, eds., *"Half Brother, Half Son": The Letters of Louis D. Brandeis to Felix Frankfurter* (Norman: University of Oklahoma Press, 2002), 209.

19. Urofsky, "Justice Louis Brandeis," p. 13; and Sarna, "'The Greatest Jew in the World,'" 348.

20. Urofsky, *Brandeis: A Life*, 17–18.

21. Halpern, *A Clash of Heroes*, 65.

22. Urofsky, *Brandeis: A Life*, 19.

23. Halpern, *A Clash of Heroes*, 65.

24. Urofsky, *Brandeis: A Life*, 20.

25. Allon Gal, *Brandeis of Boston* (Cambridge: Harvard University Press, 1980), 153–54.

26. Urofsky, *Brandeis: A Life*, 29.

27. Gal, *Brandeis of Boston*, 9.

28. Mason, *Brandeis: A Free Man's Life*, 48.

29. Urofsky, *Brandeis: A Life*, 39.

30. Mason, *Brandeis: A Free Man's Life*, 48.

31. Ibid., ch. 4.

32. Louis D. Brandeis, letter to Alfred Brandeis, July 31, 1879, in *LDB Letters* 1: 45.

33. Mason, *Brandeis: A Free Man's Life*, 64, 570.

34. Urofsky, *Brandeis: A Life*, 57.

35. Ibid., 54.

36. Gal, *Brandeis of Boston*, 12.

37. Ibid., 36; and Urofsky, *Brandeis: A Life*, 97.

38. Philippa Strum, *Louis D. Brandeis: Justice for the People* (Cambridge: Harvard University Press, 1984), 45.

39. Jonathan D. Sarna and Ellen Smith, eds., *The Jews of Boston* (Boston: Combined Jewish Philanthropies, 1995), 9.

40. Gal, *Brandeis of Boston*, 36–37.

41. Sarna and Smith, *The Jews of Boston*, 9.

42. Mason, *Brandeis: A Free Man's Life*, 63–64.

43. Gal, *Brandeis of Boston*, 36.

44. Quoted in Sarna and Smith, *The Jews of Boston*, 10.

45. Urofsky, "Louis D. Brandeis," 26.

46. Urofsky, *Brandeis: A Life*, 98.

47. Mason, *Brandeis: A Free Man's Life*, 88.

48. Louis D. Brandeis, letter to Alfred Brandeis, March 8, 1908, *LDB Letters*, II: 96.

49. Louis D. Brandeis, letter to Alfred Brandeis, March 10, 1913, *LDB Letters*, III: 42; and Louis D. Brandeis, letter to Alfred Brandeis, February 6, 1921, *LDB Letters*, IV: 529.

50. Urofsky, *Brandeis: A Life*, 73–74.

51. Halpern, *A Clash of Heroes*, 81.

52. Urofsky, *Brandeis: A Life*, 165.

53. Link, *Wilson*, 2: 11.

54. Ibid., 54.

55. Gal, *Brandeis of Boston*, 190.

56. Alden L. Todd, *Justice on Trial: The Case of Louis D. Brandeis* (New York: McGraw-Hill, 1964), 60–61.

57. Strum, *Louis D. Brandeis*, 114.

58. Ibid., 120–22.

59. Halpern, *A Clash of Heroes*, 139.

60. Louis D. Brandeis, letter to Alfred Brandeis, August 29, 1912, *LDB Letters*, 2: 661, fn. 1.

61. Urofsky, *Brandeis: A Life*, 344.

62. Louis D. Brandeis, letter to Alfred Brandeis, August 29, 1912, *LDB Letters*, 2: 61.

63. Ibid.

64. Urofsky, *Brandeis: A Life*, 343.

65. Louis D. Brandeis, letter to William Gibbs McAdoo, October 2, 1912, in *LDB Letters*, 2: 697–98.

66. Urofsky, *Brandeis: A Life*, 372.

67. Ibid., 227.

68. Urofsky, *Brandeis: A Life*, 372.

69. Gal, *Brandeis of Boston*, 192.

70. Ibid.

71. W. Barksdale Maynard, *Woodrow Wilson: Princeton to the Presidency* (New Haven: Yale University Press, 2008), 284.

72. Alexander L. George and Juliette L. George, *Woodrow Wilson and Colonel House: A Personality Study* (New York: Dover Publications, 1964), xix.

73. Cooper, *Woodrow Wilson*, 183.

74. Ibid., 189.

75. Baker, *Brandeis and Frankfurter*, 87.

76. Halpern, *A Clash of Heroes*, 103.

77. Colonel Edward M. House to Woodrow Wilson, November 22, 1912, in Arthur S. Link et. al., *Papers of Woodrow Wilson*, Vol. 25 (Princeton, NJ: Princeton University Press, 1978), 559; hereafter cited as Link, *Wilson*.

78. Louis D. Brandeis, letter to Alfred Brandeis, March 10, 1913, in *LDB Letters*, 3: 42.

79. Link, *Wilson*, Vol. 2, 95, and Vol. 4, 324.

80. Baker, *Brandeis and Frankfurter*, 89.

81. Bruce Allen Murphy, *The Brandeis/Frankfurter Connection: The Secret Political Activities of Two Supreme Court Justices* (New York: Oxford University Press, 1982), 28.

82. Ibid., 27.

83. Ibid., 28.

84. Ibid.

85. Ibid.

86. David N. Atkinson, *Leaving the Bench: Supreme Court Justices at the End* (Lawrence: University Press of Kansas, 1999), 88.

87. Melvin I. Urofsky, *American Zionism: From Herzl to the Holocaust* (Lincoln: University of Nebraska Press, 1995), 124.

88. "An Interview with Louis D. Brandeis," *American Hebrew*, December 10, 1910, as cited and quoted in Alpheus Thomas Mason's authorized biography, *Brandeis: A Free Man's Life*, 443.

89. Mason, *Brandeis: A Free Man's Life*, 443; and Robert A. Burt, *Two Jewish Justices: Outcasts in the Promised Land* (Berkeley: University of California Press, 1988), 117.

90. Ibid.

91. Strum, *Louis D. Brandeis*, 231.

92. Louis D. Brandeis, letter to Charles A. Cowen, April 6, 1916, *LDB Letters*, IV: 152.

93. Gal, *Brandeis of Boston*, 178.

94. Urofsky, *Brandeis: A Life*, 404.

95. Louis D. Brandeis, letter to Alfred Brandeis, January 7, 1912, in *LDB Letters*, 2: 537.

96. Louis D. Brandeis, letter to Norman Hapgood, January 16, 1914, in *LDB Letters*, 3: 117.

97. Strum, *Louis D. Brandeis*, 235.

98. Evan Moffic, "Brandeis and Zionism, In and Out of Love," *Jewish Ideas Daily*, June 19, 2012.

99. Ibid.

100. Ibid.

101. Yonathan Shapiro, "American Jews in Politics: The Case of Louis D. Brandeis," *American Jewish Historical Quarterly* 55 (December 1965): 199–211, as quoted and discussed in Urofsky, *Brandeis: A Life*, 406.

102. Halpern, *A Clash of Heroes*, 100.

103. Jerold S. Auerbach, *Rabbis and Lawyers: The Journey from Torah to Constitution* (Bloomington: Indiana University Press, 1990), 126–27.

104. Sarna, "'The Greatest Jew in the World,'" 357–58.

105. Ibid., 359.

106. Ibid., 353.

107. Jacob de Haas, *Louis D. Brandeis: A Biographical Sketch* (New York: Bloch Publishing Company, 1929), 49–50; as also quoted in Sarna, "'The Greatest Jew in the World,'" 354.

108. Sarna, "'The Greatest Jew in the World,'" 353.

109. Ibid.

110. Melvin I. Urofsky, *Louis D. Brandeis and the Progressive Tradition* (Boston: Little, Brown and Company, 1981), 96–97.

111. Sarna, "'The Greatest Jew in the World,'" 357.

112. Ibid.

3. Mr. Justice Brandeis: The Court Years

1. David N. Atkinson, *Leaving the Bench: Supreme Court Justices at the End* (Lawrence: University Press of Kansas, 1999), 88.

2. Thomas Karfunkel and Thomas W. Ryley, *The Jewish Seat: Anti-Semitism and the Appointment of Jews to the Supreme Court* (Hicksville, NY: Exposition Press, 1978), 40.

3. Louis D. Brandeis, letter to Alfred Brandeis, January 28, 1916, in Melvin I. Urofsky and David W. Levy, eds., *Letters of Louis D. Brandeis*, Vol. IV (Albany: State University of New York Press, 1975), 25; hereafter cited as *LDB Letters*.

4. Philippa Strum, *Louis D. Brandeis: Justice for the People* (Cambridge: Harvard University Press, 1984), 291.

5. Quoted in Melvin I. Urofsky, *Louis D. Brandeis and the Progressive Tradition* (Boston: Little, Brown and Company, 1981), 106.

6. William Howard Taft, letter to Gus Karger, January 31, 1916; as cited in Arthur S. Link et al., *Papers of Woodrow Wilson*, Vol. 4 (Princeton, NJ: Princeton University Press, 1964), 325.

7. Quoted in Urofsky, *Louis D. Brandeis and the Progressive Tradition*, 106.

8. Leonard Baker, *Brandeis and Frankfurter: A Dual Biography* (New York: Harper & Row, 1984), 104.

9. Henry J. Abraham, *Justices, Presidents, and Senators: A Political History of Appointments to the Supreme Court* (Lanham, MD: Rowman & Littlefield, 1999), 136.

10. Allon Gal, *Brandeis of Boston* (Cambridge: Harvard University Press, 1980), 196.

11. Alden L. Todd, *Justice on Trial: The Case of Louis D. Brandeis* (New York: McGraw-Hill, 1964), 92.

12. Ibid., 106.

13. Ibid.

14. Alpheus Thomas Mason, *Brandeis: A Free Man's Life* (New York: Viking Press, 1946), 501.

15. Ibid.

16. Strum, *Louis D. Brandeis*, 291.

17. Baker, *Brandeis and Frankfurter*, 102.

18. Strum, *Louis D. Brandeis*, 297–98.

19. Baker, *Brandeis and Frankfurter*, 105.

20. Todd, *Justice on Trial*, 216–17.

21. Henry Pringle, *The Life and Times of William Howard Taft*, Vol. 2 (Newtown, CT: American Political Biography Press with Henry Holt and Company, 1967), 970. In 1923, after two court sessions, Taft wrote his daughter Helen: "I have come to like Brandeis very much indeed . . . he is a very hard worker . . . He thinks much of the Court and is anxious to have it consistent and strong, and he pulls his weight in the boat." See William Howard Taft, letter to Helen Taft Manning, June 11, 1923, as quoted in Pringle, *The Life and Times of William Howard Taft*.

22. Todd, *Justice on Trial*, 83–85.

23. Urofsky, *Brandeis: A Life*, 458.

24. Strum, *Louis D. Brandeis*, 297–98.

25. Baker, *Brandeis and Frankfurter*, 101.

26. Cyrus Adler to Louis Marshall, undated handwritten note, 1916, Louis Marshall Papers, box 47, American Jewish Archives; quoted in Jonathan D. Sarna, "Two Jewish Lawyers Named Louis," *American Jewish History* 94, nos. 1–2 (March–June 2008): 16.

27. Cyrus Adler, letter to Jacob Schiff, June 15, 1916, in Ira Robinson, ed., *Cyrus Adler: Selected Letters*, Vol. 1 (Philadelphia: Jewish Publication Society, 1985), 308; and as quoted in Sarna, "Two Jewish Lawyers," 17.

28. William Howard Taft, letter to Henry W. Taft, as quoted in Todd, *Justice on Trial*, 80, and Sarna, "Two Jewish Lawyers Named Louis," 17.

29. Urofsky, *Brandeis: A Life*, 460–61.

30. Atkinson, *Leaving the Bench*, 88.

31. Abraham, *Justices, Presidents, and Senators*, 127.

32. Todd, *Justice on Trial*, 18–19.

33. Urofsky, *Brandeis: A Life*, 462.

34. Ibid., 464.

35. Louis D. Brandeis, letter to Felix Frankfurter, October 23, 1922, as quoted in Urofsky, *Brandeis: A Life*, 465.

36. William E. Nelson et al., "The Liberal Tradition of the Supreme Court Clerkship: Its Rise, Fall, and Reincarnation?" *Vanderbilt Law Review* 62, no. 6 (2009): 1759.

37. Eric Pace, "Paul A. Freund, Authority on Constitution, Dies at 83," *New York Times*, February 6, 1992.

38. Robert A. Burt, *Two Jewish Justices: Outcasts in the Promised Land* (Berkeley: University of California Press, 1988), 64.

39. Louis D. Brandeis, letter to Felix Frankfurter, October 13, 1929, in Melvin I. Urofsky and David W. Levy, eds., *"Half Brother, Half Son": The Letters of Louis D. Brandeis to Felix Frankfurter* (Norman: University of Oklahoma Press, 2002), 395; hereafter cited as *"Half Brother, Half Son"*; and Burt, *Two Jewish Justices*, 65.

40. Louis D. Brandeis, letter to Felix Frankfurter, October 13, 1929, in *"Half Brother, Half Son"*; and Burt, *Two Jewish Justices*, 65.

41. Dan A. Oren, *Joining the Club: A History of Jews and Yale* (New Haven: Yale University Press, 1985), 126.

42. Ibid., 279.

43. Urofsky, *Brandeis: A Life*, 465.

44. Paul A. Freund, "Justice Brandeis: A Law Clerk's Remembrance," *American Jewish History* 68 (September 1978): 11.

45. Melvin I. Urofsky, "Justice Louis Brandeis," in *The Jewish Justices of the Supreme Court*

Revisited: From Brandeis to Fortas, ed. Jennifer M. Lowe (Washington, DC: Supreme Court Historical Society, 1994), 18.

46. Ibid.; Strum, *Louis D. Brandeis*, 355.

47. Quoted in Strum, *Louis D. Brandeis*, 309.

48. *Schenck v. United States*, 249 U.S. 47 (1919), 51, as quoted in Baker, *Brandeis and Frankfurter*, 246.

49. *Schenck v. United States*, 249 U.S. 47 (1919), 52, as quoted in Urofsky, "Justice Louis Brandeis," 19.

50. *Schenck v. United States*, 249 U.S. 47 (1919), 52, as quoted in Strum, *Louis D. Brandeis*, 316.

51. Strum, *Louis D. Brandeis*, 320.

52. Baker, *Brandeis and Frankfurter*, 247.

53. Urofsky, "Justice Louis Brandeis," 20.

54. Strum, *Louis D. Brandeis*, 317–18.

55. Baker, *Brandeis and Frankfurter*, 248.

56. Ibid.

57. Urofsky, *Brandeis: A Life*, 561.

58. Mason, *Brandeis: A Free Man's Life*, 70.

59. Louis D. Brandeis and Samuel D. Warren, "The Right to Privacy," *Harvard Law Review* 4 (1890): 192.

60. Ibid., as quoted in Urofsky, "Justice Louis Brandeis," 27.

61. *Olmstead v. United States*, 277 U.S. (1928), as quoted in Strum, *Louis D. Brandeis*, 323–24.

62. Baker, *Brandeis and Frankfurter*, 215.

63. Urofsky, "Justice Louis Brandeis," 30.

64. Ibid.

65. Ibid.

66. Liva Baker, *The Justice from Beacon Hill: The Life and Times of Oliver Wendell Holmes* (New York: HarperCollins, 1991), 616; as quoted in Urofsky, "Justice Louis Brandeis," 28.

67. *Olmstead v. United States*, 277 U.S. (1928), as quoted in Urofsky, "Justice Louis Brandeis," 28.

68. Sarna, "Two Jewish Lawyers," 13.

69. Urofsky, *Brandeis: A Life*, 20.

70. Ibid.

71. Burt, *Two Jewish Justices*, 84; as also cited in Sarna, "Two Jewish Lawyers," 13.

72. *Pierce v. Society of Sisters of the Holy Names of Jesus and Mary*, 268 U.S. 510 (1925), as cited and discussed in Sarna, "Two Jewish Lawyers," and Jonathan D. Sarna and David G. Dalin, *Religion and State in the American Jewish Experience* (Notre Dame, IN: University of Notre Dame Press, 1997), 24, 209.

73. A.L.A. Schechter Poultry Corporation v. United States 295 U.S. 495 (1935).

74. Jonathan Alter, *The Defining Moment: FDR's Hundred Days and the Triumph of Hope* (New York: Simon & Schuster, 2006), 302.

75. Sarna and Dalin, *Religion and State*, 276–77.

76. Amity Shlaes, *The Forgotten Man: A New History of the Great Depression* (New York: Harper Perennial, 2008), 215.

77. Jim Powell, *FDR's Folly: How Roosevelt and His New Deal Prolonged the Great Depression* (New York: Three Rivers Press, 2005), 163.

78. Jeff Shesol, *Supreme Power: Franklin Roosevelt vs. The Supreme Court* (New York: W. W. Norton, 2010), 131.

79. Ibid.

80. Ibid., 131–32.

81. Shlaes, *The Forgotten Man*, 220.

82. Ibid.

83. Shesol, *Supreme Power*, 133.

84. Ibid., 134.

85. Bruce Allen Murphy, *The Brandeis/Frankfurter Connection: The Secret Political Activities of Two Supreme Court Justices* (New York: Oxford University Press, 1982), 157.

86. Conrad Black, *Franklin Delano Roosevelt: Champion of Freedom* (New York: Public Affairs, 2003), 352.

87. Shesol, *Supreme Power*, 136.

88. Urofsky, *Brandeis: A Life*, 460.

89. Murphy, *The Brandeis/Frankfurter Connection*, 345–62.

90. Ibid., 356–57, 360–61.

91. Ibid., 361–62.

92. Ibid., 362.

93. Ibid., 363.

94. Phyllis Lee Levin, *Edith and Woodrow: The Wilson White House* (New York: Scribner / Lisa Drew, 2001), 163.

95. Strum, *Louis D. Brandeis*, 378.

96. Urofsky, *Louis D. Brandeis and the Progressive Tradition*, 130.

97. Strum, *Louis D. Brandeis*, 378.

98. Urofsky, *Louis D. Brandeis and the Progressive Tradition*, 130.

99. Urofsky, *Brandeis: A Life*, 475.

100. Ibid., 506.

101. Nelson L. Dawson, "Louis D. Brandeis, Felix Frankfurter and Franklin D. Roosevelt: The Origins of a New Deal Relationship," *American Jewish History* 68, no. 1 (September 1978): 34.

102. Urofsky and Levy, *"Half Brother, Half Son,"* 5.

103. Urofsky, *Brandeis: A Life*, 503.

104. Strum, *Louis D. Brandeis*, 375.

105. Murphy, *The Brandeis/Frankfurter Connection*, 10.

106. Louis D. Brandeis, letter to Felix Frankfurter, November 19, 1916, in *LDB Letters*, IV: 266.

107. Louis D. Brandeis letter to Felix Frankfurter, November 25, 1916, in Urofsky and Levy, *"Half Brother, Half Son,"* 27.

108. Urofsky, *Brandeis: A Life*, 504.

109. Louis D. Brandeis, letter to Felix Frankfurter, September 24, 1925, in Urofsky and Levy, *"Half Brother, Half Son,"* 212.

110. Noah Feldman, *Scorpions: The Battles and Triumphs of FDR's Great Supreme Court Justices* (New York: Twelve, 2010), 29.

111. Strum, *Louis D. Brandeis*, 373.

112. Nelson L. Dawson, *Louis D. Brandeis, Felix Frankfurter and the New Deal* (Hamden, CT: Archon Books, 1980), 3.

113. Strum, *Louis D. Brandeis*, 381.

114. Murphy, *The Brandeis/Frankfurter Connection*, 113.

115. Ibid., 114.

116. Ibid.

117. Ibid.

118. Ibid., 117.

119. Ibid., 131.

120. Strum, *Louis D. Brandeis*, 383–84.

121. Dawson, *Louis D. Brandeis, Felix Frankfurter and the New Deal*, 140.

122. Urofsky, *Brandeis: A Life*, 726.

123. Ibid., 718, 741.

124. Ibid.

125. Atkinson, *Leaving the Bench*, 111.

126. Freund, "Justice Brandeis," 17.

127. Ibid.; Urofsky, *Brandeis: A Life*, 737.

128. Freund, "Justice Brandeis," 17.

129. Alan M. Dershowitz, "The Practice," *New York Times*, Book Review, September 27, 2009.

130. Ibid.

131. Sarna, "The Jewish Legacy of Louis D. Brandeis," 346.

132. Ibid.

133. Ibid., 361.

134. Dershowitz, "The Practice."

135. Sarna, "The Jewish Legacy of Louis D. Brandeis," 363.

4. Benjamin N. Cardozo: Redeeming the Family Name

1. Andrew L. Kaufman, *Cardozo* (Cambridge: Harvard University Press, 1998), 18–19.

2. Richard Polenberg, *The World of Benjamin Cardozo: Personal Values and the Judicial Process* (Cambridge: Harvard University Press, 1997), 24.

3. Richard A. Posner, *Cardozo: A Study in Reputation* (Chicago: University of Chicago Press, 1990), 17.

4. Ibid., 11.

5. Andrew L. Kaufman, "The First Judge Cardozo: Albert, Father of Benjamin," *Journal of Law and Religion* 11, no. 1 (1994–1995): 291.

6. Ibid., 12–13.

7. Stephen Birmingham, *The Grandees: America's Sephardic Elite* (New York: Harper & Row, 1971), 292.

8. Cited in Polenberg, *The World of Benjamin Cardozo*, 26.

9. Alexander B. Callow Jr., *The Tweed Ring* (New York: Oxford University Press, 1966), vii.

10. Andrew L. Kaufman, "Benjamin N. Cardozo, Sephardic Jew," in *The Jewish Justices*

of the Supreme Court Revisited: Brandeis to Fortas, ed. Jennifer M. Lowe (Washington, DC: Supreme Court Historical Society, 1994), 36.

11. Kenneth D. Ackerman, *Boss Tweed: The Rise and Fall of the Corrupt Pol Who Conceived the Soul of Modern New York* (New York: Carroll & Graf, 2005), 51.

12. Kaufman, "Benjamin N. Cardozo, Sephardic Jew," 36.

13. Polenberg, *The World of Benjamin Cardozo*, 25.

14. Ibid., 27.

15. Kaufman, *Cardozo*, 15.

16. Ibid.

17. Ibid.

18. Polenberg, *The World of Benjamin Cardozo*, 29.

19. Ackerman, *Boss Tweed*, 68.

20. Kaufman, *Cardozo*, 14.

21. Ibid., 19.

22. Kaufman, "The First Judge Cardozo," 312.

23. Ibid.

24. Ibid.

25. Ibid.

26. Kaufman, *Cardozo*, 6.

27. Ibid., 6–8.

28. Jerold L. Jacobs, "Is It Time for a Jewish Justice?" *Moment*, October 1990, 25.

29. Birmingham, *The Grandees*, 71.

30. Kaufman, "The First Judge Cardozo," 272.

31. Kaufman, *Cardozo*, 7.

32. Kaufman, "The First Judge Cardozo," 273.

33. Ibid., 274.

34. Egal Feldman, *Dual Destinies: The Jewish Encounter with Protestant America* (Urbana: University of Illinois Press, 1990), 83.

35. Ibid.

36. Ibid.

37. Ibid., 68.

38. Ibid., 23.

39. Ibid., 24.

40. Ibid.; Polenberg, *The World of Benjamin Cardozo*, 17.

41. Kaufman, "Benjamin N. Cardozo, Sephardic Jew," 41.

42. Ibid.

43. Ibid.

44. Kaufman, *Cardozo*, 69.

45. Kaufman, "Benjamin N. Cardozo, Sephardic Jew," 37.

46. Polenberg, *The World of Benjamin Cardozo*, 22.

47. Ibid., 18.

48. Ibid., 18–19.

49. Kaufman, *Cardozo*, 26.

50. Polenberg, *The World of Benjamin Cardozo*, 34.

51. Darryl Lyman, *Great Jewish Families* (Middle Village, NY: Jonathan David Publishers, 1997), 263.

52. Birmingham, *The Grandees*, 296.

53. Shalom Kassan, "Benjamin Nathan Cardozo (1870–1938) — In Memoriam," *Israel Law Review* 9 (April 1975): 160.

54. Ibid.

55. Milton R. Konvitz, "Benjamin Nathan Cardozo," *Midstream* (May/June 1999): 5.

56. Polenberg, *The World of Benjamin Cardozo*, 44.

57. Kaufman, *Cardozo*, 99.

58. Konvitz, "Benjamin Nathan Cardozo," 5.

59. Kaufman, *Cardozo*, 87.

60. Polenberg, *The World of Benjamin Cardozo*, 180.

61. Ibid.

62. Kaufman, *Cardozo*, 69–70.

63. Ibid., 70.

64. Ibid.; Konvitz, "Benjamin Nathan Cardozo," 9.

65. Kaufman, "Benjamin N. Cardozo, Sephardic Jew," 42.

66. Kaufman, *Cardozo*, 70.

67. Konvitz, "Benjamin Nathan Cardozo," 9.

68. Kaufman, *Cardozo*, 147.

69. Ibid., 147–48.

70. Ibid., 79.

71. Ibid.

72. Louis Marshall, letter to A. Bleecker Banks, December 4, 1902, and Louis Marshall, letter to Benjamin Cardozo, December 4, 1902, Louis Marshall Papers, box 1572, Jacob Rader Marcus Center of the American Jewish Archives, Cincinnati (hereafter cited as Louis Marshall Papers, American Jewish Archives), as cited in Kaufman, *Cardozo*, 89.

73. Kaufman, *Cardozo*, 89.

74. Ibid., 92.

75. Kaufman, "Benjamin N. Cardozo, Sephardic Jew," 46.

76. Kaufman, *Cardozo*, 98.

77. Ibid., 94.

78. Kaufman, "Benjamin N. Cardozo, Sephardic Jew," 46.

79. Polenberg, *The World of Benjamin Cardozo*, 49.

80. Kaufman, *Cardozo*, 118.

81. Ibid., 119.

82. Ibid.; Kaufman, "Benjamin N. Cardozo, Sephardic Jew," 46.

83. Louis Marshall, letter to Benjamin N. Cardozo, August 15, 1913, Louis Marshall Papers, box 1582, American Jewish Archives, as cited in Kaufman, *Cardozo*, 612.

84. David G. Dalin, "Louis Marshall, the Jewish Vote and the Republican Party," *Jewish Political Studies Review* 4, no. 1 (Spring 1992): 55, 61.

85. Louis Marshall, letters to the editor of the *Jewish Morning Journal, Jewish Daily News*, and *Warheit*, October 27, 1913, Louis Marshall Papers, box 1582, American Jewish Archives, as cited in Kaufman, *Cardozo*, 122.

86. Kaufman, *Cardozo*, 119.

87. Ibid., 127.

88. Ibid.; Posner, *Cardozo: A Study in Reputation*, 3.

89. Minutes of the Congregation Shearith Israel board of trustees meeting, February 3, 1914, as cited in Kaufman, *Cardozo*, 129.

90. Posner, *Cardozo: A Study in Reputation*, 3.

91. Ibid.

92. Edmund H. Lewis, "The Contribution of Judge Irving Lehman to the Development of the Law," *Columbia Law Review* 51, no. 6 (June 1951): 734.

93. Konvitz, "Benjamin Nathan Cardozo," 5–6.

94. Clarence I. Freed, "Wisdom Sits with Him: Judge Benjamin Nathan Cardozo, Legal Scientist and Philosopher, Holds Highest Judicial Office in the State of New York" (New York: Sage Publications, 1927), 381.

95. Konvitz, "Benjamin Nathan Cardozo," 5.

96. Kaufman, *Cardozo*, 199.

97. Ibid., 199–200.

98. Ibid., 204.

99. Ibid.

100. Polenberg, *The World of Benjamin Cardozo*, 89.

101. Ibid.

102. Kaufman, *Cardozo*, 174.

103. Polenberg, *The World of Benjamin Cardozo*, 89–90.

104. Kaufman, *Cardozo*, 178.

105. Ibid., 179.

106. Ibid., 181.

107. Stephen S. Wise, letter to Richard W. Montague, June 2, 1927, in Carl Hermann Voss, ed., *Stephen S. Wise: Servant of the People; Selected Letters* (Philadelphia: Jewish Publication Society, 1969), 150, as quoted in Polenberg, *The World of Benjamin Cardozo*, 122.

108. Kaufman, *Cardozo*, 181.

109. *New York Times*, September 15, 1926, as quoted in Polenberg, *The World of Benjamin Cardozo*, 122.

110. Kaufman, *Cardozo*, 182.

111. Polenberg, *The World of Benjamin Cardozo*, 121.

112. Robert A. McCaughey, *Stand, Columbia: A History of Columbia University in the City of New York, 1754–2004* (New York: Columbia University Press, 2003), 311.

113. Ibid.; Harold S. Wechsler, *The Qualified Student: A History of Selective College Admissions in America, 1870–1979* (New York: Wiley, 1977).

114. McCaughey, *Stand, Columbia*, 257.

115. Ibid.

116. Nicholas Murray Butler, letter to Stephen G. Williams, November 1, 1927, cited in McCaughey, *Stand, Columbia*, 311.

117. McCaughey, *Stand, Columbia*, 311.

118. Ibid., 312.

119. Ibid.

120. Ibid., 311.

121. Ibid., 312.

122. Stephen G. Williams, letter to Nicholas Murray Butler, as cited in McCaughey, *Stand, Columbia*, 311.

123. Ibid.

124. Kaufman, *Cardozo*, 176.

125. Kaufman, "Benjamin N. Cardozo, Sephardic Jew," 48; and Konvitz, "Benjamin Nathan Cardozo," 9.

126. Kaufman, "Benjamin N. Cardozo, Sephardic Jew," 48.

127. Kaufman, *Cardozo*, 186.

128. Ibid.

129. Ibid.

130. Kaufman, *Cardozo*, 455.

131. Ira H. Carmen, "The President, Politics and the Power of Appointment: Hoover's Nomination of Mr. Justice Cardozo," *Virginia Law Review* 55 (1969): 616.

132. Ibid.

133. Barbara A. Perry, *A "Representative" Supreme Court? The Impact of Race, Religion, and Gender on Appointments* (New York: Greenwood Press, 1991), 68.

134. Ibid., 69.

135. Kaufman, *Cardozo*, 172; and Kaufman, "Cardozo's Appointment to the Supreme Court," *Cardozo Law Review* 1 (1979): 24.

136. Nicholas Murray Butler, letter to Warren G. Harding, October 16, 1922, as cited in Kaufman, "Cardozo's Appointment to the Supreme Court," 24.

137. Thomas W. Swan, letter to Warren G. Harding, November 3, 1922, as cited in Carmen, "The President, Politics and the Power of Appointment," 618.

138. Ibid.

139. Frank Hiscock, letter to Charles Evans Hughes, October 26, 1922, as cited in Kaufman, "Cardozo's Appointment to the Supreme Court," 25.

140. George W. Wickersham, letter to William Howard Taft, September 25, 1922, as cited in Kaufman, "Cardozo's Appointment to the Supreme Court," 26–27.

141. William Howard Taft, letter to Warren G. Harding, December 4, 1922, as cited in Kaufman, "Cardozo's Appointment to the Supreme Court," 27.

142. Henry J. Abraham, *Justices, Presidents, and Senators: A History of the U.S. Supreme Court Appointments from Washington to Clinton* (Lanham, MD: Rowman & Littlefield, 1999), 140.

143. Kaufman, "Cardozo's Appointment to the Supreme Court," 28–29.

144. Ibid., 29–30.

145. Kaufman, *Cardozo*, 456.

146. Ibid., 464–465.

147. Urofsky and Levy, *"Half Brother/Half Son,"* 477.

148. Kaufman, *Cardozo*, 465.

149. Ibid., 466.

150. Samuel Seabury, letter to Herbert Hoover, January 24, 1932, as cited in Carmen, "The President, Politics and the Power of Appointment," 632.

151. Ibid., 633.

152. Franklin Fort, letter to Herbert Hoover, January 26, 1932, as cited in Polenberg, *The World of Benjamin Cardozo*, 168.

153. Ibid.

154. Carmen, "The President, Politics and the Power of Appointment," 633.

155. Ibid., 627–28.

156. Ibid., 628.

157. Jacob Billikopf, letter to Marcus Sloss, January 20, 1932, as cited in Carmen, "The President, Politics and the Power of Appointment," 628.

158. Marcus Sloss, telegram to Herbert Hoover, January 21, 1932, cited in Carmen, "The President, Politics and the Power of Appointment," 629.

159. Jacob Billikopf, letter to Abba Hillel Silver, January 20, 1932, as cited in Carmen, "The President, Politics and the Power of Appointment," 628–29.

160. Polenberg, *The World of Benjamin Cardozo*, 168–69.

161. Ibid., 169.

162. David G. Dalin and Alfred J. Kolatch, *The Presidents of the United States and the Jews* (Middle Village, NY: Jonathan David Publishers, 2000), 163.

163. Carmen, "The President, Politics and the Power of Appointment," 627.

164. Joseph P. Pollard, *Mr. Justice Cardozo: A Liberal Mind in Action* (New York: Yorktown Press, 1935), 281.

165. Ibid., 283.

166. Paul A. Freund, "Foreword: Homage to Mr. Justice Cardozo," *Cardozo Law Review* 1 (1979): 1.

167. Ibid.

168. Kaufman, *Cardozo*, 469–70.

169. Ibid., 470.

170. Dalin and Kolatch, *The Presidents*, 163.

171. Ibid.

172. Stephen S. Wise, letter to Richard W. Montague, January 20, 1932, as cited in Kaufman, *Cardozo*, 470–71.

173. Ibid., 554–55.

174. Ibid., 555.

175. Polenberg, *The World of Benjamin Cardozo*, 172.

176. Ibid., 194.

177. Ibid.

178. Ibid.

179. Jeff Shesol, *Supreme Power: Franklin D. Roosevelt vs. The Supreme Court* (New York: W. W. Norton, 2010), 50.

180. Lyman, *Great Jewish Families*, 145.

181. Benjamin N. Cardozo, letter to Learned Hand, July 6, 1932, as cited in Polenberg, *The World of Benjamin Cardozo*, 194.

182. Ibid., 195.

183. Arthur L. Goodhart, *Five Jewish Lawyers of the Common Law* (New York: Oxford University Press, 1971), 61.

184. Polenberg, *The World of Benjamin Cardozo*, 195.

185. Ibid.

186. Ibid, 201.

187. Kaufman, *Cardozo*, 193.

188. Ibid., 195.

189. Ibid.

190. Benjamin N. Cardozo, letter to Louise Wise, April 28, 1932, as cited in Polenberg, *The World of Benjamin Cardozo*, 170.

191. Ibid.

192. Ibid., 170–71.

193. Kaufman, *Cardozo*, 485 and fn. 1, 686.

194. Ibid., 473.

195. Polenberg, *The World of Benjamin Cardozo*, 171.

196. Kaufman, *Cardozo*, 477.

197. Polenberg, *The World of Benjamin Cardozo*, 171.

198. Ibid.

199. Kaufman, *Cardozo*, 478.

200. Ibid.

201. Ibid.

202. Posner, *Cardozo: A Study in Reputation*, 4–5.

203. Andrew L. Kaufman, *Cardozo* (Cambridge: Harvard University Press, 1998), 478.

204. Melvin I. Urofsky, *Louis D. Brandeis: A Life* (New York: Pantheon Books, 2009), 677; hereafter cited as Urofsky, *Brandeis: A Life*.

205. Ibid.

206. Louise W. Wise, letter to Louis D. Brandeis, March 8, 1932, as cited in Polenberg, *The World of Benjamin Cardozo*, 174.

207. Polenberg, *The World of Benjamin Cardozo*, 174.

208. Ibid.

209. Urofsky, *Brandeis: A Life*, 388.

210. Ibid., 479.

211. Ibid.

212. Polenberg, *The World of Benjamin Cardozo*, 170.

213. Ibid.; Kaufman, *Cardozo*, 479–80.

214. Polenberg, *The World of Benjamin Cardozo*, 170.

215. Kaufman, *Cardozo*, 480.

216. Ibid.

217. Ibid., 482.

218. Polenberg, *The World of Benjamin Cardozo*, 173.

219. Kaufman, *Cardozo*, 474.

220. Posner, *Cardozo: A Study in Reputation*, 8.

221. Ibid.

222. Kaufman, *Cardozo*, 483.

223. Ibid., 482.

224. Ibid., 483.

225. Ibid.

226. Alan M. Stroock, "A Personal View of Justice Benjamin N. Cardozo: Recollections of Four Cardozo Law Clerks," *Cardozo Law Review* 1 (1979): 22.

227. Kaufman, *Cardozo*, 483.

228. Ibid., 487.

229. Ibid., 488.

230. Ibid.

231. Michael Feldberg, "Justice Cardozo, Sephardic Jew," in *Blessings of Freedom: Chapters in American Jewish History*, ed. Michael Feldberg (Hoboken, NJ: KTAV Publishing House with the American Jewish Historical Society, 2002), 73.

232. Michael Feldberg, "Justice Cardozo, Sephardic Jew," in *Blessings of Freedom: Chapters in American Jewish History*, ed. Michael Feldberg (Hoboken, NJ: KTAV Publishing House and American Jewish Historical Society, 2002), 73; Kaufman, *Cardozo*, 488.

233. Benjamin N. Cardozo, letter to Aline Goldstone, September 14, 1935, as cited in Kaufman, *Cardozo*, 488.

234. Ibid.

235. Ibid.

236. Benjamin N. Cardozo, letter to Felix Frankfurter, January 31, 1936, as cited in Kaufman, *Cardozo*, 488–89.

237. Ibid., 183.

238. Benjamin N. Cardozo, letter to Annie Nathan Meyer, June 8, 1935, as cited in Polenberg, *The World of Benjamin Cardozo*, 182.

239. Kaufman, *Cardozo*, 489.

240. Ibid.

241. Ibid.

242. Ibid.

243. Dalin and Kolatch, *The Presidents*, 163.

244. Kaufman, *Cardozo*, 552.

245. Polenberg, *The World of Benjamin Cardozo*, 217.

246. Richard H. Weisberg, "Law, Literature and Cardozo's Judicial Poetics," *Cardozo Law Review* 1 (1979): 332.

247. Konvitz, "Benjamin Nathan Cardozo," 8.

248. Ibid.

249. Kaufman, *Cardozo*, 552.

250. Palko v. Connecticut 302 U.S. (1937) at 325, as cited in Kaufman, *Cardozo*, 552–53.

251. Ibid., 553.

252. Ibid.

253. Posner, *Cardozo: A Study in Reputation*, 121.

254. Konvitz, "Benjamin Nathan Cardozo," 8.

255. Polenberg, *The World of Benjamin Cardozo*, 236.

256. David N. Atkinson, *Leaving the Bench: Supreme Court Justices at the End* (Lawrence: University Press of Kansas, 1999), 107.

257. Kaufman, *Cardozo*, 195.

258. Atkinson, *Leaving the Bench*, 107.

259. Ibid.

260. Ibid.

261. Kaufman, *Cardozo*, 567.

262. Atkinson, *Leaving the Bench*, 107.

263. Goodhart, *Five Jewish Lawyers*, 62.

264. Polenberg, *The World of Benjamin Cardozo*, 238.

265. Kaufman, *Cardozo*, 578; Atkinson, *Leaving the Bench*, 109.

266. Kaufman, *Cardozo*, 578.

267. Polenberg, *The World of Benjamin Cardozo*, 238.

268. Ibid.

269. Kaufman, *Cardozo*, 577–78.

270. Posner, *Cardozo: A Study in Reputation*, 121.

271. Ibid., 128.

272. Konvitz, "Benjamin Nathan Cardozo," 5.

273. Ibid.

274. Abraham, *Justices, Presidents, and Senators*, 155.

275. Ibid.

276. Ibid.

277. Shesol, *Supreme Power*, 453.

278. Posner, *Cardozo: A Study in Reputation*, 123.

279. Ibid., 568–69.

280. Posner, *Cardozo: A Study in Reputation*, ch. 5.

281. Abraham, *Justices, Presidents, and Senators*, 369.

282. Ibid., 371.

283. Feldberg, "Justice Cardozo, Sephardic Jew," 73.

284. G. Edward White, *The American Judicial Tradition: Profiles of Leading American Judges*, 3rd ed. (New York: Oxford University Press, 2007), 210.

285. Birmingham, *The Grandees*, 307–8.

286. Ibid., 308.

287. Neil A. Lewis, "Was a Hispanic Justice on the Court in the '30s?" *New York Times*, May 26, 2009; Robert Schlesinger, "Would Sotomayor Be the First Hispanic Supreme Court Justice or Was It Cardozo?" *USA Today*, May 26, 2009; Antonio Olivo, "Would Sotomayor Really Be the First Supreme Court Latino?" *Los Angeles Times*, May 31, 2009; and Brad A. Greenberg, "Sotomayor or Cardozo? Supreme Court's First Hispanic?" *Jewish Journal*, May 26, 2009.

288. Lewis, "Was a Hispanic Justice on the Court in the '30s?"

289. F. Arturo Rosales, *The Dictionary of Latino Civil Rights History* (Houston: Arte Publico Press, 2007), 59.

290. Lewis, "Was a Hispanic Justice on the Court in the '30s?"

291. Should Obama's nominee Merrick Garland, named after Antonin Scalia's death, somehow be confirmed, the number would rise to four.

292. Zachary Baron Shemtob, "The Catholic and Jewish Court: Explaining the Absence of Protestants on the Nation's Highest Judicial Body," *Journal of Law and Religion* 27, no. 2 (2011–2012): 369.

5. Felix Frankfurter: City College to the New Deal

1. Noah Feldman, *Scorpions: The Battles and Triumphs of FDR's Great Supreme Court* (New York: Twelve, 2010), 3.

2. Will Swift, *The Roosevelts and the Royals: Franklin and Eleanor, the King and Queen of England, and the Friendship That Changed History* (Hoboken, NJ: John Wiley & Sons, 2004), 5–7.

3. Feldman, *Scorpions*, 1; Liva Baker, *Felix Frankfurter: A Biography* (New York: Coward-McCann, 1969), 18.

4. Feldman, *Scorpions*, 7–8; Liva Baker, *Felix Frankfurter*, 24.

5. Liva Baker, *Felix Frankfurter*, 24–25; Michael E. Parrish, *Felix Frankfurter and His Times: The Reform Years* (New York: Free Press, 1982), 200.

6. Leonard Baker, *Brandeis and Frankfurter: A Dual Biography* (New York: Harper & Row, 1984), 41; James F. Simon, *The Antagonists: Hugo Black, Felix Frankfurter and Civil Liberties in Modern America* (New York: Simon & Schuster, 1989), 24.

7. Helen Shirley Thomas, *Felix Frankfurter: Scholar on the Bench* (Baltimore: Johns Hopkins University Press, 1960), 3.

8. Parrish, *Felix Frankfurter and His Times*, 7.

9. Leonard Baker, *Brandeis and Frankfurter*, 41.

10. Parrish, *Felix Frankfurter and His Times*, 9.

11. Leonard Baker, *Brandeis and Frankfurter*, 41.

12. Feldman, *Scorpions*, 5.

13. Liva Baker, *Felix Frankfurter*, 20; Simon, *The Antagonists*, 25.

14. Simon, *The Antagonists*, 26.

15. Liva Baker, *Felix Frankfurter*, 20.

16. Parrish, *Felix Frankfurter and His Times*, 14; Liva Baker, *Felix Frankfurter*, 20.

17. Simon, *The Antagonists*, 27–28.

18. Marianne R. Sanua, *"Here's to Our Fraternity": One Hundred Years of Zeta Beta Tau, 1898–1998* (Hanover, NH: Zeta Beta Tau Foundation and University Press of New England, 1998), 109, 125.

19. Simon, *The Antagonists*, 28; Michael Alexander, *Jazz Age Jews* (Princeton, NJ: Princeton University Press, 2001), 77.

20. Liva Baker, *Felix Frankfurter*, 21.

21. Parrish, *Felix Frankfurter and His Times*, 19.

22. Ibid., 34.

23. Parrish, *Felix Frankfurter and His Times*, 15.

24. Joseph P. Lash, ed., *From the Diaries of Felix Frankfurter* (New York: W. W. Norton, 1975), 10.

25. Liva Baker, *Felix Frankfurter*, 36.

26. Feldman, *Scorpions*, 7.

27. Simon, *The Antagonists*, 35.

28. Liva Baker, *Felix Frankfurter*, 18.

29. Ibid.

30. Simon, *The Antagonists*, 35–36.

31. Feldman, *Scorpions*, 8–9.

32. Simon, *The Antagonists*, 36.

33. Feldman, *Scorpions*, 9.

34. Ibid.

35. Ibid.

36. Henry L. Stimson, letter to Felix Frankfurter, July 1, 1911, as cited in H. N. Hirsch, *The Enigma of Felix Frankfurter* (New York: Basic Books, 1981), 29.

37. Quoted in Leonard Baker, *Brandeis and Frankfurter*, 64–65.

38. Hirsch, *The Enigma*, 29.

39. Quoted in ibid.

40. Simon, *The Antagonists*, 36.

41. Feldman, *Scorpions*, 9.

42. Liva Baker, *Felix Frankfurter*, 36.

43. Ibid.

44. Liva Baker, *Felix Frankfurter*, 36.

45. Kai Bird, *The Color of Truth: McGeorge Bundy and William P. Bundy; Brothers in Arms; A Biography* (New York: Simon & Schuster, 1998), 30.

46. Parrish, *Felix Frankfurter and His Times*, 51.

47. Jeffrey O'Connell and Nancy Dart, "The House of Truth: Home of the Young Frankfurter and Lippmann," *Catholic University Law Review* 35 (1985): 79.

48. Bird, *The Color of Truth*, 30.

49. Ibid., 30–31; Liva Baker, *Felix Frankfurter*, 35.

50. Robert M. Mennel and Christine L. Compston, *Holmes and Frankfurter: Their Correspondence, 1912–1934* (Hanover: University of New Hampshire Press, 1996), xi.

51. Oliver Wendell Holmes Jr., letter to Felix Frankfurter, March 8, 1912, as cited in Mennel and Compston, *Holmes and Frankfurter*, xiii, 6.

52. Ibid.

53. Liva Baker, *Felix Frankfurter*, 35–36.

54. Hirsch, *The Enigma*, 37.

55. O'Connell and Dart, "The House of Truth," 88; Parrish, *Felix Frankfurter and His Times*, 52.

56. Lash, *From the Diaries*, 104.

57. Parrish, *Felix Frankfurter and His Times*, 52.

58. Bruce Allen Murphy, *The Brandeis/Frankfurter Connection: The Secret Political Activities of Two Supreme Court Justices* (New York: Oxford University Press, 1982), 89–91; Lash, *From the Diaries*, 16, 32; and Hirsch, *The Enigma*, 45, 77.

59. Bird, *The Color of Truth*, 27–28, 30.

60. O'Connell and Dart, "The House of Truth," 87; Lash, *From the Diaries*, 16.

61. O'Connell and Dart, "The House of Truth," 89–90.

62. Liva Baker, *Felix Frankfurter*, 40; Parrish, *Felix Frankfurter and His Times*, 76.

63. Hirsch, *The Enigma*, 37.

64. Parrish, *Felix Frankfurter and His Times*, 76.

65. Liva Baker, *Felix Frankfurter*, 75–76.

66. Parrish, *Felix Frankfurter and His Times*, 123.

67. Ibid.

68. Felix Frankfurter, letter to Justice Oliver Wendell Holmes Jr., July 4, 1913, in Mennel and Compston, *Holmes and Frankfurter*, 10.

69. O'Connell and Dart, "The House of Truth," 90.

70. Feldman, *Scorpions*, 10.

71. Feldman, *Scorpions*, 10; O'Connell and Dart, "The House of Truth," 90–91; and Hirsch, *The Enigma*, 60.

72. Felix Frankfurter, letter to Marion Denman, June 21, 1917, cited in Feldman, *Scorpions*, 10 and 438, fn. 19.

73. O'Connell and Dart, "The House of Truth," 91; Leonard Baker, *Brandeis and Frankfurter*, 224

74. O'Connell and Dart, "The House of Truth," 91.

75. Ibid.

76. Ibid., 91–92.

77. Leonard Baker, *Brandeis and Frankfurter*, 68.

78. Felix Frankfurter, letter to Emory Buckner, January 6, 1912, as cited in Lash, *From the Diaries*, 11.

79. Hirsch, *The Enigma*, 38; Liva Baker, *Felix Frankfurter*, 41.

80. Wilfred Dennison, letter to Edward H. Warren, June 12, 1913, as cited in Liva Baker, *Felix Frankfurter*, 41.

81. Louis D. Brandeis, letters to Roscoe Pound, July 12, 1913, and November 5, 1913, in Melvin I. Urofsky and David W. Levy, eds., *Letters of Louis D. Brandeis*, Vol. III (Albany, NY: State University of New York Press, 1973), 135–36, 209; Murphy, *The Brandeis/Frankfurter Connection*, 38.

82. Liva Baker, *Felix Frankfurter*, 41; Charles A. Madison, *Eminent American Jews* (New York: Frederick Ungar, 1970), 289.

83. Liva Baker, *Felix Frankfurter*, 42.

84. Parrish, *Felix Frankfurter and His Times*, 60.

85. Ezra Thayer, letter to Henry Stimson, June 24, 1913, as cited in Parrish, *Felix Frankfurter and His Times*, 60.

86. Ibid.

87. Leonard Baker, *Brandeis and Frankfurter*, 69–70.

88. Feldman, *Scorpions*, 11.

89. Ibid.

90. Parrish, *Felix Frankfurter and His Times*, 108.

91. Feldman, *Scorpions*, 11; Eleanor Roosevelt, letter to Sara Delano Roosevelt, May 12, 1918, as cited in Parrish, *Felix Frankfurter and His Times*, 108, and elsewhere.

92. Jean Edward Smith, *FDR* (New York: Random House, 2007), 148; Richard Breitman and Allan J. Lichtman, *FDR and the Jews* (Cambridge: Harvard University Press, 2013), 17.

93. Smith, *FDR*, 148.

94. Blanche Wiesen Cook, *Eleanor Roosevelt*, Vol. 2 (New York: Viking Press, 1999), 317; and cited in Smith, *FDR*, 148.

95. Harlan B. Phillips, ed., *Felix Frankfurter Reminisces* (New York: Reynal and Company, 1960), 289–90.

96. Ibid., 290; Robert A. Burt, *Two Jewish Justices: Outcasts in the Promised Land* (Berkeley: University of California Press, 1988), 38.

97. Simon, *The Antagonists*, 34.

98. William Lasser, *Benjamin V. Cohen: Architect of the New Deal* (New Haven: Yale University Press, 2002), 16.

99. Phillips, *Felix Frankfurter Reminisces*, 37; Hirsch, *The Enigma*, 22–23.

100. Hirsch, *The Enigma*, 23.

101. Lasser, *Benjamin V. Cohen*, 16; Phillips, *Felix Frankfurter Reminisces*, 290.

102. Michael E. Parrish, "Justice Frankfurter and the Supreme Court," in *The Jewish Justices of the Supreme Court: Brandeis to Fortas*, ed. Jennifer M. Lowe (Washington, DC: Supreme Court Historical Society, 1994), 61; Madison, *Eminent American Jews*, 298; and Melvin I. Urofsky, *Felix Frankfurter: Judicial Restraint and Individual Liberties* (Boston: Twayne Publishers, 1991), 16.

103. Parrish, *Felix Frankfurter and His Times*, 138.

104. Urofsky, *Felix Frankfurter: Judicial Restraint*, 16.

105. Parrish, *Felix Frankfurter and His Times*, 138–39.

106. Liva Baker, *Felix Frankfurter*, 83.

107. Parrish, *Felix Frankfurter and His Times*, 141.

108. Simcha Berkowitz, "Felix Frankfurter's Zionist Activities" (DHL [Doctor of Hebrew Letters] diss., Jewish Theological Seminary, 1971), 60.

109. Ibid., 59.

110. Ibid.

111. Lash, *From the Diaries*, 27.

112. Quoted in Liva Baker, *Felix Frankfurter*, 84.

113. Feldman, *Scorpions*, 30.

114. Lash, *From the Diaries*, 26.

115. Feldman, *Scorpions*, 30.

116. Berkowitz, "Felix Frankfurter's Zionist Activities," 70.

117. Simcha Berkowitz, "The Faisal-Frankfurter Letters: An Unending Story," in *Community and Culture: Essays in Jewish Studies*, ed. Nahum M. Waldman (Philadelphia: Seth Press, 1987), 2.

118. Berkowitz, "The Faisal-Frankfurter Letters," 3.

119. Ibid.

120. Simon, *The Antagonists*, 24.

121. Liva Baker, *Felix Frankfurter*, 98.

122. Ibid., 98–99.

123. Lash, *From the Diaries*, 26.

124. Ibid., 11; Alexander, *Jazz Age Jews*, 84.

125. Alexander, *Jazz Age Jews*, 84.

126. Feldman, *Scorpions*, 11.

127. Alexander, *Jazz Age Jews*, 85–86; Parrish, *Felix Frankfurter and His Times*, 97–101.

128. Feldman, *Scorpions*, 13–14; Alexander, *Jazz Age Jews*, 71.

129. Alexander, *Jazz Age Jews*, 73.

130. Feldman, *Scorpions*, 14.

131. Robert N. Rosen, *Saving the Jews: Franklin D. Roosevelt and the Holocaust* (New York: Thunder's Mouth Press, 2006), 38.

132. Feldman, *Scorpions*, 14.

133. Alexander, *Jazz Age Jews*, 72.

134. Feldman, *Scorpions*, 14.

135. Alexander, *Jazz Age Jews*, 72–73.

136. Ibid., 96; Simon, *The Antagonists*, 55.

137. Rosen, *Saving the Jews*, 38; Urofsky, *Felix Frankfurter: Judicial Restraint*, 22.

138. Simon, *The Antagonists*, 54–56.

139. Ibid.; Feldman, *Scorpions*, 21.

140. Liva Baker, *Felix Frankfurter*, 100.

141. Leonard Baker, *Brandeis and Frankfurter*, 231.

142. A. Lawrence Lowell, letter to Judge Julian Mack, cited in Leonard Baker, *Brandeis and Frankfurter*, 231, 529.

143. Leonard Baker, *Brandeis and Frankfurter*, 231; Liva Baker, *Felix Frankfurter*, 101.

144. Liva Baker, *Felix Frankfurter*, 102.

145. Henry L. Feingold, *A Time for Searching: Entering the Mainstream, 1920–1945* (Baltimore: Johns Hopkins University Press, 1992), 17.

146. Marianne R. Sanua, *Going Greek: Jewish College Fraternities in the United States, 1895–1945* (Detroit: Wayne State University Press, 2003), 126.

147. Ibid.

148. Ibid.

149. Feldman, *Scorpions*, 27.

150. Ibid.

151. Felix Frankfurter, "Why I Shall Vote for La Follette," in *The Faces of Five Decades: Selections from Fifty Years of The New Republic, 1914–1964*, ed. Robert B. Luce (New York: Simon & Schuster, 1964), 120–23.

152. Feldman, *Scorpions*, 27.

153. Quoted in Hirsch, *The Enigma*, 71–72.

154. Liva Baker, *Felix Frankfurter*, 106.

155. Ibid.

156. Swift, *The Roosevelts and the Royals*, 27.

157. Feldman, *Scorpions*, 33.

158. Swift, *The Roosevelts and the Royals*, 27.

159. Ibid., 28.

160. Swift, *The Roosevelts and the Royals*, 31.

161. Feldman, *Scorpions*, 34.

162. Felix Frankfurter, letter to Franklin D. Roosevelt, October 9, 1928, in Max Freedman, ed., *Roosevelt and Frankfurter: Their Correspondence, 1928–1945* (Boston: Little, Brown and Company, 1967), 38; as also cited in Feldman, *Scorpions*, 36.

163. Feldman, *Scorpions*, 37.

164. Parrish, *Felix Frankfurter and His Times*, 200.

165. Ibid., 201.

166. Ibid., 200.

167. Quoted in ibid., 202.

168. Feldman, *Scorpions*, 37–38.

169. Ibid.

170. Parrish, *Felix Frankfurter and His Times*, 200.

171. Urofsky, *Felix Frankfurter: Judicial Restraint*, 35.

172. Phillips, *Felix Frankfurter Reminisces*, 233; also cited in Urofsky, *Felix Frankfurter: Judicial Restraint*, 34.

173. Felix Frankfurter, letter to Joseph B. Ely, June 29, 1932, as cited in Urofsky, *Felix Frankfurter: Judicial Restraint*, 35.

174. Urofsky, *Felix Frankfurter: Judicial Restraint*, 35.

175. Leonard Baker, *Brandeis and Frankfurter*, 272.

176. Parrish, *Felix Frankfurter and His Times*, 210.

177. Urofsky, *Felix Frankfurter: Judicial Restraint*, 36.

178. Parrish, *Felix Frankfurter and His Times*, 210.

179. Ibid., 211.

180. Ibid., 220.

181. Ibid., 220–21.

182. Ibid.

183. Leonard Baker, *Brandeis and Frankfurter*, 280.

184. Thomas D. Thacher, letter to Felix Frankfurter, February 25, 1933, as cited in Leonard Baker, *Brandeis and Frankfurter*, 280.

185. Urofsky, *Felix Frankfurter: Judicial Restraint* 36.

186. Ibid.

187. Leonard Baker, *Brandeis and Frankfurter*, 281.

188. Parrish, *Felix Frankfurter and His Times*, 222.

189. Leonard Baker, *Brandeis and Frankfurter*, 281.

190. Ibid., 281–82.

191. Urofsky, *Felix Frankfurter: Judicial Restraint*, 36.

192. Leonard Baker, *Brandeis and Frankfurter*, 282.

193. Amity Shlaes, *The Forgotten Man: A New History of the Great Depression* (New York: HarperCollins, 2007), 65–66.

194. Ibid., 66.

195. Urofsky, *Felix Frankfurter: Judicial Restraint*, 36.

196. Murphy, *The Brandeis/Frankfurter Connection*, 131.

197. Michael E. Parrish, *Citizen Rauh: An American Liberal's Life in Law and Politics* (Ann Arbor: University of Michigan Press, 2010), 32–33.

198. Arthur M. Schlesinger Jr., *The Politics of Upheaval* (Boston: Houghton Mifflin, 1960), 227; and cited in Hirsch, *The Enigma*, 110.

199. Michael Hiltzik, *The New Deal: A Modern History* (New York: Free Press, 2011), 202.

200. Hirsch, *The Enigma*, 110.

201. Parrish, *Citizen Rauh*, 31; and William Lasser, *Benjamin V. Cohen: Architect of the New Deal* (New Haven: Yale University Press, 2002), 8 and 12–13.

202. Parrish, *Citizen Rauh*, 31.

203. Ibid.

204. Ibid.

205. Ibid.

206. Urofsky, *Felix Frankfurter: Judicial Restraint*, 37.

207. Benjamin Ginsberg, *The Fatal Embrace: Jews and the State* (Chicago: University of Chicago Press, 1994), 105.

208. Urofsky, *Felix Frankfurter: Judicial Restraint*, 37.

209. Bird, *The Color of Truth*, 32.

210. Henry J. Abraham, *Justices, Presidents, and Senators: A History of the U.S. Supreme Court Appointments from Washington to Clinton* (Lanham, MD: Rowman & Littlefield, 1999), 166.

211. Parrish, *Felix Frankfurter and His Times*, 223.

212. James Chace, *Acheson: The Secretary of State Who Created the American World* (New York: Simon & Schuster, 1998), 62.

213. Feldman, *Scorpions*, 383.

214. Quoted in Michael Janeway, *The Fall of the House of Roosevelt* (New York: Columbia University Press, 2004), 83 and 245, fn. 66; and Chace, 74 and 450, fn. 20.

215. Chace, *Acheson*, 415.

6. Mr. Justice Frankfurter: The Court Years

1. Michael E. Parrish, *Felix Frankfurter and His Times: The Reform Years* (New York: Free Press, 1982).

2. Ibid., 6, 274–75.

3. Henry J. Abraham, *Justices, Presidents, and Senators: A History of the U.S. Supreme Court Appointments from Washington to Clinton* (Lanham, MD: Rowman & Littlefield, 1999), 166–67.

4. Ibid., 167; Parrish, *Felix Frankfurter and His Times*, 275.

5. Harlan P. Phillips, ed., *Felix Frankfurter Reminisces* (New York: Reynal and Company, 1960), 282–83; and cited in Abraham, *Justices, Presidents, and Senators*, 167, and Noah Feldman, *Scorpions: The Battles and Triumphs of FDR's Great Supreme Court Justices* (New York: Twelve, 2010), 160–61.

6. Felix Frankfurter, letter to Franklin D. Roosevelt, January 30, 1939, in Max Freedman, ed., *Roosevelt and Frankfurter: Their Correspondence, 1928–1945* (Boston: Little Brown and Company, 1967), 485; quoted in Parrish, *Felix Frankfurter and His Times*, 278.

7. Leonard Baker, *Brandeis and Frankfurter: A Dual Biography* (New York: Harper & Row, 1984), 363–64.

8. James F. Simon, *The Antagonists: Hugo Black, Felix Frankfurter and Civil Liberties in Modern America* (New York: Simon & Schuster, 1989), 17; Leonard Baker, *Brandeis and Frankfurter*, 364.

9. Leonard Baker, *Brandeis and Frankfurter*, 364.

10. Parrish, *Felix Frankfurter and His Times*, 274; Feldman, *Scorpions*, 158.

11. Michael Beschloss, *The Conquerors: Roosevelt, Truman and the Destruction of Nazi Germany, 1941–1945* (New York: Simon & Schuster, 2002), 113.

12. Feldman, *Scorpions*, 158.

13. Ibid.

14. Richard Breitman and Allan J. Lichtman, *FDR and the Jews* (Cambridge: Harvard University Press, 2013), 145; Feldman, *Scorpions*, 158.

15. Marianne R. Sanua, *"Here's to Our Fraternity": One Hundred Years of Zeta Beta Tau, 1898–1998* (Hanover, NH: Zeta Beta Tau Foundation and University Press of New England, 1998), 114.

16. Leonard Baker, *Brandeis and Frankfurter*, 365.

17. Ibid., 367.

18. Simon, *The Antagonists*, 14.

19. James Chace, *Acheson: The Secretary of State Who Created the American World* (New York: Simon & Schuster, 1998), 75.

20. Chace, *Acheson*; Leonard Baker, *Brandeis and Frankfurter*, 367.

21. Liva Baker, *Felix Frankfurter: A Biography* (New York: Coward-McCann, 1969), 209–10; Chace, *Acheson*, 75.

22. Liva Baker, *Felix Frankfurter*, 210.

23. Michael E. Parrish, *Citizen Rauh: An American Liberal's Life in Law and Politics* (Ann Arbor: University of Michigan Press, 2010), 48.

24. Michael E. Parrish, "Justice Frankfurter and the Supreme Court," in *The Jewish Justices of the Supreme Court: Brandeis to Fortas*, ed. Jennifer M. Lowe (Washington, DC: Supreme Court Historical Society, 1994), 65.

25. Ibid.

26. Bruce Allen Murphy, *The Brandeis/Frankfurter Connection: The Secret Political Activities of Two Supreme Court Justices* (New York: Oxford University Press, 1982), 315; Parrish, *Felix Frankfurter and His Times*, 226.

27. Melvin I. Urofsky, *Louis D. Brandeis: A Life* (New York: Pantheon Books, 2009), 722.

28. Felix Frankfurter, letter to Learned Hand, February 16, 1939, as cited in Murphy, *The Brandeis/Frankfurter Connection*, 315.

29. Murphy, *The Brandeis/Frankfurter Connection*, 315–16.

30. Ibid., 317–18.

31. Ibid., 318.

32. Michael A. Kahn, "The Politics of the Appointment Process: An Analysis of Why Learned Hand Was Never Appointed to the Supreme Court," *Stanford Law Review* 25 (January 1973): 253.

33. G. Edward White, "On the Other Hand . . . The Judicial Temperament, in Private," review of *Reason and Imagination: The Selected Correspondence of Learned Hand*, edited by Constance Jordan, *Weekly Standard*, February 25, 2013, 36.

34. Kahn, "The Politics of the Appointment Process," 253.

35. Harold Laski, letter to Oliver Wendell Holmes Jr., September 9, 1922, as cited in Kahn, "The Politics of the Appointment Process," 254–55.

36. Kahn, "The Politics of the Appointment Process," 263.

37. Ibid., 271, 277–78.

38. Ibid.

39. Bruce Allen Murphy, "A Supreme Court Justice as Politician: Felix Frankfurter and Federal Court Appointments," *The American Journal of Legal History*, Vol. XXI (1977), 320.

40. Felix Frankfurter, letters to Franklin D. Roosevelt, September 30 and December 3, 1942, as cited in Murphy, *The Brandeis/Frankfurter Connection*, 319, and in Max Freedman, ed., *Roosevelt and Frankfurter: Their Correspondence, 1928–1945* (Boston: Little, Brown and Company, 1967), 670–73.

41. Murphy, *The Brandeis/Frankfurter Connection*, 319.

42. Felix Frankfurter, letter to Franklin D. Roosevelt, November 3, 1942, as cited in Murphy, *The Brandeis/Frankfurter Connection*, 319.

43. William O. Douglas, *Go East, Young Man* (New York: Random House, 1974), 331.

44. Learned Hand, letter to Felix Frankfurter, January 11, 1943, as cited in Murphy, "A Supreme Court Justice as Politician," 320.

45. Parrish, "Justice Frankfurter and the Supreme Court," 65.

46. Ibid., 65–66.

47. Ibid., 66.

48. Ibid.

49. Ibid.

50. Murphy, "A Supreme Court Justice as Politician," 320–25; Murphy, *The Brandeis/Frankfurter Connection*, 328–38.

51. Liva Baker, *Felix Frankfurter*, 199.

52. Ibid.

53. Ibid., 200.

54. Ibid.

55. Leonard Baker, *Brandeis and Frankfurter*, 350.

56. Ibid.

57. Ibid., 351.

58. Ibid.

59. Ibid.; Liva Baker, *Felix Frankfurter*, 200–1.

60. Kai Bird, *The Chairman: John J. McCloy and the Making of the American Establishment* (New York: Simon & Schuster, 1992), 205.

61. Robert N. Rosen, *Saving the Jews: Franklin D. Roosevelt and the Holocaust* (New York: Thunder's Mouth Press, 2006), 293.

62. David Engel, "Jan Karski's Mission to the West, 1942–1944," *Holocaust and Genocide Studies* 5, no. 4 (1990), as cited in Rosen, *Saving the Jews*, 293, and Bird, *The Chairman*, 205.

63. Breitman and Lichtman, *FDR and the Jews*, 227. The Office of Strategic Services, or OSS, was a precursor of the Central Intelligence Agency.

64. Bird, *The Chairman*, 206.

65. E. Thomas Wood and Stanislaw M. Jankowski, *Karski: How One Man Tried to Stop the Holocaust* (New York: John Wiley & Sons, 1994), 188.

66. Ibid.

67. Ibid.

68. Quoted in Bird, *The Chairman*, 206; and Rosen, *Saving the Jews*, 294.

69. David G. Dalin and Arthur J. Kolatch, *The Presidents of the United States and the Jews* (Middle Village, NY: Jonathan David Publishers, 2000), 176.

70. Quoted in Henry L. Feingold, *The Politics of Rescue: The Roosevelt Administration and the Holocaust, 1938–1945* (New York: Walden Press, 1980), 257.

71. Ibid., 305.

72. Dalin and Kolatch, *The Presidents*, 176.

73. Bird, *The Chairman*, 125.

74. *Minersville School District v. Gobitis* 310 U.S. 586 (1940).

75. Simon, *The Antagonists*, 106.

76. Joseph P. Lash, ed., *From the Diaries of Felix Frankfurter* (New York: W. W. Norton, 1975), 68.

77. Melvin I. Urofsky, "Conflict among the Brethren: Felix Frankfurter, William O. Douglas and the Clash of Personalities and Philosophies on the United States Supreme Court," *Duke Law Journal* 71 (1988): 84.

78. Simon, *The Antagonists*, 107.

79. Liva Baker, *Felix Frankfurter*, 242.

80. Ibid.

81. Liva Baker, *Felix Frankfurter*, 242.

82. Simon, *The Antagonists*, 107.

83. Quoted in ibid., 113, and Lash, *From the Diaries*, 69–70.

84. Simon, *The Antagonists*, 107.

85. Ibid., 17–18.

86. Feldman, *Scorpions*, 32.

87. Fred Rodell, *Nine Men: A Political History of the Supreme Court of the United States from 1750 to 1955* (New York: Knopf, 1955), 271; and cited in Abraham, *Justices, Presidents, and Senators*, 168.

88. Simon, *The Antagonists*, 108–9.

89. Ibid.

90. Jerold S. Auerbach, *Rabbis and Lawyers: The Journey from Torah to Constitution* (Bloomington: Indiana University Press, 1990), 161.

91. Ibid.; Richard Danzig, "Justice Frankfurter's Opinions in the Flag Salute Cases: Blending Logic and Psychologic in Constitutional Decision-Making," *Stanford Law Review* 36 (1984): 690–701.

92. H. N. Hirsch, *The Enigma of Felix Frankfurter* (New York: Basic Books, 1981), 148.

93. *West Virginia Board of Education v. Barnette*, 319 U.S. 624, at 646, quoted in Simon, *The Antagonists*, 118.

94. Ibid.

95. Jonathan D. Sarna and David G. Dalin, *Religion and State in the American Jewish Experience* (Notre Dame, IN: University of Notre Dame Press, 1997), 9.

96. Ibid., 139.

97. Ibid., 140.

98. Ibid., 63.

99. Ibid., 63–64.

100. Ibid., p. 64.

101. Leonard Baker, *Brandeis and Frankfurter*, 395.

102. Melvin I. Urofsky, *Felix Frankfurter: Judicial Restraint and Civil Liberties* (Boston: Twayne Publishers, 1991), 69.

103. Liva Baker, *Felix Frankfurter*, 289.

104. Feldman, *Scorpions*, 227.

105. Urofsky, *Felix Frankfurter: Judicial Restraint*, 70.

106. Ibid.

107. Feldman, *Scorpions*, 226–27.

108. Ibid., 227.

109. Lash, *From the Diaries*, 211; and cited in Feldman, *Scorpions*, 227, and Hirsch, *The Enigma*, 169.

110. Liva Baker, *Felix Frankfurter*, 304.

111. Parrish, "Justice Frankfurter and the Supreme Court," 62; Feldman, *Scorpions*, 406.

112. Feldman, *Scorpions*, 386, 388.

113. Leonard Baker, *Brandeis and Frankfurter*, 473.

114. Ibid.; Parrish, "Justice Frankfurter and the Supreme Court," 62; and Murphy, *The Brandeis/Frankfurter Connection*, 321.

115. Parrish, "Felix Frankfurter and the Supreme Court," 62–63.

116. Leonard Baker, *Brandeis and Frankfurter*, 473–74.

117. Feldman, *Scorpions*, 382–83.

118. Ibid., 383.

119. Ibid., 383–84.

120. Adam J. White, "The Lost Greatness of Alexander Bickel," *Commentary*, March 2012, 35, 38.

121. Feldman, *Scorpions*, 417.

122. Ibid.

123. Simon, *The Antagonists*, 247.

124. Leonard Baker, *Brandeis and Frankfurter*, 487.

125. Simon, *The Antagonists*, 247.

126. Baker v. Carr, 369 U.S. 186 (1962), as cited in Feldman, *Scorpions*, 418.

127. Feldman, *Scorpions*, 418.

128. Baker v. Carr, 369 U.S. 186 (1962), as cited in Lash, *From the Diaries*, 84.

129. Feldman, *Scorpions*, 378.

130. Adam J. White, "The Lost Greatness," 36.

131. Feldman, *Scorpions*, 378.

132. Adam J. White, "The Lost Greatness," 36.

133. Feldman, *Scorpions*, 378–79.

134. Adam J. White, "The Lost Greatness," 36.

135. Ibid.

136. Alexander M. Bickel, "The Original Understanding and the Segregation Decision," *Harvard Law Review* 69, no. 1 (1955): 58–59, as cited in Feldman, *Scorpions*, 379.

137. Feldman, *Scorpions*, 379.

138. Adam J. White, "The Lost Greatness," 35.

139. Joshua Henkin, "Sleeping on Felix Frankfurter's Couch," blog post, *Forward*, June 22, 2012.

140. "Justices in Agreement—No Arguments on Yom Kippur," JWeekly.com, September 18, 2003.

141. Henkin, "Sleeping on Felix Frankfurter's Couch"; "Justices in Agreement," JWeekly. com.

142. Robert Schlesinger, *White House Ghosts: Presidents and Their Speechwriters* (New York: Simon & Schuster, 2008), 117.

143. Ibid.

144. Ibid.

145. Patrick Anderson, *The President's Men: White House Assistants of Franklin D. Roo-*

sevelt, Harry S. Truman, Dwight D. Eisenhower, John F. Kennedy and Lyndon B. Johnson (Garden City, NY: Anchor Books, 1969), 264.

146. Ibid., 265; Schlesinger, *White House Ghosts*, 117–18.

147. Schlesinger, *White House Ghosts*, 119; Anderson, *The President's Men*, 265.

148. Ibid.

149. Ibid., 264.

150. Anderson, *The President's Men*, 264.

151. Ibid.

152. Geoffrey Kabaservice, *The Guardians: Kingman Brewster, His Circle, and the Rise of the Liberal Establishment* (New York: Henry Holt and Company, 2004), 125, 131.

153. Kai Bird, *The Color of Truth: McGeorge Bundy and William P. Bundy; Brothers in Arms; A Biography* (New York: Simon & Schuster, 1998), 118; Kabaservice, *The Guardians*, 131.

154. Anderson, *The President's Men*, 315.

155. Bird, *The Color of Truth*, 69.

156. Ibid., 80.

157. Anderson, *The President's Men*, 315.

158. Bird, *The Color of Truth*, 100.

159. Ibid.

160. Ibid., 100–1.

161. Linda Bayer, *Ruth Bader Ginsburg* (Philadelphia: Chelsea House Publishers, 2000), 41.

162. Elinor Slater and Robert Slater, *Great Jewish Women* (Middle Village, NY: Jonathan David Publishers, 2004), 97.

163. Ibid.; "Ruth Bader Ginsburg," *Current Biography*, February 1994, 29.

164. Jill Abramson and Barbara Franklin, *Where They Are Now: The Story of the Women of Harvard Law 1974* (Garden City, NY: Doubleday, 1986), 9.

165. Ibid., 10.

166. Jeffrey Toobin, *The Nine: Inside the Secret World of the Supreme Court* (New York: Anchor Books, 2007), 82.

167. Ibid., 132.

168. Leonard Baker, *Brandeis and Frankfurter*, 489.

169. Ibid., 489–90.

170. Ibid., 490.

171. Quoted in David N. Atkinson, *Leaving the Bench: Supreme Court Justices at the End* (Lawrence: University Press of Kansas, 1999), 132.

172. Simon, *The Antagonists*, 255.

173. Felix Frankfurter, letter to John F. Kennedy, July 5, 1963, quoted in Leonard Baker, *Brandeis and Frankfurter*, 490.

174. Atkinson, *Leaving the Bench*, 133.

175. Urofsky, *Felix Frankfurter: Judicial Restraint*, 173.

176. Leonard Baker, *Brandeis and Frankfurter*, 491.

177. Liva Baker, *Felix Frankfurter*, 332.

178. Leonard Baker, *Brandeis and Frankfurter*, 491.

179. Urofsky, *Felix Frankfurter: Judicial Restraint*, 174.

180. Lash, *From the Diaries*, 89.

181. Garson Kanin, "Trips to Felix," in *Felix Frankfurter: A Tribute*, ed. Wallace Mendelson (New York: Reynal and Company, 1964), 57; Lash, *From the Diaries*, 89.

182. Ibid.

183. Hirsch, *The Enigma*, 3.

184. Ibid., 198.

185. Andrew L. Kaufman, *Cardozo* (Cambridge: Harvard University Press, 1998), ix.

186. Urofsky, *Felix Frankfurter: Judicial Restraint*, ix.

187. Quoted in ibid.

188. Ibid.

189. Quoted in ibid.

190. Hirsch, *The Enigma*.

191. Ibid., 5.

192. Leonard Baker, *Brandeis and Frankfurter*, 380.

193. Feldman, *Scorpions*, 418.

194. Parrish, "Justice Frankfurter and the Supreme Court," 71.

195. Urofsky, *Felix Frankfurter: Judicial Restraint*, ix.

196. Lash, *From the Diaries*, 87.

197. Parrish, "Justice Frankfurter and the Supreme Court," 71.

198. Ibid., 70.

199. Ibid., 71.

200. Ibid.

201. Alexander M. Bickel, "Justice Frankfurter at Seventy-Five," *New Republic*, November 18, 1957, 9; quoted in Parrish, "Justice Frankfurter and the Supreme Court," 71.

202. Abraham, *Justices, Presidents, and Senators*, 211.

203. Parrish, *Felix Frankfurter: The Reform Years*, 6.

204. Philip B. Kurland, *Mr. Justice Frankfurter and the Constitution* (Chicago: University of Chicago Press, 1971), xiii; and cited in Thomas H. Peebles, "Mr. Justice Frankfurter and the Nixon Court: Some Reflections on Contemporary Judicial Conservatism," *American University Law Review* 24, no. 1 (1974): 1.

205. Adam Liptak, "Ronald Dworkin, Scholar of the Law, Is Dead at 81," *New York Times*, February 14, 2013.

206. Kurland, *Mr. Justice Frankfurter and the Constitution*, xiii.

207. Lash, *From the Diaries*, 83.

208. Feldman, *Scorpions*, 406.

209. Hirsch, *The Enigma*, 190.

210. Ibid., 177.

211. Ibid.; and especially Lash, *From the Diaries*, 309–38.

212. Hirsch, *The Enigma*, 178.

213. Parrish, "Justice Frankfurter and the Supreme Court," 64.

214. Urofsky, "Conflict among the Brethren," 90.

215. Ibid.

216. Ibid.

217. Hirsch, *The Enigma*, 180.

218. Ibid., 190.

219. Ibid., 187.

220. Parrish, "Justice Frankfurter and the Supreme Court," 64.

221. Hirsch, *The Enigma*, 66, 206.

222. Ibid., 206.

223. Auerbach, *Rabbis and Lawyers*, 160.

224. Parrish, "Justice Frankfurter and the Supreme Court," 64.

225. Ibid., 71.

226. Hirsch, *The Enigma*, 5.

227. Parrish, "Justice Frankfurter and the Supreme Court," 71.

228. Urofsky, "Conflict among the Brethren," 77.

229. Hirsch, *The Enigma*, 69.

230. Simon, *The Antagonists*, 57; Hirsch, *The Enigma*, 69.

231. Simon, *The Antagonists*, 57.

232. Parrish, "Justice Frankfurter and the Supreme Court," 61.

233. Simon, *The Antagonists*, 34.

234. Parrish, "Justice Frankfurter and the Supreme Court," 61.

235. Liva Baker, *Felix Frankfurter*, 332.

236. Feldman, *Scorpions*, 29.

237. Ibid.

238. Auerbach, *Rabbis and Lawyers*, 158.

239. Ibid.

240. Parrish, "Justice Frankfurter and the Supreme Court," 61.

241. Quoted in Auerbach, *Rabbis and Lawyers*, 162–63.

242. William Lasser, *Benjamin V. Cohen: Architect of the New Deal* (New Haven: Yale University Press, 2002), 30.

243. Parrish, "Felix Frankfurter and the Supreme Court," 65.

7. Arthur J. Goldberg: A Promising Tenure Cut Short

1. Victor Lasky, *Arthur J. Goldberg, The Old and the New* (New Rochelle, NY: Arlington House, 1970), 7.

2. Ibid.

3. David Stebenne, *Arthur J. Goldberg: New Deal Liberal* (New York: Oxford University Press, 1996), 375–76.

4. Alan Dershowitz, *Taking the Stand: My Life in the Law* (New York: Crown Publishers, 2013), 82.

5. Stebenne, *Arthur J. Goldberg*, 377.

6. Ibid., 4; Irving Cutler, *The Jews of Chicago: From Shtetl to Suburb* (Urbana: University of Illinois Press, 1996), 64, 100, 101; Ira Berkow, *Maxwell Street* (Garden City, NY: Doubleday, 1977), 182–83, 245–47, 299–301.

7. Cutler, *The Jews of Chicago*, 64, 152.

8. Ibid., 83.

9. Stebenne, *Arthur J. Goldberg*, 4; Berkow, *Maxwell Street*, 301; and Emily Field Van Tassel, "Justice Arthur Goldberg," in *The Jewish Justices of the Supreme Court Revisited: Brandeis to Fortas*, ed. Jennifer M. Lowe (Washington, DC: Supreme Court Historical Society, 1994), 84.

10. Stebenne, *Arthur J. Goldberg*, 5.

11. Van Tassel, "Justice Arthur Goldberg," 85.

12. Stebenne, *Arthur J. Goldberg*, 6.

13. Ibid., 6–7.

14. Van Tassel, "Justice Arthur Goldberg," 85.

15. Dorothy Goldberg, *A Private View of Public Life* (New York: Charterhouse, 1975), 3.

16. Stebenne, *Arthur J. Goldberg*, 5; and Van Tassel, "Justice Arthur Goldberg," 86.

17. Dorothy Goldberg, *A Private View*, 3; and Van Tassel, "Justice Arthur Goldberg," 85.

18. Van Tassel, "Justice Arthur Goldberg," 86; Stebenne, *Arthur J. Goldberg*, 12–18.

19. Stephen J. Friedman, "Arthur J. Goldberg," in *The Justices of the United States Supreme Court, 1789–1969: Their Lives and Major Opinions*, ed. Leon Friedman and Fred Israel, Vol. IV (New York: R. R. Bowker Company, 1969): 2977; and Dershowitz, *Taking the Stand*, 74.

20. Youngstown Sheet & Tube Co. v. Sawyer, 343 U.S. 579 (1952); Dershowitz, *Taking the Stand*, 74–75.

21. Van Tassel, "Justice Arthur Goldberg," 86.

22. Stebenne, *Arthur J. Goldberg*, 157, 174.

23. Theodore Sorensen, *Kennedy* (New York: Harper & Row, 1965), 52; and cited in Stebenne, *Arthur J. Goldberg*, 446, fn. 72.

24. Stebenne, *Arthur J. Goldberg*, 174.

25. Ibid., 233.

26. Arthur M. Schlesinger Jr., *A Thousand Days: John F. Kennedy in the White House* (Boston: Houghton Mifflin, 1965), 130.

27. Richard Pfau, *No Sacrifice Too Great: The Life of Lewis L. Strauss* (Charlottesville: University Press of Virginia, 1984), 223–39.

28. Van Tassel, "Justice Arthur Goldberg," 88.

29. Stebenne, *Arthur J. Goldberg*, 310; Schlesinger, *A Thousand Days*, 698.

30. Schlesinger, *A Thousand Days*, 698; Michal R. Belknap, *The Supreme Court under Earl Warren, 1953–1969* (Columbia: University of South Carolina Press, 2005), 102.

31. Arthur M. Schlesinger Jr., *Robert Kennedy and His Times* (New York: Ballantine Books, 1978), 407.

32. Lucas A. Powe Jr., *The Warren Court and American Politics* (Cambridge: Harvard University Press, 2000), 210; Henry J. Abraham, *Justices, Presidents, and Senators: A History of the U.S. Supreme Court Appointments from Washington to Clinton* (Lanham, MD: Rowman & Littlefield, 1999), 209.

33. Stephen G. Breyer, "Clerking for Justice Goldberg," *Journal of Supreme Court History* (1990): 4, cited in Alan M. Dershowitz, *Chutzpah* (Boston: Little, Brown and Company, 1991), 60.

34. Schlesinger, *Robert Kennedy and His Times*, 407.

35. Belknap, *The Supreme Court under Earl Warren*, 103.

36. Dorothy Goldberg, *A Private View*, 136.

37. Laura Krugman Ray, "The Legacy of a Supreme Court Clerkship: Stephen Breyer and Arthur Goldberg," *Penn State Law Review* 115, no. 1 (2010): 83.

38. Clare Cushman, "Stephen G. Breyer," in *The Supreme Court Justices: Illustrated Biographies, 1789–1995*, ed. Clare Cushman (Washington, DC: Supreme Court Historical Society and Congressional Quarterly Press, 1995), 537.

39. Ray, "The Legacy of a Supreme Court Clerkship," 109.

40. Dershowitz, *Taking the Stand*, 55, 57.

41. Powe, *The Warren Court*, 210; Stebenne, *Arthur J. Goldberg*, 317.

42. Van Tassel, "Justice Arthur Goldberg," 90.

43. Powe, *The Warren Court*, 211.

44. Arthur J. Goldberg, "The Judicial Task," in *The Defense of Freedom: The Public Papers of Arthur J. Goldberg*, ed. Daniel Patrick Moynihan (New York: Harper & Row, 1966), cited in Van Tassel, "Justice Arthur Goldberg," 90, 101.

45. Kennedy v. Mendoza-Martinez, 372 U.S. 144 (1963).

46. Friedman, "Arthur J. Goldberg," 2983.

47. Watson v. Memphis, 373 U.S. 526 (1963).

48. Friedman, "Arthur J. Goldberg," 2984.

49. Cushman, "Stephen G. Breyer," 468–69.

50. Escobedo v. Illinois, 378 U.S. 478 (1964).

51. Van Tassel, "Justice Arthur Goldberg," 90; Dershowitz, *Taking the Stand*, 80–81.

52. Escobedo v. Illinois, 490; quoted in Dershowitz, *Taking the Stand*, 81.

53. Van Tassel, "Justice Arthur Goldberg," 90–91.

54. Quoted in Lucas A. Powe Jr., *The Supreme Court and the American Elite, 1789–2008* (Cambridge: Harvard University Press, 2009), 265.

55. Powe, *The Warren Court*, 391.

56. Powe, *The Supreme Court and the American Elite*, 265.

57. Edward Lazarus, *Closed Chambers: The Rise, Fall, and Future of the Modern Supreme Court* (New York: Penguin Books, 1999), 85.

58. Dershowitz, *Taking the Stand*, 75–76.

59. Van Tassel, "Justice Arthur Goldberg," 92; Lazarus, *Closed Chambers*, 86; and Dershowitz, *Taking the Stand*, 75–76.

60. Arthur J. Goldberg and Alan M. Dershowitz, "Declaring the Death Penalty Unconstitutional," *Harvard Law Review* 83 (1969–1970): 1774–1819.

61. Van Tassel, "Justice Arthur Goldberg," 92; Dershowitz, *Taking the Stand*, 211.

62. Dorothy Goldberg, *A Private View*, 198.

63. Van Tassel, "Justice Arthur Goldberg," 82.

64. David N. Atkinson, *Leaving the Bench: Supreme Court Justices at the End* (Lawrence: University Press of Kansas, 1999), 134.

65. Laura Kalman, *Abe Fortas: A Biography* (New Haven: Yale University Press, 1990), 241.

66. Dorothy Goldberg, *A Private View*, 194, 197.

67. Stebenne, *Arthur J. Goldberg*, 348; Abraham, *Justices, Presidents, and Senators*, 213.

68. Arthur J. Goldberg Oral History Transcript, March 25, 1983, Lyndon Baines Johnson Library, p. 1., cited in Van Tassel, "Justice Arthur Goldberg," 100, fn. 5.

69. Quoted in Van Tassel, "Justice Arthur Goldberg," 97.

70. Van Tassel, "Justice Arthur Goldberg," 96.

71. Bruce Allen Murphy, *Fortas: The Rise and Ruin of a Supreme Court Justice* (New York: William Morrow and Company, 1988), 170–71.

72. Van Tassel, "Justice Arthur Goldberg," 97.

73. Atkinson, *Leaving the Bench*, 135.

74. Quoted in ibid., 136.

75. Daniel Schorr, "Remembrances of Justice Goldberg," *Hastings Constitutional Law Quarterly* 17 (1990): 285; quoted in Van Tassel, "Justice Arthur Goldberg," 98.

76. Michael Oren, *Power, Faith, and Fantasy: America in the Middle East, 1776 to the Present* (New York: W. W. Norton, 2007), 526.

77. Stebenne, *Arthur J. Goldberg*, 354–55.

78. Ibid., 355.

79. Ray, "The Legacy of a Supreme Court Clerkship," 107.

80. Stebenne, *Arthur J. Goldberg*, 358.

81. Cushman, "Stephen G. Breyer," 470.

82. Berkow, *Maxwell Street*, 312.

83. Stuart Banner, *The Baseball Trust: A History of Baseball's Antitrust Exemption* (New York: Oxford University Press, 2013), 189.

84. Ibid., 204.

85. Cushman, "Stephen G. Breyer," 470.

86. Stebenne, *Arthur J. Goldberg*, 381.

87. Van Tassel, "Justice Arthur Goldberg," 83.

88. School District of Abington Township Pa. v. Schempp 374 US 203, 306 (1963); and quoted in Van Tassel, "Justice Arthur Goldberg," 84.

89. Quoted in Stebenne, *Arthur J. Goldberg*, 38.

90. Dershowitz, *Chutzpah*, 60.

91. Stebenne, *Arthur J. Goldberg*, 6–7.

92. Berkow, *Maxwell Street*, 305.

93. Ibid., 314.

94. This story is recounted in Ruth Bader Ginsburg, "Remembering the First Five Jewish Justices of the Supreme Court," *Forward*, January 9, 2004.

95. Dershowitz, *Chutzpah*, 61.

96. Quoted in Van Tassel, "Justice Arthur Goldberg," 83–84.

97. Dershowitz, *Chutzpah*, 61.

98. Van Tassel, "Justice Arthur Goldberg," 81.

99. Powe, *The Warren Court*, 210.

100. Van Tassel, "Justice Arthur Goldberg," 89.

101. Dershowitz, *Taking the Stand*, 75.

102. Ibid., 79.

103. Dershowitz, *Chutzpah*, 53, 56; and Dershowitz, *Taking the Stand*, 72.

8. Abe Fortas: A Tale of Achievement and Scandal

1. Robert Shogan, *A Question of Judgment: The Fortas Case and the Struggle for the Supreme Court* (Indianapolis: Bobbs-Merrill Company, 1972), 80.

2. Bruce Allen Murphy, *Fortas: The Rise and Ruin of a Supreme Court Justice* (New York: William Morrow and Company, 1988), 91; Robert Dallek, *Lone Star Rising: Lyndon Johnson and His Times, 1908–1960* (New York: Oxford University Press, 1991), 332; and Robert A. Caro, *The Years of Lyndon Johnson: Means of Ascent* (New York: Alfred A. Knopf, 1990).

3. Shogan, *A Question of Judgment*, 83.

4. Murphy, *Fortas*, 91.

5. Shogan, *A Question of Judgment*, 30.

6. Murphy, *Fortas*, 4–5; Laura Kalman, *Abe Fortas: A Biography* (New Haven: Yale University Press, 1990), 8–9.

7. Kalman, *Abe Fortas*, 8; Bruce Allen Murphy, "Through the Looking Glass: The Legacy of Abe Fortas," in *The Jewish Justices of the Supreme Court Revisited: Brandeis to Fortas*, ed. Jennifer M. Lowe (Washington, DC: Supreme Court Historical Society, 1994), 104.

8. Murphy, *Fortas*, 8; and Kalman, *Abe Fortas*, 14.

9. Quoted in Murphy, *Fortas*, 13.

10. Dan A. Oren, *Joining the Club: A History of Jews and Yale* (New Haven: Yale University Press, 1985), 125.

11. Noah Feldman, *Scorpions: The Battles and Triumphs of FDR's Great Supreme Court Justices* (New York: Twelve, 2010), 60–62, 172–74; Bernard Schwartz, *A History of the Supreme Court* (New York: Oxford University Press, 1993), 239–40; and Clare Cushman, ed., *The Supreme Court Justices: Illustrated Biographies, 1789–1995* (Washington, DC: Supreme Court Historical Society and Congressional Quarterly Press, 1995), 391–92.

12. Quoted in Kalman, *Abe Fortas*, p. 14.

13. Kalman, *Abe Fortas*, 14–15, 25.

14. David M. Dorsen, *Henry Friendly: Greatest Judge of His Era* (Cambridge: Belknap Press, 2012), 32.

15. Quoted in Kalman, *Abe Fortas*, 27.

16. Ibid., 28.

17. Jonathan Alter, *The Defining Moment: FDR's Hundred Days and the Triumph of Hope* (New York: Simon & Schuster, 2006), 281.

18. Shogan, *A Question of Judgment*, 35.

19. Murphy, *Fortas*, 25; and Shogan, *A Question of Judgment*, 114.

20. Shogan, *A Question of Judgment*, 41.

21. Murphy, "Through the Looking Glass," 105.

22. Kalman, *Abe Fortas*, 76.

23. Shogan, *A Question of Judgment*, 55; Kalman, *Abe Fortas*, 125.

24. Shogan, *A Question of Judgment*, 56; Kalman, *Abe Fortas*, 126.

25. Anthony Lewis, *Gideon's Trumpet* (New York: Random House, 1964), 51.

26. Shogan, *A Question of Judgment*, 71; Lewis, *Gideon's Trumpet*, 51; and Kalman, *Abe Fortas*, 158.

27. Murphy, *Fortas*, 74.

28. Kalman, *Abe Fortas*, 166–68.

29. Kalman, *Abe Fortas*, 195.

30. Shogan, *A Question of Judgment*, 72; Isaac Stern with Chaim Potok, *My First 79 Years* (New York: Alfred A. Knopf, 1999), 176–77; and Kalman, *Abe Fortas*, 193.

31. Eric F. Goldman, *The Tragedy of Lyndon Johnson* (New York: Alfred A. Knopf, 1969), 39–40; Murphy, *Fortas*, 79–80.

32. Abe Fortas, letters to Lyndon Johnson, August 9, 1956, and August 20, 1957: both cited in Kalman, *Abe Fortas*, 203.

33. Lyndon Johnson, letter to Abe Fortas, August 24, 1956, as quoted in Murphy, *Fortas*, 104.

34. Murphy, *Fortas*, 105; Kalman, *Abe Fortas*, 177; "Institute Honors Fortas," *Washington Post*, November 22, 1965, cited in Kalman, *Abe Fortas*, 441, fn. 183.

35. Lewis, *Gideon's Trumpet*, 51; Kalman, *Abe Fortas*, 159; Murphy, *Fortas*, 105; and Dallek, *Lone Star Rising*, 561.

36. Shogan, *A Question of Judgment*, 90; Kalman, *Abe Fortas*, 210–12; and Murphy, *Fortas*, 109.

37. Quoted in Murphy, *Fortas*, 111.

38. Abe Fortas, letter to Isaac Stern, November 18, 1961, quoted in Kalman, *Abe Fortas*, 177, and cited in Kalman, 441, fn. 179.

39. Shogan, *A Question of Judgment*, 97.

40. Murphy, *Fortas*, 114–16.

41. Ibid., 117–18.

42. Stern with Potok, *My First 79 Years*, 268–69.

43. Shogan, *A Question of Judgment*, 136.

44. Ibid., 96.

45. Peter Irons, *A People's History of the Supreme Court* (New York: Penguin Books, 2000), 415; Shogan, *A Question of Judgment*, 74–75.

46. Murphy, *Fortas*, 158; Shogan, *A Question of Judgment*, 104.

47. Shogan, *A Question of Judgment*, 105.

48. Sheldon Goldman, *Picking Federal Judges: Lower Court Selection from Roosevelt through Reagan* (New Haven: Yale University Press, 1997), 181.

49. Kalman, *Abe Fortas*, 241–42; Henry J. Abraham, *Justices, Senators, and Presidents: A History of the U.S. Supreme Court Appointments from Washington to Clinton* (Lanham, MD: Rowman & Littlefield, 1999), 215; Murphy, *Fortas*, 172.

50. Murphy, *Fortas*, 180.

51. Kalman, *Abe Fortas*, 245; Murphy, *Fortas*, 180.

52. Murphy, *Fortas*, 180–81.

53. Ibid., 181; and Kalman, *Abe Fortas*, 245.

54. Murphy, *Fortas*, 175.

55. Ibid.

56. David G. Dalin and Alfred J. Kolatch, *The Presidents of the United States and the Jews* (Middle Village, NY: Jonathan David Publishers, 2000), 232–33.

57. Quoted in Shogan, *A Question of Judgment*, 112–13.

58. Kalman, *Abe Fortas*, 245.

59. Ibid.; Shogan, *A Question of Judgment*, 113–114.

60. Kalman, *Abe Fortas*, 245.

61. Murphy, *Fortas*, 182; Kalman, *Abe Fortas*, 242–43.

62. Murphy, *Fortas*, 184; Shogan, *A Question of Judgment*, 110; and Kalman, *Abe Fortas*, 242.

63. Kalman, *Abe Fortas*, 255–56; Cushman, *The Supreme Court Justices*, 464–65, 474.

64. Cushman, *The Supreme Court Justices*, 474; Shogan, *A Question of Judgment*, 124; Kalman, *Abe Fortas*, 250–54; and Murphy, *Fortas*, 532.

65. Shogan, *A Question of Judgment*, 124.

66. Kalman, *Abe Fortas*, 254–55.

67. Abraham, *Justices, Senators, and Presidents*, 216; Murphy, *Fortas*, 235.

68. Bruce Allen Murphy, *The Brandeis/Frankfurter Connection: The Secret Political Activities of Two Supreme Court Justices* (New York: Oxford University Press, 1982), 4; David M.

O'Brien, *Storm Center: The Supreme Court in American Politics* (New York: W. W. Norton, 2005), 92.

69. Shogan, *A Question of Judgment*, 139; O'Brien, *Storm Center*, 91–92.

70. Shogan, *A Question of Judgment*, 137.

71. Kalman, *Abe Fortas*, 301; Shogan, *A Question of Judgment*, 139; and Warren Bass, *Support Any Friend: Kennedy's Middle East and the Making of the U.S.-Israeli Alliance* (New York: Oxford University Press, 2003), 59.

72. Michael B. Oren, *Power, Faith, and Fantasy: America in the Middle East, 1776 to the Present* (New York: W. W. Norton, 2007), 524; Kalman, *Abe Fortas*, 301.

73. Kalman, *Abe Fortas*, 300–1, 312; Shogan, *A Question of Judgment*, 139.

74. Kalman, *Abe Fortas*, 312.

75. Laura Kalman, "Abe Fortas: Symbol of the Warren Court?" in *The Warren Court in Historical and Political Perspective*, ed. Mark Tushnet (Charlottesville: University Press of Virginia, 1993), 164.

76. Murphy, *Fortas*, 235; Abraham, *Justices, Senators, and Presidents*, 216.

77. Kalman, "Abe Fortas: Symbol of the Warren Court?" 164–65.

78. Shogan, *A Question of Judgment*, 235; Murphy, *Fortas*, 234.

79. Shogan, *A Question of Judgment*, 140.

80. Murphy, "Through the Looking Glass," 109; John W. Dean, *The Rehnquist Choice: The Untold Story of the Nixon Appointment That Redefined the Supreme Court* (New York: Free Press, 2001), 2.

81. Fred Graham, "Abe Fortas," in *The Justices of the United States Supreme Court, 1789–1969: Their Lives and Opinions*, ed. Leon Friedman and Fred L. Israel (New York: Chelsea House Publishers, 1969), 3024; Murphy, "Through the Looking Glass," 112; and Abraham, *Justices, Senators, and Presidents*, 218.

82. John Massaro, "LBJ and the Fortas Nomination for Chief Justice," *Political Science Quarterly* 97, no. 4 (1982–1983): 609.

83. U.S. Senate debate, September 30, 1968, *Congressional Record* 114, no. 28762, as quoted in Murphy, *The Brandeis/Frankfurter Connection*, 4, 365.

84. Murphy, *Fortas*, 380–82.

85. Ibid., 382.

86. Graham, "Abe Fortas," 3025; Dean, *The Rehnquist Choice*, 3.

87. Alexander Charns, *Cloak and Gavel: FBI Wiretaps, Bugs, Informers, and the Supreme Court* (Urbana: University of Illinois Press, 1992), 96.

88. Graham, "Abe Fortas," 3025; Dean, *The Rehnquist Choice*, 3–4.

89. Graham, "Abe Fortas," 3025; Dean, *The Rehnquist Choice*, 4.

90. Kalman, *Abe Fortas*, 300 and 465, fn. 31.

91. Murphy, "Through the Looking Glass," 114.

92. Robert Dallek, *Flawed Giant: Lyndon Johnson and His Times, 1961–1973* (New York: Oxford University Press, 1998), 559; Barbara A. Perry, *A "Representative" Supreme Court: The Impact of Race, Religion, and Gender on Appointments* (New York: Greenwood Press, 1991), 78.

93. Murphy, *Fortas*, 473–74.

94. Murphy, "Through the Looking Glass," 116–17 and 125, fn. 42.

95. Shogan, *A Question of Judgment*, 185.

96. Graham, "Abe Fortas," 325–26; Dean, *The Rehnquist Choice*, 5, 8.

97. Dean, *The Rehnquist Choice*, 5, 9; Clare, "Abe Fortas," 475.

98. Kalman, *Abe Fortas*, 382; Murphy, *Fortas*, 582.

99. Howard Ball and Phillip J. Cooper, *Of Power and Right: Hugo Black, William O. Douglas, and America's Constitutional Revolution* (New York: Oxford University Press, 1992), 316.

100. Kalman, *Abe Fortas*, 387–90; Murphy, *Fortas*, 582–83.

101. David Atkinson, *Leaving the Bench: Supreme Court Justices at the End* (Lawrence: University Press of Kansas, 1999), 142.

102. Kalman, *Abe Fortas*, 401.

103. Stern with Potok, *My First 79 Years*, 178.

104. Abraham, *Justices, Senators, and Presidents*, 217.

105. Kalman, *Abe Fortas*, 183.

106. Lucas A. Powe Jr., *The Warren Court and American Politics* (Cambridge: Belknap Press, 2000), 385.

107. Kalman, *Abe Fortas*, 379; Murphy, *Fortas*, 379, 592.

108. Murphy, "Through the Looking Glass," 104.

109. Kalman, *Abe Fortas*, 300.

110. Ibid., 401.

111. Marianne R. Sanua, *Let Us Prove Strong: The American Jewish Committee, 1945–2006* (Hanover, NH: University Press of New England, 2007), 140–41; Dallek, *Flawed Giant*, 427.

112. Kalman, *Abe Fortas*, 302; Isaac Stern, letter to Abe Fortas, August 11, 1967, quoted in Kalman, *Abe Fortas*, 302, and cited on p. 466.

113. Perry, *A "Representative" Supreme Court*, 80.

114. Quoted in Charns, *Cloak and Gavel*, 107.

115. Perry, *A "Representative" Supreme Court*, 79.

9. Three Jewish Justices: Ginsburg, Breyer, and Kagan Join the Court

1. David G. Dalin, "Presidents, Presidential Appointments and Jews," in *Jews in American Politics*, ed. L. Sandy Maisel and Ira N. Forman (Lanham, MD: Rowman & Littlefield, 2001), 45–46; Henry J. Abraham, *Justices, Presidents, and Senators: A History of U.S. Supreme Court Appointments from Washington to Clinton* (Lanham, MD: Rowman & Littlefield, 1999), 316; Jeffrey Toobin, *The Nine: Inside the Secret World of the Supreme Court* (New York: Anchor Books, 2008), 72; and Ruth Lampson Roberts, "Ruth Bader Ginsburg," in *The Supreme Court Justices: Illustrated Biographies, 1789–2012*, ed. Clare Cushman, 3rd. ed. (Thousand Oaks, CA: Supreme Court Historical Society and Congressional Quarterly Press, 2013), 489.

2. Abraham, *Justices, Presidents, and Senators*, 317–18; Toobin, *The Nine*, 71–78.

3. Toobin, *The Nine*, 75–76.

4. Ibid., 79–80.

5. Ibid., 80.

6. Abraham, *Justices, Presidents, and Senators*, 318.

7. Ibid., 318; Roberts, "Ruth Bader Ginsburg," 489.

8. Toobin, *The Nine*, 83.

9. Abraham, *Justices, Presidents, and Senators*, 322–23; Toobin, *The Nine*, 89–90.

10. Abraham, *Justices, Presidents, and Senators*, 324–25.

11. Roberts, "Ruth Bader Ginsburg," 486; Nichola D. Gutgold, *The Rhetoric of Supreme Court Women: From Obstacles to Options* (Lanham, MD: Lexington Books, 2012), 47; Elinor Slater and Robert Slater, *Great Jewish Women* (Middle Village, NY: Jonathan David Publishers, 2004), 96; and Linda Bayer, *Ruth Bader Ginsburg* (Philadelphia: Chelsea House Publishers, 2000), 14–17.

12. "James Madison High School," *Wikipedia*; Roberts, "Ruth Bader Ginsburg," 489; Gutgold, *The Rhetoric of Supreme Court Women*, 47–48; Malvina Halberstam, "Ruth Bader Ginsburg," in *Jewish Women in America: An Historical Encyclopedia*, Vol. 1, ed. Paula E. Hyman and Deborah Dash Moore (New York: Routledge, 1997), 516; Jason Horowitz, "Sanders's 100% Brooklyn Roots Are as Unshakable as His Accent," *New York Times*, July 25, 2015, A14; Bayer, *Ruth Bader Ginsburg*, 17–18, 23–26; and Irin Carmon and Shana Knizhnik, *Notorious RBG: The Life and Times of Ruth Bader Ginsburg* (New York: Dey Street Books, 2015), pre-publication copy, 26.

13. Halberstam, "Ruth Bader Ginsburg," 517; Gutgold, *The Rhetoric of Supreme Court Women*, 48; Roberts, "Ruth Bader Ginsburg," 487; Bayer, *Ruth Bader Ginsburg* (Philadelphia: Chelsea House Publishers, 2000), 37; and Jill Abramson and Barbara Franklin, *Where They Are Now: The Story of the Women of Harvard Law 1974* (Garden City, NY: Doubleday, 1986), 10.

14. Slater and Slater, *Great Jewish Women*, 97.

15. Ibid.; "Ruth Bader Ginsburg," *Current Biography*, February 1994, 29.

16. Bayer, *Ruth Bader Ginsburg*, 43; Halberstam, "Ruth Bader Ginsburg," 517.

17. Halberstam, "Ruth Bader Ginsburg"; Gutgold, *The Rhetoric of Supreme Court Women*, 49; and Clare Cushman, ed., *Supreme Court Decisions and Women's Rights: Milestones to Equality*, 2nd ed. (Washington, DC: Supreme Court Historical Society and Congressional Quarterly Press, 2011), 257.

18. Gutgold, *The Rhetoric of Supreme Court Women*, 49; Halberstam, "Ruth Bader Ginsburg," 517–18; Cushman, *Supreme Court Decisions*, 257; Bayer, *Ruth Bader Ginsburg*, 43.

19. Gutgold, *The Rhetoric of Supreme Court Women*, 54; Edward Lazarus, *Closed Chambers: The Rise, Fall, and Future of the Supreme Court* (New York: Penguin Books, 1999), 513–14; Roberts, "Ruth Bader Ginsburg," 489.

20. Lazarus, *Closed Chambers*, 514; Halberstam, "Ruth Bader Ginsburg," 518.

21. Goldman v. Secretary of Defense, 739 F2nd 657 (1984); United States v. Pollard 959 F2nd 1011 (D.C. Cir. 1991).

22. Jonathan D. Sarna and David G. Dalin, *Religion and State in the American Jewish Experience* (Notre Dame, IN: University of Notre Dame Press, 1997), 278–79; Samuel Rabinove, "Justice Ginsburg and the 'Jewish Agenda,'" *Reform Judaism* (Spring 1994): 75; Bayer, *Ruth Bader Ginsburg*, 71; and John D. Inazu, "Justice Ginsburg and Religious Liberty," *Legal Studies Research Paper Series*, Paper No. 12-01-01 (St. Louis: Washington University School of Law, 2012), 5–6.

23. Rabinove, "Justice Ginsburg and the 'Jewish Agenda,'" 75; Peter Perl, "The Spy Who's Been Left in the Cold," *Washington Post*, July 5, 1998; and Editorial, "Netanyahu's Plea for Pollard," *New York Sun*, January 6, 2011.

24. Former Harvard Law School dean and U.S. solicitor general Erwin Griswold has said of Tribe's treatise: "It may well be that no book . . . has ever had a greater influence on the development of American constitutional law." Quoted in Ethan Bronner, *Battle for Justice: How The Bork Nomination Shook America* (New York: W. W. Norton, 1989), 132.

25. Ibid., 330.

26. Ibid.; Abraham, *Justices, Presidents, and Senators*, 299.

27. Bronner, *Battle for Justice*, 330–35.

28. Laura Krugman Ray, "The Legacy of a Supreme Court Clerkship: Stephen Breyer and Arthur Goldberg," *Penn State Law Review* 115, no. 1 (2010): 108; Elinor Slater and Robert Slater, *Great Jewish Men* (Middle Village, NY: Jonathan David Publishers, 2005), 73; Jeffrey Toobin, "Breyer's Big Idea," *The New Yorker*, October 31, 2015, 37; and Jeffrey Toobin, *The Oath: The Obama White House and The Supreme Court* (New York: Random House, 2012), 88.

29. Ray, "The Legacy of a Supreme Court Clerkship," 108–9; Jennifer L. Jack, "10 Things You Didn't Know about Stephen Breyer," *U.S. News & World Report*, October 1, 2007.

30. Abraham, *Justices, Presidents, and Senators*, 323; Toobin, *The Nine*, 225; Joan Alpert et al., "Religion and the Current Supreme Court Justices," *Moment*, September/October 2008, 46; Jane Manners, "Stephen G. Breyer," in *The Supreme Court Justices: Illustrated Biographies, 1789–2012*, ed. Clare Cushman, 3rd ed. (Thousand Oaks, CA: Supreme Court Historical Society and Congressional Quarterly Press, 2013), 493.

31. Manners, "Stephen G. Breyer," 493; Toobin, *The Nine*, 94–95; Toobin, *The Oath*, 84; and Abraham, *Justices, Presidents, and Senators*, 324.

32. Manners, "Stephen G. Breyer," 493; Toobin, *The Nine*, 95; Sheldon Goldman, *Picking Federal Judges: Lower Court Selection from Roosevelt through Reagan* (New Haven: Yale University Press, 1997), 261; and Nathan Lewin, "Stephen Gerald Breyer," in *Encyclopedia Judaica*, 2nd ed., Vol. 4 (Farmington Hills, MI, and Jerusalem: Thomson Gale and Keter Publishing House, 2007), 174.

33. Manners, "Stephen G. Breyer," 494; Jeffrey Rosen, "Breyer Restraint," *New Republic*, July 11, 1994, 25.

34. Manners, "Stephen G. Breyer," 494; Slater and Slater, *Great Jewish Men*, 74.

35. Eli Wald, "The Rise and Fall of the WASP and Jewish Law Firms," *Stanford Law Review* 60 (April 2008): 136.

36. Nancy Lisagor and Frank Lipsius, *A Law unto Itself: The Untold Story of the Law Firm Sullivan and Cromwell; 100 Years of Creating Power and Wealth* (New York: Paragon House, 1989), 57–59.

37. Alan M. Dershowitz, *Abraham: The World's First (but Certainly Not Last) Jewish Lawyer* (New York: Nextbook, 2015), 176, fn. 8.

38. Wald, "The Rise and Fall," 119.

39. Jerold S. Auerbach, *Against the Grain: A Historian's Journey* (New Orleans: Quid Pro Books, 2012), 23–24; and Jerold S. Auerbach, "From Rags to Robes: The Legal Profession, Social Mobility, and the American Jewish Experience," *American Jewish Historical Quarterly* 66 (December 1976): 273.

40. Lisagor and Lipsius, *A Law unto Itself*, 106; Dershowitz, *Abraham*, 125.

41. Toobin, *The Oath*, 173–74; Clare Cushman, "Elena Kagan," in *The Supreme Court Justices: Illustrated Biographies, 1789–2012*, ed. Clare Cushman, 3rd ed. (Thousand Oaks, CA: Supreme Court Historical Society and Congressional Quarterly Press, 2013), 507.

42. Lisa W. Foderaro, "Growing up, Kagan Tested Boundaries of Her Faith," *New York Times*, May 12, 2010, A25.

43. Toobin, *The Oath*, 175; and Jeffrey Toobin, "Supreme Sacrifice," in *Portraits of Amer-*

ican Politics: A Reader, ed. Bruce Allen Murphy, 3rd ed. (Boston: Houghton Mifflin, 2000), 419–21.

44. Cushman, "Elena Kagan," 508.

45. Toobin, *The Oath*, 176; Cushman, "Elena Kagan," 507.

46. Toobin, *The Oath*, 177; Cushman, "Elena Kagan," 507; Gutgold, *The Rhetoric of Supreme Court Women*, 107.

47. Toobin, *The Oath*, 178–79; Cushman, "Elena Kagan," 507.

48. Neil A. Lewis, "Abner Mikva, Lawmaker, Judge and Mentor to Obama, Dies at 90," *New York Times*, July 5, 2016.

49. Toobin, *The Oath*, 28, 179–80.

50. Ibid., 164, 180; Cushman, "Elena Kagan," 508.

51. Laurence Tribe and Joshua Matz, *Uncertain Justice: The Roberts Court and the Constitution* (New York: Henry Holt and Company, 2014), 2, 88–120.

52. Bruce Allen Murphy, *Scalia: A Court of One* (New York: Simon & Schuster, 2014), 406; Tribe and Metz, *Uncertain Justice*, 88.

53. Toobin, *The Oath*, 170–71; Michael Scherer, "Citizens United v. Federal Election Commission," in *The Supreme Court: Decisions That Changed America* (New York: Time Inc. Books, 2015), 82.

54. Gutgold, *The Rhetoric of Supreme Court Women*, 112–13; Toobin, *The Oath*, 226–29.

55. Toobin, *The Oath*, 174.

56. Toobin, "Breyer's Big Idea," 40; Toobin, *The Oath*, 121.

57. Tribe and Metz, *Uncertain Justice*, 285; Brian Lamb, Susan Swain, and Mark Farkas, *The Supreme Court: A C-Span Book Featuring the Justices in Their Own Words* (New York: Public Affairs, 2010), 138.

58. Toobin, *The Nine*, 238, 284.

59. Joan Biskupic, *American Original: The Life and Constitution of Supreme Court Justice Antonin Scalia* (New York: Sarah Crichton Books, 2009), 89.

60. Quoted in Joan Biskupic, *Sandra Day O'Connor: How the First Woman on the Supreme Court Became Its Most Influential Justice* (New York: HarperCollins, 2005), 289–90.

61. Biskupic, *Sandra Day O'Connor*, 89, 304; Bayer, *Ruth Bader Ginsburg*, 88–89; Toobin, *The Oath*, 201–2.

62. Veronica Stracqualursi, "Ruth Bader Ginsburg's Birthday: 10 Gifts to Get the Supreme Court Justice," ABCNews.com, March 15, 2015.

63. Toobin, *The Oath*, 252–53; Elissa Goldstein, "Justices Elena Kagan and Ruth Bader Ginsburg Share Personal Trainer, Mutual Admiration," *Tablet*, February 10, 2014.

64. United States v. Virginia 518 US (1996), quoted in Roberts, "Ruth Bader Ginsburg," 489.

65. United States v. Virginia 518 US (1996), quoted in Nina Totenberg, "Notes on a Life," in *The Legacy of Ruth Bader Ginsburg*, ed. Scott Dodson (New York: Cambridge University Press, 2015), 10.

66. Cary Franklin, "A More Perfect Union: Sex, Race, and the VMI Case," in *The Legacy of Ruth Bader Ginsburg*, ed. Scott Dodson (New York: Cambridge University Press, 2015), 91–92; Gutgold, *The Rhetoric of Supreme Court Women*, 58.

67. Jeffrey Toobin, "DOMA and the Court," *The New Yorker*, July 8–15, 2013, 27; Adam

Liptak, "Supreme Court Ruling Makes Same-Sex Marriage a Right Nationwide," *New York Times*, June 26, 2015.

68. Toobin, "Breyer's Big Idea," 39; Toobin, *The Nine*, 352.

69. Jay Alan Sekulow, *Witnessing Their Faith: Religious Influence on Supreme Court Justices and Their Opinions* (Lanham, MD: Rowman & Littlefield, 2006), 321.

70. Sekulow, *Witnessing Their Faith*, 321.

71. Quoted in Linda Greenhouse, "The Ten Commandments Reach the Supreme Court," *New York Times*, February 28, 2005.

72. Toobin, "Breyer's Big Idea," 39; Toobin, *The Nine*, 353.

73. Richard H. Fallon Jr., "A Salute to Justice Breyer's Concurring Opinion in *Van Orden v. Perry*," *Harvard Law Review* 128, no. 1 (November 2014): 429.

74. Ibid.

75. Toobin, *The Nine*, 353.

76. Sekulow, *Witnessing Their Faith*, 327.

77. Ibid.

78. Toobin, *The Oath*, 85–86.

79. Michael J. Klarman, "Judicial Statesmanship: Justice Breyer's Concurring Opinion in *Van Orden v. Perry*," *Harvard Law Review* 128, no. 1 (November 2014): 452, 456.

80. Adam Liptak, "Town Meetings Can Have Prayer, Justices Decide," *New York Times*, May 5, 2014; Gerard V. Bradley, "The Supreme Court on Prayer," *Public Discourse*, May 28, 2014.

81. Liptak, "Town Meetings Can Have Prayer."

82. Ibid.

83. Quoted in Yair Rosenberg, "Elena Kagan's Very Jewish Dissent—and Mistake," *Tablet*, May 5, 2014.

84. Rosenberg, "Elena Kagan's Very Jewish Dissent"; and Yair Rosenberg, "Supreme Court Corrects Kagan Dissent," *Tablet*, May 19, 2014.

85. Zachary Baron Shemtob, "The Catholic and Jewish Court: Explaining the Absence of Protestants on the Nation's Highest Judicial Body," *Journal of Law and Religion* 27, no. 2 (2012): 388; Juliet Eilperin, "Obama Takes Step to Mend Relations with Speech at Adas Israel Synagogue," *Washington Post*, May 21, 2015.

86. Alpert et al., "Religion and the Current Supreme Court Justices," *Moment*, 46; Robert Barnes, "Religion and the High Court: Ginsburg Is Latest Justice to Reflect on Faith," On Faith, *Washington Post*, January 15, 2008.

87. Lauren Markoe, "Justice Ginsburg Writes a Feminist Opinion for Passover," Religion News Service, March 19, 2015; Michael Stokes Paulsen, "Passover, Abortion, and Rabbi Ruth Bader Ginsburg," *Public Discourse*, April 3, 2015; and Michelle Boorstein, "Justice Ginsburg Has Released a New Feminist Take on the Passover Narrative," *Washington Post*, March 18, 2015.

88. Quoted from Ginsburg's address to the 1995 Annual Meeting of the American Jewish Committee, as reprinted in the *New York Times*, January 14, 1996.

89. Shemtob, "The Catholic and Jewish Court," 380.

90. "Justices in Agreement—No Arguments on Yom Kippur," JWeekly.com, September 18, 2003; Slater and Slater, *Great Jewish Men*, 75.

91. Stephen G. Breyer, "Zion's Justice," *New Republic*, October 5, 1998, 18–19.

92. Sheryl Gay Stolberg, "An Aging Court Raises the Stakes of the Presidential Election," *New York Times*, June 28, 2012, A18.

93. Randall Kennedy, "The Case for Early Retirement," *New Republic*, April 28, 2011; Carmon and Knizhnik, *Notorious RBG*, 171–73.

94. Joan Biskupic, "Exclusive: Supreme Court's Ginsburg Vows to Resist Pressure to Retire," Reuters, July 4, 2013; Gail Collins, "The Unsinkable R.B.G.: Ruth Bader Ginsburg Has No Interest in Retiring," *New York Times*, February 20, 2015; and Carmon and Knizhnik, *Notorious RBG*, 174.

95. Randy E. Barnett and Josh Blackman, "The Next Justices," *Weekly Standard*, September 14, 2015, 22.

96. Carmon and Knizhnik, *Notorious RBG*.

97. Goldman, *Picking Federal Judges*, 233.

98. Ruth Bader Ginsburg, "From Benjamin to Brandeis to Breyer: Is There a Jewish Seat?" *Brandeis Law Journal* 41 (2002): 235.

99. Slater and Slater, *Great Jewish Men*, 75.

100. Robert A. Burt, "On the Bench: The Jewish Justices," in *Jews in American Politics*, ed. L. Sandy Maisel and Ira N. Forman (Lanham, MD: Rowman & Littlefield, 2001), 75.

101. Shemtob, "The Catholic and Jewish Court," 388–89; Foderaro, "Growing up, Kagan Tested Boundaries."

SELECTED BIBLIOGRAPHY

Abraham, Henry J. 1999. *Justices, Presidents, and Senators: A History of the U.S. Supreme Court Appointments from Washington to Clinton*. Revised edition. Lanham, MD: Rowman & Littlefield.

Abramson, Jill, and Barbara Franklin. 1986. *Where They Are Now: The Story of the Women of Harvard Law 1974*. Garden City, NY: Doubleday.

Ackerman, Kenneth D. 2005. *Boss Tweed: The Rise and Fall of the Corrupt Pol Who Conceived the Soul of Modern New York*. New York: Carroll & Graf.

Alexander, Michael. 2001. *Jazz Age Jews*. Princeton, NJ: Princeton University Press.

Atkinson, David N. 1999. *Leaving the Bench: Supreme Court Justices at the End*. Lawrence: University Press of Kansas.

Auerbach, Jerold S. 1976 (December). "From Rags to Robes: The Legal Profession, Social Mobility, and the American Jewish Experience." *American Jewish Historical Quarterly* 66: 249–84.

———. 1990. *Rabbis and Lawyers: The Journey from Torah to Constitution*. Bloomington: Indiana University Press.

Baker, Leonard. 1984. *Brandeis and Frankfurter: A Dual Biography*. New York: Harper & Row.

Baker, Liva. 1969. *Felix Frankfurter: A Biography*. New York: Coward-McCann.

Banner, Stuart. 2013. *The Baseball Trust: A History of Baseball's Antitrust Exemption*. New York: Oxford University Press.

Barnard, Harry. 1974. *The Forging of an American Jew: The Life and Times of Judge Julian W. Mack*. New York: Herzl Press.

Bayer, Linda. 2000. *Ruth Bader Ginsburg*. Philadelphia: Chelsea House Publishers.

Berkow, Ira. 1977. *Maxwell Street*. Garden City, NY: Doubleday.

Berkowitz, Simcha. 1971. "Felix Frankfurter's Zionist Activities," Doctor of Hebrew Letters [DHL] diss., Jewish Theological Seminary.

———. 1987. "The Faisal-Frankfurter Letters: An Unending Story." In *Community and Culture: Essays in Jewish Studies*, edited by Nahum M. Waldman. Philadelphia: Seth Press.

Bird, Kai. 1992. *The Chairman: John J. McCloy and the Making of the American Establishment*. New York: Simon & Schuster.

———. 1998. *The Color of Truth: McGeorge Bundy and William Bundy; Brothers in Arms*. New York: Simon & Schuster.

Biskupic, Joan. 2005. *Sandra Day O'Connor: How the First Woman on the Supreme Court Became Its Most Influential Justice*. New York: HarperCollins.

———. 2009. *American Original: The Life and Constitution of Supreme Court Justice Antonin Scalia*. New York: Farrar, Straus and Giroux.

Brandeis, Louis D. 1914. *Other People's Money and How the Bankers Use It*. New York: Stokes.

Brandeis, Louis D., and Samuel D. Warren Jr. 1890–1891. "The Right to Privacy," *Harvard Law Review* 4: 193–220.

Breitman, Richard, and Allan J. Lichtman. 2013. *FDR and the Jews*. Cambridge: Harvard University Press.

Bronner, Ethan. 1989. *Battle for Justice: How the Bork Nomination Shook America*. New York: W. W. Norton.

Breyer, Stephen G. 1998 (October 5). "Zion's Justice." *New Republic*. 18–19.

———. 2005. *Active Liberty: Interpreting Our Democratic Constitution*. New York: Alfred A. Knopf.

———. 2015. *The Court and the World: American Law and the New Global Realities*. New York: Alfred A. Knopf.

Burt, Robert A. 1988. *Two Jewish Justices*. Berkeley: University of California Press.

———. 2001. "On the Bench: The Jewish Justices." In *Jews in American Politics*, edited by L. Sandy Maisel and Ira N. Forman. Lanham, MD: Rowman & Littlefield, 65–80.

Cardozo, Benjamin N. 1921. *The Nature of the Judicial Process*. New Haven: Yale University Press.

———. 1924. *The Growth of the Law*. New Haven: Yale University Press.

Carmen, Ira H. 1969 (May). "The President, Politics and the Power of Appointment: Hoover's Nomination of Mr. Justice Cardozo," *Virginia Law Review* 55 (4): 616–59.

Carmon, Irin, and Shana Knizhnik. 2015. *Notorious RBG: The Life and Times of Ruth Bader Ginsburg*. New York: Dey Street Books.

Caro, Robert A. 1990. *Means of Ascent: The Years of Lyndon Johnson*. New York: Alfred A. Knopf.

Chace, James. 1998. *Acheson: The Secretary of State Who Created the American World*. New York: Simon & Schuster.

Clinton, Bill. 2005. *My Life*. Vintage Books.

Cohen, Naomi W. 1969. *A Dual Heritage: The Public Career of Oscar S. Straus*. Philadelphia: Jewish Publication Society of America.

Cooper, John Milton, Jr. 2009. *Woodrow Wilson: A Biography*. New York: Vintage Books.

Cushman, Clare, ed. 2011. *Supreme Court Decisions and Women's Rights: Milestones to Equality*. Second edition. Washington, DC: Congressional Quarterly Press.

———, ed. 2013. *The Supreme Court Justices: Illustrated Biographies, 1789–2012*. Third edition. Washington, DC: Congressional Quarterly Press.

Dalin, David G. 1992 (Spring). "Louis Marshall, the Jewish Vote, and the Republican Party." *Jewish Political Studies Review* 4 (1): 55–84.

———. 2001. "Presidents, Presidential Appointments and Jews." In *Jews in American Politics*, edited by L. Sandy Maisel and Ira N. Forman. Lanham, MD: Rowman & Littlefield, 29–47.

———. 2008. "Jews and the American Presidency." In *Religion, Race, and the American Presidency*, edited by Gaston Espinosa. Lanham, MD: Rowman & Littlefield, 129–52.

———. 2016. "Old Isaiah." Review of *Louis D. Brandeis: American Prophet*, by Jeffrey Rosen (New Haven: Yale University Press), in *Jewish Review of Books* 9, no. 2 (Summer 2016): 26–27.

Dalin, David G., and Alfred J. Kolatch. 2000. *The Presidents of the United States and the Jews*. Middle Village, NY: Jonathan David Publishers.

Dallek, Robert. 1991. *Lone Star Rising: Lyndon Johnson and His Times, 1908–1960*. New York: Oxford University Press.

———. 1998. *Flawed Giant: Lyndon Johnson and His Times, 1961–1963*. New York: Oxford University Press.

Dawson, Nelson L. 1980. *Louis D. Brandeis, Felix Frankfurter and the New Deal*. Hamden, CT: Archon Books.

Dean, John W. 2001. *The Rehnquist Choice: The Untold Story of the Nixon Appointment That Redefined the Supreme Court*. New York: Free Press.

de Haas, Jacob. 1929. *Louis D. Brandeis: A Biographical Sketch*. New York: Bloch Publishing Company.

Dershowitz, Alan M. 1991. *Chutzpah*. Boston: Little, Brown and Company.

———. 2013. *Taking the Stand: My Life in the Law*. New York: Crown Publishers.

———. 2015. *Abraham: The World's First (but Certainly Not Last) Jewish Lawyer*. New York: Nextbook.

Dodson, Scott, ed. 2015. *The Legacy of Ruth Bader Ginsburg*. New York: Cambridge University Press.

Evans, Eli N. 1988. *Judah P. Benjamin: The Jewish Confederate*. New York: Free Press.

Fallon, Richard H., Jr. 2014 (November). "A Salute to Justice Breyer's Concurring Opinion in *Van Orden v. Perry*." In "Essays in Honor of Justice Stephen G. Breyer," edited by Martha Minow, *Harvard Law Review* 128 (1): 429–33.

Feldman, Noah. 2010. *Scorpions: The Battles and Triumphs of FDR's Great Supreme Court Justices*. New York: Twelve–Hachette Book Group.

Foderaro, Lisa W. 2010 (May 12). "Growing up, Kagan Tested the Boundaries of Her Faith," *New York Times*.

Frankfurter, Felix. 1927. *The Case of Sacco and Vanzetti: A Critical Analysis for Lawyers and Laymen*. Boston: Little, Brown and Company.

———. 1939. *Mr. Justice Holmes and the Supreme Court*. Cambridge: Harvard University Press.

Freedman, Max, ed. 1967. *Roosevelt and Frankfurter: Their Correspondence, 1928–1945*. Boston: Little, Brown and Company.

Freund, Paul A. 1957. "Mr. Justice Brandeis: A Centennial Memoir," *Harvard Law Review* 70: 769–92.

———. 1978 (September). "Justice Brandeis: A Law Clerk's Remembrance," *American Jewish History* 68 (1): 7–18.

Friedman, Leon, and Fred L. Israel, eds. 1969. *The Justices of the United States Supreme Court, 1789–1969: Their Lives and Majority Opinions*, Vols. 3–4. New York: R. R. Bowker Company.

Gal, Allon. 1980. *Brandeis of Boston*. Cambridge: Harvard University Press.

Ginsburg, Ruth Bader. 1994. Introduction to *The Jewish Justices of the Supreme Court Revisited: Brandeis to Fortas*, edited by Jennifer M. Lowe. Washington, DC: Supreme Court Historical Society, 3–4.

———. 2002. "From Benjamin to Brandeis to Breyer: Is There a Jewish Seat?" *Brandeis Law Journal* 41: 229–36.

———. 2016. *My Own Words*. New York: Simon & Schuster.

Ginsburg, Justice Ruth Bader, and Rabbi Lauren Holtzblatt. 2015 (March). "The Heroic and Visionary Women of Passover." American Jewish World Service, Chag V'Chesed series: 1–5.

Goldberg, Arthur J. 1971. *Equal Justice: The Warren Era of the Supreme Court*. Evanston, IL: Northwestern University Press.

Goldberg, Arthur J., and Alan M. Dershowitz. 1969–1970. "Declaring the Death Penalty Unconstitutional," *Harvard Law Review* 83: 1773–1819.

Goldberg, Dorothy. 1975. *A Private View of Public Life*. New York: Charterhouse.

Goldman, Sheldon. 1997. *Picking Federal Judges: Lower Court Selection from Roosevelt through Reagan*. New Haven: Yale University Press.

———. 2006. "The Politics of Appointing Catholics to the Federal Court." *University of St. Thomas Law Journal* 4, 2 (2006): 193–220.

Goldman, Solomon, ed. 1942. *Brandeis on Zionism*. Washington, DC: Zionist Organization of America.

Goodhart, Arthur L. 1971. *Five Jewish Lawyers of the Common Law*. New York: Oxford University Press.

Gutgold, Nichola D. 2012. *The Rhetoric of Supreme Court Women: From Obstacles to Options*. Lanham, MD: Lexington Books.

Hacker, Louis M., and Mark D. Hirsch. 1978. *Proskauer: His Life and Times*. Tuscaloosa: University of Alabama Press.

Halberstam, Malvina. 1997. "Ruth Bader Ginsburg." In *Jewish Women in America: An Historical Encyclopedia*, Vol. 1, edited by Paula E. Hyman and Deborah Dash Moore. New York: Routledge: 515–20.

Halpern, Ben. 1987. *A Clash of Heroes: Brandeis, Weizmann, and American Zionism*. New York: Oxford University Press.

Hirsch, H. N. 1981. *The Enigma of Felix Frankfurter*. New York: Basic Books.

Hirshman, Linda. 2015. *Sisters in Law: How Sandra Day O'Connor and Ruth Bader Ginsburg Went to the Supreme Court and Changed the World*. New York: HarperCollins.

Kahn, Michael A. 1973 (January). "The Politics of the Appointment Process: An Analysis of Why Learned Hand Was Never Appointed to the Supreme Court." *Stanford Law Review* 25: 251–85.

Kalman, Laura. 1990. *Abe Fortas: A Biography*. New Haven: Yale University Press.

Karfunkel, Thomas, and Thomas W. Ryley. 1978. *The Jewish Seat: Anti-Semitism and the Appointment of Jews to the Supreme Court*. Hicksville, NY: Exposition Press.

Katz, Irving. 1968. "Henry Lee Higginson vs. Louis Dembitz Brandeis: A Collision between Tradition and Reform," *New England Quarterly* 41: 67–80.

Kaufman, Andrew L. 1994. "Benjamin N. Cardozo, Sephardic Jew." In *The Jewish Justices of the Supreme Court Revisited: Brandeis to Fortas*, edited by Jennifer M. Lowe. Washington, DC: Supreme Court Historical Society, 35–59.

———. 1994–1995. "The First Judge Cardozo: Albert, Father of Benjamin," *Journal of Law and Religion* 11, (1): 271–315.

———. *Cardozo*. 1998. Cambridge: Harvard University Press.

Kennedy, Randall. 2011 (April 28). "The Case for Early Retirement," *New Republic*.

Klarman, Michael J. 2014 (November). "Judicial Statesmanship: Justice Breyer's Concurring Opinion in *Van Orden v. Perry*." In "Essays in Honor of Justice Stephen G. Breyer," edited by Martha Minow, *Harvard Law Review* 128, (1): 452–56.

SELECTED BIBLIOGRAPHY

Kurland, Philip B. 1971. *Mr. Justice Frankfurter and the Constitution*. Chicago: University of Chicago Press.

Lash, Joseph P., ed. 1975. *From the Diaries of Felix Frankfurter*. New York: W. W. Norton.

Lasky, Victor. 1970. *Arthur J. Goldberg: The Old and the New*. New Rochelle, NY: Arlington House.

Lasser, William. 2002. *Benjamin V. Cohen: Architect of the New Deal*. New Haven: Yale University Press.

Lazarus, Edward. 1999. *Closed Chambers: The Rise, Fall, and Future of the Modern Supreme Court*. New York: Penguin Books.

Lewis, Anthony. 1964. *Gideon's Trumpet*. New York: Random House.

Lisigor, Nancy, and Frank Lipsius. 1989. *A Law unto Itself: The Untold Story of the Law Firm Sullivan and Cromwell; 100 Years of Creating Power and Wealth*. New York: Paragon House.

Mason, Alpheus T. 1946. *Brandeis: A Free Man's Life*. New York: Viking Press.

Massaro, John. 1982–1983. "LBJ and the Fortas Nomination for Chief Justice," *Political Science Quarterly* 97 (603): 603–21.

Maynard, W. Barksdale. 2008. *Woodrow Wilson: Princeton to the Presidency*. New Haven: Yale University Press.

McClennen, Edward F. 1948. "Louis D. Brandeis as a Lawyer." *Massachusetts Law Quarterly*, 33: 1–28.

Mendelson, Wallace, ed. 1964. *Felix Frankfurter: A Tribute*. New York: Reynal and Company.
———. 1966. *Justices Black and Frankfurter: Conflict in the Court*. Chicago: University of Chicago Press.

Mennel, Robert M., and Christine L. Compston. 1996. *Holmes and Frankfurter: Their Correspondence, 1912–1934*. Hanover, NH: University Press of New England.

Minow, Martha, ed. 2013 (November). "Essays in Honor of Justice Ruth Bader Ginsburg." *Harvard Law Review* 127 (1): 423–85.
———, ed. 2014 (November). "Essays in Honor of Justice Stephen G. Breyer." *Harvard Law Review* 128 (1): 416–516.

Morgenthau, Henry, III. 1991. *Mostly Morgenthaus: A Family History*. New York: Ticknor and Fields.

Murphy, Bruce Allen. 1977 (October). "A Supreme Court Justice as Politician: Felix Frankfurter and Federal Court Appointments." *American Journal of Legal History* 21 (4): 316–34.
———. 1982. *The Brandeis/Frankfurter Connection: The Secret Political Activities of Two Supreme Court Justices*. New York: Oxford University Press.
———. 1988. *Fortas: The Rise and Ruin of a Supreme Court Justice*. New York: William Morrow and Company.
———. 1994. "Through the Looking Glass: The Legacy of Abe Fortas." In *The Jewish Justices of the Supreme Court Revisited: Brandeis to Fortas*, edited by Jennifer M. Lowe. Washington, DC: Supreme Court Historical Society, 103–26.

Murphy, Walter F. 1961. "In His Own Image: Mr. Justice Taft and Supreme Court Appointments," *Supreme Court Review*: 159–93.

Nathanson, Nathanial L. 1963. "Mr. Justice Brandeis: A Law Clerk's Recollections of the October Term, 1934," *American Jewish Archives* 15: 6–13.

O'Brien, David. 1986. *Storm Center: The Supreme Court in American Politics*. New York: W. W. Norton.

O'Connell, Jeffrey, and Nancy Dart. 1985 (Fall). "The House of Truth: Home of the Young Frankfurter and Lippman," *Catholic University Law Review* 35 (1): 79–95.

Oren, Dan A. 1985. *Joining the Club: A History of Jews and Yale*. New Haven: Yale University Press.

Oren, Michael B. 2007. *Power, Faith, and Fantasy: America in the Middle East, 1776 to the Present*. New York: W. W. Norton.

Paper, Lewis J. 1993. *Brandeis*. Secaucus, NJ: Citadel Press.

Parrish, Michael E. 1982. *Felix Frankfurter and His Times: The Reform Years*. New York: Free Press.

———. 1994. "Justice Frankfurter and the Supreme Court." In *The Jewish Justices of the Supreme Court Revisited: Brandeis to Fortas*, edited by Jennifer M. Lowe. Washington, DC: Supreme Court Historical Society, 61–80.

———. 2010. *Citizen Rauh: An American Liberal's Life in Law and Politics*. Ann Arbor: University of Michigan Press.

Peppers, Todd C. 2006. *Courtiers of the Marble Palace: The Rise and Influence of the Supreme Court Law Clerk*. Stanford, CA: Stanford University Press.

———. 2009. "Isaiah and His Young Disciples: Justice Brandeis and His Law Clerks," *Journal of Supreme Court History* 34 (1): 75–97.

Perry, Barbara A. 1991. *A "Representative" Supreme Court? The Impact of Race, Religion, and Gender on Appointments*. New York: Greenwood Press.

Phillips, Harlan P., ed. 1960. *Felix Frankfurter Reminisces*. New York: Reynal and Company.

Polenberg, Richard. 1997. *The World of Benjamin Cardozo: Personal Values and the Judicial Process*. Cambridge: Harvard University Press.

Posner, Richard A. 1990. *Cardozo: A Study in Reputation*. Chicago: University of Chicago Press.

Powe, Lucas A., Jr. 2009. *The Supreme Court and the American Elite, 1789–2008*. Cambridge: Harvard University Press.

Proskauer, Joseph M. 1950. *A Segment of My Times*. New York: Farrar, Straus.

Rabinove, Samuel. 1994 (Spring). "Justice Ginsburg and the 'Jewish Agenda.'" *Reform Judaism*, 74–75.

Ray, Laura Krugman. 2010. "The Legacy of a Supreme Court Clerkship: Stephen Breyer and Arthur Goldberg." *Penn State Law Review* 115 (1): 83–134.

Rosen, Jeffrey. 1993 (May 10). "Court Watch: The List." *New Republic*, 12–15.

———. 1993 (August 2). "The Book of Ruth." *New Republic*, 19–20, 29–31.

———. 2006. *The Supreme Court: The Personalities and Rivalries That Defined America*. New York: Times Books.

———. 2014 (October 13). "'RBG Presides': Interview with Ruth Bader Ginsburg." *New Republic*: 18–25.

———. 2016. *Louis D. Brandeis: American Prophet* (New Haven: Yale University Press).

Rosenberg, Yair. 2014 (May 5). "Elena Kagan's Very Jewish Dissent—and Mistake," *Tablet*.

———. 2014 (May 19). "Supreme Court Corrects Kagan Dissent," *Tablet*.

Sanua, Marianne R. 1998. *"Here's to Our Fraternity": One Hundred Years of Zeta Beta Tau, 1898–1998*. Hanover, NH: Zeta Beta Tau Foundation and University Press of New England.

———. 2003. *Going Greek: Jewish College Fraternities in the United States, 1895–1945.* Detroit: Wayne State University Press.

Sarna, Jonathan D. 1994 (Spring/Summer 1994). "'The Greatest Jew in the World since Jesus Christ': The Jewish Legacy of Louis D. Brandeis." *American Jewish History* 81 (3–4): 346–64.

———. 2008 (March–June). "Two Jewish Lawyers Named Louis." *American Jewish History* 94 (1–2): 1–19.

———. 2012. *When General Grant Expelled the Jews.* New York: Nextbook.

Sarna, Jonathan D., and David G. Dalin. 1997. *Religion and State in the American Jewish Experience.* Notre Dame, IN: University of Notre Dame Press.

Scherer, Michael. 2015. *"Citizens United v. Federal Election Commission."* In *The Supreme Court: Decisions That Changed America.* New York: Time Inc. Books, 80–83.

Schlesinger, Arthur M., Jr. 1978. *Robert Kennedy and His Times.* New York: Ballantine Books.

Schlesinger, Robert. 2008. *White House Ghosts: Presidents and Their Speechwriters.* New York: Simon & Schuster.

Schwarz, Jordan A. 1981. *The Speculator: Bernard Baruch in Washington, 1917–1965.* Chapel Hill: University of North Carolina Press.

Sekulow, Jay Alan. 2006. *Witnessing Their Faith: Religious Influence on Supreme Court Justices and Their Opinions.* Lanham, MD: Rowman & Littlefield.

Shemtob, Zachary Baron. 2012 (January). "The Catholic and Jewish Court: Explaining the Absence of Protestants on the Nation's Highest Judicial Body." *Journal of Law and Religion* 27 (2): 359–96.

Shesol, Jeff. 2010. *Supreme Power: Franklin Roosevelt vs. The Supreme Court.* New York: W. W. Norton.

Shlaes, Amity. 2008. *The Forgotten Man: A New History of the Great Depression.* New York: Harper Perennial.

Shogan, Robert. 1972. *A Question of Judgment: The Fortas Case and the Struggle for the Supreme Court.* Indianapolis: Bobbs-Merrill Company.

Simon, James F. *The Antagonists: Hugo Black, Felix Frankfurter and Civil Liberties in Modern America.* New York: Simon & Schuster, 1989.

Slater, Elinor, and Robert Slater. 1998. *Great Jewish Men.* Middle Village, NY: Jonathan David Publishers.

———. 2004. *Great Jewish Women.* Middle Village, NY: Jonathan David Publishers.

Starr, Kenneth W. 2002. *First among Equals: The Supreme Court in American Life.* New York: Warner Books.

Stebenne, David L. 1996. *Arthur J. Goldberg: New Deal Liberal.* New York: Oxford University Press.

Strum, Philippa. 1984. *Louis D. Brandeis: Justice for the People.* Cambridge: Harvard University Press.

Swift, Will. 2004. *The Roosevelts and the Royals: Franklin and Eleanor, the King and Queen of England, and the Friendship That Changed History.* Hoboken, NJ: John Wiley & Sons.

Todd, A. L. 1964. *Justice on Trial: The Case of Louis D. Brandeis.* New York: McGraw-Hill.

Toobin, Jeffrey. 2005 (October 31). "Breyer's Big Idea," *The New Yorker*, 36–43.

———. 2008. *The Nine: Inside the Secret World of the Supreme Court.* New York: Anchor Books.

———. 2012. *The Oath: The Obama White House and the Supreme Court*. New York: Doubleday.

Tribe, Laurence H. 1986. *God Save This Honorable Court: How the Choice of Supreme Court Justices Shapes Our History*. New York: Penguin Group / Mentor.

Tribe, Laurence, and Joshua Matz. 2014. *Uncertain Justice: The Roberts Court and the Constitution*. New York: Henry Holt and Company.

Tushnet, Mark, ed. 1993. *The Warren Court in Historical and Political Perspective*. Charlottesville: University Press of Virginia.

Urofsky, Melvin I. 1981. *Louis D. Brandeis and the Progressive Tradition*. Boston: Little, Brown and Company.

———. 1988 (February). "Conflict among the Brethren: Felix Frankfurter, William O. Douglas and the Clash of Personalities and Philosophies on the United States Supreme Court." *Duke Law Journal* 71 (1): 71–113.

———. 1991. *Felix Frankfurter: Judicial Restraint and Individual Liberties*. Boston: Twayne Publishers.

———. 1994. "Justice Louis Brandeis." In *The Jewish Justices of the Supreme Court Revisited: Brandeis to Fortas*, edited by Jennifer M. Lowe. Washington, DC: Supreme Court Historical Society, 9–34.

———. 2009. *Louis D. Brandeis: A Life*. New York: Pantheon Books.

Urofsky, Melvin I., and David W. Levy, eds. 1971–1978. *Letters of Louis D. Brandeis*, Vols. I–V. Albany: State University of New York Press.

———, eds. 1991. *"Half Brother, Half Son": The Letters of Louis D. Brandeis to Felix Frankfurter*. Norman: University of Oklahoma Press.

———, eds. *The Family Letters of Louis D. Brandeis* (Norman: University of Oklahoma Press, 2002).

Van Tassel, Emily Field. 1994. "Justice Arthur J. Goldberg." In *The Jewish Justices of the Supreme Court Revisited: Brandeis to Fortas*, edited by Jennifer M. Lowe. Washington, DC: Supreme Court Historical Society, 81–102.

Wald, Eli. 2008 (April). "The Rise and Fall of the WASP and Jewish Law Firms." *Stanford Law Review* 60: 101–65.

White, Adam J. 2012 (March). "The Lost Greatness of Alexander Bickel." *Commentary*, 35–38.

Yarbrough, Tinsley E. 2000. *The Rehnquist Court and the Constitution*. New York: Oxford University Press.

INDEX

Brandeis family members, 23–24, 26–30, 33, 41, 45, 52
Brandeis, Louis D., life and career, 22–44; Brandeis family, 23–26; Frankfurter and, 127, 128, 130, 140, 141, 142, 144; Goldberg, comparison with, 187; House of Truth and, 123; introduction to, 22–23; Jewishness, 24–25, 39, 73–74, 75; Mack and, 18; mentioned, 6, 8; mentors, 18; in New England, 26–33; as public advocate, 33–35; reputation, 111; Weizmann and, 132–33; Wilson and, 12, 35–39; Zionism and, 35, 39–44, 75–76, 277
Brandeis, Louis D., as Supreme Court justice, 45–76; appointment of, 45–52; Cardozo and, 103; death, 73–74; extrajudicial activities, 65–69; Frankfurter and, 148; on free speech and right to privacy, 56–61; as holder of Jewish seat, 282; law clerks, 20, 53–56; legacy, 74–76; mentioned, 21; New Deal and, 69–72; retirement, 72–73; Schechter case, 62–65; Schwimmer case, 165; swearing in, 52–53; Taft on, 294n21; Wilson and, 6; Wyzanski and, 151
Brandeis University, 75
Braunfeld v. Brown, 162–63
Breaking the Vicious Cycle: Toward Effective Risk Regulation (Breyer), 257
Bremen incident, 105–7
Brennan, William, 180, 194, 227
Breyer, Stephen G.: antisemitism against, 259; appointment of, 114, 244, 247; in *Citizens United*, 265; collegiality, 266–67; Jewishness, 276–77, 282–83; as law clerk, 205; liberalism, 269–70; life and career, 192–93, 254–57; as possible justice, 244–46; retirement question, 279, 280; as swing vote, 270; Ten Commandments cases and, 269–73
Brown v. Board of Education, 155, 165–68, 179, 195
Bryan, William Jennings, 4, 38
Buckner, Emory, 119, 120, 127
Bundy, Harvey Hollister, 124, 145
Bundy, McGeorge and William, 172–73

Burger, Warren E., 61, 179, 242, 279
Burlingham, Charles C., 152
Burt, Robert, 62
Bush, George H. W., 253, 278, 279
Bush, George W., 262
Bush v. Gore, 269–70
Butler, Nicholas Murray, 84, 92, 93, 96
Byrnes, James, 153, 197–98

capital punishment, 193, 196–97
Cardozo: A Study in Reputation (Posner), 112
Cardozo, Benjamin N., 77–114; antisemitism and, 107; appointment of, 95–100, 153; *Bremen* incident and, 105–7; on Columbia University board of trustees, 92–95; death, 72, 109–10; early life, 82–83; education and law practice, 7, 83–87; father's career, 77–80; Frankfurter and, 125, 142; as holder of Jewish seat, 282; as justice, 100–105; law clerks, 104–5, 114; legacy, 110–14; legal and judicial career, 87–91; on New York State Court of Appeals, 91–92; *Palko v. Connecticut* and, 107–9; Schechter case and, 64; Sephardic heritage, 80–82, 113
Cardozo family members, 80–81
Carswell, G. Harrold, 242
Carter, Jimmy, 193, 202, 251, 256, 280
Carter, John Franklin, 141
Casals, Pablo, 211, 217, 220, 239
The Case of Sacco and Vanzetti (Frankfurter), 136
Chafee, Zechariah, 99, 160
"A Chapter of Erie" (Adams), 79
Chase, Salmon P., 65
Chattanooga Times, 226
Chilton, William, 46, 47, 48
church-state separation, 163
Ciechanowski, Jan, 157–58
Citizens United v. Federal Election Commission, 264–66
Clarke, John Hessin, 152, 197
Clark, Grenville, 116, 118, 119, 160
Clayton Antitrust Act (1914), 38
"clear and present danger" standard, 57–58

Cleveland, Grover, 3, 4, 30, 33
Clinton, Bill, 114, 243, 244, 254, 261–62, 280, 281, 282, 283
Cohen, Benjamin V., 44, 64, 65, 70, 71, 130, 142–44, 147, 182, 226
Cohen, Morris Raphael, 119
Coleman, William T., Jr., 168
The Common Law (Holmes), 52, 91
concentration camps, 157–59, 182–83
confessions, forced, 195
Constitution. *See specific amendments and clauses*
Cook, Blanche Wiesen, 129
Coolidge, Calvin, 96–97, 138, 152
Corcoran, Thomas, 64, 65, 70, 71, 142–44, 147, 177
Cox, Archibald, 191
Craig v. Boren, 251
Cravath, Swaine, and Moore (law firm), 258
criminal defendants, rights of, 227–28
Croly, Herbert, 124, 127, 137
Cummings, Homer, 145, 148
Cuomo, Mario, 244–45
currency, Jews pictured on, 8

Davis, David, 65
Davis, John W., 258–59
Davis, Polk, and Wardwell (law firm), 258–59
death penalty, 193, 196–97, 205, 206
Debs, Eugene V., 12, 57–58
de Haas, Jacob, 26, 40, 43, 132
Dembitz family members, 23, 25, 26, 32, 40
Denman, Marion, 124–26
Dennison, Wilfred, 127
Dershowitz, Alan, 74, 183, 185, 192, 193–94, 196, 197, 205, 207, 208, 253
Digest of the Reported Decisions of the Superior Court of the Late Territory of Orleans . . . (Benjamin and Slidell), 9
Dirksen, Everett, 234–35, 237
Dodge, Cleveland, 36–37
double jeopardy, 108
Douglas, William O.: appointment of, 72–73, 146; early life and career, 212–13; Fortas and, 209, 213, 215, 218, 239, 240;

Frankfurter and, 154, 177, 179–80; Johnson and, 235; Kennedy and, 191; law clerks, 114; as liberal justice, 194; in *Miranda v. Arizona*, 227; predecessor to, 282; tenure of, 176; on wiretaps, 61
due process provisions, 108–9
Dulles, John Foster and Allen, 258
Dworkin, Ronald, 179

Eastland, James, 233–34, 236
Eighth Amendment, 196, 197
Eisenhower, Dwight D., 168, 180, 190, 278
Eliot, Charles William, 26, 48
Elkus, Abram I., 5, 7, 15, 87, 91
Elman, Philip, 155, 166, 180
Emerson, Ralph Waldo, 31
equal protection clause, 100
Escobedo v. Illinois, 193, 195–96, 206
establishment clause, 203, 270, 271, 272
Evans, Eli, 10, 287n44
extrajudicial activities: Brandeis's, 65–69, 72, 103, 150; Cardozo's, 94–95; of early justices, 151; Fortas's, 229–32; Frankfurter's, 150–55, 180, 183; of nineteenth-century justices, 65–66

Feisal ibn Husayn, Emir, 131–32, 182
Field, Stephen, 65
Fifth Amendment, 108, 227, 228
Filene, A. Lincoln, 39
Fillmore, Millard, 10
First Amendment, 56, 203, 252, 265, 270, 271, 272, 274
flag salute cases, 159–62, 178
Flood v. Kuhn, 202
forced confessions, 195
Ford, Gerald, 168, 225, 278, 282
Fortas, Abe, 209–43; Agricultural Adjustment Administration, role in, 144; antisemitism against, 259; appointment of, 222–27; Brandeis and, 70; death, 239–40; early life and career, 210–15; extrajudicial activities, 183, 229–32; *Gideon v. Wainwright* and, 221–22; as holder of Jewish seat, 114, 282; Johnson and, 197, 209–10,

Griswold, Erwin, 174, 249
Griswold v. Connecticut, 255

Hand, Billings Learned, 55, 101, 111, 112, 119, 125, 151–54, 156, 172, 179
Hapgood, Norman, 41, 44, 48, 51
Harding, Warren, 96, 138, 152, 197
Harman, Avraham, 230–31, 242
Harrison, Benjamin, 4, 11
Harvard Law Review, 32, 169
Harvard Law School: antisemitism at, 257; Breyer and, 255; Frankfurter and, 6, 118–19, 126–29, 133; Jewish faculty, 55; Jews attending, 6–7; Kagan at, 259, 262–63; law clerks from, 53–55; women at, 174, 249
Harvard University: German Jewish professors and, 155–56; Jewish students at, 136–37
Hastie, William, 166
Hatch, Orrin, 245, 247, 256
Hayes, Rutherford B., 65
Haynsworth, Clement, 242
Heller, Joseph, 64
Henkin, Louis, 159, 170, 175
"The Heroic and Visionary Women of Passover" (Ginsburg and Holtzblatt), 276
Higginson, Henry Lee, 32, 34, 36, 49
Hirsch, Maurice de, 4
Hirsch, Solomon, 4, 286n19
Hiss, Alger, 214
Hitler, Adolf, 155
Holmes, Oliver Wendell, Jr.: Brandeis and, 28–29, 31–32, 52–53, 56; in *Debs v. U.S.*, 57; Frankfurter and, 119, 122, 127, 140, 141, 142, 161, 181; House of Truth and, 122–23; law clerks, 53; law firms of, 27; legacy, 112; movie portrayal of, 281; in *Olmstead vs. United States*, 61; reputation, 111; in *Schenck v. United States*, 57; Schwimmer case and, 165; successor to, 282
Holmes, Oliver Wendell, Sr., 29
Holocaust, 157–59, 182–83
Hoover, Herbert, 95, 97, 98–99, 153, 197, 282
Hoover, J. Edgar, 134

House, Edward M. ("Colonel"), 37, 45, 66, 131, 132
House of Truth (Frankfurter residence), 122–24, 126
Hughes, Charles Evans, 16, 52, 64, 73, 99, 153, 197–99, 205

Ickes, Harold, 69–70, 71, 140, 144, 147, 177, 215
In re Gault, 228, 240
Israel: Fortas's support for, 242; Six Day War, 200, 229, 230–31, 242. *See also* Zionism

Jackson, Hugh, 140
Jackson, Robert H., 147, 180, 264
Jaffee, Louis, 54, 55, 70
Javitz, Jacob, 236, 237
Jay, John, 151
Jehovah's Witnesses, 159–62, 163
Jewish justices: antisemitism's decline in legal profession, 257–59; Brandeis, 22–76; Breyer, 244, 245–46, 247, 254–57, 266–67, 269–73, 276–77; Cardozo, 77–114; Fortas, 209–43; Frankfurter, 115–83; Ginsburg, 246–52, 265, 267–70, 275–76, 277–81; Goldberg, 184–208; Jewish seat, end of, 282–84; Kagan, 259–67, 273–75, 280; presidential appointments before Brandeis, 1–21
Jewishness: Brandeis's, 24–25, 39, 73–74, 75; Breyer's, 276–77; Cardozo's, 82–83, 86, 113; Frankfurter's, 129–30, 181–82; Ginsburg's, 275–76; Goldberg's, 202–5, 207; Kagan's, 275
Jewish Publication Society, 25
Jewish seat (on Supreme Court), 4, 72, 114, 191, 224, 242–43, 282–84
Johnson, Lyndon B., 114, 197, 198, 201, 209–10, 218–26, 229–36, 239, 242
judicial activism, 194
judicial restraint, 159, 160–61, 167, 168, 175, 178–79, 191
justices. *See individual justices by name*
juvenile criminal defendants, 228

Shapiro, Yonathan, 41

Sharansky, Natan, 194

Shearith Israel synagogue, 81, 82, 83, 85–86, 89, 109–10, 113

Shulman, Harry, 54, 55, 257

Silberman, Laurence, 252, 253

Silver, Abba Hillel, 98

Six Day War, 200, 229, 230–31, 242

Sixth Amendment, 195

Slidell, John, 9–10

Slidell, Thomas, 9

Sloss, Marcus C., 6–7, 98

social justice, 276–77

Social Security Act (1935), 70, 101, 107, 111, 144

Sorensen, Ted, 171, 189–90

Sotomayor, Sonia, 113, 260, 265, 266, 283

Souter, David, 267, 270, 278, 279

Soviet Union, as U.S. ally, 164

Stebenne, David, 198

Stern, Isaac, 211, 218, 220, 221, 239–40, 241, 242

Stevens, John Paul, 225, 265–66, 270, 278, 279, 283

Stevenson, Adlai, 214

Stevenson, Coke, 210

Stewart, Potter, 266

Stimson, Henry L., 67, 97, 119–24, 126–27, 145, 152, 154, 157–59, 172–73, 183

Stone, Harlan Fiske, 97, 101, 102–3, 147, 155, 160, 162, 165, 166, 266

Story, Joseph, 112, 151

Straus, Isidor, 3, 4

Straus, Nathan, 51

Straus, Oscar, 3–5, 7, 11, 12, 17, 21, 94, 190

Stroock, Alan M., 104, 105, 107

Sullivan and Cromwell (law firm), 258

Sulzberger, Arthur Hays, 149

Sulzberger, Mayer, 12, 14–16

Summers, Lawrence, 262, 263

Sunday (blue) laws, 162–63

Supreme Court. See individual justices by name

Sutherland, George, 71, 146, 152

Szold, Henrietta, 43

Taft, William Howard: advisors to, 2; appointments by, 5, 14, 15–16, 33, 122, 123, 152; Brandeis and, 46, 49, 51, 294n21; Cardozo and, 96; on Holmes's *Olmstead* dissent, 61; Mack and, 17–18, 20–21, 289n84; presidential campaign (1912), 12–13; as solicitor general, 264; Stimson and, 120; on Supreme Court, 56, 60, 142

Tammany Hall, 77–80, 88

Taney, Roger, 151

Taussig, Frank W., 27

Taussig, James, 28

Taylor, Zachary, 9

Ten Commandments cases, 270–73

Thacher, Thomas D., 119, 120, 141

Thayer, Ezra, 29, 127

Thomas, Clarence, 266, 268, 270, 279

Thornberry, Homer, 233

Thurmond, Strom, 256

Toobin, Jeffrey, 256, 261

Town of Greece v. Galloway, 273–75

Treatise on the Law of Sale of Personal Property . . . (Benjamin), 8

Tribe, Laurence, 253, 261, 263, 327n24

Truman, Harry, 190, 234–35

Trump, Donald, 284

Tugwell, Rexford, 70–71

Tulin, Leon, 212

Turkey, Straus as minister to, 3–5

Ullman, Isaac, 15

United Nations, Goldberg at, 200–201

United States, cases against. See opposing party by name

UN Security Council Resolution 242 (1967), 200

Untermeyer, Samuel, 5, 7, 11, 12, 15, 38, 87

Urofsky, Melvin I., 18

USS *Pueblo*, seizure of, 201

Valentine, Robert Grosvenor, 122

Van Devanter, Willis, 53, 71, 146

Van Doren, Charles, 171

Van Orden v. Perry, 270, 271s–73